STRUCTURE AND MEANING
in HUMAN SETTLEMENTS

STRUCTURE AND MEANING

University of Pennsylvania Museum of Archaeology and Anthropology • Philadelphia, PA

in Human Settlements

Tony Atkin and Joseph Rykwert, Editors

University of Pennsylvania Museum of Archaeology and Anthropology
3260 South Street
Philadelphia, PA 19104-6324
First Edition

See page 371 for illustration credits

Mexcaltitan Village, Nayarit, Mexico, is located in a lagoon on the Pacific coast northwest of Guadalajara. The cross made by the intersection of the four main streets represents the division of the heavens into the "four corners of the world."

Library of Congress Cataloging-in-Publication Data
Structure and meaning in human settlements / Tony Atkin and Joseph Rykwert, editors.-- 1st ed.
   p. cm.
 Includes index.
 ISBN 1-931707-83-9 (alk. paper)
 1. Human settlements. 2. Human ecology. 3. Architecture, Domestic. 4. Space (Architecture) I. Atkin, Tony. II. Rykwert, Joseph, 1926-
 GF101.S77 2005
      307.1'4--dc22
                              2005017756

Printed in China on acid-free paper

Contents

FOREWORD

The essays in this volume examine varieties of settlement patterns and spatial organization. They consider the physical remains of ancient cultures and surviving indigenous settlements as well as contemporary cities, and examples are included of extreme settlement conditions and places of cultural and environmental conflict. The authors have come together to explore a common interest in architectural theories of dwelling and place, anthropological research into settlement archaeology, and the study of cultural landscapes.

Archaeologists and settlement planners are natural allies, yet their pursuits begin from opposite ends. The archaeologist asks: what do these traces of past (or artifacts of present) settlements tell me about the state and evolution of the society that inhabited them? How did site and circumstance shape the material culture of a specific time and place, and how was it embodied in rituals and patterns of life? The object is to generalize about a society from the specific instances found in the field. The settlement planner, however, is faced with pragmatic decisions about how to extend or renovate an existing place or to build a new settlement in the future. Her task is to distill, from the broad understandings of a society, particular insights and ultimately prescriptions about place and change. She needs to know: how did the special and ordinary places of this settlement acquire their value or meaning? What special blend of social conventions should be respected in making changes to the physical form of settlements, and in new places what is valuable and durable enough to be emulated?

Quite clearly, social understanding can inform decisions about settlement form. But it may be less obvious that an understanding of the pragmatics of designing and building a settlement can also yield important insights about the relations or capacity of a society, extending well beyond its infrastructure or built fabric. At least, testing these propositions was the motivation for a wide-ranging conference organized at the University of Pennsylvania in October 2000 that brought together researchers in a host of disciplines including archaeology, architecture, classical studies, geography, landscape studies, and urban and regional planning. The chapters that follow are further developed versions of the contributions of those who participated in the conference.

In the second half of the 20th century, the study of human settlement became a significant area of research in a variety of disciplines. In archaeology, for example, it has been more than 50 years since Gordon R. Willey (also see his Chapter 3) so clearly argued the potential significance of the study of settlement patterns, which he took to include the way in which man disposed himself over the landscape on which he lived. It refers to dwellings, to their arrangement, and to the nature and disposition of other buildings pertaining to community life. These settlements reflect the natural environment, the level of technology on which the builders operated, and various institutions of social interaction and control which the culture maintained (*Prehistoric Settlement Patterns in the Viru Valley* 1953, 1).

"Of all those aspects of man's prehistory which are available to the archaeologist," Willey wrote, "perhaps the most profitable for such an understanding are settlement patterns. . . . Because settlement patterns are, to a large extent, directly shaped by human needs, they offer a strategic starting point for the functional interpretation of archaeological cultures."

In the ensuing years, studies of settlement patterns have had profound effects on scholarly understandings of ancient cultures. They have played a crucial role in enriching and strengthening research on a wide variety of cultural groups from mobile hunter-gatherers to complex urban states. On a basic level, such studies have stimulated new insights into human-environment interaction. In addition, archaeological research on settlements has helped broaden scholarly views of the archaeological record. In Sabloff's field of Maya studies, for instance, settlement research has helped shift scientific focus from just the impressive visible remains of the ancient elite to the full range of society, including the houses and activity areas of the peasants who helped build and support the Maya cities. With the advent of a host of new technological tools, such as satellite photography and side-looking radar, settlement pattern research has grown in sophistication, while advances in survey methodology and sampling have increased its impact on the archaeological knowledge of cultural developments through time and space.

However, what makes the study of archaeological settlement patterns so relevant to architects and planners today are a number of recent innovations in archaeological thinking. In the broadest sense, these new studies are looking beyond the material links between environment and human use to more holistic attempts to integrate human perception of the environment into settlement research. Although such studies have sometimes been labeled "landscape archaeology," these new research directions can also be seen as more systemic attempts to comprehend ancient human ecology with ideology playing as crucial a role as economics, politics, or social organization in research design and interpretation.

This significantly broader view of settlement in archaeology has the potential to be much more relevant to architects and planners (see the chapter by Ashmore, for example), because it fits so well with current concerns by the latter with comprehending the perceptions of clients or people affected by the planning, rather than simply imposing their ideas on the built environment—the "meaning" in the title of this volume. In particular, these new directions in archaeology can provide time depth and context to modern planning (see the chapters by Ferguson and Preucel and by Atkin, for instance) and hopefully lead to greater insights into long-term human relationships with the land.

Only in the past several decades have designers and planners sought such insights. The early decades of the 20th century spawned an ideology of modernism, where little of the past was considered relevant. Buildings and settlements were seen as the instruments of social change, seeking to reconstruct the society in ways that discarded hidebound traditions. A progressive international culture would take its place, where buildings and settlements would have much the same character wherever in the world they were found. Out of this ideology was born the European new towns movement, the reconstruction of city centers on several continents to accommodate automobiles and promote high-rise offices, and the ubiquitous spread of suburban housing forms that began in America and only lately have found their way to the four corners of the earth (see Campanella's chapter on recent Chinese urbanization and highway building). American public housing developments also owe their origins to heroic modernism, and their failures and reconstruction that Lawrence Vale chronicles argue for a much more nuanced understanding of the (evolving) culture of its inhabitants, the changing cultural meaning of such places, and the realistic possibilities of physical and social integration with neighbors.

Of course, few settlements are formed instantaneously, and even those that are become modified through use and changing activities. If the fit between culture and place matters, an important question is the manner by which cultural understandings or traditions in place-making are transmitted from generation to generation. What are the instruments of ensuring that settlements match the cultures of their inhabitants?

The chapters that follow identify at least three social processes that have resulted in well-adapted places. One is the co-evolution of place and society, in an unselfconscious way, through a process of trial and error. A society may be largely formed around the necessities of maintaining existence in a hostile place, and the settlement pattern follows evolving rules of ownership of land and resources and maintenance of common infrastructure. Often difficult geographic conditions demand such a process. The compelling images of Laureano's description of the oasis settlement shaped by the conservation of scarce water resources are an example.

A second, quite different, process sees the rules of settlement codified in some form of documented social understanding. This can take a variety of forms: formal settlement rules such as the Law of the Indies, the geomancer's dictates, models that are to be emulated (see Ashmore's description of the Maya town) or even the analogic understandings of literary works (as Fung describes). More the mark of mature societies that have resources to support the pursuit of symbolic purposes, such narratives or codes serve as a conservative rudder on social processes, limiting experimentation while maintaining social conventions.

Over the past several centuries, in a period dominated by the ideology of progress, a third process may be distinguished. Sorkin's utopian visions which follow are the most recent in a long line of reconstructive visions of society, rooted in a critique of current social processes. William Mitchell has described the outcome as "recombinant urbanism," where reinvention of social and economic institutions in light of new technological possibilities results in new settlement form. Unlike the two other processes just mentioned, these visions argue that a discontinuity of settlement form is either inevitable or desirable.

Several of the chapters offer insights about the dialectic of settlement form and social change, including Ferguson and Preucel's account of the Mesa Villages of the Pueblo revolt period and Blier's description of building destruction in a turbulent period of Dahomey political history. Whether cataclysmic or the slow transformation brought about by technological advances, it is often useful to see such change in ecological terms. Olin provides a language drawn from landscape ecology that seems equally powerful for observation or prescription. Ultimately, it is essential to see settlements and society as an integral process.

We are optimistic about the productive potential of future collaborations among archaeologists, architects, and planners to lead to better comprehension of human settlements and the use of this knowledge to improve planning, and we hope that this volume can serve as a stimulus to such work.

Gary Hack

an architect and planner, is Dean, University of Pennsylvania School of Design, and
Paley Professor of City and Regional Planning at the University of Pennsylvania

Jeremy A. Sabloff

an archaeologist, is Director Emeritus of the University Museum, the Edmund J. and Louise W. Kahn Endowed Term
Professor in the Social Sciences, and Curator of Mesoamerican Archaeology,
University of Pennsylvania Museum of Archaeology and Anthropology

ACKNOWLEDGMENTS

The editors wish to thank all the contributors from all over the world for their important and thoughtful work and for their enthusiasm and curiosity about the meaning of human settlements. We appreciate their patience and good will during the sometimes arduous process of organizing, editing, and producing the book.

We gratefully acknowledge the Samuel H. Kress Foundation for its timely and ongoing support of the conference and the publication; the Graham Foundation for Advanced Studies in the Fine Arts for its support of the original conference and its encouragement to publish the results; and the Center for Ancient Studies for its generous contribution to both the conference and the preparation of this text. We are tremendously grateful to the J. M. Kaplan Fund for its grant making it possible to include the many color illustrations.

This book is based on an international conference held at the University of Pennsylvania during October 2000 on the subject of Structure and Meaning in Human Settlements, jointly sponsored by the University of Pennsylvania School of Design, the Department of Architecture, the Department of Anthropology, and the University of Pennsylvania Museum of Archaeology and Anthropology. We greatly appreciate the roles of Gary Hack, Dean of the School of Design, and Jeremy A. Sabloff, then Director of the University Museum, for their early and consistent support and enthusiasm for both the conference and the book, as well as their financial contributions. We wish to gratefully acknowledge Walda Metcalf, Director of Museum Publications, who attended the original conference, proposed the book, and has been unflagging in her enthusiasm since. Our thanks go to her and her staff, especially Matthew Manieri.

A book of this size and complexity requires tremendous planning, hard work, and sustained attention to detail on the part of many. We are very grateful for the intelligence, talent, and organizational skills of those involved in producing and preparing the manuscript. Virginia Jacobs, our wonderful chief assistant editor, Evan Mull, our tireless and proficient copy editor, Christopher Ford, illustrations editor, and Maggie Boccella, Mary Mottola, and William Hayes, copy and illustration assistants, deserve our great thanks and acknowledgment for the many hours they have spent shaping, organizing, and editing the manuscript. Without them, the publication of this book would not have been possible. We also deeply appreciate the work and contributions of Catherine Vieth, then a graduate student in the Department of Architecture, now an architect living in San Francisco, and Mary O'Toole, Assistant to the Chair in the Department of Architecture, who helped tremendously with the organization and running of the original conference.

We would also like to thank the members of the firm of Atkin Olshin Lawson-Bell Architects, and especially the partners, for their support and understanding of the time, energy, and office resources that have been required in seeing this project to completion.

Tony Atkin and Joseph Rykwert

Philadelphia and London, June 2005

Before a support was transformed into a column, a roof into a pediment,

and stone heaped upon stone, man put stone upon the ground in order

to recognize place in the midst of an unknown universe

and thereby measure and modify it.

V. Gregotti, "Territory and Architecture," *Architectural Design* 55:28.

BUILDING AND KNOWING

Joseph Rykwert and Tony Atkin

S ettlements, and the relationships and patterns they embody, provide a primary record and reading of human existence—they organize our social and productive activities in every kind of ecological setting and technical horizon. As the following essays show, we can find social, productive and cosmological order embedded in the physical structure of every human community, even in those of the most marginal and unprepossessing hunter-gatherer societies.

What defines settlements as human? All animals inhabit a terrain; they respond to cold, heat, hunger; they move around or change their environment to avoid discomforts, predators, or the dangers of exposure. Many band together to forage or hunt, to defend themselves, or to care for their young. Some socialize their space by marking it with body smells or excreta; others do it through sometimes elaborate burrowing or building. There are animal habitats that are wonders of technological and organizational efficiency as well as ecological balance. Sometimes these structures incorporate intricate methods of ventilation and elaborate defense mechanisms. Complex patterns of behavior, social hierarchy, and forms of communication that are characteristic of human settlements exist in some form among many other species. Human beings sometimes make symbolic reference to animals and take on what we believe to be the attributes of successful species around us, and in our shelters or dress or social organization deliberately imitate them to appropriate their power, stealth, or industriousness.

However, since all other animals build by instinct, modification in the forms or methods of their building results only from a genetic or environmental change. Humans, on the other hand, have created settlements and built forms of tremendous variety throughout history as a species with no noticeable genetic modification. They reflect, compare, and often make elaborate preparations before beginning to build. We have a great need to recognize ourselves in our environment and find it important to convey this knowledge of our place to ourselves and to others. We reassure and remind ourselves of this knowledge by devising and making boundaries, and instituting productive and cultural acts that locate and distinguish our place from the rest of its unmodified surroundings, as well as the spaces occupied by others.

A human mark or trace made on the terrain may look to outsiders like an accident, yet for those who make it the distinction between that mark and what is around it is obvious and essential. It may show the way to a water source or a hunting ground: such a reading may be the beginning of settlement. Elaborate geometries, heavenly alignments, and precise measurements give assurance of place in more complex societies. Patterns of settlement are sometimes rigorously defined and obvious, or based on subtle and nearly indistinguishable variations.

Much of what we have learned about the beginnings of settlement and the earliest humans comes from evidence that continues to appear about the burial of the dead. Ancient burials have been found in Lebanon, Southern France, and Northern Iran. Some of the earliest discovered so far are accompanied by grave goods and floral offerings—this practice seems to have begun sometime before 50,000 BCE.

We do not know how our ancestors spread all over the earth; we are *homo sapiens sapiens*, man doubly wise in all our varieties from Australian Aborigines to Lapland Eskimos. But we have only been doubly-wise for about fifty thousand years, while for some half a million years before that *homo sapiens* inhabited the world. Although less wise than us—to go by the label—some of these ancestors or cousins of ours had brains about 2% more capacious on average than ours—or so we are told by paleontologists who called them Neanderthals after one of the first findings of their remains in the valley of the river Neander in the Rhineland. And we, their successors, are identified with a burial cave at Cro-Magnon in the Dordogne, which is still the earliest site in Europe with *homo sapiens sapiens* remains.

The two species of man seem either to have co-habited for a while, or succeeded each other quickly in this part of the world, the eastern shore of the Mediterranean. Whether by development, by conquest, or by interbreeding, our ancestors were left as the only sub-species of humanity. Shortly before this changeover, but apparently independent of any genetic change, a remarkable alteration occurred in the makeup of humans. What exactly caused it or how it proceeded is not clear.

The archaeological evidence has been taken to imply that those earliest buriers, probably Neanderthals, had some notion—call it moral or intentional—about their own existence. Where burial custom originated and whether it did so in several places at once or was diffused from one center is not clear (and probably never will be). Burials are sometimes the only or at least the most obvious remains from remote antiquity, but they tell us little of those beliefs about death and the dead that prompted them and even less about the context and ritual in which they took place. However, they are often quite elaborate—evidence that they were the work of people who had ritual practices, and therefore a language of action. Language and ritual presuppose the catastrophic realization that things have meaning—or rather, that everything has meaning. "Things," Claude Lévi-Strauss pointed out half a century ago, "could not have come to take on meaning gradually . . . a passage was made from one stage, in which nothing had any meaning, to another, where everything signified. . . . In other words, to when the whole Universe suddenly became meaningful" (Levi-Strauss 1950:xlvii).

Meaning and therefore language: once meaning can be ascribed to anything, it can be ascribed to everything, and there can be no return to beastly unthinking. All the techniques and endeavors that we share with animals are continuous and tend to be progressive—as are many skills. Meaning, on the other hand, being inevitably metaphoric, must always have a subject (p means q), and will therefore be discontinuous. The first funerals imply the acquisition of certain mental skills and of language, which also involves a symbolic reading of the world, an interpretation of existence, and this in turn demands the burial of the dead.

Unlike their earliest ancestors, those burying and those buried had bare skins. *Homo* probably lost his primate hair-cover soon after he learned the skill of walking upright. It follows that once they were bare-skinned, our ancestors required clothing, shelter, and controlled fire. Vitruvius relates the antique tradition, which he took over from Lucretius, that associates language and the control of fire with the origin of building (Vitruvio 1997:172 ff). The legend which Vitruvius and Lucretius tell probably took form sometime around three thousand years ago, though building is, of course, infinitely older than that. For millennia, hunter-gatherers sheltered in caves, on rock ledges, or brushwood shelters such as are still to be found all over the world. These devices used basic techniques, sometimes little different from that of the other higher primates.

Even in the earliest burials coloring was used: red ochre has been taken to signify blood—and therefore life—in many cultures; including red ochre powder with the dead is a custom as

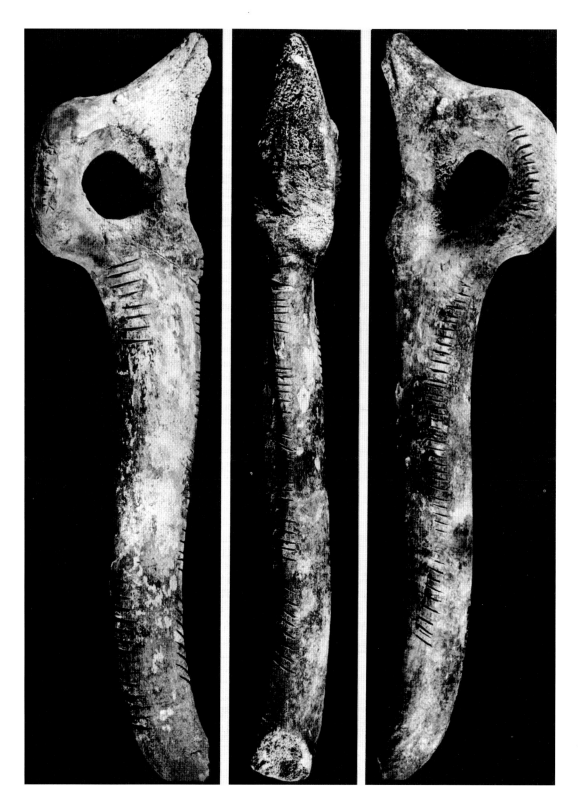

1.1 The three sides of a *bâton* of antler, 13.75 in long, from Le Placard (Charente), containing a hole, the sculpted head of a fox, and sets of engraved marks. Lower Magdelenian.

old, it seems, as is the practice of burial itself (Clark 1977:20 f, 34 ff; Leroi-Gourhan 1964:150 ff; Mithen 2003:30 ff, 168 ff). The use of pigment also led some to the coloring of objects, and painted pebbles may be the earliest works of art to have survived. What has not survived, however, though it surely preceded the decorating of inanimate objects, is body-painting and marking. Neanderthals and the first Cro-magnon certainly went in for body decorations: we know of shell and bone necklaces, bracelets and rings from various burials. Even if no tattooed or scarified skin fragments have survived older than about 500 BCE, it is fair to surmise from the evidence of paintings and decorated statues that the practice was probably common. What is more, carved bits of bone and wood, statuettes, and what seem to be ceremonial objects (sometimes called *bâtons de commandement* or scepters) have been found in connection with painted caves. Many of them are marked or scratched—apparently rhythmically—and not much sense was made of them for a century after they were first found and recorded (some of the early interpretations were that they represented animal kills, like the notches on a gunslinger's six shooter). In 1972 Alexander Marshack published his reading of the marks, and following him many of them have been interpreted as astronomical observations. Some of the biggest of the many objects that have been found in burials as well as in dwellings are elephant and mammoth tusks that were probably treated as semi-precious objects.

At Pushkari, in the Ukraine, there are remains of communal dwellings sheltering fireplaces. These long-houses, partly hollowed out of the ground and built up, often using mammoth and elephant bones (particularly tusks and ribs) as well as wood for structure, appear in Eastern and Central Europe at the period of the great frost—about 30,000 BCE. They were probably covered with mammoth hides or other animal skins to provide enclosure. At this time most of Europe north of the Carpathians, most of the British Isles, the Alps and the Caucasus were covered with a thick ice sheet which absorbed so much water that the seas were rather smaller than they are now. The ice cap withdrew over the next six or seven millennia and produced other climatic changes, and in the meantime humanity acquired another skill closely tied to metaphoric understanding—representational art.

The huts in the Ukraine seem to have been contemporary with the cave and rock paintings of central France and northern Spain that we still find astonishing, and more of which come to light all the time. They were painted by people who were flaking quite fine flints, but otherwise had rudimentary technical equipment, and this labels their time as Paleolithic, the old stone age. The mammoth-tusk huts and the paintings testify to a self awareness and ambitions that went far beyond their elementary technology.

We know of peoples who have survived as hunter-gatherers into our time and who continue to have very limited technical knowledge: for example, the Pitjantjatara who live in the foothills of the Barrow Range in Central Australia. They employ spears and spear-throwers, but do not have bows and arrows, nor do they cultivate their food or bake pots or build permanent shelters—though they do make use of quern-stones (stones with flat surfaces used for grinding corn or grain) and digging sticks. On the other hand, they have bull-roarers (wooden or stone tablets, pierced at one end, and swung on a stick to make a whirring sound) to accompany their ceremonies. When their rituals require it, they paint rocks as well as their skins, and they practice an elementary division of labor in that they have specialists—medicine men, singers, ceremonial experts—to nurture an intellectual-speculative as well as a ritual life for which they also make elaborate, if temporary, enclosures (Turner 1970:299 ff; Leroi-Gourhan 1964:164 ff;

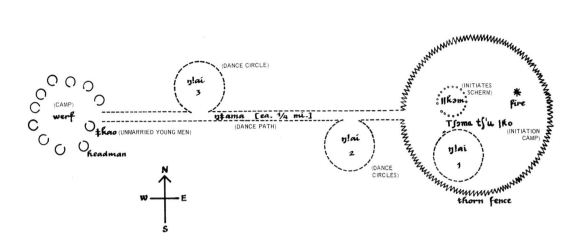

Sahlins 1979:78 ff). Had they died out or vanished, their physical remains would have been even thinner than those of some Neanderthal groups.

Such discontinuity between technique and materiality and speculation was demonstrated neatly by Lévi-Strauss in his examination of a Bororo village. One of us has already quoted this in an earlier publication, but the example still seems valid to us (Rykwert 1988:169 ff). These Bororo are a hunting and gathering people of the Upper Amazon basin who wear little more than a belt and a penis wrapper normally, though for ceremonial occasions, such as burials or marriages, they deck themselves out in elaborate feather and fur costumes. Their villages, like the one called Kejara (described by Lévi-Strauss), are shoddily built to last only a few years, and when the ground is exhausted the village moves on. In spite of this messy, almost informal appearance, the Bororo consider their villages, which consist of a rectangular men's house in the center of a rough circle of huts with a dancing ground before it, to be an image of their social order. Firstly, the village is bisected into two moieties, each one consisting of twenty-four huts, articulated as eight groups of three—the geometry of the plan makes this quite explicit. The circle of the enclosure, however, contrasts with the rough rectangle of the men's house. Its conceptual division, as of a cross in a square, is instantly recognizable to the inhabitants.

This kind of ordering may be reproduced in an even more complex form among people whose dwellings may look even shabbier and more disorderly than the Bororo village. The 'Gui and 'Gana Kalahari Bushmen—the last human grouping in whose speech the clicking phoneme has remained from what is assumed to be a primitive linguistic substratum—build villages which are roughly enclosed and outlined with stones but which consist of wind shelter-screens rather than huts. Yet they also carry out lengthy initiation ceremonies for which they construct semi-permanent grounds fenced with stones and thorns to the east of the village, and they edge a path for the dance-procession directed in the same way. The geometry of the circle is used to create a ritual environment, and the ceremony is ordered on the east-west axis, as in many different cultures (Rykwert 1988:45, 175; Wheatley 1971:423 ff; Brentjes 1981:26 ff).

One of the curious characteristics of a settlement circle is that it is usually divided into symmetrical moieties and often subdivided into four, eight, or even sixteen sectors. The squaring of the circle is an ancient conundrum—it is a practice of many societies to divide the circle of the horizon into the four directions, sometimes more (the Chinese also included up and many North American Indians included up and down, the zenith and the nadir), and

1.3 Santa Ana Cosmology. At the center is *Tamaya*—the Keresan word for the pueblo.

NW Corner

Middle North
(Yellow)

NE Corner

Leaf House
Home of Thought Woman

Shipap

Ya'takana House
Home of Mockingbird Youth

Gotsa's Home

White House

Dawn Mt

Cattail House

Tamaya

Place of Sunrise
Home of Koshari

Middle West
(Blue)

Wenima
Home of Katcinas

Shell Spring
Home of Quirana

Middle East
(White)

Home of
Whirlwind Old Man

Wood House
Home of Spider Grandmother

Gowawaima

Turquoise House
Home of Boraika

SW Corner

Middle South
(Red)

SE Corner

1.4 *Tienten*, the Temple of Heaven in Beijing, China, used for rituals and sacrifice by the Ming and Qing emperors. The circular temple represents the sky. It rests on a three-level platform that divides the horizon into segments aligned with the cardinal points.

1.5 NWT hieroglyph (third from top, upper right corner) on detail of a painted limestone doorway indicating 'town' or 'place' from the west wall of the tomb chapel of Ka(i)pura, late V or early VI dynasty (2415-2298 BCE).

sometimes to give positive or negative attributes, even colors, to phenomena originating from those locations. These divisions are used by various kinds of diviners as a token of a heaven-instituted world-order. The cross in the square is a standard device—for example it had a long life in the NWT hieroglyph, signifying 'town,' a cosmogram which was maintained in Egypt into Roman Imperial times.

The daily arc of the sun and seasonal changes are often recognized in the orientation and location of dwellings and community structures, as are the changes in the night sky. Many pre-industrial cultures built solar clocks and calendars to connect their ritual and community structures to the cosmos, as well as determine annual events, such as planting or harvest time, or seasonal floods. A remarkable solar calendar built by ancient Puebloans still remains at Chaco Canyon in northwestern New Mexico.

1.6 The Templum of the Sky. Miniature illustrating Hyginus Gromaticus's "Constitutio Limitum" in the most ancient surviving manuscript of the *Corpus Agrimensorum*, the "Codex Arcerianus," a 6th century collection of writings on surveying.

A community of settlers, a society, or even a commonwealth is sometimes thought about and presented as a functioning human body, as when the forum is called the heart of the city, the king the head of his kingdom, or a highway likened to the circulatory system. Mid-20th century urban theorists such as Candilis, Soltan, and Bakema, even a group called the Metabolists in Japan, made much of these biological analogies—describing "urban organisms" with systemic arrangements of "cells," "arteries," and "spines"—comparing the health of cities with healthy bodies.

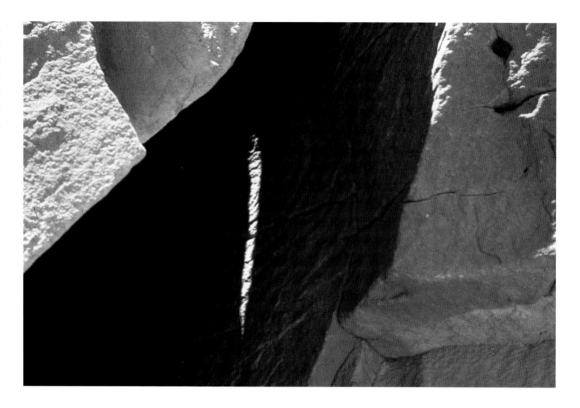

Orientation, bilateral symmetry, and the differentiated functions of human organs are commonly represented in the patterns and working of the settlement. In this way, the individual can project his or her intimate and corporeal workings onto the form of the community. The Dogon, who build admirable, complex, mud-vaulted and thatch-roofed houses, consider their villages to be beings—or bodies—like themselves, and explain their community structure as locations on a body. In the northern part of the village, the men's house (and the smithy associated with it) is read as the head. The main dwelling section is the chest, and the two women's houses are the hands. South of this are oil-crushing stones and the village altar, representing the female and male genitals. The ancestral altars in the south are the feet (Griaule 1965). The descriptions of the houses and villages of the Batammaliba and the Danhome of West Africa are analogous. These societies make remarkable houses with explicit corollaries to body parts and functions, and spaces segregated by gender identity (Blier 1987 and Chapter 13 in this volume).

Our buildings sometimes literally embody—they project the human figure into their construction through bodily measurements, such as the distance between the elbow and the hand, the length of a foot, a man's height (such as the Japanese *ken*, used to determine the length of a tatami or the height of a doorway), or idealized human proportions. These measures have often been (and in unmechanized cultures still are) used by builders as the basis of their rule-of-thumb building procedures. The Dong in southern China build beautiful and complex drum towers and bridges using this method (Ruan 2001).

Settlement begins, therefore, through cognitive appropriation and modifications of our surroundings and the conveying of this information to others. It is made up of explicit spatial and temporal relationships that define human existence. These relationships are embedded in ways of making things and of building, and they are often recollected and re-enacted in daily and seasonal rituals. Settlement forms provide culture with physical continuity and a setting for the individual

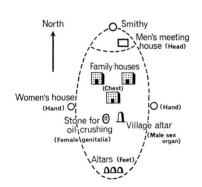

1.8 Ideal schema of Dogon village. Mali, Africa.

within the community. Everyone is born into some form of settlement, and we learn our place in the world from our dwelling. Like language, the shapes, forms, and relationships we gather from our environment create a way of thinking and apprehending the world.

The form of our settlement is a major part of our cultural and emotional makeup, whether we stay put or wander to some other town or village, even if we choose to live in isolation like a hermit whose renunciation of society is itself a social and cultural act. After emigration, people will often recreate the forms and relationships of their prior existence in the new setting, even if the original materials are unavailable.

The ability to perceive a difference between the first artificial mark and nature, or even the relative significance of settlement forms, separates the settler from outsiders. The inhabitants of Zuni Pueblo in New Mexico mark the approximate time of the midwinter solstice with the annual celebration of *Shalako*, when the *kachina* gods return to bless the village. On the first day, the "Council of the Gods" including *Shulawitsi*, the young Fire-god, and representatives from each of the six Zuni cardinal directions visit small excavations freshly made at points around the village, where they deposit prayer feathers and corn meal (Stevenson 1904; Atkin observation, 1994). At any other time, the locations of these sites are unremarkable and unmarked to outsiders, but they are well understood and sacred to the Zuni.

Separation and marking make a claim over something that was once an integral part of nature. Many peoples believe that they must make amends to nature or the gods for what they have taken away. They sometimes do so through sacrifice and ritual or by making the settlement itself a model of the ordered world, of the cosmos: they explain its order and its workings through orientation and the primary geometry and location of the settlement features.

This cognitive and physical transformation is extended when natural features of the landscape—both in and out of settlement boundaries—are given names and assigned roles in the community's life. Examples of this abound—Mt. Taylor in northwest New Mexico was a point of alignment and sacred feature for the builders of Chaco Canyon, many miles away, as well as for the later inhabitants of Acoma Pueblo to the south; Mt. Fuji in Japan provided a symbolic ancestor mountain as well as street orientations in Edo (Tokyo before the Meiji restoration). Landscape features provide orientation and location—often the entire visible landscape is anthropomorphized and woven into cultural narratives.

Food gathering, production, trade, and distribution, or the allotment of water resources, can provide a basis for community organization and spatial structure. Scarce water resources have assumed a formative role in desert cultures for millennia just as the shape and productive requirements of rice paddies have organized many communities in southeastern Asia. The specialization of functions, the movement of goods, technology, and defense mechanisms often result in surprising and beautiful physical forms. Sometimes these forms are greatly elaborated or decorated to spiritually enhance their operations.

The making of a new settlement will inevitably modify, transform, and mold the perceptions of its founders, and it will provide a new framework for the actions and self-awareness of its inhabitants. The choice of a site and the work of builders often seem to defy the demands of rationality, as, for example, the remote and ecologically precarious cliff dwellings at Mesa Verde or Betatakin in the American southwest. The idea of comfort is highly mediated by historical and social factors. Effective shelter and ecological balance are usually preferred—certainly in theory—but are not essential. The physical requirements for shelter and sustenance can be met in very different ways; sometimes they are mostly ignored or overcome with great effort and expenditure of resources. Emotional and empathic considerations, even chance, may trump reason.

The form of a settlement reflects and conditions not only its physical structure but also, of course, its history. There is often a founding event—"this is the place"—in which the god/hero finds the site and fixes the form and its boundaries. He or she may have done this by some direct inspiration, as in a dream, or by consulting divine indications: the Greeks consulted the Delphic Oracle, the Etruscans and Roman Augurs read sheep's entrails and the flight of birds, while in China geomancers made a wind-and-water reading of the site, Feng Shui. Only when divine sanction has been given were the limits of the site set out, usually by some solemn method, and the land subdivided. Such rituals are repeated regularly so that their memory becomes part of the life of the settlement: the birthday of Rome and its story have been celebrated on April 21 almost continuously for 2,700 years, and even today in certain Tokyo neighborhoods, a palanquin from the local temple is ritually carried around the community every year on the shoulders of its residents to again mark the boundaries of the settlement (Jinnai 1995).

Over time, the fabric of the settlement becomes a container and transmitter of cultural memory. Its materiality provides support, resistance, and contention for the individuals' everyday living as it conditions communal action. The fabric is tightly woven into the life of some communities. The nomadic Indians of the North American Plains were wedded to the circle that defined the pattern of their camps. At war on the Little Big Horn in Montana, where General Custer and his battle troops were sheltered in strictly aligned rectangular tents, the Sioux and their Cheyenne and Omaha allies camped in a series of circles. These circles were arranged in moieties, each with its particular lodges on a particular side. The teepees which

1.9 Plan showing four different arrangements of camp circles. Plains Indians.

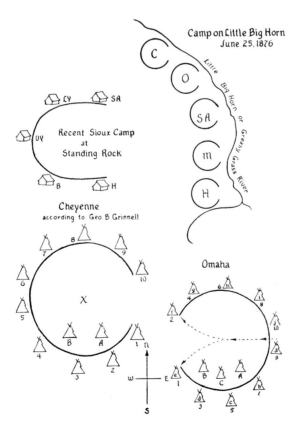

made up the camp were themselves circular, of course, and the ordering of the camp echoed their shape—almost as if these Indian nations were obeying Alberti's injunction to see the house as a small town and the town as a large house (*De Re Aedificatoria* I:9 and V:2).

The diffusion or imposition of settlement patterns may also be a powerful weapon, as the Romans knew well. The Cardo and the Decumanus are still a sign of ancient Roman presence all over the Mediterranean, as are the ensuing orthogonal divisions of the land in Italy that have survived two millennia. When conflicts destroy a pattern, it is sometimes accepted as an equally powerful sign that can also provoke disorientation and confusion, as it did in 2001 in New York City. The destruction and rebuilding of settlements due to war or natural calamity is a commonplace of history. Most of the time, buildings and cities are rebuilt in the same place, even illogically. In some cases, villages and towns, as well as cities, were not only physically razed to the ground, but could also be ritually "unfounded" to prohibit rebuilding, as Carthage was by the Romans in 146 BCE by marking out its boundary backwards and pouring salt on the "wound," rendering the site fallow and sterile.

Major disruptions in built form and in temporal relationships have been a common experience for many societies in the 20th and 21st centuries. These discontinuities raise the question whether meaningful structures continue to exist in human settlements after they are transformed by international consumer culture and place-defying technology like that of the present day. The growing concern with ethnic identity and anti-globalization movements might signal a return to the significance of settlements and places—or it may be just a further indication of a groping for lost moorings. Periods of rapid social and economic change such as ours raise the question of how we can understand the ongoing significance of settlement practice—the effect on ourselves—when the world view incorporated in the existing forms of settlement atrophies or is violently disrupted.

Settlement archaeology and the study of situation and spatial patterns in anthropology have proven to be a rich source of cultural investigation that connects artifacts to their milieu and reveals the conditions and meaning of their original production. The complex relationships between artifacts, settlement forms, and landscapes can provide powerful insights into the ways of being for a society—how they view and explain themselves and their existence, to themselves and to outsiders.

Conversely, architects and planners can study the principles that have guided and informed past settlements in order to foster their appreciation and understanding of the social and material processes that have created enduring and complex places. We might then learn to see architecture as not just a possibly desirable aesthetic supplement, but as the embodiment of social intentions and cultural meaning.

References

Alberti, Leon Battista. *De Re Aedificatoria* [On the Art of Building in Ten Books], trans. J. Rykwert, N. Leach, and R. Tavernor. Cambridge, MA: MIT Press, 1988.

Blier, Suzanne Preston. *The Anatomy of Architecture: Ontology and Metaphor in Batammaliba Architectural Expression*. Cambridge: Cambridge University Press, 1987.

Brentjes, Burchard. *Die Stadt des Yima*. Leipzig: Seemann Verlag, 1981.

Clark, Grahame. *World Prehistory*. Cambridge: Cambridge University Press, 1977

Griaule, Marcel. *Conversations with Ogotemmeli*. London: Oxford University Press, 1965.

Jinnai, Hidenobu. *Tokyo, a Spatial Anthropology*. Translated by Kimiko Nishimara. Berkeley, CA: University of California Press, 1995.

Leroi-Gourhan, André. *Le Geste et la Parole*. Paris: A. Michel, 1964.

Lévi-Strauss, Claude. "Introduction l'Oeuvre de Marcel Mauss." In *Sociologie et Anthropologie,* by Marcel Mauss. Paris: Presses Universitaires de France, 1950.

Marshack, Alexander. *The Roots of Civilization*. New York: McGraw Hill, 1972.

Mithen, Alexander. *After the Ice*. London: Weidenfeld & Nicholson, 2003.

Ruan, Xing. "Myth and Architectonics: The Case of the Dong Drum Tower and Its Social Life." Paper presented at the Center for East Asian Studies, University of Pennsylvania, April 2001.

Rykwert, Joseph. *The Idea of a Town*. Cambridge, MA: MIT Press, 1988.

Sahlins, Marshall. *Stone-Age Economics*. London: Tavistock, 1979.

Stevenson, Matilda Coxe. *The Zuni Indians: Their Mythology, Esoteric Fraternities, and Ceremonies*. Orig. pub. as *Bureau of American Ethnology Report* 23(1904):227–61. Glorieta, NM: Rio Grande Press, 1985.

Turner, Victor. *The Forest of Symbols*. Ithaca, NY: Cornell University Press, 1970.

Wheatley, Paul. *The Pivot of the Four Quarters*. Edinburgh: Edinburgh University Press, 1971.

ANIMAL SETTLEMENTS
ECOLOGICAL FUNCTIONALISM OF ANIMAL ARCHITECTURE

Juhani Pallasmaa

2

"The bird nest is absolute functionalism, because the bird is not conscious of its death"
—*Sverre Fehn, Architect, 1997 Pritzker Prize Winner, personal communication, 1985.*

ARCHITECTURAL MARVELS AND THE EXTENDED PHENOTYPE

The study of animal building behavior reveals astonishingly refined structures and complex architectural principles can teach us important lessons. Animal community structures and organizations are equally elaborate. It is evident that the structures which various animal species build for themselves and their offspring are just as essential for their survival as architecture is for human existence and culture.

The notion of extended phenotype unites an animal species, its behavioral patterns, survival strategies and constructions into a singular concept. Thus the beaver's dam and nest, for instance, are inseparable parts of the extended phenotype of the beaver. In the same way architecture and technology, as well as societal and cultural institutions, are ingredients of the extended phenotype of man. Richard Dawkins (1999) argues that "in a very real sense [the spider's] web is a temporary functional extension of her body, a huge extension of the effective catchment area of her predatory organs" (198). In his view, there is no principal difference between genetic control of morphology and genetic control of behavior (199).

Animal constructions serve the same fundamental purposes as human constructions; they alter the immediate environment for the benefit of the species by increasing the level of order and predictability in the habitat.

Animal constructions are surprisingly varied. Some degree of building behavior is practiced throughout the entire animal kingdom, and skillful building species are scattered throughout the phyla from protozoa to primates. Pockets of special architectural skill can be found among birds, insects, and spiders.

It is thought provoking to realize that the constructions of higher animals are among the least ingenious in the animal kingdom. Apes, for example, only construct a haphazard and temporary shelter each night, as compared to termite metropoli of millions of inhabitants, which may be utilized for centuries.

Gaston Bachelard included a chapter on nests in *The Poetics of Space*. He quotes Ambroise Paré's view: "The enterprise and skill with which animals make their nests is so efficient that it is not possible to do better, so entirely do they surpass all masons, carpenters and builders; for there is not a man who would be able to make a house better suited to himself and to his children than these little animals build for themselves. This is so true, in fact, that we have a proverb according to which men can do everything except build a bird's nest" (Bachelard 1964:72).

2.1 A gigantic nest of sociable weaverbirds.

Spiders and their web-building skills have evolved during 400 million years; when this period of evolution is compared with the meager few million years of human development since *Homo erectus* stood up on two legs, we may expect animal building skills to exceed ours in many respects.

There were animal architects on earth for millions of years before *Homo sapiens* put together his first clumsy structures. Our conventional concepts of architecture are restricted to the building that has taken place over roughly 5,000 years of Western high culture. In the past few decades, however, the architects have turned their attention toward the wisdom and beauty of the building traditions among the highly diverse indigenous communities beyond western culture. Bernard Rudofsky's eye-opening book, *Architecture Without Architects* (1964), initiated a growing body of publications on indigenous and vernacular building traditions. These studies have revealed the cultural, symbolical, functional, and technical refinements of the unselfconscious processes of construction mediated by illiterate and embodied traditions.

Two thousand years ago wasps taught the Chinese how to make paper, and the nesting chambers of potter wasps are believed to have served as models of clay jars for the American Indians. The Chinese learned how to use the fine silk line spun by the larva of the silk moth 4,600 years ago, and even today we are using several million kg of raw silk annually. In addition to being used as material for fine cloth, silk thread was earlier used to produce fishing rods and strings of musical instruments.

2.2 A chimpanzee lying on its sleeping platform built of branches for a single night.

2.3 Cells of the potter wasp (*Eumenes*). The egg of the wasp is suspended from a thread above the paralyzed larvae that are food for the offspring.

2.4 A wasp's nest exemplifies absolute functionalism born through millions of years of direct response to the ecological context of the animal's life cycle.

14   STRUCTURE AND MEANING IN HUMAN SETTLEMENTS

SIGNIFICANCE OF ANIMAL ARCHITECTURE

The constructions of animals and their structural principles bear striking similarities to human constructions utilizing similar materials. The clay structures of various swallows and wasps resemble structures of American Indians. In traditional African cultures, beavers' curved dam walls fight the pressure of water in the same way as some of our largest and most advanced dams. A tiny butterfly larva may protect its case with a dome assembled of its own larval hair, echoing the geometry of Buckminster Fuller's geodesic structures, which are among the most efficient human constructions in their ratio of enclosed volume to weight.

A Green Building research project (1990) by Future Systems utilizing a jar-like external shape and a system of natural ventilation strikingly evokes the internal nest shape and automated air-conditioning system of certain termites species (*Macrotermes bellicosus*), one of the finest constructions in the animal kingdom.

Constructions increase the life expectancy of the animals themselves or of their offspring and improve their chances of procreation.

SCALE AND PRECISION OF ANIMAL CONSTRUCTIONS

In relation to the size of their builders many animal constructions exceed the scale of human constructions. Others are constructed with a precision unimaginable in normal human construction.

The largest single animal construction in absolute size is the beaver dam; the largest known dam is 1,200 m long. The continuous additive capture net of certain orb weaver spiders (*Araneus sermoniferus*, *Uloborus republicanus*), built by thousands of individuals, may reach the size of 100 m, which would be almost 20 km if transferred to human scale. The highest termite

2.5 A nest of Australian termite species. The largest nests are nearly 6 m high, and if this height were transposed to the scale of man, the structure would be almost two kilometers high.

2.6 Microscopic animal architecture. The sand-grain house of an unidentified species of caddis larva (*Heliopsychidae*) collected in Borneo.

nests are 8 m high, which equals the height of nearly 3 km in human scale. The weight of a large termite nest may amount to about 12,000 kg.

In the microscopic end of the scale of animal structures, the normal thread thickness of a grown-up large orb spider is 0.010–0.012 mm. But the cribellate spiders produce capture woof from up to 50,000 individual threads of only 0.0002 mm in diameter. The capture net of a certain caddis fly larva, the size of a human fingernail, stretched across a narrow passage in their heart-like architectural device constructed of sand grains, may contain a 100 million meshes.

The bee cell has been mathematically shown to be the most efficient way of storing honey in structures of wax. The hexagonal bee cell has two angles of 70°34' and four angles of 109°26', which is exactly the mathematical optimum. The standard cell thickness of the bee's honeycomb is 0.073 mm, and it is produced with the staggering tolerance of 0.002 mm, which is far beyond the precision of human builders.

Animal Master Builders

The appearance of builders through the phyla is rather unpredictable; there are concentrations of architectural talent, as among the gastropod mollusks and birds. The species do not have to be particularly intelligent or advanced in order to be skillful builders; impressive construction takes place among the protozoa and many capable builder species appear in the lower metazoa.

Artifact-building animals teach us that the organization of even simple animal life is complex and subtle. Close studies by scanning electron microscope reveal mind-boggling refinements of structures in a scale invisible to the human eye and totally beyond the capabilities of human builders, such as the microscopic structural ingenuities of spider or caddis fly larva constructions.

Most of the animal species that build have a high manipulative skill, and this is particularly true of the three major classes of builders. The spiders and insects derive their skill from their multiple-jointed legs and subtle mouthparts, whereas birds have a narrow beak attached to their mobile heads to allow precise movements. This manipulative building skill is exemplified by the almost human weaving, intertwining, and knotting practice of weaverbirds.

Functions of Animal Constructions

Many of the structural and functional achievements of animal construction are examples of functional causality and perfection. Through millions of years of evolutionary development and adaptation, the merciless struggle for survival has perfected animal constructions as flawless responses to their life conditions. Functions of animal architecture can be listed as follows: (1) protection from the physical environment including temperature control, water management, humidity control, gas exchange and ventilation, and waste management; (2) protection from predators including avoidance of detection or recognition, mechanical protection, and protective nesting association; (3) food gathering, cultivation, feeding, prey capture, leaf rolling, and food storage; (4) communication including structures that assist transmission, structures that are signals, and mate selection and reproduction; (5) decoration.

The various functional principles of animal architecture could be illustrated by numerous impressive and astonishing examples from the temperature control of compass termites, bees, or various bird species, to the stunning communications systems, such as the tiktokkic, a South African longbreath locust transmitting waves, which can be sensed by another locust at a distance of at least eight miles. In this context, however, I shall only discuss the most controversial of the architectural functions, that of decoration and the notion of beauty.

DECORATION, RITUAL, AND BEAUTY

Animal constructions are often impressively beautiful, although beauty is clearly a category of the human mind and eye. The extraordinary beauty of their constructions derives from the same characteristics as the most convincing beauty in human constructions; their shapes and structures are born from subtle contextual responses and the inevitability of functional and structural logic. The real beauty of animal architecture, however, is in its total integration of the life pattern of its builder, and dynamically balanced natural systems.

The suggestion that animal architects might apply ornament to their constructions is provocative. Some animal behavior related with nest construction, however, appears as superfluous decoration without other evident function in the performance of the structure. Bowerbirds display quasi-decorative behavior in which the Nobel Prize winning ethnologist Karl von Frisch recognized a seed of aestheticism (1974:244–45).

Flower decorations are frequently used to court the female by male Black-throated weavers (*Ploceus benghalensis*) and Striated weavers (*P. manyar*) living in India; the male dabs wet mud onto the nest chamber and implants brightly colored—red, orange, yellow, blue, or white— flowers or flower petals in it. The Paradise riflebird (*Ptiloris paradiscus*) living in Australia often decorates its nest with a discarded snakeskin, while the Crested bellbird (*Oreoica gutturalis*), another Australian bird, puts hairy caterpillars on the rim of its nest.

The avenues, stages, bowers, and maypoles of the bowerbirds possess distinct decorative qualities. The bowerbirds decorate their courts and bowers with colorful fruits, berries, and flowers, shiny objects such as insect exoskeletons, and a variety of other materials—feathers, leaves, moss, lichens, stones, bones, snail shells, and pieces of charcoal. They even paint their bowers using crushed colorful berries as paint and a piece of bark as a brush.

Different species of bowerbirds prefer different colors: the avenue builders *Ptilonorhynchus* prefer blue, while *Chlamydera* prefer white, green, or blue, whereas the maypole builders *Amblyornis* favor red and yellow objects. The shiny blue objects selected by the male Satin bowerbird (*Ptilinorhynchus violaceus*) resemble the lilac-blue color of his eyes and his shiny blue-black plumage. This observation suggests that the decoration is used as a visual extension of the bird itself.

Richard Dawkins points out that bowerbird species that build particularly elaborate bowers tend to have relatively drab plumage, while species with bright plumage tend to construct rather simple bowers. He suggests that some species may have shifted from adaptation through bodily phenotype to adaptation through the extended phenotype of bower architecture (Dawkins 1999:199–200).

The ritual presentation of an empty silk cocoon, or a mere stone as a gift to the female, by males of certain insect species, such as the balloon fly or some spiders, might appear first as an example of aestheticized behavior, but a closer inspection reveals the evolutionary strategy behind the gesture; the gift both improves the male's visibility and protects him from the

2.7 The great grey bowerbird (*Chlamydera nuchalis*) male decorating his bower with bones and brightly colored flowers.

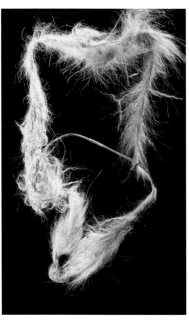

2.8 Ako's necklace.

danger of being eaten by the female. The governing principle of life is to spread one's own genes as efficiently as possible. This goal may lead the males of certain spider species to allow the female to eat him during copulation in order to make sure that another male will not interfere in the process of reproduction.

After having killed and eaten a colobus monkey, a group of chimpanzees living in the wild were observed carrying pieces of its skin. A female chimp called Ako wore a piece of the skin, knotted to form a loop, around her neck. What is the significance of Ako's necklace? Does it indicate the beginning of decoration? Recent research attempts to reveal the evolutionary role of beauty as well as the brain functions related with aesthetic experiences (Rentschler et al. 1988).

Methods of Construction

Any manufactured artifact results from two interrelated choices, those of materials and those of methods of manufacture. Most of the materials used by animals are also used by man, and due to the constraints imposed by these materials, the construction methods of animal architects have close parallels with our own constructions.

The methods which animals use in their constructions can be classified in seven processes: sculpting and burrowing; piling up; molding, modeling, and extrusion molding and spinning; rolling and folding; sticking together; weaving; and sewing.

The Institute of Light Tensile Structures at the University of Stuttgart, directed by Frei Otto, has for decades carried out extensive microscopic studies of the refined structural principles and details of animal constructions as a basis for the design of lightweight and tensile structures. Spider webs, for instance, have numerous structural subtleties, such as end fittings and shock-absorbing devices, which are currently being applied to the design of advanced tensile structures.

Structural, Economic, and Ecological Refinements

Animal architecture is in a perfect dynamic balance with its ecological context; the animal builders do not exhaust natural resources or cause problems of waste and pollution, as their activities are kept in balance by other processes of life. Under abrupt environmental changes, such as natural calamities or senseless human interference, which detach animal behavior from its normal ecological constraints and interactions, animal communities may, however, become ecologically unbalanced and eventually self-destructive.

Animal constructions are structurally efficient, and natural selection has gradually optimized both the forms of structures and the use of materials. The vertically suspended cell wall of the bee, for instance, has two layers of cells, built back to back with half a cell's shift in the position of the cell walls, to create a continuous three-dimensional folded structure made of pyramidal units at the boundary surface. The structure is amazingly strong: a cell cake made of 40 g of beeswax can contain up to 1,800 g of honey.

The inner cell of the abalone is twice as tough as human-made high-tech ceramics; instead of breaking, the shell deforms under stress like a metal. Mussel adhesive works underwater and sticks to anything, whereas rhino horn repairs itself although it contains no living cells. All these miraculous materials are produced in body temperatures without toxic byproducts and they return back to the cycles of nature.

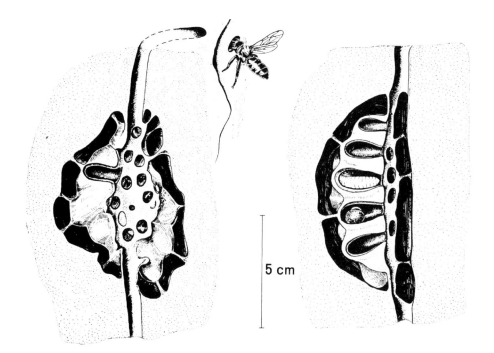

2.9 The delicate subterranean clay comb of the mining bee (*Halictus quadricinctus*). The comb is suspended in its cavity by slender supports, and the two passages leading to the comb form a ventilation shaft.

5 cm

The extraordinary strength of spider drag line is another example of the technical miracles of evolutionary processes. None of the man-made metals or high-strength fibers of today can even come close to the combined strength and energy-absorbing elasticity of spider drag line. The tensile strength of the line spun by the spider is more than three times that of steel. The elasticity of spider drag line is even more amazing; its extension at break point is 229% as compared with the meager 8% of steel. The spider silk consists of small crystallites embedded in a rubbery matrix of organic polymer—a composite material developed 380 million years before our current age of composite materials. The spider silk line is even tougher than polyaramid Kevlar, the material used in bulletproof vests and facial masks; it can absorb five times the impact force of Kevlar without breaking. According to *Science News*, January 21, 1995, a spider web simulating a normal human fishing net in its thickness of thread and the scale of its mesh could catch a passenger plane in flight.

The spider line is produced with low energy at spider body temperature, whereas in the production of Kevlar petroleum-derived molecules are poured into a pressurized vat of concentrated sulfuric acid and boiled at several hundred degrees in order to force it into a liquid crystal form. The energy input is very high and there are extremely problematic toxic byproducts.

Animal constructions follow strict budgets and satisfy rigorous criteria of cost-effectiveness. The cost of animal architecture is measured in terms of energy and time used in the construction process. The animal architect has to consider availability and appropriateness of materials, factors affecting manufacturing costs, such as transportation, as well as the functional effectiveness of the product itself. Also in animal construction the cost will be lower if the process is kept simple.

Animals tend to schedule their construction at times when cost is lowest. The red oven bird (*Furnarius rufus*) for example, builds its laborious nest of mud with a high cost. The building activity is, however, spread over the winter months, and takes place in bouts that coincide with mild weather and rainfall when soft mud is easily available.

Prolonged utilization and reuse are also important economic considerations. Termite nests may be used for centuries and large stick nests of birds, as well as the nests of cliff swallows, are often reused for many seasons. Recycling of nest materials is also common among bees, wasps and ants. The dwarf honey bees (*Apis florea*), for instance, gnaw off the wax of their abandoned house and carry it in their leg baskets to make a new one of the same material, and save energy in wax production. Empty used cocoons are used by carder bees (*Bombus agrorum*) as storage jars for nectar and pollen. The ponerine ant (*Prionopelta amabilis*) uses fragments of former silk cocoons to line pupal nest chambers to control humidity, whereas many small birds use spider or caterpillar silk in their nest construction.

In order to minimize the use of material the Bolas spider has devised a virtual net. The spider spins a single line and attaches sticky droplets to the far end of the line. When a prey insect approaches, lured by the smell generated by the spider, the spider starts to whirl its line around to create a virtual net surface.

Since the building material which spiders use—the protein of the thread—is metabolically expensive, they have evolved a parsimonious solution: the thread is eaten but, in an unknown way, the protein bypasses the digestive system and is soon available in the spinnerets for a new net without having the valuable proteins broken down in the process of recycling.

Composite Animal

A thought-provoking perspective to the idea of the extended phenotype is the notion of the composite animal.

In his influential book *The Soul of the White Ant*, Eugene Marais conceives the termitary as an organism comparable with the cellular entity of higher organisms (Marais 1939:53–81). The royal chamber with its queen functions as the brain processing information and initiating intentions, the termite fungus gardens function as a metabolic organ (termites can only use liquid food), and the soldier and worker termites perform the tasks of white and red corpuscles, respectively. The nest architecture performs as an artificial lung. The complex construction creates an automated ventilation system that functions in the following manner: air in the chambers, where the fungus is cultivated, is heated by the fermentation processes, and heat is also produced by the breathing of the animals themselves. The hot air rises and is forced by the pressure of the continuous flow into the wide horizontal ridge ducts. The exterior and interior walls of the ridges are porous, and they enable gas exchange to take place; carbon dioxide seeps out and is replaced by oxygen, which penetrates into the multitude of thin ducts from outside. The ridges function as artificial lungs for the colony. As the air is cooled during its flow through the ridges, the heavier regenerated and cooled air falls into the cellar through the bottom air space. This air returns to the nest from the bottom through the air space surrounding the nest, and replaces the rising warm air.

The royal couple lives inside a hard, thick-walled chamber, barely large enough to house the couple and the workers tending them. This chamber is rebuilt up to six times in accordance with the growth of the queen. The monstrously swollen queen is the reproductive center of the community, which lays 50,000 eggs per day. Every individual in the community of millions derives from this single mother. The millions of individuals appear to have a collective group psyche. The queen seems to adjust the relative number of soldiers and workers, for instance, in relation to external conditions (such as wars between ants and termites) communicated chemically to her by workers.

The queen exudes a mysterious power over her subjects through signals that we do not know. When an entire nest is experimentally dissected in two separate parts by a thick steel plate, the inhabitants of the two disconnected halves continue to construct their nest symmetrically as if the separation did not exist. But very soon after the queen dies, the entire community dies and the nest begins to disintegrate. The surface of the termitary wall is always repaired from inside outwards in the same manner that living skin repairs itself. The nest structure seems to possess the cohesion and flexibility of living skin as long as the queen and the community lives, but it begins to erode into earth when communal life is extinguished. Injuries of the queen weaken her influence in proportion to the wound.

The communication of the queen seems entirely mystical in relation to human capacities, but it might not be entirely unique in the animal kingdom. Marais argues that termites possess perceptive powers a million times more acute than human senses.

There are actually composite animals in the animal world. In the sea around the African coast there are a hundred kinds of a marine creature, called *Hydromedusa*, and of *Siphonophora*, a related species. The peculiarity of this animal is that a full-grown specimen is a composite animal composed of hundreds of individuals. The animals are born as complete independent creatures with mouth, stomach, swimming aparatus, and sexual organs. Later a group of individuals create an organic union; one group becomes the complicated swimming aparatus, another the stomach and digestive system, and a third group develops into the sexual organs of the composite animal. One group even takes on hepatic functions and becomes the liver (Marais 1939:78–79).

Who is the Architect?

The purposefulness and refinement of animal architecture pose the questions: who is the architect, and how is the blueprint passed on to the next generation?

Building behavior clearly has some genetic base and genetic change may therefore result in phenotypic novelty in the completed artifact. This novelty will then be exposed to the forces of natural selection. If it is advantageous, it will become more widely used and, perhaps, eventually replace the former architectural style.

According to *The Animal Mind* by James L. Gould and Carol Grant Gould, "higher degrees of mental activity are called cognition, which is defined . . . as the act or process of knowing. Cognition can be innate—passive knowledge encoded in an animal's genes and used as instructions for wiring a nervous system to generate particular inborn abilities and specializations" (Gould and Gould 1999:8).

Most of animal behavior is driven by instinctual reactions triggered by certain external stimuli. The reactions form a closed chain, which progresses through a pre-coded sequence. The sexually active termites, for instance, mate only after they have taken their nuptial flight and shed their wings; they do not break off their wings before they have flown and they do not mate before they have shed their wings.

The microscopic marvels of insect architecture are guided by hormonal changes. When an insect reaches a certain age, its endocrine hormones prepare it for a certain action, for instance, rolling a leaf. It carries a model to do this in its nervous system. Further hormonal changes

2.10 Weaver ants (*Oecophylla*) use their own larva, clasped between their mandibles, as a spindle and shuttle to weave their leaf nest together.

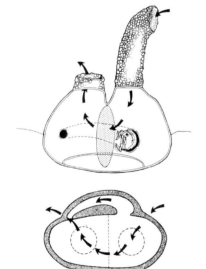

2.11 A combined house and capture device shown in the vertical and horizontal section of the house of *Macronema transversum*. Water enters through the inhalent funnel, is filtered through the incredibly refined net which divides the main chamber, and exits through the exhalent funnel. The larva is positioned in a side chamber next to the capture net.

make it ready to pupate and weave a cocoon. The adult hatching from the pupa has its own behavioral model that makes it take off to search for food and a sexual mate.

An interesting detail is that the larva can make certain preparations for its next developmental stage. Because the adult butterfly or moth has sucking mouthparts, the larva must make sure that the adult is able to get out of its case. They prepare a weaker area in the end of the cocoon, or create a round hatchway, which is only weakly attached to the cocoon proper.

The more complex animal constructions, however, seem to call for goal-oriented behavior, i.e., an awareness of the purpose of the behavior or architectural construction. When pondering on the complex building task of the air-conditioned termitary, the authors of *The Animal Mind* reason, "it seems simpler to account for the feat by supposing that the individual termites have some functional picture of the end result and, from an array of innate motor programs, choose the behavior most appropriate in the circumstance to bring the work closer to that goal" (Gould and Gould 1999:118).

The African termite species (*Macrotermes bellicosus*) is capable of constructing two different systems of air-conditioning depending on whether they do their construction in the coastal climate of the Ivory Coast or the drier and less forested circumstances of Uganda. How the termites are capable of choosing between two different principles of physics for their system is mind-boggling.

Another example of a capacity among termites which seems to exceed mere genetically derived instinctual behavior is the fact that when a nest is experimentally covered by a plastic sheet which prevents normal flow of air required for cooling and CO_2 disposal, the insects are capable of devising an emergency system of cone-shaped chimneys to save the community.

REHEARSAL AND SELF-ORGANIZATION

Rehearsal and learning are an essential part of the behavior of weavers and bowerbirds. Young males begin to practice nest construction early on and this "apprenticeship" can last up to two years among the latter. Young bowerbird males frequently visit completed bowers and observe the building process of adult males as well as the subsequent courtship. The owner male of a bower keeps constantly maintaining and repairing his structure. He also experiments with his bower and optimizes its effect by repositioning ornamental elements and exchanging fading flowers for fresh blossoms.

The authors of *The Animal Mind* argue that "[the beaver's] natural history makes it hard to believe that dam building behavior is not, at the very least, goal-oriented rather than task-directed" (Gould and Gould 1999:130). The beaver's capacity for flexible problem solving is expressed in the animal's capacity to appropriate existing structures and encounter experimental situations that could hardly be coded in their natural habitat. In repairing damage in their dams, they often project an understanding of hydrodynamics that humans could hardly grasp.

The evolutionary process in many ant species appears to have favored a flexible nesting strategy adapting both the use of building material and the architectural design to the spatial and temporal variations of the environment.

Lessons of Animal Architecture

The slow evolution of animal artifacts can be compared with the processes of tradition in traditional human societies. Tradition is a force of cohesion that slows down change and ties individual invention securely to its patterns established through endless time and the test of life. It is this interaction of change and rigorous testing by forces of selection that is lost in human architecture of the industrial era. Human architecture evolves more under forces of cultural and social values than those of the natural world do.

It is becoming increasingly essential that our own constructions are studied in their anthropological, socio-economic, and ecological frameworks, in addition to the traditional aesthetic sphere of the architectural discipline. It is equally important that our aesthetic understanding of architecture is expanded to the biocultural foundations of human behavior and construction. As builders, we could learn from studying the gradual and slow development

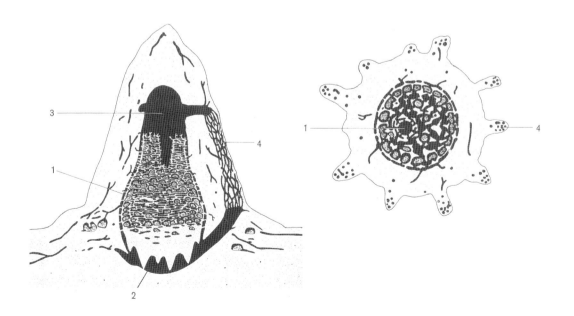

2.12 Horizontal and vertical section through the nest of *Macrotermes bellicosus* termites. The nest mound easily reaches the height of some 4 m and contains more than two million termites. These live, work, and breathe within the closed volume of the nest. Their consumption of oxygen is considerable, and without a proper system of air-conditioning the termites would suffocate quickly in their stone-hard skyscraper.

and adaptation of animal constructions over the course of millions of years, as we, human architects of the communication age, tend, on the contrary, to invent a new architectural style for each new season of architectural fashion.

Animal constructions open up an important window on the processes of evolution, ecology, and adaptation. Ants have the biggest biomass and they are most numerous and widespread of all animals, including man, as a consequence of their skills in adapting to a wide variety of environmental conditions. They are among the most highly social of all creatures, and the study of ants has produced insights into the origins of altruistic behavior (Hölldobler and Wilson 1990:179–96, 297).

The ecological rationality and functionality of human building is bound to be compromised, because our architecture is also a means of attempting to understand and symbolize the world, and an attempt to achieve immortality. Human architecture is always more about cultural, metaphysical, and aesthetic aims than pure functionality and reason.

"Architecture is not only about domesticating space," writes philosopher Karsten Harries, "it is also a deep defense against the terror of time. The language of beauty is essentially the language of timeless reality" (Harries 1982:59–69). Or, as the young Alvar Aalto put it, "form is nothing else but a concentrated wish for everlasting life on earth" (Schildt 1984:192).

Greater efficiency and technical sophistication are clearly the successful strategies of the evolutionary processes of animal architecture. An investigation of animal species and their shelters suggests that a proper way toward an ecologically sound human architecture is not through a regression back to primitive forms of construction, but through progressive technological sophistication. We are beginning to grasp the ultimate refinements of the natural world. As we attempt new strategies of technology and development, the unsurpassable marvels of animal construction should teach us all a welcome sense of humility.

REFERENCES

Allaby, Michael. *Animal Artisans*. New York: Alfred A. Knopf, 1982.

Bach, Klaus et al., ed. under the direction of J. G. Helmcke and Frei Otto. *Nets in Nature and Technics* (IL 8). Stuttgart: Institute for Lightweight Structures, University of Stuttgart, 1975.

Bach, Klaus et al., ed. under the direction of Eda Schaur et al. *Pneus in Nature and Technics* (IL 9). Stuttgart: Institute for Lightweight Structures, University of Stuttgart, 1976.

Bachelard, Gaston. *The Poetics of Space*. Boston: Beacon Press, 1964.

Beck, Benjamin B. *Animal Tool Behaviour: The Use and Manufacture of Tools by Animals*. New York: Garland STPM Press, 1980.

Benyus, Janine M. *Biomimicry*. New York: William Morrow, 1997.

Collias, Nicholas E., and Elsie C. Collias. *Nest Building and Bird Behaviour*. Princeton, NJ: Princeton University Press, 1984.

Campbell, Bruce, and Elizabeth Lack, eds. *A Dictionary of Birds*. Calton: T&AD Poyser, 1985.

Dawkins, Richard. *The Extended Phenotype: The Long Reach of the Gene*. New York: Oxford University Press, 1999.

Ellis, Malcolm, ed. *Animal Specialists: Builders*. London: J. M. Dent and Sons, 1979.

Evans, Howard E., and Mary Jane West Ebenhard. *The Wasps*. Ann Arbor, MI: University of Michigan Press, 1970.

Fabre, J. H. *Muistelmia hyönteismaailmasta*. Porvoo: WSOY, 1965.

von Frisch, Karl. *Animal Architecture*. New York: Harcourt Brace Jovanovich, 1974.

Gould, James L., and Carol Grant Gould. *The Animal Mind*. New York: Scientific American Library (1994), 1999.

Guidoni, Enrico. *Primitive Architecture*. New York: Electa/Rizzoli, 1987.

Hancocks, David. *Animals and Architecture*. London: Hugh Evelyn, 1971.

Hansell, Michael H. *Animal Architecture & Building Behaviour*. London: Longman, 1984.

———. *The Animal Construction Company*. Glasgow: Hunterian Museum and Art Gallery, 1999.

———. "The Ecological Impact of Animal Nests and Burrows." *Functional Ecology* (1993).

———. "What's So Special about Using Tools?" *New Scientist* 8(January 1987).

Harries, Karsten. "Building and the terror of time." In *Perspecta, The Yale Architectural Journal*. Cambridge, MA: MIT Press, 1982.

Havas, Paavo, and Sulkava Seppo. *Suomen luonnon talvi*. Kirjayhtymä, 1987.

Hildebrand, Grant. *Origins of Architectural Pleasure*. Berkeley, CA: University of California Press, 1999.

Hölldobler, Bert, and Edward O. Wilson. *The Ants*. Cambridge, MA: Harvard University Press, 1990.

Kaija Kangasniemi, ed. *Kodin suuri eläinkirja*. Espoo: osat 1–10 Weilin & Göös, 1981.

Leakey, Richard E., and Roger Lewin. *Origins*. London: Macdonald and Jane's, 1979.

Lee, K. E., and T. G. Wood. *Termites and Soils*. London: Academic Press, 1971.

Marais, Eugen N. *The Soul of the White Ant*. London: Methuen, 1939.

Morgan, Lewis. *The American Beaver*. New York: Dover, (orig. ed. 1868).

Morris, Desmond. *Miksi seepralla on raidat*. Porvoo: WSOY, 1991.

Mound, Laurence. *Le peuple des insectes*. Paris: Gallimard, 1990.

Mitchell, James, and Jess Stein, eds. *The Random House Encyclopedia*. New York: Random House, 1990.

Otto, Frei. *Lightweight Structures in Architecture and Nature* (Exhibition catalogue) (IL 32). Stuttgart: Institute for Lightweight Structures, University of Stuttgart, 1983.

Pallasmaa, Juhani, ed. *Animal Architecture*. Helsinki: Museum of Finnish Architecture, 1995.

Rentschler, Ingo, Barbara Herzberger, and David Epstein, eds. *Beauty and the Brain: Biological Aspects of Aesthetics*. Basel: Birkhäuser Verlag, 1988.

Reuter, O. M. *De lägre djurens själslif*. Stockholm: Samson & Wallin, 1886.

Rudofsky, Bernard. *Architecture Without Architects*. New York: Museum of Modern Art, 1964.

———. *The Prodigious Builders*. New York: Harcourt Brace Jovanovich, 1977.

Schildt, Goran. *Alvar Aalto: The Early Years*. New York: Rizzoli, 1984.

Sire, Marcel. *The Social Life of Animals*. London: Studio Vista, 1965.

Spoczynska, Joy O. I. *The World of the Wasp*. London: Frederich Muller, 1975.

Tinbergen, Niko. *Animal Behaviour*. Life Nature Library. Time-Life International, 1966.

Vander Wall, Stephen B. *Food Hoarding in Animals*. Chicago, IL: University of Chicago Press, 1990.

Settlement Patterns in Americanist Archaeology

Gordon R. Willey

3

The manner in which people have arranged themselves over and built upon the surfaces of the earth must inevitably tell us something about the societies and cultures of which they were a part. This, in brief, is the logic behind settlement pattern studies in archaeology. The idea is neither esoteric nor profound but basic and obvious, as is the corollary proposition that settlement arrangements and constructions, in their turn, help form and shape society and culture. In a word, settlement pattern study is a necessary, indeed, an inevitable, part of archaeology.

In trying to answer questions about the relationships of settlements to society and culture, the archaeologist must rely not only upon constructions and modifications of land forms but upon all aspects of the archaeological record—artifacts, burial arrangements, the human remains themselves—the totality of what can be recovered from the past. Indeed, when I began settlement pattern research in the late 1940s, I never thought of what I was doing as a replacement of any part of the methodological arsenal of archaeology that had gone before; rather, the focus on settlements was simply something to be added to our archaeological procedures, one more way to appraise and look at the record of the past.

To stand back for a moment and think of the history of the discipline of archaeology, we can see that it has proceeded through three major and overlapping phases or stages. First, there was a time of discovery, and the initial descriptions of these discoveries were not infrequently laced with fanciful interpretations. In the Americas, this first phase began to be replaced by a second in the early 20th century. This second phase was characterized by somewhat more objective descriptions of the data and by their typological, distributional, and chronological orderings. Then, in the mid-20th century, archaeologists began a third phase by placing a greater emphasis on a search for the meanings in their data, that is, by asking and trying to answer questions about the causes behind social and cultural change. Not surprisingly, in venturing onto such ground, there have been disagreements, with divergent schools of thought emerging in this third phase. Arguments between those who categorize themselves as "processual archaeologists" versus "post-processual" archaeologists are a well-known example. The larger goals of the field, however, are essentially agreed upon: to understand why and how ancient societies developed and changed in the ways that they did. The study of settlement patterns has been one of the early features in this third phase of Americanist archaeology.

My own beginnings in settlement pattern archaeology certainly came about in what was then a very traditional archaeological context. In 1946, a number of us, including some with previous interests in Peruvian archaeology, had decided to run a cooperative archaeological-anthropological project in a single valley, the Virú, on the Peruvian north coast. At the outset,

our objectives were traditional ones: determining the cultural chronology in the valley through stratigraphic digging and grave-lot and surface collection potsherd seriations and identifying and describing major architectural monuments.

Before we departed for the field, however, a senior colleague of mine at the Smithsonian Institution, Julian H. Steward, suggested that I do something else. There would be a sufficient number of my colleagues from other institutions attending to these conventional archaeological matters, so why didn't I, instead, launch into a study of what he called "settlement patterns." Steward wasn't very explicit about what he meant by this term, but he indicated that it would be an examination of the way the valley's population had arranged their living spaces and built upon them through time. In this I would obviously be aided and abetted by my colleagues who would be dating sites stratigraphically and by potsherd surface collections.

I took Steward's advice, and for several months examined the form, layout, and architectural features of over 300 archaeological sites in the Virú Valley, together with their relationships to ancient irrigation canals and other prehistoric features or landscape modifications. While doing this I received relative ceramic dating information on these sites and features from my colleagues who were digging Virú sites and, particularly, from James Ford who was making an extensive potsherd surface collection survey of the sites that I was examining. Clearly, my job would have been impossible in so short a field period if I had not received the help I did from these colleagues who were engaged in what we might think of as "traditional archaeology."

As a result, from my Virú settlement study I was able to tell a story which began with small villages, occupied by shellfish gatherers and early farmers, continuing through successive periods of settled agriculturists who lived in increasingly large apartment-like dwelling complexes covering densely settled acres of terrain (Willey 1953). Pacing along with these dwelling changes were the constructions of associated pyramids and public buildings, as well as increasingly complex canal irrigation systems and associated garden-plot arrangements.

It would be impossible even to list the places in Americanist archaeology, let alone those in non-American settings, where settlement pattern study has gone forward as a part of the general archaeological endeavor, but let me refer to a few of the outstanding settlement studies in the Americas. We can begin by continuing here on the Peruvian coast. These essentially rainless, coastal valleys, all much like Virú in this respect, are particularly well adapted to settlement research. With minimal present-day vegetation, archaeological features—including architecture, ancient roadways, canals, and irrigation-cultivation systems—are readily visible on aerial photographs. I benefited from these in my Virú Valley survey, as has David J. Wilson in an impressive monograph, *Prehispanic Settlement Patterns in the Lower Santa Valley, Peru* (1988). The Santa empties into the Pacific, about 50 km south of Virú and is one of the largest valleys of the north coast. While its cultural chronology parallels that for Virú, running from late preceramic times up through the Inca Conquest, its populations were much larger. Wilson carefully traces their growth, the development of irrigation agriculture in the valley, and the nature and role of inter-valley warfare in the rise of the state there and elsewhere on the north coast. The Moche conquest of the Santa Valley was a part of this story. A long article by Brian Billman, "Reconstructing Prehistoric Political Economies and Cycles of Political Power in the Moche Valley, Peru" (1999), details the political economy and power of the Moche state which was centered there and is another closely related contribution to settlement pattern archaeology from the Peruvian coast. The Billman article carefully plots out the architectural and agricultural record of the rise and growth of this coastal state and empire from its beginnings (CE 200) to its eventual downfall (CE 800).

Another American area in which settlement pattern archaeology has been pursued vigorously in recent years is Mesoamerica. William T. Sanders has been a leader in this, carrying out early settlement surveys in the Valley of Mexico (Sanders 1956; Sanders, Parsons, and Santley 1979) and at the huge site of Kaminaljuyü in the Guatemalan Highlands (Sanders and Michels 1969). At both these places there has been considerable attention to the rise of large-scale urbanism and how this comes about in its relationships to governmental controls, religion, and trade. Settlement archaeology similarly has been a major part of the long-term research conducted by Kent V. Flannery and Joyce Marcus and their colleagues in Oaxaca in tracing out the rise and growth of the Zapotec and Mixtec civilizations (Flannery and Marcus 1983).

Moving farther south in Mesoamerica, the Maya Lowlands of southern Mexico, Guatemala, and Belize has also been another area of settlement pattern interest; and, if I may be permitted to continue to refer to my own experiences in settlement archaeology, my next settlement venture, after Peru, was in this region. This came about as I was confronting what was for me the new field of Maya archaeology. It was an Americanist field for which there was a much greater and more complex body of knowledge than was the case for Peru. Nevertheless, it struck me that despite the research that had been done in Maya ceramics, sculpture, and architecture, to say nothing of the many studies into the arcane matters of hieroglyphics, calendrics, and art, very little was really known about settlement patterns and settlement systems. Not surprisingly, previous archaeological attention had been given over almost entirely to the "cities" or "ceremonial centers." Indeed, so little was known of overall Maya Lowlands settlement that the term "city"

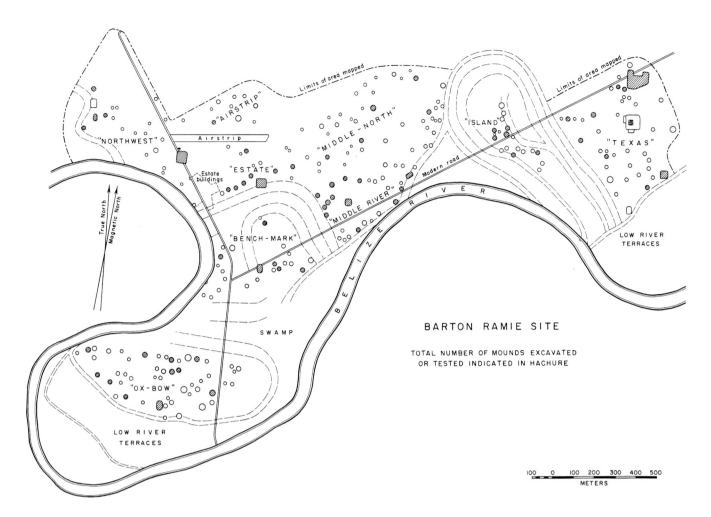

3.2 Map of Barton Ramie
site showing mounds
excavated or tested
in hachure symbol.

was used rather questionably, and most Maya archaeologists were more comfortable with the term "ceremonial center." These were the places of the magnificent pyramids, temples, and palaces with their elaborately carved monuments, inscriptions, and lavishly furnished tombs. But to what degree were these "ceremonial centers" true cities in an urban sense? Where were the residences of the people who built and sustained them?

Relatively little attention had been given to this question, so I decided it might be an appropriate place for a tyro in Maya archaeology to make a beginning. I did this, along with graduate student colleagues (Willey, Bullard, Glass, and Gifford 1965), in the Belize Valley of what was then British Honduras (now the Commonwealth of Belize) at a location not far from the Guatemalan frontier called Barton Ramie.

The name derived from an agricultural station, which had been established on the river terraces there to grow an Asian fiber plant, ramie. The ramie agricultural program turned out to be a failure in that the ramic plants would not grow to their appropriate commercial heights without constant fertilization that would have been too costly; however, the extensive cultivated fields of the stunted ramie had revealed numerous small Maya mounds.

On excavation, these mounds proved to be dwelling sites. On the approximate 2 km² of the river terraces that had been cleared of jungle and planted with ramie, we mapped 260 such small mounds. Most were small earth and rough-stone masonry platforms, 2 to 3 m in height and 10 to 15 m in diameter; however there was one larger complex with a 10 m high pyramid and three smaller buildings arranged around a little courtyard which, in effect, looked like a very small ceremonial center, albeit one without any carved stone monuments or elaborations that might be found in a larger center.

We continued our surveys in the Belize Valley over three seasons (1954–56), mapping and doing more excavations on the Barton Ramie mounds and exploring elsewhere. Continuing along the river in a westerly direction, we came to Baking Pot, where excavations had been carried out many years before (Ricketson 1929) and where there was a ceremonial center substantially larger than the little one at Barton Ramie. In slowly exploring the 7 km between Barton Ramie and Baking Pot, which was in dense undergrowth, we came upon numerous other small mounds or house mounds like those at Barton Ramie. Indeed, we came away from our Belize Valley surveys with the knowledge that residential settlement was pretty much solid, with little mounds being found all along the river terraces as far as the Guatemalan border. We knew then of a sizable ceremonial center, Benque Viejo, or Xunantunich, with large pyramids and carved stone stelae, about 25 km west of Barton Ramie and not far from the Guatemalan border. Since then, research by several other archaeologists has disclosed the presence of several large-to-medium ceremonial centers in this stretch of the Belize Valley and its hinterlands. Moreover, other centers of this size and numerous residential mounds have been found in the hills farther back from the immediate river valleys.

As this and much other Maya Lowland settlement pattern research has shown, we now have knowledge pertaining not only to degrees of true city formation or urbanization—which appears to vary from region to region and also from period to period—but also to Maya settlement arrangement over much larger stretches of territory.

What seems quite likely from the data now at hand is a hierarchical arrangement of settlement that undoubtedly reflects political structuring. In the Belize Valley, by Late Classic times (ca. CE 600–1000) if not earlier, there appear to be at least three and possibly more levels of ceremonial centers, or cities, in the hierarchy. At the lowest level there would be a very small center, such as the one in the Barton Ramie cluster of house mounds. Then coming up the scale of political importance would be a center like the one at Baking Pot, a few km up river from Barton Ramie. After this, and still higher on the political scale, there would be the impressive site of Xunantunich, with its very large buildings and carved stone stelae. Nor might a hierarchy stop there. Perhaps still bigger and grander centers, such as Yaxhá and even Tikal farther to the west in the Guatemalan Petén, may, at times, have had political control of centers in the Belize Valley as far east as Barton Ramie.

It should be noted here that the recent successes in translating the Maya hieroglyphic texts have coincided nicely with settlement studies in giving archaeologists a new understanding of ancient political systems and political histories. This began with the identification of emblem glyphs, which are a sort of dynastic coat-of-arms, and which identify centers or cities and their rulers. The distributions of these, their appearances, and their replacements by rival emblem glyphs offered some of the first clues to the political meanings of settlement arrangements and the hierarchical linkings of primary, secondary, and tertiary centers. In a general way, of course, the archaeologist operates with the assumption that site, center, or city size denotes ancient power and importance, and I would think that it usually does; however, in the Maya Lowlands, with its numerous hieroglyphic texts and monuments, the archaeologist has an additional advantage, now that these can be read, of knowing somewhat more specifically about political arrangements and how these changed through time.

There have now been many settlement pattern studies in Lowland Maya archaeology (Ashmore 1981). Indeed, the "settlement dimension" is now a "must" in most ongoing Maya field research. A good example is the article, "Deducing Social Organization from Classic Maya Settlement Patterns: A Case Study from the Copan Valley," by William L. Fash (1983). Another, reviewing the problems confronting archaeologists as they set about understanding the social, economic, political, and religious institutions and forces behind settlement arrangements, is Jeremy A. Sabloff's "Classic Maya Settlement Pattern Studies: Past Problems, Future Prospects" (1983).

Perhaps because conscious settlement pattern study had its Americanist beginnings in the areas of the "high" or "complex" cultures, namely those of Peru and Mesoamerica, it is best known, or thought to be most applicable, in such settings. However, it has had its impact elsewhere and is growing in importance in other American areas. Shortly after the Virú publication, I organized, jointly with my Harvard ethnological colleague, Professor Evon Z. Vogt, a symposium for the 1954 Annual Meeting of the American Anthropological Association, with the title *Prehistoric Settlement Patterns in the New World*. A number of American archaeological colleagues were invited to participate and offer regional papers on the subject. Later, with the addition of still other contributors, a volume of these papers was published (Willey 1956). There are 21 articles in the volume, and while a few of them treat Mesoamerica or Peru, the majority deal with other areas of North and South America. The Southwestern United States is represented by four papers; the Eastern United States by five; attention also was given to the West Indies, Tropical South America, the northern marginal peripheries of Mesoamerica, and even the non-agricultural cultures of California. I think the symposium and the book began to stimulate American archaeologists in general to think about the importance of settlement patterns and the way they could be interpreted to tell us more about the people who were responsible for them.

It was not until much more recently, however, that stronger indications of settlement pattern interest began to emerge in these non-nuclear parts of the Americas. The volume *Settlement Pattern Studies in the Americas. Fifty Years Since Virú* (Billman and Feinman 1999), in addition to articles treating Peru and Mesoamerica, has two from non-agricultural settings, one about hunter-gatherers and their sedentism in the Owens Valley of California (Bettinger 1999), and the other with village life on the Lower Alaska Peninsula (Maschner 1999). It also has two papers that deal with the Eastern United States, one on the Central Mississippi Valley, by George R. Milner and James S. Oliver (1999), and another by David J. Hally on north Georgia (1999). Both of these treat the relatively late (post–CE 1000) Middle Mississippian temple mound and large village sites which characterized the alluvial valleys of the middle and lower Eastern United States. The sites here and their arrangements pose problems of sociopolitical hierarchies reminiscent of those of Mesoamerica or Peru. Of particular interest on this theme is a monograph, *The Cahokia Chiefdom: The Archaeology of a Mississippian Society* (Milner 1998). Cahokia, in the river bottomlands near East St. Louis, is noted for the largest earth pyramid mound in the Eastern United States and also for its subsidiary temple and platform mounds as well as for its evidences of extensive village or large townsite populations. The nature of its domain of political or politico-religious control has been much debated, and Milner takes a critical look at the data which would appear, at least in a developmental sense, to adumbrate or foreshadow the kinds of processes that were going on in Mesoamerica.

3.3 Gordon R. Willey at Virú Valley, Peru.

Settlement pattern archaeology draws us in many fascinating directions. For example, one of these, *Archaeologies of Landscape*, has been treated in various parts of the world in a collection of essays under this title (Ashmore and Knapp 1999). Another direction or obvious alliance is with architecture, to which this volume is a testament.

I can only close by repeating that settlement pattern study is, inevitably and inescapably, a major dimension of archaeology, and I am pleased to have had a small role in its more conscious recognition and development.

References

Ashmore, Wendy, ed. *Lowland Maya Settlement Patterns*. Albuquerque, NM: University of New Mexico Press, 1981.

Ashmore, Wendy, and A. Bernard Knapp, eds. *Archaeologies of Landscape: Contemporary Perspectives.* Oxford: Blackwell, 1999.

Bettinger, Robert L. "From Traveler to Processor: Regional Trajectories of Hunter-Gatherer Sedentism in the Inyo-Mono Region, California." In *Settlement Pattern Studies in the Americas. Fifty Years Since Virú*, ed. Brian R. Billman and Gary N. Feinman. Washington, DC: Smithsonian Institution Press, 1999.

Billman, Brian R. "Reconstructing Prehistoric Political Economies and Cycles of Political Power in the Moche Valley, Peru." In *Settlement Pattern Studies in the Americas. Fifty Years Since Virú*, ed. Brian R. Billman and Gary M. Feinman. Washington, DC: Smithsonian Institution Press, 1999.

Billman, Brian R., and Gary M. Feinman, eds. *Settlement Pattern Studies in the Americas. Fifty Years Since Virú*. Washington, DC: Smithsonian Institution Press, 1999.

Fash, William L. "Deducing Social Organization from Classic Maya Settlement Patterns: A Case Study from the Copan Valley." In *Civilization in the Ancient Americas. Essays in Honor of Gordon R. Willey*, ed. Richard M. Leventhal and Alan L. Kolata. Albuquerque, NM: University of New Mexico Press, and Cambridge, MA: Peabody Museum, Harvard University, 1983.

Flannery, Kent V., and Joyce Marcus, eds. *The Cloud People: Divergent Evolution of the Zapotec and Mixtec Civilizations*. New York: Academic Press, 1983.

Hally, David J. "The Settlement Pattern of Mississippian Chiefdoms in Northern Georgia." In *Settlement Pattern Studies in the Americas. Fifty Years Since Virú*, ed. Brian R. Billman and Gary N. Feinman. Washington, DC: Smithsonian Institution Press, 1999.

Maschner, Herbert D. G. "Sedentism, Settlement, and Village Organization on the Lower Alaska Peninsula: A Preliminary Assessment." In *Settlement Pattern Studies in the Americas. Fifty Years Since Virú*, ed. Brian R. Billman and Gary N. Feinman. Washington, DC: Smithsonian Institution Press, 1999.

Milner, George R. *The Cahokia Chiefdom: The Archaeology of a Mississippian Society*. Washington, DC: Smithsonian Institution Press, 1998.

Milner, George R., and James S. Oliver. "Late Prehistoric Settlements and Wetlands in the Central Mississippi Valley." In *Settlement Pattern Studies in the Americas. Fifty Years Since Virú*, ed. Brian R. Billman and Gary N. Feinman. Washington, DC: Smithsonian Institution Press, 1999.

Ricketson, Oliver G., Jr. *Excavations at Baking Pot, British Honduras*. Carnegie Institution of Washington, Publication No. 403, Contributions to American Archaeology No. 1. Washington, DC: Carnegie Institution of Washington, 1929.

Sabloff, Jeremy A. "Classic Maya Settlement Pattern Studies: Past Problems, Future Prospects." In *Civilization in the Ancient Americas. Essays in Honor of Gordon R. Willey*, ed. Richard M. Leventhal and Alan L. Kolata. Albuquerque, NM: University of New Mexico Press, and Cambridge, MA: Peabody Museum, Harvard University, 1983.

Sanders, William T. "The Central Mexican Symbiotic Region: A Study in Prehistoric Settlement Patterns." In *Prehistoric Settlement Patterns in the New World*, ed. Gordon R. Willey. Viking Fund Publications in Anthropology No. 23. New York: Wenner-Gren Foundation for Anthropological Research, 1956.

Sanders, William T., and Joseph W. Michels, eds. *The Excavations. The Pennsylvania State University Kaminaljuyú Project—1968 Season, Part I*. Occasional Papers in Anthropology 2. University Park, PA: Dept. of Anthropology, Pennsylvania State University, 1969.

Sanders, William T., Jeffrey R. Parsons, and Robert S. Santley. *The Basin of Mexico: Ecological Processes in the Evolution of a Civilization*. New York: Academic Press, 1979.

Willey, Gordon R. *Prehistoric Settlement Patterns in the Virú Valley, Peru*. Bulletin 155, Bureau of American Ethnology. Washington, DC: Smithsonian Institution, 1953.

Willey, Gordon R., ed. *Prehistoric Settlement Patterns in the New World*. Viking Fund Publications in Anthropology No. 23. New York: Wenner-Gren Foundation for Anthropological Research, 1956.

Willey, Gordon R., William R. Bullard, John B. Glass, and James C. Gifford. *Prehistoric Maya Settlements in the Belize Valley*. Papers of the Peabody Museum of Archaeology and Ethnology, Harvard University 52. Cambridge, MA: Peabody Museum, 1965.

Wilson, David J. *Prehispanic Settlement Patterns in the Lower Santa Valley, Peru*. Washington, DC: Smithsonian Institution Press, 1988.

The Idea of a Maya Town

Wendy Ashmore

4

Despite more than four centuries' attention from conquerors, travelers, and scholars, the structure and meaning of Maya settlement continue to yield new insights. Some observers see Maya farmsteads, towns, and cities as evincing relatively informal, at times even haphazard arrangement. Increasing numbers of scholars today, however, view Maya settlement as richly imbued with spatial order and symbolism. In this chapter, I consider briefly some influential explications of the structure of Maya settlement, focusing especially on towns and cities of pre-Columbian times. From those more established views, I turn to recent research that discerns even greater intricacies in ancient Maya spatial structure and in meanings embodied in the ancient built environment. My central contentions are (1) that current research underscores the complex texture of Maya spatial order, and (2) that both similarities and difference among recorded towns and cities express shared worldviews as shaped by local political history. In short, those who commissioned ancient Maya civic construction drew on an array of shared beliefs about the proper arrangement and constitution of the human habitat. Like counterparts in many societies, they materialized a cosmically sanctified authority by creating and acting within appropriately formed buildings and spaces.

The title of this chapter is appropriated from Joseph Rykwert's (1998) seminal work on ancient Roman towns and on the norms and protocols followed in civic planning. Although focusing on Rome, his inferences have far wider resonance cross-culturally. I want to note the liberties I have taken in using his term "town" in a discussion treating both towns and cities. The theoretical and functional distinctions between the two categories are undeniably important, and their definitions are debated widely. Although I recognize that the two terms are not equivalent, they serve equally well, and almost interchangeably, for this discussion. That is, although scholars debate whether the individual settlements I consider are best labeled "cities," "towns," or some other socio-spatial category, all are more likely to agree that in each case, they are both a recognizable architectural focus and formalized arenas in which civic events are held, for social assembly at larger than a domestic scale. What I address here are ideas behind the structure of these settlements and the meanings in their well-structured arrangement—that is, the idea of a Maya town.

I would also note that the time frame for discussion here encompasses the span of Maya civilization in pre-Columbian times. The Classic period, generally placed between about CE 250 and CE 900 or 1000, is the one for which the planning patterns I describe are clearest. The Preclassic or Formative, conventionally 1000 BCE to CE 250, lacks the wealth of ancient texts characteristic of Classic times, and as argued later, evinces significant differences from the Classic in town planning principles and their inferred meaning. The Postclassic period, ca. CE 1000–

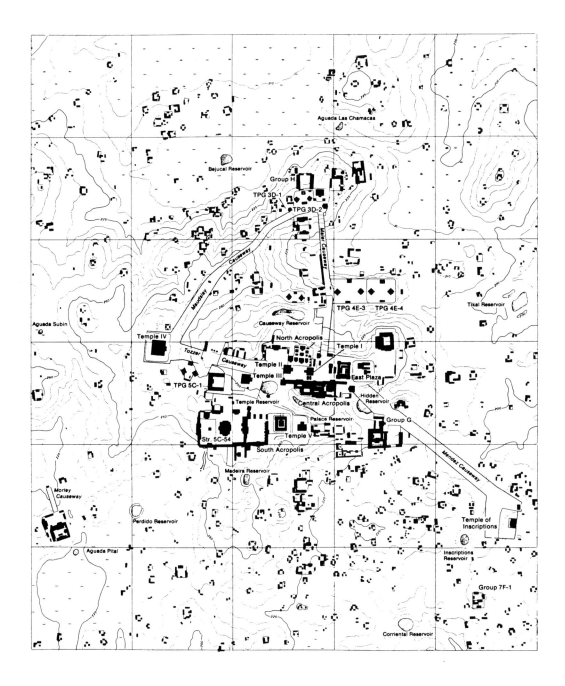

1526, yields continuities and differences in planning as well as the most direct links with living communities and with a new world of descriptive literature spawned by the Spanish Conquest.

BACKGROUND MODELS

Many authors have considered the form of and meaning behind Maya settlement. From 16th century descriptions aimed at justifying colonial and proselytizing efforts to ecclesiastical authorities through the structural, functional, and symbolic interpretations of 20th century analysts written for scholarly audiences, the varying interpretations reflect well the social and intellectual milieux in which their authors wrote. Whereas some authors have focused on the Maya specifically, others situate Maya towns and cities within larger comparative frameworks.

Comparative and theoretical treatises on towns, cities, city space, and their social correlates are legion, with even the literature of only the most recent decades yielding truly diverse perspectives from many disciplines. For Mesoamerica and the Maya, specifically, archaeologist Gordon Willey (1956, 1981) has led the way in characterizing settlement patterns at the town, city, and community level. The late architect George Andrews (1975) wrote of modular units through which Maya cities and settlement were structured. William Sanders and David Webster, following Richard Fox, have argued that the diversity among ancient Mesoamerican cities could be partitioned with three functional categories: regal-ritual, administrative, and mercantile cities (Sanders and Webster 1988; see Ball and Taschek 1991; Chase, Chase, and Haviland 1990). Although many other authors have also offered provocative insights on Maya and other towns and cities, I single out three sets of ideas that have been particularly influential for preparing this chapter. These are the writings of Bishop Landa and Diane Chase's critique, Joyce Marcus's incisive discussion of models for Mesoamerican cities, and Joseph Rykwert's volume on Roman towns.

Fray Diego de Landa, second Bishop of Yucatan, is commonly credited with describing the essential spatial order of Maya towns in early Spanish colonial times. Having been called to account for his efforts by his overlords in the Spanish Inquisition, Landa produced a detailed description of Maya customs in the later 16th century, the oft-cited *Relación de las Cosas de Yucatan* (Tozzer 1941). Landa described a concentric organization of the towns by social class, with close packing of houses and provisioning resources, the inferred rationale of the arrangement being at least partly defensive:

> Before the Spaniards had conquered that country, the natives lived together in towns in a very civilized fashion. They kept the land well cleared and free from weeds, and planted very good trees. Their dwelling place was as follows: in the middle of the town were their temples with beautiful plazas, and all around the temples stood the houses of the lords and the priests, and then (those of) the most important people. Thus came the houses of the richest and those who were held in the highest estimation nearest to these, and at the outskirts of the town were the houses of the lower class. And the wells, if there were but few of them, were near the houses of the lords; and they had their improved lands planted with wine trees and they sowed cotton, pepper and maize, and they lived thus close together for fear of their enemies, who took them captive, and it was owing to the wars of the Spaniards that they scattered in the woods. (Tozzer 1941:62–64)

Although the foregoing is cited frequently as a key to understanding Maya townscapes, Diane Chase (1986) has asserted categorically that the "concentric-ring class-linked residence pattern described by Landa does not appear to have existed" (366), at least not for Yucatan near the time of the Spanish Conquest. From her critical ethnohistoric research and archaeological investigations at Santa Rita Corozal, plausibly the 16th-century capital of the Maya province of Chetumal (349), Chase suggests that Landa may have drawn on earlier Spanish accounts and on Spanish concepts of proper town planning, rather than his own first-hand analysis of local Maya town form (362–63). She further suggests that Maya towns at that time were more likely organized in sectors or *barrios*; although some, such as the confederation capital of Mayapan, also had a discernible civic center, Santa Rita Corozal and some other settlements lacked a distinct center (Chase 1986:364–66).

Writing at about the same time as Chase, Joyce Marcus (1983) reviewed a range of morphological and functional characterizations for Mesoamerican cities, including those of the Maya. Among the morphology alternatives she discussed were concentric and sector models, similar in the forms encompassed to the constructs described by Chase but stemming in Marcus's discussion from theoretical models of urban growth, from sociology and cultural geography (198–202). Marcus found evidence of concentric, sector, and related patterns in discrete pre-Columbian cases of diverse age and cultural affiliation, but like Chase, saw no models as applicable universally for either Mesoamerica or the Maya. Indeed, she found that "Mesoamerican cities display, in microcosm, much of the diversity of ancient cities elsewhere" (Marcus 1983:239). A city's morphology, she argued, was related most strongly to its growth history (240). Her analysis and my own diverge in focus at this point, although not through disagreement. Two particular further points from her review are especially important to the current essay.

The first point is that, following Doxiadis, Marcus distinguished "planned" from "unplanned" cities, the former formalized in rectangular or axially ordered layouts, and the latter evincing less formal, radial morphology. At the same time, she notes significantly that "many Mesoamerican cities combine both aspects, having a clearly planned 'inner city,' which is the locus for public secular and religious structures, and an unplanned 'outer city,' which shows haphazard residential growth" (Marcus 1983:197).

For city morphology, her focus was the city in its entirety. For me, however, it is what Marcus calls the "inner city," or civic center, and it is their forms and meaning that we are coming to understand more clearly.

Marcus's second point to note here comes from her important discussion of native views of the city. From linguistic and ethnohistoric analysis in multiple Mesoamerican traditions, Marcus concludes that towns and cities were understood only within their larger social and political contexts. The native point of reference is that one "belonged to a particular region controlled by a specific native ruler, to whom he owed allegiance and tribute and from whom he received protection and civic-ceremonial leadership" (1983:208; see Quezada 1993). City size and growth history, so important to our Western analytic models today, were not central to native people. In their words, the essence of town or city was that it was where the ruler lived.

What emerges from the foregoing discussion is the importance to a town of its central civic and ceremonial precinct, and of its resident ruler. No single models for form or growth pattern account for settlement morphology universally. I contend below that specific morphology is contingent on the political history of the town or city, set within the builders' wider understanding of acceptable town and city forms. I turn now to processes of establishing settlements and of creating proper town plans.

Here I draw on Joseph Rykwert's work, cited at the outset, for the importance he places on the acts in establishing a town, and on what the town means for its inhabitants. He discusses the rituals and protocols for choosing a site, establishing boundaries, and building the place. Although his central cases are Rome and Roman towns, he makes wide-ranging comparisons across societies in Old and New Worlds, from ancient and modern times. Toward the close of the book, he notes that he has "been concerned to show the town as a total mnemonic symbol, or at any rate a structured complex of symbols; in which the citizen, through a number of bodily exercises, such as processions, seasonal festivals, sacrifices, identifies himself with his town, with its past and its founders" (Rykwert 1998:189). More expansively, he describes Roman and perhaps earlier towns as having

4.2 On Str. A–6, Xunan-tunich, a plaster frieze identifies the local king as re-enacting the creation of the cosmos, by placing a statue of him amid gigantic deity masks, as well as lunar and other celestial symbols. Although the statue is no longer there, the serpent-headed throne on which his image sat is preserved, immediately above the un-excavated central mask.

been founded by the procedure which the Romans and Etruscans probably shared in some way with the whole of the ancient world: it consisted of the following elements: (1) the acting out, at the founding of any settlement (or temple maybe, even a mere house) of a dramatic show of the creation of the world; (2) the incarnation of that drama in the plan of the settlement, as well as in its social and religious institution; (3) the achieving of this second aim by the alignment of its axes with those of the universe; and finally (4) the rehearsal of the foundation cosmogony in regularly recurrent festivals, and its commemorative embodiment in the monuments of the settlement. (194)

And again, with more specific reference to individual Romans' lived experience:

It is difficult to imagine a situation when the formal order of the universe could be reduced to a diagram of two intersecting co-ordinates in one plane. Yet this is exactly what did happen in antiquity: the Roman who walked along the *cardo* knew that his walk was the axis around which the sun turned, and that if he followed the *decumanus*, he was following the sun's course. *The whole universe and its meaning could be spelt out of his civic institutions— so he was at home in it*. (202, emphasis added)

The conclusions Rykwert draws about how cosmology, ritual, and local history shape town form and meaning certainly resonate strongly with a wider literature on cities, the built environment generally, and now landscapes as well (Basso 1996; Eliade 1959; Rapoport 1982; Tuan 1977; Wheatley 1971).

The key points to note here are the cross-cultural, perhaps even universal importance of the three shaping factors—cosmology, ritual, and local history—and the set of acts by which they are linked to a specific town. That is, for the ancient Maya, as for town planners in many settings, we recognize increasingly the formative roles played by the acting out of creation, its incarnation in the town plan, the town's alignment with cosmic axes, and the repetitive re-enactment of creation within the properly situated town. I contend further that, as in many other societies, those who commissioned the civic built environment used the sanctified space and the timely rituals to establish and then underscore their own authority to rule the populace identified with the town.

Recent Research on Maya Town and City Planning

To demonstrate the role of the foregoing factors in Maya civic planning, I briefly review several related factors widely accepted as at least partial plan determinants—astronomy, landscape mimicry, cosmology—and then place them within a planning model where these factors offer a vocabulary through which those who commissioned the construction created well-structured and highly meaningful political expressions in stone, earth, and bounded space.[1]

Beginning with astronomy, much has been written about the astronomical sophistication of the ancient Maya, by skilled astronomers such as Anthony Aveni (1980). The heavens also shaped the built environment, as attested in such famed observatories as the Caracol of Chichén Itzá, Venus-sighting windows in Copán and other places, or the widespread solstice-equinox observation stations known prosaically as "E-Groups," for their first recognition in Group E of Uaxactún (Ruppert 1940). The latter complexes well illustrate that more than an astronomical dimension was involved. As Vilma Fialko (1988) has argued, many E-Groups are misaligned with respect to guiding solstice-equinox sunrise observations; she suggests that we consider them, instead, to commemorate the idea of such observation. I agree, and as asserted shortly, believe E-Groups are among multiple sufficient but not individually necessary markers of a well-planned and well-governed Maya town.

Because the rich legacy of Classic period inscriptions is being deciphered at what often seems a dizzying clip, we also appreciate ever more the astrological role of the ancient astronomy in guiding political and personal actions. This recent explosion of textual information yields many other insights relevant here, especially concerning landscape mimicry and mapping of the cosmos. Epigraphers can now tell us the names of buildings and open spaces (Schele and Freidel 1990; Schele and Mathews 1998; compare Stuart and Houston 1994). Among other things, the names confirm long-standing recognition that, as is common cross-culturally, the Maya built environment mimics the surrounding landscape (Townsend 1992). A Maya pyramid does not just resemble a mountain; it is a mountain, or *witz* (Benson 1985; Schele and Freidel 1990; Stone 1992; Stuart 1987; Vogt

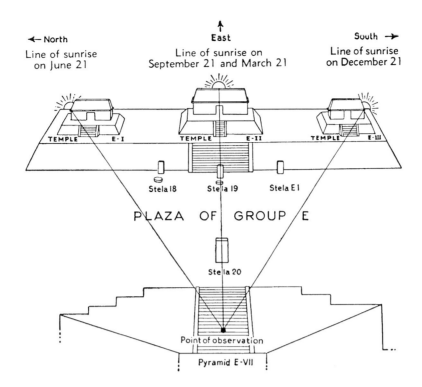

◄— North

Line of sunrise
on June 21

East

Line of sunrise on
September 21 and March 21

South —►

Line of sunrise
on December 21

TEMPLE   E-I

TEMPLE   E-II

TEMPLE   E-III

Stela 18

Stela 19

Stela E1

PLAZA   OF   GROUP   E

Stela 20

Point of observation

Pyramid E-VII

1964). Like observed mountains, the constructed ones shelter caves, either as what we call rooms or what we recognize as burial chambers (Brady and Ashmore 1999; Freidel and Schele 1989). The caves, in turn, are portals to the supernatural underworld beneath the mountain, often literally or metaphorically a watery place, as is appropriate for the karstic Maya lowlands.

Moreover, thanks to research on ancient water management, especially by Vernon Scarborough (1996, 1998) and his colleagues, we also now know that scarce water resources within Maya cities were often controlled and enhanced by intricate human engineering (Dunning et al. 1999; Scarborough and Gallopin 1991). By allotment and construction of waterholes, the king controlled and provided sustenance, and the distribution of reservoirs was well planned and meaningfully placed: at Tikal, for example, the four largest are "located roughly in the cardinal directions from the epicenter" (Scarborough 1996:305; 1998:141; see Figure 4.1). Beyond serving as a critical *practical* resource, the exposed water may have signaled a portal to the underworld, and its mirror-like reflective properties may have encouraged divination and sacrifice (Brady and Ashmore 1999; Taube 1992). Certainly Maya rituals and sacrifice at bodies of water are well known, the most famous evidence being offerings documented from Chichén Itzá's Cenote of Sacrifice (Coggins 1992).

Town plans mimic landscapes in tightly controlled ways. Both, in turn, map the cosmos. Epigraphers describe the use of civic buildings and spaces as stages and arenas for enacting primordial sagas of creation and for rituals to safeguard the continuance of human and other life within the cosmos. Perhaps the clearest material expression of such mapping is a series

of complexes at Tikal known as Twin Pyramid Groups (Coggins 1980; Jones 1969). In these groups flat-topped pyramids flank east and west edges of a spacious open platform where hundreds could gather. To the south is a low building with nine doorways into its single room. On the north edge of the platform, an unroofed enclosure embraces a single pair of sculptures, the upright stela of which displays a portrait of the then-current king of the city. Clemency Coggins (1980) describes this as a map of the cosmos, of the vertical path of the sun turned 90° on its side to accommodate the practicalities of construction. The two pyramids mark rise and set directions of the sun's path, and the nine-doorwayed building is the realm of the Nine Lords of the Underworld, the sun at nadir and thus, metaphorically, "down." To complete the solar circuit, the northern building would represent "up" and would thereby place the ruler, through his portrait, in the celestial realm, with his ancestors and other powerful supernaturals—especially with the sun at its most powerful midday position overhead.

I have argued elsewhere (1989, 1991, 1992) that Tikal's Twin Pyramid Groups offer a key to understanding the significance of the pervasive north-south axis in Classic period civic centers. Although the specific scale and disposition of buildings vary among settlements, the dominance of a north-south axis is indisputably prevalent for Classic Maya civic centers. My inference is that this axial emphasis maps the cosmos in such a way as to situate the king and his arenas for public action in metaphorically powerful, supernaturally potent positions, especially in the heavens to the north or the underworld to the south. It even holds in some non-Maya places, such as Gualjoquito, in west-central Honduras (Ashmore 1987), where the directions are slightly more askew, but suggest to me that the builders—known from other evidence to be influenced, if not governed, by Maya Copán to the west—that these local builders were creating *or approximating* a

4.5 The northernmost mask on the Str. A–6 frieze portrays a *Pax* god, and with its twin on the south end, represents the world tree at the center of the cosmos. To the left of the mask is a U-shaped lunar symbol.

proper arena for hosting their distinguished Maya visitors on politically, ritually, and economically important occasions. As with the "misaligned" E-Groups mentioned earlier, it is the idea of proper spatial order and its recognizable materialization that counts, not the precision of its rendering.

What is the meaning of this north-south directional dimension? At first, I could suggest only that it complemented the clear solar dimension of the east-west axis and related to dynastic rulership (Ashmore 1989, 1991). Several further observations augment this suggestion, linking it more directly with the celebration of rulership in a sanctified, cosmic setting. One is the notable shift in dominant axial planning orientation between Preclassic and Classic times. In the Preclassic, east-west is the dominant axis of the planned precincts of Maya towns and cities, such as El Mirador or Nakbe. This was also a time when sculpture depicted the sun, Venus, and other celestial deities, not identifiable humans. With the onset of the Classic, however, sculptures commonly depicted and glorified kings. Writing, already well developed by the time of its first-known renderings in stone, provided another medium to extol the kings, their deeds, and their dynasties. It seems to me more than coincidence that this same transition should also have corresponded, at least approximately, with the time when the planning axis shifted to north-south, away from the previously solar axis (Ashmore 1995; Freidel and Schele 1988a, 1988b; Taube 1998).

More important, ethnographic, epigraphic, iconographic, and astronomical evidence jointly suggest that the north-south dimension represents a man, specifically a king, as incarnation of First Father, or the Maize God, and architect of cosmic creation. Many scholars have written of the royal portrait stelae as metaphorical trees and of these full-length human images arrayed in a civic plaza as marking a "forest of kings" (Newsome 1991; Schele and Freidel 1990). Freidel, Schele, and Parker (1993) interpret the symbolism of such trees in their discussion of the World Tree as depicted at Palenque: "The [hieroglyphically recorded] name of the tree literally meant 'raised-up sky.' The Classic texts at Palenque tell us that the central axis of the cosmos was called the 'raised-up sky' because First Father had raised it at the beginning of creation in order to separate the sky from the earth. Each World Tree was, therefore, a representation of the *axis of creation*" (55, emphasis added).

This was not the first act of creation, that having been achieved in First Father's laying of a three-stone hearth at a place called "Lying-Down-Sky" (75). These three stones are also commemorated architecturally, by triadic arrangements particularly characteristic of Preclassic times (e.g., Freidel, Schele, and Parker 1993:140). Next, however, was when he "entered the sky" by raising the world tree: "we learn that First Father's 'entering the sky' also created a house and that it was made of eight partitions. . . . [Further depictive evidence shows that] the Maya thought of the entire north direction as a house erected at Creation with the World Tree, the Wakah-Chan, penetrating its central axis. First Father 'entered the sky' by raising this tree out of a plate of sacrifice" (Freidel, Schele, and Parker 1993:71).

In raising up the sky, First Father not only separated the earth from the sky, and founded a house in the north, but according to Freidel, Schele, and Parker (1993), he thereby also established the eight cardinal and intercardinal directions of the world: "First Father's house [in the north] thus orders the entire upper cosmos, the world of humanity, of plants and animals, and of the sky beings, by establishing the center, the periphery, and the partitions of the world. Even today the Maya practice this partitioning and ordering of the world in their rituals" (73).

The point here is not that this raising of the world tree was the only act of creation, but that it was one equated with a north-south dimension, and with a male figure. To be sure, First Father is a supernatural male, but just as movements of the Milky Way perpetually depict and re-enact creation events in the sky (Cook 2000), so too, I would argue, establishing a town or a civic precinct with a dominant north-south axis mapped this central creation act on the ground.[2] He who literally commanded construction of the civic complex could be equated with First Father, he who ordered the entire cosmos by raising the World Tree. Rituals in varied forms, as processions, dances, and pilgrimages, repeatedly recalled the architect of this act to all witnesses and participants assembled in the materialized cosmic map of the civic center (Schele and Mathews 1998:173; Ringle 1999).

Two other matters of planning require comment here, both concerning variability among specific town or city plans. Despite the Classic period dominance of a north-south axis, Maya cities and towns clearly differ from one another in arrangement of buildings and plazas. There are surely many reasons for this, but at least two are worth noting here.

The first stems from realization that because what we observe today is a "site plan" of ruins, we must recognize and sort out the cumulative nature of planning and construction at what was originally a town or city. Jeremy Sabloff and I examined the civic plans of the sites we knew best at first hand—Quiriguá, Copán, Seibal, Sayil, and Xunantunich—plus that of Tikal, one of the most studied of Maya sites. Our conclusion, perhaps unsurprising in retrospect, was that the complexity of the observed palimpsest correlates with the length of occupation span and the turbulence of political history (Ashmore and Sabloff 2002).

That is, for three of the sites examined—Quiriguá, Copán, and Sayil—political history seems to have been relatively untroubled. Documented dynastic rule at the three ranged from

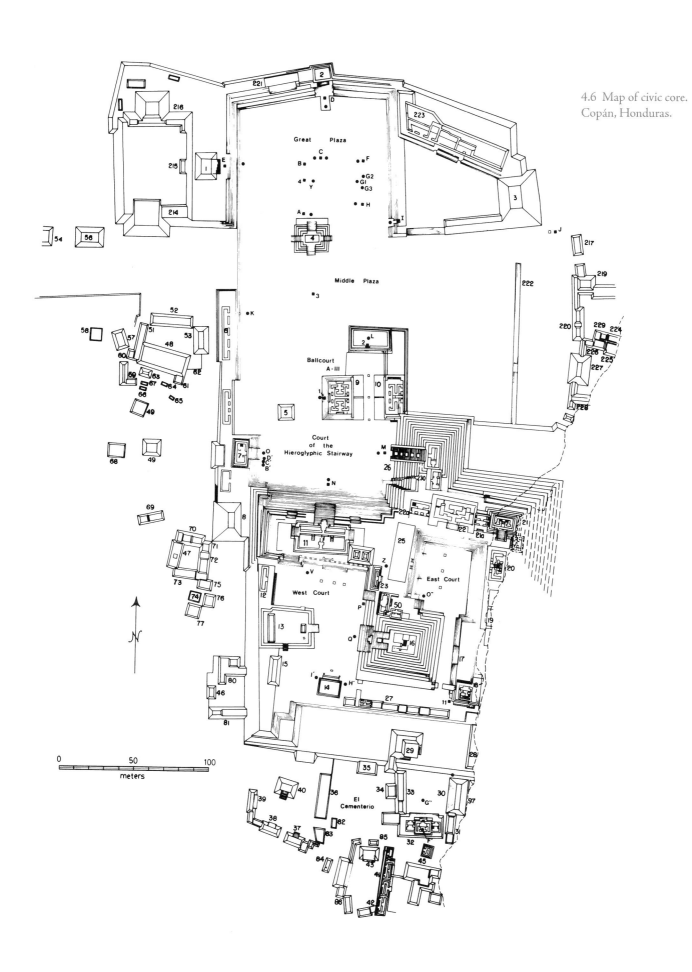

4.6 Map of civic core.
Copán, Honduras.

Great Plaza

Middle Plaza

Ballcourt
A-III

Court
of the
Hieroglyphic Stairway

West Court

East Court

El Cementerio

N

0   50   100
meters

4.7 Map of civic core.
Seibal, Guatemala.

perhaps one to perhaps four centuries in duration, but the rebellion of Quiriguá against Copán notwithstanding, there is no indication that the ruling house of any was overthrown during the span of major, documented construction. There is no evidence that anyone sought to change the local civic plan significantly.

Seibal had a deeper history, nearly two millennia (ca. 900 BCE–CE 900), from Preclassic times through the end of the Classic, with a turbulent upheaval in governance during the final years. The major re-orientation of city plan, however, is most plausibly linked to the Preclassic-Classic shift in dominant orientation inferred earlier for the lowlands as a whole.

Tikal was the most complicated case, the hardest to figure out spatially, and the one with the most intricate text-documented history, with total occupation span roughly equivalent to that at Seibal. Not only does Tikal span the Preclassic-Classic shift, it also underwent major struggles within and between dynasties, as well as protracted warfare and its attendant disruptions. The Tikal civic plan does make sense to modern observers, however, if examined as successive building programs by kings who sought to glorify themselves and their ruling house and either glorify or eradicate memory of their diverse predecessors (Ashmore and Sabloff 2002; Jones 1991; Laporte and Fialko 1995).

Tikal's plan and political history bring us to our final point. Some of the distinctions and similarities among sites I have examined may also be explicable in political terms. In 1989, I defined what I saw as a "template" for civic planning, rooted in the spatial symbolism of Tikal's Twin Pyramid Groups. The template fit the layouts of Quiriguá, Copán, and a number of other cities and towns. Bret Houk (1996) has applied it at Dos Hombres in northern Belize, and Olivier de Montmollin (1995) has discussed it in relation to sites in and adjoining the Upper

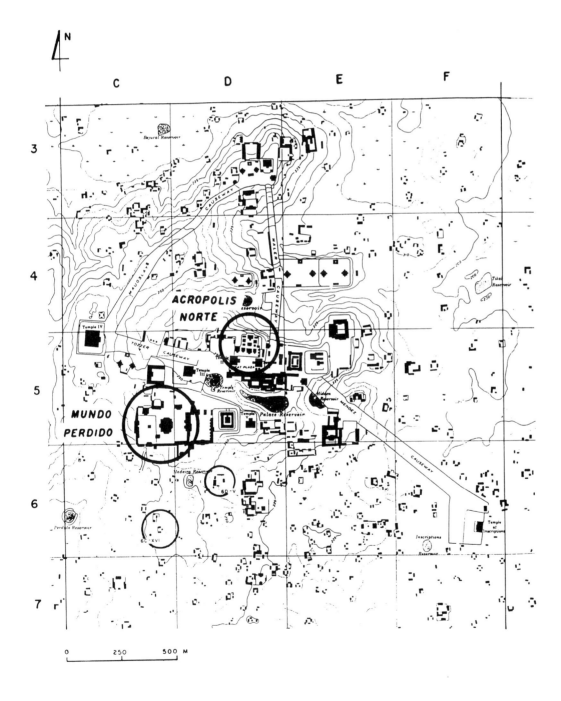

4.8 Map of greater civic core highlighting temporally distinct foci of royal architectural planning. Tikal, Guatemala

4.9 Map of civic core.
Xunantunich, Belize.

Grijalva basin of Chiapas. However, as Norman Hammond noted to me about 1990, the template failed to fit many Maya centers in Belize. That led me to research at Xunantunich, in which I have observed that a different pattern—with the same underlying cosmos-based spatial vocabulary, including a dominant north-south axis—seemed to copy the civic cores of Naranjo and Calakmul (Ashmore 1998; Ashmore and Leventhal 1993).

In the mid-1990s, epigraphers Simon Martin and Nikolai Grube began reporting their far-reaching research, concluding that lowland Maya political history was dominated by centuries of struggle between two "superstates" based at Tikal and Calakmul (Martin and Grube 1995, 2000). Alliances, intrigue, and warfare all studded the emerging history, but what struck me was that, quite independently, examination of civic plans seem to echo the texts, suggesting membership in one or the other super-alliance. That is, Quiriguá and Copán were

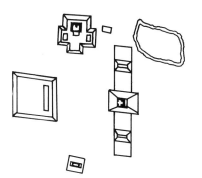

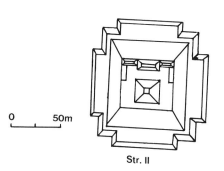

0   50m

Str. II

documented textually as allies of Tikal and shared its core civic plan—the exception was the period embracing Quiriguá's rebellion against its overlord, Copán, in the mid-8th century; the rupture lasted no more than a few decades but was apparently supported by temporary alliance with distant Calakmul (Looper 1995). In contrast, Naranjo is linked textually with Calakmul, and both Naranjo and its plausible subordinate or heir, Xunantunich, evinced a core plan similar to Calakmul (Ashmore 1998).

The sparse, terse, and badly eroded texts of Xunantunich have yielded an apparent reference to Naranjo, but we lack inscriptions situating it within its own or any larger political history. Although I would not argue that "reading" civic plans will reveal all about such history, I would suggest, particularly for sites where literal references are absent, that study of civic plans may provide clues to political history. The cosmically sanctified civic plans were as much a vehicle for royal promotion and political opinion shaping as were the public texts found within their confines (Marcus 1992; Schele and Mathews 1998; cf. Steinhardt 1986 for Chinese capital-city plans). They still have much to tell us.

Concluding Remarks

At the outset, I reviewed briefly some influential conceptions about spatial order in Maya towns. I then turned to Rykwert's recognition of the formative roles played in town planning by the acting out of creation, its incarnation in the town plan, the town's alignment with cosmic axes, and the repetitive re-enactment of creation within the properly situated town. I have sought to illustrate the operation of each of these processes and principles in a range of Classic Maya civic centers, and to link their expression to political motives of those directing planning and construction. Together, these illustrations support the contentions (1) that current research underscores the complex texture of Maya spatial order, and (2) that both similarities and difference among recorded towns and cities express shared worldview as shaped by local political history. Acknowledging that there is much more yet to learn about the form and meaning of Maya settlements, I would suggest that the idea of a Maya town was fundamentally one of cosmically sanctioned political expression.

NOTES

1. Discussions of town and city planning, and of the idea of what constitutes a proper town, range far more widely than can be treated here. Most important is more extended consideration than has been included hereon the social construction and moral fabric of settlements (Smith 2003). Other partial determinants of town and city form generate fruitfully provocative discussion, and omission of their discussion stems only from their being neither central to nor incompatible with arguments of this volume. For example, Peter Harrison (1994) has argued intriguingly that, at Palenque and in the Central Acropolis of Tikal, particular geometric relationships account for the position and orientation of some successive constructions—see related arguments for Quiriguá and Copán by Vogrin (1989). John Carlson (1981) inferred operation of principles akin to Chinese *feng shui* in situating Mesoamerican settlements generally. Defensive factors cited by Bishop Landa for the 16th century were clearly important for some earlier times, especially in places like the war-torn Petexbatún region. Even for astronomy-related factors, I have omitted recognition here of important light-and-shadow hierophanies—and their consequent celebration of a particular king's authority—arising from orientation of buildings, and particularly doorways, to sunrise or sunset on particular dates (e.g., Palenque: Schele 1977; Yaxchilán: Tate 1985).

2. House foundation rituals were likewise important creation events in Classic times, and remain important among the Maya today (e.g., Gillespie 2000; Stuart 1998; Vogt 1969 and 1976).

REFERENCES

Andrews, George F. *Maya Cities: Placemaking and Urbanization.* Norman, OK: University of Oklahoma Press, 1975.

Ashmore, Wendy. "Cobble Crossroads: Gualjoquito Architecture and External Elite Ties." In *Interaction on the Southeast Mesoamerican Periphery: Prehistoric and Historic Honduras and El Salvador*, ed. Eugenia J. Robinson. BAR International Series 327. Oxford: BAR, 1987:28–48.

———. "Construction and Cosmology: Politics and Ideology in Lowland Maya Settlement Patterns." In *Word and Image in Maya Culture: Explorations in Language, Writing and Representation*, ed. William F. Hanks and Don S. Rice. Salt Lake City, UT: University of Utah Press, 1989, 272–86.

———. "Site-planning Principles and Concepts of Directionality among The Ancient Maya." *Latin American Antiquity* 2(1991):199–226.

———. "Deciphering Maya Site Plans." In *New Theories on the Ancient Maya*, ed. Elin Danien and Robert J. Sharer. Philadelphia, PA: University of Pennsylvania Museum of Archaeology and Anthropology, 1992, 173–84.

———. "Ritual Landscapes in the Xunantunich Area." Paper presented at the First International Symposium on Maya Archaeology, San Ignacio, Belize, 1995.

———. "Monumentos Políticos: Sitios, Asentamiento, y Paisaje por Xunantunich, Belice." In *Anatomía de una Civilización: Aproximaciones Interdisciplinarias a la Cultura Maya*, ed. Andrés Ciudad Ruiz, Yolanda Fernández Marquínez, José Miguel García Campillo, Ma. Josefa Iglesias Ponce de León, Alfonso Lacadena García-Gallo, Luis T. Sanz Castro. Publ. No. 4. Madrid: Sociedad Española de Estudios Mayas, 1998, 161–83.

Ashmore, Wendy, and Richard M. Leventhal. "Xunantunich Reconsidered." Paper presented at Conference on Belize, University of North Florida, Jacksonville, 1993.

Ashmore, Wendy, and Jeremy A. Sabloff. "Spatial Orders in Maya Civic Plans." *Latin American Antiquity* 13(2002):201–15.

Aveni, Anthony F. *Skywatchers of Ancient Mexico*. Austin, TX: University of Texas Press, 1980.

Ball, Joseph W., and Jennifer Taschek. "Late Classic Lowland Maya Political Organization and Central-place Analysis: New Insights from the Upper Belize Valley." *Ancient Mesoamerica* 2(1991):149–65.

Basso, Keith H. *Wisdom Sits in Places: Landscape and Language among the Western Apache*. Albuquerque, NM: University of New Mexico Press, 1996.

Benson, Elizabeth P. "Architecture as Metaphor." In *Fifth Palenque Round Table, 1983*, ed. Merle Greene Robertson and Virginia M. Fields. San Francisco, CA: Pre-Columbian Art Research Institute, 1985, 183–8.

Brady, James E., and Wendy Ashmore. "Mountains, Caves, and Water: Ideational Landscapes of the Ancient Maya." In *Archaeologies of Landscape: Contemporary Perspectives*, ed. Wendy Ashmore and A. Bernard Knapp. Oxford: Blackwell, 1999, 124–45.

Carlson, John. "A Geomantic Model for the Interpretation of Mesoamerican Sites: An Essay in Cross-cultural Comparison." In *Mesoamerican Sites and World-Views*, ed. Elizabeth P. Benson. Washington, DC: Dumbarton Oaks, 1981, 143–215.

Chase, Diane Z. "Social and Political Organization in the Land of Cacao and Honey: Correlating the Archaeology and Ethnohistory of the Postclassic Lowland Maya." In *Late Lowland Maya Civilization: Classic to Postclassic*, ed. Jeremy A. Sabloff and E. Wyllys Andrews V. Albuquerque, NM: University of New Mexico Press, 1986, 347–77.

Chase, Diane Z., Arlen F. Chase, and William A. Haviland. "The Classic Maya City: Reconsidering the 'Mesoamerican Urban Tradition.'" *American Anthropologist* 92(1990):499–506.

Coggins, Clemency. "The Shape of Time: Some Political Implications of a Four-part Figure." *American Antiquity* 45(1980):727–39.

———. "Artifacts from the Cenote of Sacrifice, Chichén Itzá, Yucatan." *Memoirs of the Peabody Museum of Archaeology and Ethnology* 10, 3. Cambridge, MA: Peabody Museum, Harvard University, 1992.

Cook, Garrett W. *Renewing the Maya World: Expressive Culture in a Highland Maya Town*. Austin, TX: University of Texas Press, 2000.

de Montmollin, Olivier. "Settlement and Politics in Three Classic Maya Polities." *Monographs in World Archaeology* 24. Madison, WI: Prehistory Press, 1995.

Dunning, Nicholas P., Vernon Scarborough, Fred Valdez, Jr., Sheryl Luzzadder-Beach, Timothy Beach, and John G. Jones. "Temple Mountains, Sacred Lakes, and Fertile Fields: Ancient Maya Landscapes in Northwestern Belize." *Antiquity* 73(1999):650–60.

Eliade, Mircea. *The Sacred and the Profane*. New York: Harcourt Brace, 1959.

Fialko, Vilma. "Mundo Perdido, Tikal: Un Ejemplo de Complejos de Conmemoración Astronómica." *Mayab* 4(1988):13–21.

Freidel, David, and Linda Schele. "Symbol and Power: A History of the Lowland Maya Cosmogram." In *Maya Iconography*, ed. Elizabeth P. Benson and Gillett Griffin. Princeton, NJ: Princeton University Press, 1988a, 44–93.

———. "Kingship in the Late Preclassic Maya Lowlands: The Instruments and Places of Royal Power." *American Anthropologist* 90(1988b):547–67.

———. "Dead Kings and Living Temples: Dedication and Termination Rituals among the Ancient Maya." In *Word and Image in Maya Culture: Explorations in Language, Writing and Representation*, ed. William F. Hanks and Don S. Rice. Salt Lake City, UT: University of Utah Press, 1989, 233–43.

Freidel, David, Linda Schele, and Joy Parker. *Maya Cosmos: Three Thousand Years on the Shaman's Path*. New York: William Morrow, 1993.

Gillespie, Susan D. "Maya 'Nested Houses': The Ritual Construction of Place." In *Beyond Kinship: Social and Material Reproduction in House Societies*, ed. Rosemary A. Joyce and Susan D. Gillespie. Philadelphia, PA: University of Pennsylvania Press, 2000, 135–60.

Harrison, Peter D. "Spatial Geometry and Logic in the Ancient Maya Mind, Part II: Architecture." In *Seventh Palenque Round Table, 1989, Vol. IX*, ed. Merle Greene Robertson and Virginia M. Fields. San Francisco, CA: Pre-Columbian Art Research Institute, 1994, 243–52.

Houk, Bret A. "The Archaeology of Site Planning: An Example from the Maya Site of Dos Hombres, Belize." Ph.D. dissertation, Department of Anthropology, University of Texas, Austin, 1996.

Jones, Christopher. "The Twin-Pyramid Group Pattern: A Classic Maya Architectural Assemblage at Tikal, Guatemala." Ph.D. dissertation, Department of Anthropology, University of Pennsylvania, 1969.

———. "Cycles of Growth at Tikal." In *Classic Maya Political History*, ed. T. Patrick Culbert. Cambridge: Cambridge University Press, 1991, 102–27.

Laporte, Juan Pedro, and Vilma Fialko. "Un Reencuentro con Mundo Perdido, Tikal, Guatemala." *Ancient Mesoamerica* 6(1995):41–94.

Looper, Matthew G. "The Sculpture Programs of Butz'-Tiliw, an Eighth-century Maya King of Quiriguá, Guatemala." Ph.D. dissertation, University of Texas, Austin, 1995.

Marcus, Joyce. "On the Nature of the Mesoamerican City." In *Prehistoric Settlement Patterns: Essays in Honor of Gordon R. Willey*, ed. Evon Z. Vogt and Richard M. Leventhal. Albuquerque, NM: University of New Mexico Press, and Cambridge, MA: Peabody Museum, Harvard University, 1983, 195–242.

———. *Mesoamerican Writing Systems: Propaganda, Myth, and History in Four Ancient Civilizations*. Princeton, NJ: Princeton University Press, 1992.

Martin, Simon, and Nikolai Grube. "Maya Superstates." *Archaeology* 48,6(1995):41–46.

———. *Chronicle of the Maya Kings and Queens: Deciphering the Dynasties of the Ancient Maya*. London: Thames & Hudson, 2000.

Newsome, Elizabeth. "The Trees of Paradise and Pillars of the World: Vision Quest and Creation in the Stelae Cycle of 18-Rabbit-God K, Copan, Honduras." Ph.D. dissertation, Art Department. University of Texas, Austin, 1991.

Quezada, Sergio. *Pueblos y Caciques Yucatecos, 1550–1580*. México City: El Colegio de México, 1993.

Rapoport, Amos. *The Meaning of the Built Environment: A Nonverbal Communication Approach.* Beverly Hills, CA: Sage, 1982.

Ringle, William M. "Pre-Classic Cityscapes: Ritual Politics among the Early Lowland Maya." In *Social Patterns in Pre-Classic Mesoamerica*, ed. David C. Grove and Rosemary A. Joyce. Washington, DC: Dumbarton Oaks, 1999, 183–223.

Ruppert, Karl. "A Special Assemblage of Maya Structures." In *The Maya and Their Neighbors*, ed. C. L. Hay et al. New York: Appleton-Century, 1940, 222–31.

Rykwert, Joseph. *The Idea of a Town: The Anthropology of Urban Form in Rome, Italy, and the Ancient World.* Cambridge, MA: MIT Press, 1998 [1976].

Sanders, William T., and David Webster. "The Mesoamerican Urban Tradition." *American Anthropologist* 90(1988):521–46.

Scarborough, Vernon L. "Reservoirs and Watersheds in the Central Maya Lowlands." In *The Managed Mosaic: Ancient Maya Agriculture and Resource Use*, ed. Scott L. Fedick. Salt Lake City, UT: University of Utah Press, 1996:304–14.

———. "Ecology and Ritual: Water Management and the Maya." *Latin American Antiquity* 9(1998):135–59.

Scarborough, Vernon L., and Gary G. Gallopin. "A Water Storage Adaptation in the Maya Lowlands." *Science* 251(1991):658–62.

Schele, Linda. "Palenque: The House of the Dying Sun." In *Native American Astronomy*, ed. Anthony F. Aveni. Austin, TX: University of Texas Press, 1977, 42–56.

Schele, Linda, and David Freidel. *A Forest of Kings.* New York: William Morrow, 1990.

Schele, Linda, and Peter Mathews. *The Code of Kings: The Language of Seven Sacred Maya Temples and Tombs.* New York: Scribner, 1998.

Smith, Monica L., ed. *The Social Construction of Maya Cities.* Washington, DC: Smithsonian Institution Press, 2003.

Steinhardt, Nancy Shatzman. "Why were Chang'an and Beijing so Different?" *Journal of the Society of Architectural Historians* 45(1986):339–57.

Stone, Andrea. "From Ritual in the Landscape to Capture in the Urban Center: The Recreation of Ritual Environments in Mesoamerica." *Journal of Ritual Studies* 6(1992):109–32.

Stuart, David. *Ten Phonetic Syllables. Research Reports on Ancient Maya Writing* 14. Washington, DC: Center for Maya Research, 1987.

———. "'The Fire Enters His House': Architecture and Ritual in Classic Maya Texts." In *Function and Meaning in Classic Maya Architecture*, ed. Stephen D. Houston. Washington, DC: Dumbarton Oaks, 1998, 373–425.

Stuart, David, and Stephen D. Houston. "Classic Maya Place Names." *Studies in Pre-Columbian Art and Archaeology* 33. Washington, DC: Dumbarton Oaks, 1994.

Tate, Carolyn. "Summer Solstice Ceremonies Performed by Bird Jaguar III of Yaxchilán of Yaxchilán, Chiapas, México." *Estudios de Cultura Maya* 16(1985):85–112.

Taube, Karl A. "The Iconography of Mirrors at Teotihuacan." In *Art, Ideology, and the City of Teotihuacan*, ed. Janet C. Berlo. Washington, DC: Dumbarton Oaks, 1992, 169–204.

———. "The Jade Hearth: Centrality, Rulership, and the Classic Maya Temple." In *Function and Meaning in Classic Maya Architecture*, ed. Stephen D. Houston. Washington, DC: Dumbarton Oaks, 1998, 427–78.

Townsend, Richard F., ed. *The Ancient Americas: Art from Sacred Landscapes.* Chicago, IL: Art Institute of Chicago, and Munich: Prestel Verlag, 1992.

Tozzer, Alfred M., ed. "Landa's Relación de las Cosas de Yucatan, A Translation." *Papers of the Peabody Museum of American Archaeology and Ethnology* 18. Cambridge, MA: Peabody Museum, Harvard University, 1941.

Tuan, Yi-Fu. *Space and Place: The Perspective of Experience.* Minneapolis, MN: University of Minnesota Press, 1977.

Vogrin, Annegret. "The Spatial Relationships of Monuments at Copán and Quiriguá." In *Memorias del Segundo Coloquio Internacional de Mayistas* 1. México City: Universidad Nacional Autónoma de México, 1989, 139–48.

Vogt, Evon Z. "The Genetic Model and Maya Cultural Development." In *Desarrollo Cultural de Los Mayas*, ed. Alberto Ruz L. México City: Universidad Nacional Autónoma de México, 1964, 9–48.

———. *Zinacantan.* Cambridge, MA: Harvard University Press, 1969.

———. *Tortillas for the Gods: A Symbolic Analysis of Zinacantan Ritual.* Cambridge, MA: Harvard University Press, 1976.

Wheatley, Paul. *The Pivot of the Four Quarters: A Preliminary Inquiry into the Origins and Character of the Ancient Chinese City.* Chicago, IL: Aldine, 1971.

Willey, Gordon R. "Problems Concerning Prehistoric Settlement Patterns in the Maya Lowlands." In *Prehistoric Settlement Patterns in the New World*, ed. Gordon R. Willey. Viking Fund Publications in Anthropology 23. New York: Wenner-Gren Foundation for Anthropological Research, 1956, 107–14.

———. "Maya Lowland Settlement Patterns: A Summary Review." In *Lowland Maya Settlement Patterns*, ed. Wendy Ashmore. Albuquerque, NM: University of New Mexico Press, 1981, 385–415.

Willey, Gordon R., ed. *Prehistoric Settlement Patterns in the New World.* Viking Fund Publications in Anthropology 23. New York: Wenner-Gren Foundation for Anthropological Research, 1956.

Cosmological Structures of Ancient Egyptian City Planning

David O'Connor

5

Egyptologists generally agree that ancient Egyptian temples, tombs, and palaces have a cosmological dimension. In their plans and decoration such buildings are equated with the structure and processes of the Egyptian cosmos. Thus, temple cult, the world of the dead, and royal ceremonial are empowered and legitimized by becoming incorporated into cosmos.

But Egyptian towns, and the houses making up their fabric, are not usually analyzed in cosmological terms. Scholars prefer to emphasize their functional or utilitarian purposes. In contrast, I will suggest that Egyptian houses and towns are cosmologically structured; like temples and tombs, they were microcosms, miniaturizations of the macrocosmos that gave meaning to the Egyptians' life and history. Overall, ancient Egyptian cities and towns are important for the cross-cultural study of the cosmology of settlements and towns in many cultures.

The Egyptian Concept of Cosmos

How did Egyptians understand the universe? This is well articulated in Egyptian art and literature, but it is important to note the Egyptians played many variations on basic cosmological concepts.

In art or literature, or in social practice or architecture, the Egyptians sometimes emphasized the totality of cosmic structure and process. At other times, they highlighted selected aspects of the cosmos, rather than the whole. Thus, the eastern and western aspects of the cosmos might be contrasted with each other, or the northern and the southern. Even within a single treatise or work of literature or art form or building, varied cosmological notions were brought into play in complex and interwoven ways.

Throughout these variations, however, basic Egyptian beliefs about the cosmos remain the same. A unique creator brings itself, and then the cosmos into being, operating within the endless liquidity of chaos or formlessness. The cosmos thus created is hierarchically structured, involving deities, humans, and the dead, all working together—at different levels of power and action—to maintain the processes that keep the cosmos alive and functioning.

For the Egyptians, their familiar world both masked yet revealed to their imaginations a supra-reality, a cosmos of which they and the terrestrial realm they inhabited were a part. Sky and earth (the latter, in Egypt, comprising fertile flood plain and sterile desert) were visualized as the sky goddess *Nut* overarching the earth god *Geb*. Their father, *Shu*, the atmosphere, provided the void within chaos that the cosmos occupied; he also literally supported Nut, so that the sky and earth would not collapse into each other and bring the cosmos to an end.

55

The other constituents of the cosmos were also manifest as deities, and cosmic order itself was personified as the goddess *Maat*. However, the most significant deity was the sun-god, *Re*. Re was a manifestation of the creator, often called *Atum* and sometimes *Atum-Re*. Re could be pictured as the winged sun disk itself, or as a hawk-headed human; in both cases, it was his form as *Re-Horakhty*—Re the Falcon of the Two Horizons—to which reference is made. Cosmologically, Re's most important function was to initially vitalize, via his life-giving radiance, the conceptual cosmos as imaged by Atum, and then to endlessly repeat this process (in the form of the daily sunrise) throughout eternity. However, Re was also strongly associated with kingship: as a manifestation of the creator he literally ruled cosmos, while more specifically the Egyptian pharaoh on earth functioned as Re's delegate, and was habitually titled "the son of Re."

Sailing in his boat through heaven and the netherworld, Re brought the cosmos and Egypt back to life and order every day, and every night he underwent regeneration in the netherworld so he and the cosmos would be reborn the next day.

Chaos, called *Isfet* by the Egyptians, continued to surround the cosmos. Paradoxically, chaos supplied the cosmos with potential life, which was activated and made actual by the sun god; but at the same time chaos also continually sought to re-absorb, and thus destroy, the cosmos. The aggressive and negative force of chaos took many forms, from demons and monsters directly attacking the sun god to natural disorders or societal breakdowns. All forms of negative force had to be resisted, repelled, and reduced to impotence by the deities and humans alike.

For humans, the king was central to their role in maintaining the cosmos and repelling chaos. The king mediated between humanity and the divine: only he or his surrogates could perform temple cult. Throughout Egypt's numerous temples, images of the deities received ritual treatment (such as cleansing, re-anointing, and adorning) and offerings of food and drink three times a day. In temple art, only the king was depicted performing these acts for the deities, although in fact this was done by the chief priest of the temple, an embodiment of the king. Only the latter, as the one "effective of ritual," had the qualities and knowledge that made ritual effective. Through his bureaucracy, the king brought stability to Egypt, so that it conformed to Maat or cosmic order. Those officials responsible for national government, and the control of imperial possessions, clustered around the king at royal cities such as Memphis and Thebes. In addition, in Egypt's 40 or so provinces, were local officials charged with executing the policies and practices desired by the center. This bureaucratic system (backed up by police and, when necessary, military power) provided the state with revenue, and the population with some degree of stability and sustenance, but also ensured the dominance of the kingship. The whole was legitimized as a replication of the hierarchical order of cosmos itself. More specifically, the king also repeatedly repelled chaotic force on earth, in the form of aggressive and rebellious foreigners, of whom the deities had made the Egyptian king overlord.

The Cosmology of Royal Cities

In various book chapters over the years (O'Connor 1995, 1997, 1998), I have tried to show how these cosmological ideas shaped not only the layout but also the ceremonial and even administrative and societal life of the New Kingdom royal cities of Thebes and el-Amarna.

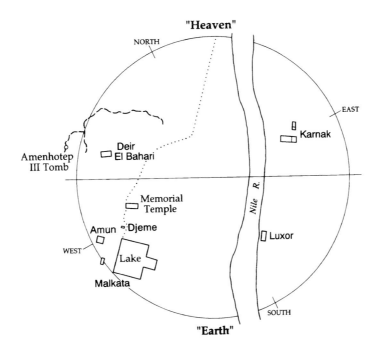

In both, city plans and functions were correlated with cosmic structure and process. In part, the correlation was dynamic, operating through the rituals, ceremonies, and general life of the city. In part, it was static, the cosmos manifest in the city's built forms—such as temples and palaces—and their spatial disposition over the cityscape.

These royal cities represented the cosmos in its constituent elements of east and west and north and south, each associated with a specific group of processes and meanings. Yet, at the same time, the city, in plan and activity, linked these different elements into a totality that corresponded to the Egyptian concept of the cosmos as a whole.

The eastern and western and the northern and southern dimensions of the cosmos represented contrasting yet interactive powers that, when taken together, were essential for the stability and productivity of the cosmos. The message of royal cities such as Thebes and el-Amarna was therefore clear. They provided a structural context in which the king and his subjects—that is Egypt as a whole—mimicked on earth the processes of the cosmos and attested themselves part of its order, an order to which they contributed.

The urban matrix of Thebes has not been excavated, but its monumental remains—temples and tombs—define its cosmic structure. The city, occupying about 500 ha, or 2 sq mi on the east bank of the Nile, was defined by temple complexes at its northern and southern ends.

Across the river, beyond a broad flood plain, was a line of royal mortuary temples servicing royal tombs set far away from them, in a valley hidden behind the cliffs. Numerous elite and other cemeteries filled the foothills.

Thebes was a royal city in that kings resided there for part of each year and its god *Amun-Re* was the divine patron of state and empire. The bureaucracy housed in Thebes administered the southern half of Egypt and its southern empire in Nubia.

Thebes' widely scattered monuments were linked together administratively, societally, and especially ceremonially. Two separate annual festivals—led by the king and involving the entire city population—required the god Amun-Re to processionally trace out ritual paths defining

5.2 Processional rituals of
Thebes: relief from the Temple
of Amun-Re, Karnak, dating to
the reign of Philip Arrhidaeus
(323–316 BCE).

the city. One ran north-south through the city proper; the other ran east-west across the river
and then north-south along the line of mortuary and other temples on the west bank.

During the Ramesside period (XIX and XX Dynasties, circa 1292–1075 BCE), apprentice
scribes copied a variety of literary compositions for instructional purposes. These compositions
included hymns of praise for "residence cities" such as Thebes in which pharaoh lived, and
performed ceremonies, for at least part of every year. In such compositions, cities like Thebes
were treated as cosmograms, representations of the cosmos traced out on the earth. "Thebes is
the pattern for every city . . . her ground was created upon the primeval mound when earth came
into being, then mankind came into being with her" (Nims 1965:69). Thebes is an embodiment
of the sun disk, of the governing and creative force of the sun god, on earth.

Under king Amenhotep III (1390–53 BCE)—and surely under other rulers as well—the
notion of Thebes as the cosmos was given literal expression in the life of the city and in the city
plan. The cosmographic aspects of Thebes referred both to the daily east-west trajectory of the
sun-god and also to his annual cycle around the world, a north-south movement along the horizon,
and then a return to the starting point over the course of the year. These cosmologically significant
trajectories were reenacted in the movements of the sun-god Amun-Re, in statue form and of the
living king through Thebes, a city laid out so as to specifically make these movements possible.

The city and its cemeteries correspond to the eastern and western dimensions of the
cosmos. Thus, the city is associated with important cosmological phenomena associated with
the eastern dimension of cosmos. These phenomena include the process of the daily rebirth
of cosmos, and the re-initiating of its orderly rulership, both manifested by the rising sun; and
also the concept that the sun disk is the sun-god's eye, which "opens" (i.e. appears in the sky at
dawn) to emit the solar radiance that brings renewed life to cosmos. In contrast, the cemeteries
and mortuary temple represent the western location of solar descent, death but ultimately
regeneration, which brings back life to both the cosmos and the city in the east.

In terms of north and south, the north half of Thebes, while not an exclusively sacred zone, equated with "heaven" and thus appropriately contained the residences of both Amun-Re and the king, the former's chief temple (Karnak) and the latter's residential palace. The southern half of Thebes was symbolically equated with the "earth" or the terrestrial realm. Its palaces and temples, in function and decoration, emphasized the relationship between king and subject, rather than between king and deity.

The northern and southern halves of Thebes were also symbolically differentiated in that they corresponded to the Egyptians' concept that—in terms of the solar year—northern Egypt was a place and time (spring and summer) of intense solar manifestation, a "heavenly" realm, while southern Egypt, in fall and winter, associated with growth and regeneration, and the sojourn of the sun-god in the netherworld. This reinforced the contrast between northern Thebes as "heaven" and southern Thebes as "earth" and the netherworld below it.

The ritual and ceremonial lives of god and king at Thebes brought cosmological unity to the cosmic diversity manifested in the city plan. Daily, the king moved north to south to perform temple cult and exercise governance, seeming to descend from heaven (northern Thebes) to earth (southern Thebes). At the same time, Amun-Re inhabited his east-west trajectory across the sky, a trajectory reflected on earth, and via which he energized and governed the cosmos.

Moreover, through the annual festivals—as at Luxor temple, in southern Thebes—god and king ritually re-affirmed the cosmic significance of the north-south and east-west axes of Thebes, city and cemetery alike.

The other archaeologically known royal city is el-Amarna, which was built for king Akhenaten (1353–36 BCE). Akhenaten developed a monotheistic form of religion out of Egypt's polytheistic practices and theology. Consequently, his capital city is a variant on the traditional idea of city as cosmos, a variant appropriate to the changes in religious belief and practice Akhenaten had initiated.

Akhenaten believed he had moved religion back to the time of creation itself, before the netherworld, and indeed before the deities themselves had come into being. Rather, humanity could focus on a single god, simultaneously creator and lord of the cosmos, which manifested itself in the sun disk, called in Egyptian the *Aten*. For Akhenaten, the Aten had chosen el-Amarna as the center of this endless creative process, and the city built there had to be an appropriately structured cosmogram, indeed one that incorporated the landscape itself.

Some scholars suggest that the notched cliff towering over el-Amarna to its east was read by the Egyptians as a gigantic form of the hieroglyph for "horizon" (in Egyptian, *akhet*). Thus,

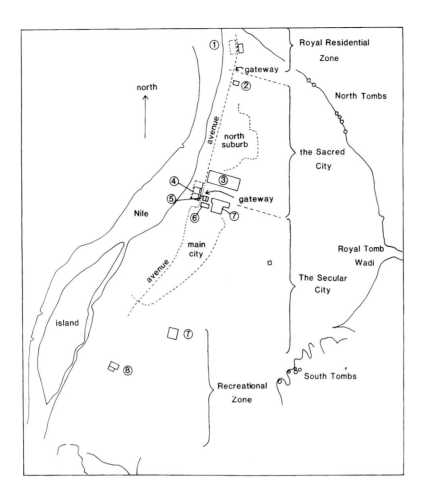

5.5 The city of Akhetaten at el-Amarna; the numbers refer to the palaces, temples, and other entities comprising the city. 1 is the King's residential palace; 3 is the Great Temple; and 6 is the city temple.

when the sun rose above the cliffs every morning, the entire universe seemed to manifest the name of the city—Akhetaten, "the horizon of the sun disk."

At Amarna, in accordance with Akhenaten's new ideas, the cemeteries—both royal and elite—were on the east, the place of birth, rather than the west, associated with solar descent and death. This automatically made the city itself the west, so that at the end of the day, or of the life cycle, god and king did not descend into a netherworld, but instead literally returned to their residences—temple and palace—in the city, where they slept through the night, to appear rejuvenated the next day.

As at Thebes, a division into northern and southern halves is also significant at el-Amarna, and similar in cosmological meaning to the other city's. North—the "sacred city"—is heavenly and contains the residential palace of the king (archaeologically attested) and the great temple, home to the Aten. The southern half, however, corresponds to "earth," to the relationship between king and subject. In the southern half is the "city temple" and the houses and offices of the bureaucrats who run state and empire on the king's behalf.

Within this cosmologically structured framework, king and god trace out trajectories defining the axes and processes of the cosmos so that the entire city and all the cosmos can be seen as one and the same. Daily, the king rides from north to south, in an electrum-plated

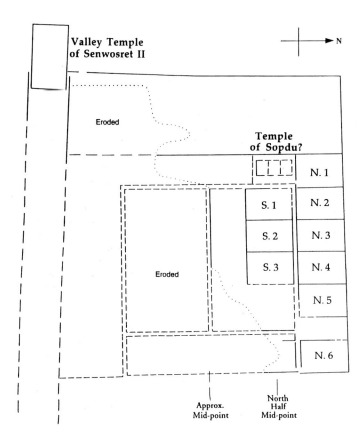

chariot. Electrum is gold with a high silver content, and hence has a particularly light color that reflects light intensely. At el-Amarna the king's chariot is specifically said to be radiant like the sun disk, moving from "heaven" (northern Amarna) to "earth" (southern Amarna) in order to bring life and order to the terrestrial realm. Simultaneously, Aten rises from his temple and, along an east-west trajectory, brings life and order to the cosmos as a whole.

Non-royal Towns

With regard to the cosmological dimension of non-royal towns in Egypt, towns with which the living king did not have a special connection, only a pre-New Kingdom town— Kahun, of the 19th century BCE—is sufficiently excavated to be taken into consideration.

Kahun serviced the pyramid and mortuary temple of king Senwosret II (1844–37 BCE). Kahun's inhabitants included priests and attendants who performed daily cult for the dead king in a large temple near the southwest corner of the town. They probably lived in the western suburb of the town, closed off from the rest by a wall.

The rest of the town was also surrounded by a wall. It housed the officials who administered the cult establishment, ran its large, revenue-producing estates on the nearby flood plain, and maintained order in the town's large service population of some 3,000 individuals.

The town (excluding its western suburb) was laid out in gridiron fashion, a highly regular checkerboard of houses and streets. Such great regularity can express a cosmological dimension, as in many Chinese towns, but at Kahun it probably simply reflects the need to rapidly build and staff an administrative center. The town occupied 9.8 hectares, about 24.2 acres.

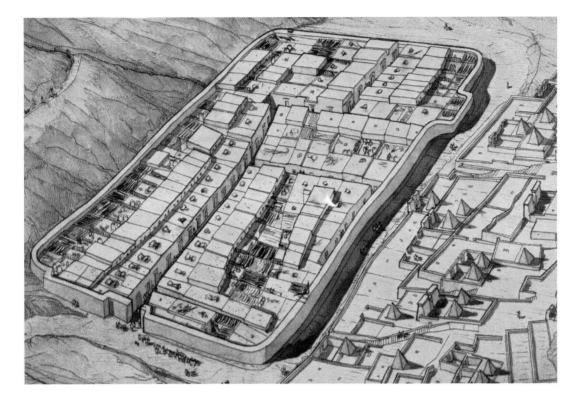

The southern half of the town has been largely eroded away, but the overall town plan was likely symmetrical. We reconstruct two entrances in the east wall, creating a pattern of main streets running east-west, then north-south, and finally west-east.

The northern half of Kahun is mostly occupied by nine very large elite households (each occupies about .25 hectare or .5 acre), very similar to each other in plan and scale. Flanking the northern main street, the houses were occupied by the chief officials of the town.

Precisely located on the transverse (east-west) axis of the northern half of Kahun was a small temple, the "city temple" dedicated to *Sopdu*, Lord of the East.

Houses other than elite ones are much smaller and presumably occupied much of the southern half of the town as well. However, documents refer to institutions such as a "prison" or "workhouse" not archaeologically identifiable in the north half, so these too may have been in the south.

One reason for thinking this town had a cosmological dimension is that its elite houses appear to be cosmograms themselves, suggesting this might be true for the town as a whole.

For example, contemporary house models indicate that house roofs were decoratively treated as skies, and hence were cosmographically equated with "heaven." Moreover, houses (like temples) had columns shaped like bundles of papyrus, or lotus buds, indicating that house floors—like temple floors—were identified as "earth," the terrestrial realm.

Further, if vertically the elite house seemed to represent the structure of the cosmos—heaven and earth—horizontally the house plan and the activities it implies seem to mimic cosmic process.

A typical elite house (one of the two types represented at Kahun) had a central residential suite for the senior male, always an important official.

This central suite was flanked by the wife's residence and an office used to administer the household's external affairs, and perhaps service some of the senior male's official responsibilities.

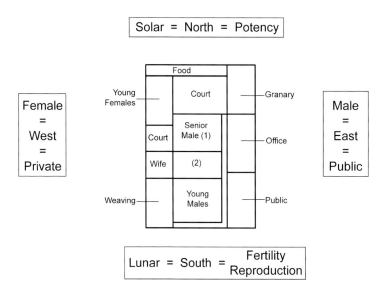

In the northeast was a large granary, and nearby were areas for storing and processing food. In the northwest was a residence perhaps for the senior couple's female children, in the south another, perhaps for the male children. To the southwest was a unit used for weaving linen, an important domestic industry, and to the southeast a cluster of "public" rooms, near the house entrance.

This spatial patterning can be read cosmologically, and thus it provided legitimization to the social hierarchy and to the variable allocations of status and power embodied in the house plan.

The central suite of the senior male (a royal delegate) corresponds to the sun god's central position in the cosmos and the king's central position in the world. The flanking suites represent the senior male's authority over the household, exercised via his wife, and over the household's external affairs, exercised through his office, much as the sun-god runs the cosmos with the aid of the other but subordinate deities, and the king runs the world through his bureaucrats.

Finally, the peripheral areas of the house can be equated with the peripheral zone of the cosmos, in which cosmos and chaos interact. This interaction subdues the negative aspects of chaotic force and transforms its life potential into the energy and life the cosmos requires.

Correspondingly, the house's peripheral zone incorporates the maturation of unruly children into responsible adults; the production of a useful material, linen, from flax; and, in the kitchens, the transformation of the "raw" into the "cooked."

Further, the houses of these elite families also refer to the constituent elements of cosmos. For example, cosmographically east associates with sunlight and the public domain, where males are especially active, and the eastern half of the house relates to the external life of the household, through its granary and office.

However, the western half of the cosmos associates with the secluded world, and the regenerative power of the netherworld, the latter often expressed in sexual terms. Correspondingly, the western half of the house represents the private realm and is associated with females and reproduction. The senior male's wife experienced intercourse, pregnancy, and birth in her suite; her female children were housed to her north; and in the south, the weaving unit was supervised by the wife and staffed largely by women.

North and south contrasts, relating to those evident in the cosmos, are also significant in the household. Cosmographically, north relates to a heavenly, solar dimension; and, correspondingly, the senior male's chief rooms lie north of the transverse, east-west axis, as does the largest and hence most sun-filled courtyard in the house. Equally appropriately, the wife's suite—associated with fertility and gestation—and the male children associated with maturation lie south of the transverse axis. These are attributes typical of the cosmographic south as well.

The rich symbolic cosmology of Kahun's elite houses therefore encourages us to look at the entire town from a cosmological perspective. Here, the north-south division, familiar to us from the later royal cities, emerges as a cosmographically significant one. The east-west division does not involve so much the town itself, as it does the contrast and relationship between the town and its cemeteries, the latter literally to the west, between the town and the pyramid.

In the town, the northern half recalls the heavenly northern zone of royal cities. Not only does it contain the most prestigious structures—the city temple and elite houses—but these are primarily residences, identical or akin to the northern temples (divine residences) and residential palaces of a royal city. Elite residences may have favored northern locations as more salubrious, since the prevailing north wind kept them free of the odors and dust of the rest of the town, but this does not preclude cosmological symbolism being present also.

Again reminiscent of later royal cities, the southern half of Kahun was occupied by smaller residences and perhaps an "official zone" of some kind. Thus, Kahun's southern half corresponds to the terrestrial, southern zone of royal cities, occupied by those who serviced both god and king.

Moreover, as in royal cities, the two halves of Kahun are tied together and unified by ritual and ceremonial activities that have cosmological significance.

If there was a southern official zone, officials would have moved from north to south to reach it, much as elsewhere the king moved from his residence to the bureaucratic zone, from northern "heaven" to southern "earth."

Further, the main street pattern suggests that the annual or periodic festival procession of the town god (here, such a procession is seen in its later form, Fig. 5.2) likely exited the town via one eastern gateway and re-entered via the other, thus circum-traversing the entire town. This was appropriately inclusive of the community, but at the same time such festival processions, involving boat-shaped palanquins as seen here, mimicked the course of the sun god around the cosmos in his boat. This provides yet another indication that Kahun—and perhaps non-royal towns in general—functioned as a cosmogram.

Conclusion

The preceding discussion has necessarily involved much that is speculative, yet is at least anchored in the reality of the relevant archaeology, and art-historical and textual sources. In these regards, in fact, the issue of the cosmography of Egyptian buildings and towns involves no more speculation than the discussion of other major issues regarding ancient Egypt, where informed speculation is taken pretty much for granted. However, to extend cosmographical meanings from temples to palaces, houses, and entire cities or towns is a relatively innovative step, and likely to provoke not only discussion but also resistance.

Nevertheless, I hope I have shown above that cosmographical readings of Egyptian urban forms, as well as of individual structures—including elite houses—are reasonable, given what we know from textual and art-historical sources about the high degree to which cosmological beliefs permeated Egyptian culture as a whole. Egyptian built forms, individually and in the aggregate, linked private, official, religious, and royal life styles and performative activities to the processes and structures imagined to be essential to the continuity of cosmos itself. On one level, this equivalence helped to maintain the normative relationships between the different categories of Egypt's population, and to ensure that the rising generation—first as children, then young adults—would in turn become accustomed to following these norms. At another level, the cosmological aspects of structures and towns provided yet another visible statement (alongside the many presented in ritual, royal ceremonies, and social action, and in literature and art) about the place of Egypt in cosmos, and the harmonious relationship between the two.

REFERENCES

Nims, Charles F. *Thebes of the Pharaohs, Pattern for Every City*. New York: Stein and Day, 1965, 69.

O'Connor, David. "Beloved of Maat, the Horizon of Re; the Royal Palace in New Kingdom Egypt." In *Ancient Egyptian Kingship*, eds. David O'Connor and David P. Silverman. Leiden: Brill, 1995, 263–300.

———. "The Elite Houses of Kahun." In *Ancient Egypt, the Aegean and the Near East: Studies in Honor of Martha Rhoads Bell*, ed. Jacke Phillips with Lanny Bell, Bruce B. William, and James Hoch and Ronald J. Leprohan. Vol. 2. San Antonio, TX: Van Sicklen, 1997, 389–400.

———. "The City and the World: Worldview and Built Forms in the Reign of Amenhotep III." In *Amenhotep III: Perspectives on His Reign*, eds. David O'Connor and Eric H. Cline. Ann Arbor, MI: University of Michigan Press, 1998, 125–72.

Mohenjo-Daro: The Symbolic Landscape of an Ancient City

Gregory Possehl

6

Mohenjo-daro, the "Mound of the Dead Men," is arguably the best-preserved Bronze Age city in the world. This ancient monument is located in Sindh Province, Pakistan, on the flood plain of the Indus River. The Indus or Harappan Civilization arose on the plains of the greater Indus Valley, Baluchistan, and Gujarat in the middle of the 3rd millennium BCE (ca. 2500–1900 BCE). Mohenjo-daro is one of the principal urban centers of this Bronze Age civilization. It appears to have been a "founder's settlement" conceived and built very early in the history of the Indus Civilization, possibly within the so-called Early Harappan–Mature Harappan Transition (2600–2500 BCE), a period of pyroxic change within which the distinctively urban features of Indus life were defined and developed.

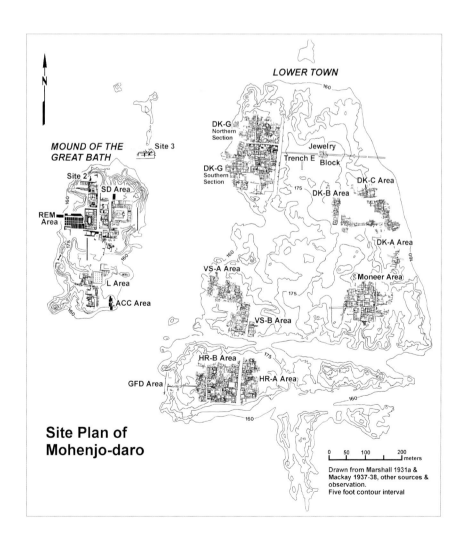

6.1 Plan of Mohenjo-daro.

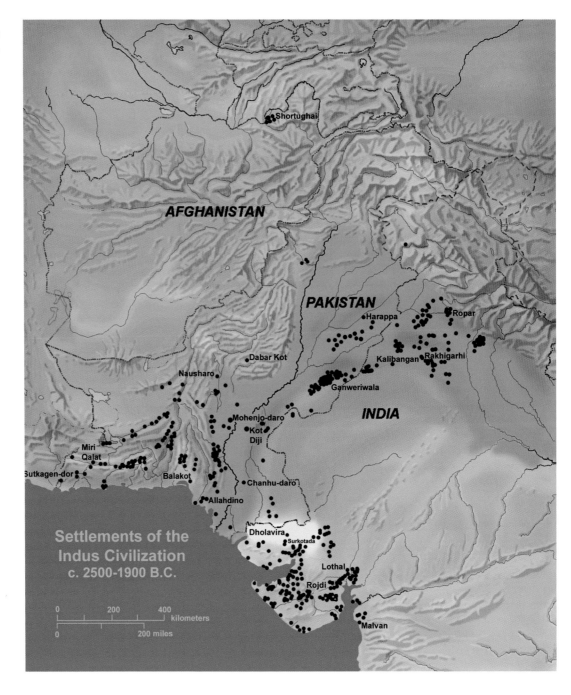

I think of Mohenjo-daro as the premier city of the Indus or Harappan Civilization. My colleague Michael Jansen, an archaeologist-architect from Aachen, who began a long-term study of Mohenjo-daro in 1979, shares this notion. We think of this ancient urban setting as a kind of metaphor for the Indus Civilization as a whole (Jansen 1994), a place where the ideology of the civilization is expressed in physical form.

The defining characteristic of the Indus Civilization would have been its ideology, those concepts about human life and culture that the peoples of the Indus Civilization used to identify themselves. Without the presence of written records, the full expression of this ideology may elude us. But, the archaeological record does seem to preserve a reflection of it in physical form as the distinctive suite of Harappan artifacts, architecture, baked-brick buildings, brick-lined wells, bathing facilities, and new or expanded technologies.

There are immense differences in the artifactual style of the Indus Civilization as compared to the Early Harappan (ca. 3200–2600 BCE). This change should be seen as a replacement of the older Early Harappan symbolic system with a new order or way of life. It is as though the peoples of the Indus Civilization turned their backs on their own past and replaced it with a new order or ideology. In this sense the peoples of the Indus Civilization were nihilists.

This is not the place to define this new ideology in detail, but it has to do with nihilism, urbanization, and sociocultural complexity, the management and symbolism of water—something Jansen calls *wasserluxus* or in English "water splendor" (1993), technological innovation, and symbolic forms of identification as with the use of writing and personal stamp seals.

The Mature Harappan ideology drew on older cultural traditions of the greater Indus region but was also a new configuration. We have not yet learned to separate the various strands of Indus history, but it seems clear that there was little change in subsistence and the sociocultural, economic, and political balances between farmer and pastoralists.

Two relatively recent sources on the importance of ideology in the understanding of sociocultural processes in complex archaic sociocultural systems (Demarest and Conrad 1992; Claessen and Oosten 1996a) stress themes that are not necessarily new, such as the importance of self-identity, group affiliation, and systems of symbolism in sociocultural systems (Adams 1992; Claessen and Oosten 1996b). What is new is the attempt to deal with these themes in deep antiquity, often without the aid of texts. This chapter will take one theme in the Harappan ideology, their use of water, and expand upon it.

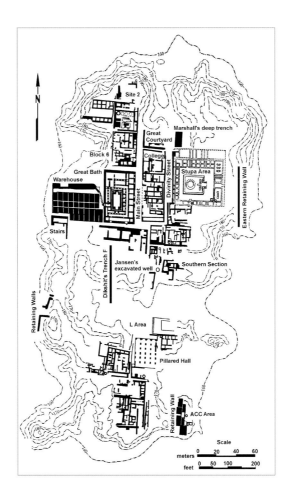

6.3 Mound of the Great Bath at Mohenjo-daro.

WATER MANAGEMENT: INDUS IDEOLOGY EXPRESSED IN ARCHITECTURE

Water and its management were central to the ideology of the Harappan peoples. This is most fully expressed at Mohenjo-daro, but it is also found at many other Indus sites such as Harappa, Dholavira, Lothal, and Chanhu-daro.

Mohenjo-daro is an urban environment that was first conceived and planned, then built, at the very beginnings of the Indus Civilization. This is one of the reasons that it reflects the new ideology of the Harappan peoples, just as the various Alexandrias reflect the ideology of the ancient Greeks. One of the clearest ideological principles of the Indus Civilization is in fact urbanization itself. Another ideological focus of the Indus peoples is water and its management. This is clearly seen at Mohenjo-daro with the many brick-lined wells, elaborate drainage system, bathing facilities in virtually all of the houses, and a ritual structure commonly called the "Great Bath." The bathing facilities in each house inform us that washing and cleanliness were important to the Harappans. We have to consider that this involved both physical cleanliness and something of a more symbolic nature. The many wells throughout the city were sources of new, pure water, essential for effective cleanliness. The drainage system served to move effluents away from the houses and their occupants, below ground, safely out of the way and out of sight, in brick-lined channels that prevented massive contamination of the earth of the city.

WELL DIGGING

Wells lined with baked bricks, often especially made for this purpose, are a distinguishing feature of many settlements of the Indus Civilization. They are, in fact, an Indus invention, probably developed in the Transitional Stage (2600–2500 BCE) between the Early and Mature Harappan.

6.4 An excavated well at Mohenjo-daro.

The Indus peoples lined their wells with baked bricks for two reasons. First, such bricks guard against cave-ins and erosion. This is especially important since many of the wells are in confined urban spaces. Properly managed brick-lined wells also deliver clean water with a minimum of silt and other large particulate contaminants.

Brick-lined wells have been found at a number of Indus sites: Harappa, Chanhu-daro, Kalibangan, and Lothal among them. At Allahdino, to the east of Karachi, two stone-lined wells and drains reveal a variation on the Harappan pattern. One of the ancient brick-lined wells discovered at Chanhu-daro was found to be badly broken at the top. On January 1, 1936, the water level in it was at -28.8 ft. Ernest Mackay, the Field Director of the Chanhu-daro excavation, raised the steening of this well and brought it into use again after an interval of some 4,500 years. It also now supplies water to the nearby village of Jamal-Kirio (Mackay 1943:17).

It has been estimated that there were about 700 wells at Mohenjo-daro (Jansen 1989:252). Archaeological observations trace the continuity of well location over the stratigraphic buildup of Mohenjo-daro. Courses of bricks were added to wells as the city mound grew. Some wells at Mohenjo-daro are as small as 60 cm (2 ft) in diameter; one was as large as 2.1 m (7 ft). There is also an oval well. The average diameter is about 1 m or about 3 ft (Mackay 1948:38). Ardeleanu-Jansen provided the information for Table 6.1 concerning the 74 wells exposed at Mohenjo-daro (1993:1). Some recomputation of data was done due to the availability of updated excavation data (Jansen 1993:266). The GFD (or UPM) Area is not included in the study of wells.

The area served by each well and the mean distance between wells is remarkably consistent in the Lower Town, another reflection of the planning that went into Mohenjo-daro from the very beginning. A few wells were abandoned during the life of the city (Mackay 1937–38:72, 96, 164–65) that Mackay suggests were abandoned because someone jumped into them (Mackay 1948:39).

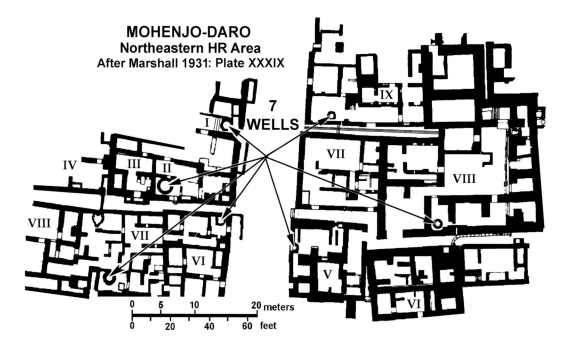

Mackay observes that the social context of wells at Mohenjo-daro seems to have changed over time: "In the early days of the city it is probable that the wells were private, as there seems to be no means of reaching them from the street, but later on, as the population grew, they were thrown open to public use. The rooms in which the wells were situated were, as a rule, carefully paved, and the floor in many cases was worn into deep depressions where countless water-jars had been set down" (1948:38).

TABLE 6.1. WELLS AT MOHENJO-DARO

EXCAVATION AREA	EXCAVATION AREA (M²)	NUMBER OF WELLS	AREA PER WELL (M²)	MEAN DISTANCE BETWEEN WELLS (M)
MOUND OF THE GREAT BATH				
D, DM, REM	16,500	4	4125	56.3
L & ACC	6.400	2	3200	36.5
Total or average	22,900	6	3662	46.4
LOWER TOWN				
DK-G	28,000	21	1333	36.5
DK-A-C	12,200	10	1525	39.0
VS	13,000	10	1300	36.0
HR	20,600	23	1030	32.0
Moneer	7,200	5	1440	38.2
GFD	2,000	—	—	—
Total or average	83,000	69	1326	36.3

THE DRAINAGE SYSTEM AND DOMESTIC WATER FACILITIES

One of the most remarkable features of Mohenjo-daro, and several other Mature Harappan settlements (e.g., Harappa, Kalibangan, Nausharo, Chanhu-daro, Allahdino, Dholavira, and Lothal) is the street drainage system. At Mohenjo-daro the streets and lanes in all of the neighborhoods were provided with drainage (see Mackay 1931b:277–82 for a general discussion). There was also provision for the management of waste water inside the houses, with intramural drains, vertical drain pipes in the walls, chutes through walls to the streets, and drains from bathing floors into street drains. Mohenjo-daro receives less than 13 cm (5 in) of rain per year, probably about what it received in the 3rd millennium. This would not seem to be enough rain to justify so elaborate a system.

At Mohenjo-daro drains were found at all levels of the site. They were a part of the original city plan and may be another technology of the Indus Civilization that was developed in the important Transitional Stage. The street drains at all sites are generally made of baked brick, although the one at Allahdino is of stone.

In SD Area, on the Mound of the Great Bath of Mohenjo-daro, the bottoms of some drains were plastered with gypsum and lime, with sides of baked brick. In most instances ordinary baked brick was used, but specially dressed brick was noted in some drains of SD and DK areas. Specially shaped bricks were also used to form the gently rounded corners of drains. The integrity of the drains was achieved by closely fitting the bricks with a bit of mud mortar. Dressed bricks made the fit even better.

Drains were often reused from building period to building period at Mohenjo-daro. This was done by simply raising the walls with more bricks. At the southern end of first street in DK-G Area the walls of a drain were repaired and raised at least twice. In its last construction phase this drain was 42 cm (16.5 in) wide, but 2 m (6 ft, 6 in) deep in places (Mackay 1937–38:27, 29, 31, 34 ff). Most of the drains had brick or stone covers because they were under the street or ground surface. Open drains have been found along the sides of streets, a feature of many modern settlements in India and Pakistan.

The most frequent drain cover was an ordinary baked brick laid flat across the side walls, although bricks laid on edge across the channel are also well documented. The wider drains were covered with large limestone blocks quarried from the nearby Rohri hills. These blocks are especially common on the Mound of the Great Bath.

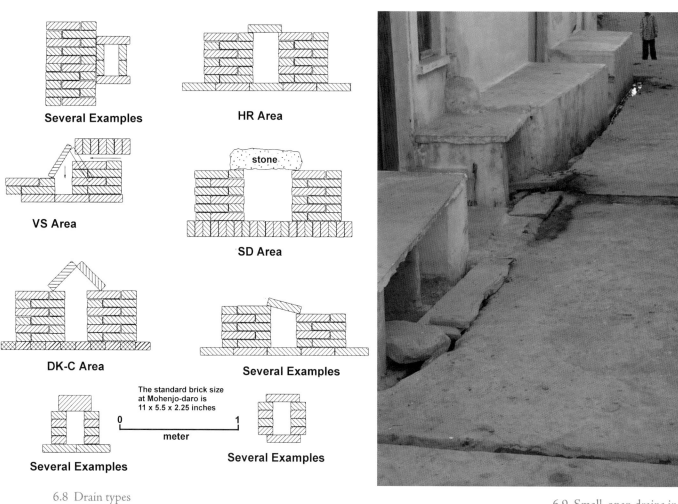

Several Examples

HR Area

stone

VS Area

SD Area

DK-C Area

The standard brick size
at Mohenjo-daro is
11 x 5.5 x 2.25 inches

0 ⊢———————————⊣ 1

meter

Several Examples

Several Examples

Several Examples

6.8 Drain types
at Mohenjo-daro.

6.9 Small, open drains in a
lane in the village of Gilund,
Rajasthan, 2001.

The drains were hidden underground, out of the way of traffic. Mackay estimates that the average depth was in the range of 46 to 60 cm (18 to 24 in). Limestone drain covers in SD Area sometimes had a distinct polish on their upper side, "polish that must have been caused by the feet of passers-by" (Mackay 1931b:278). We should imagine the tops of these covering blocks right at ground level, some slightly buried, and that as the earth of the street surface changed and moved, some were periodically exposed and the slight polish of wear was applied to them.

Small settling pools and traps were built into the system of drainage. This allowed coarse sediment and other materials to drop out of the flow in places were it could be periodically collected. "That the drains of Mohenjo-daro were cleaned out periodically is attested by the little heaps of greenish-gray sand that we frequently found alongside them. The more finely levigated clays would be readily carried off by the rush of water whereas the heavier particles of sand were deposited" (Mackay 1937–38:27).

The wider drains, or culverts, could not be covered in an ordinary way. Sometimes special bricks of extra length were baked (Mackay 1937–38:91, 428). The corbelled arch was used for the culverts, as at the Great Bath.

STRUCTURE AND MEANING IN HUMAN SETTLEMENTS

Water from inside houses was sometimes led directly into a street drain, but other facilities were used as well, such as brick-lined cess pits and pottery jars along the streets. But it was clearly important for the water from bathing floors to be moved out of the home and for it not to be allowed to sink directly into the ground. This suggests that the water from bathing (and other domestic activities?) was polluted and dirty beyond the simple "scientific" sense, leading to the close connection with ideology.

BATHING FACILITIES

One of the most common features of a house at Mohenjo-daro was a special platform for bathing. These are usually on the order of 1.5 m on a side, sometimes not square, but always rectilinear. The bricks of the floor were very carefully prepared, sawn, and ground to shape, with right angles where faces met, and smoothed upper surfaces. This was specialized work, expensive in terms of time, but then the jobs were relatively small in scale. The bricks varied in size, even within a single platform. A raised rim around the platform was achieved by ringing the platforms with a course of bricks on edge. The surfaces of these bathing platforms were slightly tilted so that water would run to a corner and out of the bathing area through a drain in the wall.

Not only were the floors of these platforms sloped, they were very smooth, probably ground down after all of the bricks had been fitted, to give a seamless floor. Then they were coated with a plaster of lime and brick dust (Mackay 1931b:273) that was polished by the plasterer and the feet of the users.

Bathing facilities are also found in abundance at Harappa, where they conform to the patterns outlined here. Somewhat different is the line of thirteen bathing platforms on the

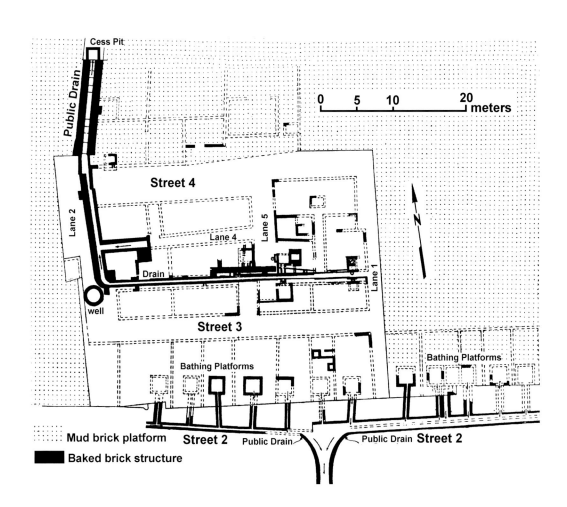

Cess Pit

Public Drain

Street 4

Lane 2

Lane 4

Lane 5

Lane 1

N

Drain

well

Street 3

Bathing Platforms

Bathing Platforms

0   5   10   20 meters

:::::: Mud brick platform   Street 2   Public Drain   Public Drain Street 2

■ Baked brick structure

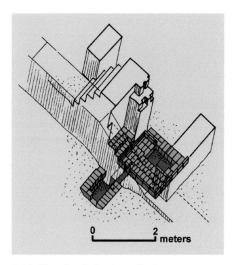

6.13 Sketch of a bathing facility at Mohenjo-daro.

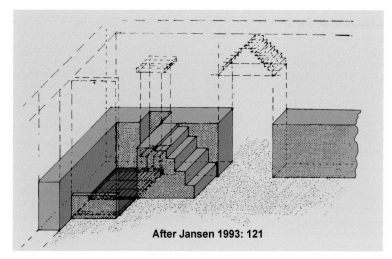

After Jansen 1993: 121

6.14 One of the privies at Mohenjo-daro.

Acropolis at Lothal. This seems to have been a public facility, open to many, not likely all, of the relatively few people at this small site.

Bathing platforms seem to be the chief source of water that went into the civic drainage system of many Indus settlements, except for those few days when there was a really good rain.

Privies

The issue of latrines, or privies, in the Indus Civilization begins with Marshall's discussion of the vertical terracotta pipe in the wall of a house: "From its small size it is clear that this vertical pipe was meant to convey fluid only, not solids; and this seems to be true of the house drains of Mohenjo-daro. . . . [However] in House XLIX of HR Area, Section B, Block 7 privies with seats (as to the character of which there can be no question) are directly connected with brick drains of the usual type, which must therefore have been designed for sewage of any kind, solid or fluid" (Marshall 1931:21).

There is one more privy as well, but that is all, and the drains of Mohenjo-daro seem not to emerge as conduits for solid human waste. There are just too many good points against it, as noted by Mackay (1931:281).

In a discussion of triangular terracotta cakes Wheeler says: "Their great abundance, especially in drains, would be consistent with a use in the toilet, either as flesh rubbers or as an equivalent to toilet paper" (1968:93).

The Great Bath at Mohenjo-Daro

The Great Bath at Mohenjo-daro was a place of ritual, probably for the civic elites. The central feature of the bath is a sunken, brick-lined pool. It was fashioned of precisely made and

6.15 The Great Bath at
Mohenjo-daro.

laid baked bricks, fitted tightly together. The exact north-south dimension of the west wall is 11.99 m (39 ft, 4 in) and the east wall is 11.96 m (39 ft, 3 in). Its breadth is 7.12 m (23 ft, 4.5 in) in the north and 6.99 m (22 ft, 11 in) in the south (Mackay 1931a:131). We may call it 12 x 7 m, while being aware of the accuracy of construction, especially in the north-south dimension. The depth is ca. 2.4 m, or 8 ft. There are flights of steps at either end, and at the foot of each a low platform for the convenience of bathers who might otherwise have found the water too deep (Marshall 1931a:24).

The finish on the bath was said by the experienced excavator Ernest Mackay to be "so good that the writer has not seen its equal in any ancient work" (1931a:131). The four walls of the bath were uniformly 1.36 m (4 ft, 5.5 in) thick, covered and made waterproof by a regular lining of bitumen (tar) 2.4 cm (1 in) thick, kept in place by a course of brick. Earth rammed between the last, innermost, course of brick and the hole excavated to hold the bath kept everything in place (Mackay 1931a:132). The bottom of the structure was not probed in sufficient depth to determine if the bitumen lining sealed the bottom as well, but that is more than a fair assumption.

The Great Bath was also strategically placed. The mound on which it sits is a separate urban environment with open ground between it and the rest of the city, where the ordinary, vulgar affairs of daily life predominated. It was also elevated above the lower town of Mohenjo-daro, out of view of the ordinary citizens of the city. In the symbolic landscape of Mohenjo-daro the Great Bath used exclusivity and elevation as defining dimensions for this unique Harappan institution. From these and other variables, I conclude that the Great Bath of Mohenjo-daro was a place for ritual bathing.

The so-called College of Great Bath Priests across Main Street from the Great Bath itself is a very large building. Its location and size suggest that it functioned as a complement to the

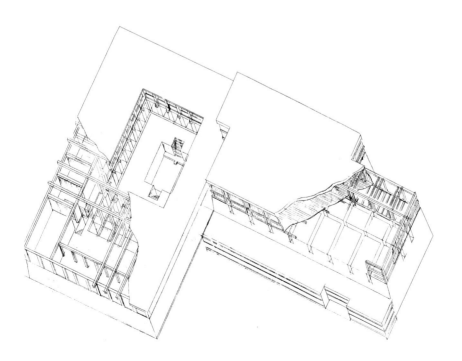

6.16 Isometric drawing of the Great Bath at Mohenjo-daro.

N

corbelled arch drain

bathroom

sump & drain

bathroom

bathroom

well

bathrooms

sump & drain

bathroom

drain

bathroom

drain

| 0 | | 5 | | 10 meters |
| 0 | 10 | 20 | 30 | feet |

6.17 Reconstruction of the Great Bath.

6.18 Stairs
in the Great Bath.

Great Bath. There is no corroborating evidence that this building was a temple. It may have been the administrative and domestic abode of the functionaries who managed and used the Great Bath.

Dholavira: Another Indus City of *Wasserluxus*

Recent finds at the Indus city of Dholavira in Kutch, a district of Gujarat State, India (Bisht 1991, 1994a, 1994b, 1997), demonstrate the importance of water at yet another Indus city. This large, 60 ha site was discovered 1967–68 and has been under large-scale excavation since 1989. Dholavira is one of the largest urban centers of the Indus Civilization.

Dholavira was a planned settlement with an exquisite system of water storage and management. There is a long sequence of habitation, and R. S. Bisht has defined seven periods of occupation, or stages, at the site. The first two fall within the Early/Mature Harappan Transition. Stages III, IV, and V are Mature Harappan with the final two stages being Post-urban Harappan.

In the early part of the Indus period (stage III) Dholavira grew from a small settlement to a large town or city with two sets of fortifications, districts, and a water storage system on a significant scale. This period marks the raising of the Citadel and Bailey. Throughout the Indus period massive drains were created to move water from huge cisterns. Some of the cisterns are shown on the site plan. Others are deep rock-cut structures.

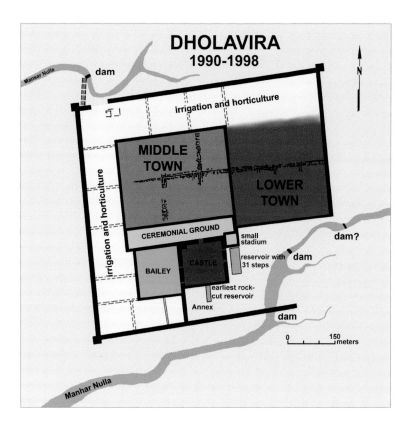

Dholavira provides a comparison to Mohenjo-daro and demonstrates the tremendous importance of water for the Indus Civilization. Some of this importance is surely functional, as we need water to live. But the Indus peoples also used another dimension of this life-giving fluid as a part of their system of beliefs.

THE INDUS CIVILIZATION AND WATER

Water was important in the Indus Civilization in two ways. It sustained the life of humans, plants, and animals, but it also played an important symbolic role as an essential part of the Indus ideology. The bathing facilities in each house inform us that washing and cleanliness were very important to the Harappans. We have to assume that this involved physical cleanliness as well as something more symbolic. The many wells throughout the city were sources of new, pure water, essential for effective cleanliness. The drainage system served to move effluents away from the houses and their occupants, below ground, safely out of the way and out of sight. The Great Bath at Mohenjo-daro was designed as a special place for the ablutions of an elite.

These distinctive features of the Indus Civilization are cultural patterns that serve to define these ancient people. They bespeak an ideology expressed in an atextual archaeological record. The symbolic nature of water and water management for the Harappans was one of their defining characteristics and of the Indian subcontinent's first urban system.

REFERENCES

Adams, Robert McC. "Ideologies: Unity and Diversity." In *Ideology and Pre-Columbian Civilizations*, eds. Arthur A. Demarest and Geoffrey W. Conrad. Santa Fe, NM: School of American Research Press, 1992:205–21.

Ardeleanu-Jansen, Alexandra. "Who Fell in the Well? Digging Up a Well in Mohenjo-Daro." In *South Asian Archaeology 1991*, eds. Adalbert J. Gail and Gerd J. R. Mevissen. Stuttgart: Franz Steiner Verlag, 1993:1–15.

Bisht, Ravi Singh. "Dholavira: A New Horizon of the Indus Civilization." *Puratattva* 20(1991):71–82.

———. "Secrets of the Water Fort." *Down to Earth* May(1994a):25–31.

———. "Planning at Dholavira: A Harappan City." In *The City and the Stars: Cosmic Urban Geometries of India*. Delhi: Indira Gandhi National Centre of the Arts, 1994b.

———. "Dholavira Excavations: 1990–94." In *Facets of Indian Civilization—Recent Perspectives (Essays in Honor of Professor B. B. Lal)*, ed. Jagat Pati Joshi. Delhi: Aryan Books International, 1997:107–20.

Claessen, Henri J. M., and Jarich G. Oosten, eds. *Ideology and the Formation of Early States*. Studies in Human Society. Leiden: Brill, 1996a.

Claessen, Henri J. M., and Jarich G. Oosten. "Introduction." In *Ideology and the Formation of Early States*, eds. Henri J. M. Claessen and Jarich G. Oosten. Studies in Human Society 11. Leiden: Brill, 1996b:1–23.

Demarest, Arthur A., and Geoffrey W. Conrad, eds. *Ideology and Pre-Columbian Civilizations*. Santa Fe, NM: School of American Research Press, 1992.

Jansen, Michael. "Some Problems Regarding the Forma Urbis Mohenjo-Daro." In *South Asian Archaeology 1985*, eds. Karen Frifelt and Per Sorensen. Scandinavian Institute of Asian Studies, Occasional Papers No. 4. London: Curzon, 1989:247–56.

———. *Mohenjo-daro: Stadt der brunnen und kanale (City of Wells and Drains), Wasserluxus vor 4500 Jahren (Water Splendor 4500 Years Ago)*. Dual German-English text. Bergisch Gladbach: Frontinus-Gesellschaft e. V., 1993.

———. "Mohenjo-daro, Type Site of the Earliest Urbanization Process in South Asia: Ten Years of Research at Mohenjo-daro, Pakistan, and an Attempt at Synopsis." In *South Asian Archaeology 1993*, eds. Asko Parpola and Petteri Koskikallio. Helsinki: Annales Academiae Scientiarum Fennicae, 1994:263–80.

Mackay, Ernest J. H. "SD Area: The Great Bath and Adjacent Buildings." In *Mohenjo-daro and the Indus Civilization*, ed. Sir John Marshall. London: Arthur Probsthain, 1931a:131–50.

———. "Architecture and Masonry." In *Mohenjo-daro and the Indus Civilization*, ed. Sir John Marshall. London: Arthur Probsthain, 1931b:262–86.

———. *Further Excavations at Mohenjo-daro*. Delhi: Government of India, 1937–38.

———. *Chanhu-daro Excavations, 1935–36*. American Oriental Series 20. New Haven, CT: American Oriental Society, 1943.

———. *Early Indus Civilizations*. 2nd ed. Rev. by Dorothy Mackay. London: Luzac, 1948.

Marshall, Sir John. "The Buildings." In *Mohenjo-daro and the Indus Civilization*, ed. Sir John Marshall. London: Arthur Probsthain, 1931:15–26.

Wheeler, Sir Mortimer. *The Indus Civilization*. 3rd ed. Supplementary Volume to *The Cambridge History of India*. Cambridge: Cambridge University Press, 1968.

HOLY MOUNTAINS

Joseph Rykwert

7

During the 3rd, and perhaps even at the end of the 4th, millennium BCE, many vast structures which we now interpret as holy mountains were built in the north of Egypt and in the south of Mesopotamia. This is generally known, and I only spell it out at the outset of my chapter because it seems to me that some questions are still worth asking about this wholly familiar phenomenon.

Like anything born, it has two parents: a seed needs to be planted in a matrix. That matrix, the ground on which the holy mountains first rose, was the fertile alluvium both of the Nile Valley and of the plain between the Two Rivers which we call Mesopotamia. Migrant populations from the south—from Nubia and the Saharan edges into Egypt, or from the surrounding high grounds of Elam and Iran into Mesopotamia, and almost certainly from the Persian Gulf, already organized into food-raising communities—seem to have brought the seed.

Why they migrated is not clear. Climatic changes in the center of Africa and population movements between the Sahara and the Nile Valley may provide some clues to the creation of the dual Nilotic state. It will not quite help us to understand the Mesopotamian changes—or the rise of the Sumerians—whose part in the process of urbanizing the south of the Tigris/Euphrates delta and the organizing of irrigation was decisive in the formation of settlements.

The most conspicuous monuments of these two cultures, known as pyramids and ziggurats, are often bunched together. By calling them both holy mountains—as I have now done, following many students—I have also raised my first problem, since even if their bulk

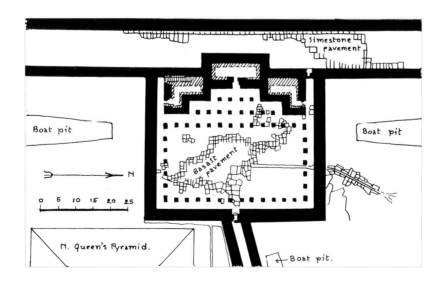

7.1 Pyramid of Cheops, Egypt. Underground plan.

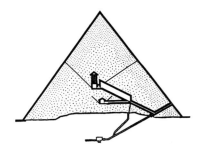

7.2 The Pyramid of Cheops, Egypt. Section.

may be roughly analogous, the differences are glaring. The largest pyramid, that of Cheops, who reigned from ca. 2605 to 2580 BCE, has a footprint of 720 ft², while the largest of the ziggurats, that of Ur-Nammu, the prince who founded the 3rd dynasty of Ur about 2150 BCE (and fragments of whose commemorative stele are now in the University of Pennsylvania Museum of Archaeology and Anthropology in Philadelphia), has a much smaller footprint, 190 by 130 ft. At that time Ur was probably the biggest city in the world, and the Sumerians had fully developed syllabic writing, which was to provide the basis of all subsequent record-keeping methods.

The differences in size and in date raise another query, which seems a non-problem to me, however. Is 400 years time enough for the influence to have diffused from one end of the fertile crescent to the other? In terms of method, I would suggest neither diffusion nor influence offer any convincing explanation for such phenomena. A people, its rulers, and its wise men do not take features from another group unless they have a use for it and can find a place for it in their world-picture and their political and religious practice. Often they need to reinterpret it so completely that the original borrowed element may be twisted out of recognition.

I wish to quarrel with another word much used in this context—"development." It is simply not true, as the word suggests, that the pyramid grew or developed from the mastaba, nor did the ziggurat develop from the temple platform. If you need to use the word, then you must make it active: they developed. But this did not happen impersonally by smooth gradations, as it does with plants or animals. Development was arrived at by a series of disjointed decisions, discontinuously and with great effort; it required much thought and great ingenuity as well as a highly organized labor force.

The differences between ziggurats and pyramids are almost as obvious as the analogies. There is, to begin with, the way in which they were "used." The pyramids were smooth and completely inaccessible tombs in which the mummified body of the divinized king was sealed for

7.3 The Ziggurat of Ur, reconstruction perspective.

7.4 The Ziggurat of Ur,
plan of terrace complex.

eternity. Their casing was probably polychrome and the capstone was itself a pyramid inscribed with invocations to Re and gilded, as it is in the surviving basalt one, that of Ammenemhet III (1842–1797 BCE) at Dashur, now in the Cairo Museum (Giedion 1964:421 ff). Recently that of the "Red" pyramid of Snefru has been reconstructed (Verner 200:185 f). They were pierced by long, thin conduits planned as mazes, which accommodated the Pharaoh's burial and his treasures—and which may have had complex astral references. The ziggurats, on the other hand, were solid brick mounds that were to be ascended by bulky exterior ramps and stairways; they probably had pavilions at various levels that served for some kind of ceremony. The royal tombs at Ur, though properly constructed and filled with sacrifices and goods, seem to have no outstanding marker above ground.

Both kinds of man-made mountains were oriented. Most pyramids have their sides precisely aligned according to world-directions, while the Sumerians—and the Babylonians and Assyrians after them—oriented the corners of their ziggurats to the cardinal points. The sites of the brick mounds were sanctified, and each rebuilding amplified their bulk. The pyramid, though, once established on its site, was to stand unchanged forever.

Pyramid and ziggurat were also very unlike materially. The Ziggurat of Ur, like some of the surviving Assyrian, Babylonian, and Elamite successors, had a soft brick core reinforced with reed matting and bonded with asphalt. It was covered with figured and brightly colored glazed tiles, which provided a hard surface—though when the tiles were broken up by various conquerors, the ziggurats sometimes degenerated into mud heaps. The pyramids (with the exception of some smaller and later ones) were built of stone and meticulously encased with limestone. Cheops's pyramid was already 2,000 years old when the accuracy of the jointing was

HOLY MOUNTAINS 87

7.5 The Stele of Ur-
Nammu, original at the
University of Pennsylvania
Museum. Original and late
reconstructions.

praised by Herodotus (Histories II:125), but that casing, like that of its neighbors, was stripped by Saladdin toward the end of the 12th century CE to build the citadel and mosques of Cairo, leaving the stone cores intact.

The very first pyramid shows it clearly. It was the tomb of Netjeri-Khet (later known as Djoser or Zoser, who ruled 2680–2645 BCE), probably the second Pharaoh of the III Dynasty at Saqqara. Legend has it that it was designed by a named individual, Imhotep. He was by repute an administrator, healer, sculptor, painter, as well as architect, and also came to be known as "the Egyptian Asklepios." He was divinized by the Ptolemaic Pharaohs who considered him a son of the wise craftsman-god, Ptah. The legend became history in 1926 when the base of a statue of the Pharaoh dedicated by Imhotep—who identified himself as "Chancellor of Lower Egypt, Second to the King in Upper Egypt, Master of the Palace, hereditary noble, High Priest of Heliopolis"—was found in the precinct of the stepped pyramid. He may have been the Pharaoh's son (but see Arnold and Zeigler 1999:4, 6, 13, 155, 280). More recently a small bronze statue of him, holding a papyrus scroll on which his name is inscribed, was found and is also in the Cairo Museum (Verner 2002:138).

Nothing is known about how the decision to raise the pyramid was taken—or the force required to build it assembled. It seems that Imhotep first had a large but conventional tomb

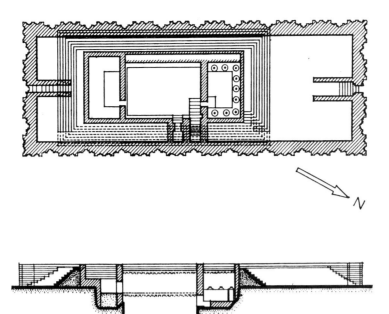

built for his king, the kind called mastaba, meaning "bench" in Arabic. This was usually not a square but a long rectangular solid with paneled sides that covered an underground tomb. That first mastaba was enlarged twice, the second time along one side to provide cover for more tombs, probably those of royal wives and children. At some later time, the decision was taken to embed the enlarged mastaba in a four-step structure, like the hieroglyph for the mound of creation. The derivation from the sun's rays under certain conditions seems too recondite by comparison (Verner 2002:116). The last stage of the building then involved increasing the number of steps to six. In the course of these operations, yet another decision led to enclosing the new pyramid in a vast monumental court of carefully cut and jointed limestone construction representing the ritual fields that were devised for a royal ceremony, the Sed festival. A model of Egypt was created near (or within) a temple precinct for this festival, with the various districts represented by more or less primitive huts through which the Pharaoh ran or danced to renew the vigor of his kingship and his divine power (Frankfort 1978:79 ff). By the time of Djoser this was an essential part of royalty, and the pyramid court represents the previous wood-and-reed pavilions in solid masonry. Very few of the pyramids had any interior spaces, but where they existed, they were decorated with colored ceramic that reproduced the reed-and-wood construction of houses and palaces. A trench, enclosing an area twice that of the court, surrounded the complex and took the form of a rectangle with one overlapping side, like the hieroglyph for "house." Userkaf, the founder of the V Dynasty tried to build a pyramid within their trench (Verner 2002:279 f).

Imhotep's work may have been the first ashlar-stone monumental building ever. Even if the step-pyramid was the product of one commanding mind, there had been a long period of preparation for it. The soil of Egypt is, of course, fertile and humid when inundated and silted by the Nile flood, but dry and hot at those edges the floodwaters do not reach. The bodies of the dead buried in such relatively stable soil dried quickly and did not rot, so that Egyptian soil

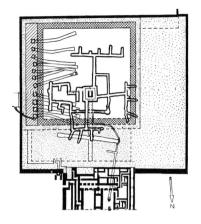

7.7 The Step Pyramid of Zoser, Sakkara, Egypt. Underground Plan.

conserved corpses without any artificial aids. The graves of the earliest inhabitants of the valley known to us—where they have escaped the attention of grave robbers—often contain grave goods around a corpse that has been buried crouching, with its head usually to the south.

As the settlements of the fertile valley grew and stabilized, the tombs became increasingly ambitious (Hoffman 1984). In the south the buried part became increasingly elaborate, while in the north the heap of sand or stones that marked them was formalized in pre-dynastic days into a mound, which would be enclosed in a rectangular flat-topped structure under which the tomb would often be artfully concealed. It is not clear when groups of settlements were organized into distinct social organizations. However, early in the 4th millennium BCE, a change occurred in the valley that some archeologists have associated with an invasion, perhaps from the east. Invasion may be too brutal a word; if there was one, it was more of an incursion or penetration, one that has been compared to the Norman invasion of Britain. The conquering group, whom archaeologists call the Dynastic race, came to be identified with a group who referred to themselves as the "Sons of Horus" (Hoffman 1984:293ff; Emery 1961:30 ff).

Some historians favor invasions or migrations as mechanisms for cataclysmic social change. Yet revolutionary developments can occur without any such impact or admixture. Invasion or no, the early articulation of Egypt into districts, which were often represented by a heraldic animal, led to their incorporation in two kingdoms—north and south. About the first document of the monarchy is a late 4th millennium stone macehead of the otherwise unknown Scorpion King, whose inscribed name is one of the earliest known hieroglyphs. It shows him carrying out irrigation works amid scenes of rejoicing—but he is only shown wearing the white crown of the south. Some time about 3200 BCE, we find mention of a southern king, who chroniclers called Menes, and who seems to have unified the country. This king may have been Hor-Aha or "fighting Horus," the founder of the I dynasty, one of whose alternative names was Men, "the established" (Verner 2002:19; Spencer 1993:63 ff).

Another early document, the palette of King Narmer, shows him wearing the white crown of the south on one side, the red crown of the north on the other. The new monarchy established two capitals, one in the north at Heliopolis, near which Hor-Aha established the city of—presumably plastered—white walls later known as Memphis, while the southern one was at Buto and Sais, then at Abydos/Thinis. Like some of his successors, Hor-Aha seems also to have had two tombs: one, a buried enclosure at Abydos, and another, probably a mastaba, on the west side of the Nile opposite Heliopolis (Emery 1961:40 ff).

Both northern and southern tombs were usually surrounded by minor burials. It is not clear whether those buried were sacrificed—as were those in the III Dynasty tombs at Ur—or buried there after a natural death. In one case, that of the Pharaoh Uadji (Djet), grandson of Hor-Aha, his mastaba at Saqqara is edged by a bench into which 300 horned (and presumably sacrificial) bull skulls are molded. In the tomb of Enezib (Anejib), the grandson of Uadji, another feature is formalized: the inner heap of earth and rubble which sometimes crowned the tomb chamber within the mastaba is given a stepped surround, almost like a miniature project for Djoser's great enclosure. Many archeologists consider that mastaba roofs were curved, while the sides of most were recessed and paneled. Whether the plastered surface covered brick or stone, they were all—as were some early stone sarcophagi—images of the impermanent wood, plaster, and reed architecture of palaces and houses (Badawy 1966:68, 116; Andrae 1933; Giedion 1964:198, 264).

After that the major pyramids were all built in lower Egypt during a relatively brief period ending in the reign of Mycerinus, the penultimate pharaoh of the IV Dynasty, who died about 2500 BCE and who closed the Saqqara building campaign with the smallest of the three great pyramids at Gizeh. Practically all pyramids were sited on the western bank of the Nile, between Cairo and Dashur, so that the funerary temples could all face the river eastward, much as the Middle Kingdom Pharaohs had built their eastward tombs on the west bank of the Nile at Thebes—now Karnak/Luxor.

During the first two dynasties Egyptian thinkers elaborated a theology of divine kingship and at the same time devised elaborate anatomical procedures to preserve the royal corpse intact. The Pharaoh was a semi-divine being whom death fully deified. The smooth sides of the pyramid show the sun's rays shining on the earth and allow the dead king within it to ascend to Re, the Sun, his father. The Egyptians maintained this theology into Imperial Roman times, so that even Hadrian could see himself reflected in it. The pyramids are the founding monuments of this theology.

Once they had become an overpowering physical presence and the type was securely established, the actual monuments no longer needed to be vast. The great pyramid age took less than a century and a half of the three Egyptian millennia—even if smaller and rougher pyramids went on being built, such as those of the Nubian kings in the south, below Aswan, or much more outlying ones—as in Rome itself, where one Caius Cestius Epulo built himself a small pyramid by the Ostian gate in the first years of the reign of Augustus.

Mesopotamian climatic and soil conditions were quite different from Egyptian ones. The alluvium of the Tigris and Euphrates Rivers and their tributaries was much harsher and more copious than the Nile silt, so that the southeast flowing Tigris-Euphrates changed course much more often and deposited much more at their mouth than the northward Nile. Silting and flooding in Mesopotamia was indeed so irregular that irrigation works had to be much more demanding. The coastline on the Persian Gulf moved much more quickly than that of the Nile delta. Constantly shifting and muddy, the alluvium gave the settlements along the two rivers no secure, dry borders where the dead might rest intact. Inevitably, tomb-deposits were, with some notable exceptions, badly preserved in Mesopotamia. Stone was hard to come by, reeds and brick the staple building material. Funerary monuments made little contribution to the growth of Mesopotamian architecture along the rivers.

Where there is a direct parallel, it is in the twin organization of the lands. Like Egypt, Mesopotamia was divided into north and south. But while Egypt seems to have spoken one language and to have been unified early, the Mesopotamians spoke two quite distinct languages: Sumerian, the language of the south, agglutinative and perhaps tonal, belongs to no known language group, while Akkadian, the northern language, is clearly Semitic, as are its later by-products, Babylonian and Assyrian (Crawford 1991:16 f, 20 ff). The term *shumer v'akkadi* refers to a linguistic-geographical rather than a racial-ethnic division. *Shumer* is the Semitic name of a people who called themselves "the black-haired" or "dwellers in reed-land," and they had legends about their arrival from elsewhere, though no obvious original homeland has so far been suggested. They first devised the notation on wet clay we now call cuneiform, in which the Semitic languages were also later written, while Sumerian, which died as a spoken language, became the vehicle for diplomatic and liturgical texts.

The two river valleys had no direct physical connection and were separated by deserts and mountain ranges. Yet some building forms—the paneled and recessed construction of Egyptian

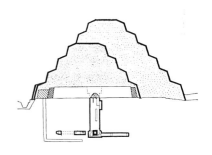

7.8 The Step Pyramid of Zoser, Sakkara, Egypt. Section.

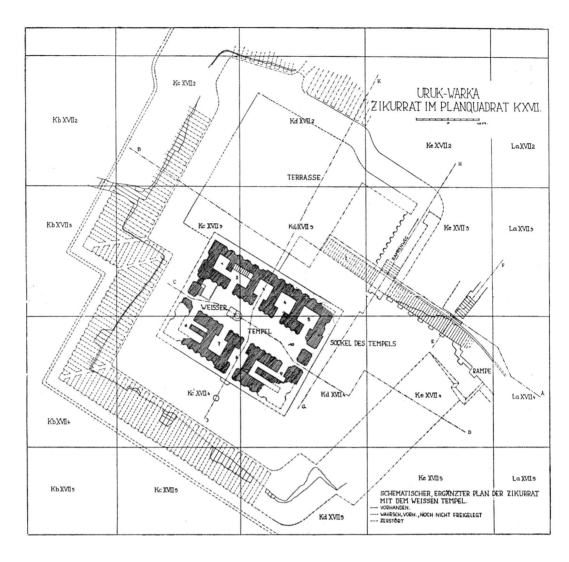

pre-dynastic and Old Kingdom buildings—are also a feature of Sumerian temples and ziggurats (Verner 2002:24; Emery 1961:42 ff). Whether Egyptian hieroglyphs, which initially appear on I Dynasty monuments, were an emulation of the Sumerian idea or devised independently is still disputed (Diringer 1968:17 ff; Amiet 1982 passim). What goes for writing goes also for the sacred mountains. Early trade certainly seems to have gone westward, first: the lapis-lazuli which even pre-dynastic Egyptians treasured so much came from the foothills of the Hindukush, and the cylinder seal may well be an import from Mesopotamia. There are no signs either of hostile or of diplomatic dealings between the valleys in early dynastic times. The exception is Naram-Sin's of Akkad victory over the shadowy Lord Mannu of Magan—which has been read as a victory over the Egyptians. "Magan" has certainly meant Egypt in later documents, and some of Naram-Sin's (2291–2255 BCE) surviving booty, such as alabaster vases, looks credibly Egyptian. He was a contemporary of the VI Egyptian Dynasty and the fall of the Old Kingdom, though the evidence remains circumstantial (Edwards et al. 1971:495 ff).

Yet even if the rulers of Mesopotamian cities and of their successor states were despotic, cruel, and imperialistic, they were not themselves divine like the Pharaohs, but remained the gods' bailiffs. Of the holy mountains in Mesopotamia, the two earliest seem to have been the "White Temple" Eanna at Uruk/Erech/Warka and the "sea-temple" mound of Enki, the water-god of wisdom and law at Eridu/Abu Shahrain, the southernmost Sumerian harbor town. At Eridu the small nuclear first temple is built on virgin soil at the outset of the Ubaid (before 3500 BCE) period, a simple buttressed square to which an altar-niche was later added. Several more temples, ever larger, are built over the same spot, enclosing the original nucleus. At the beginning of the Dynastic period, the full paneled construction appears and at a level above that there is a brick platform over which the subsequent levels finally constitute themselves into a ziggurat—a vast and solid brick mass, ascended by ramps, presumably with a shrine of some kind at the summit. At its high point, Eridu seems to have had a population of about 10,000 inhabitants, but it was stranded by the changing coastline and abandoned by the retreat of the riverbed so it eventually shrank back to being a village.

At Uruk/Warka, on the other hand, the White Temple was the highest and the biggest of several shrines at the center of the city: it was a brick "mountain," with battered, plastered sides, deeply scored by flutes, while access was by a ramp and by a stairway to the temple of Anu, the sky-god, that crowned a 40-ft high platform. The temple itself is a rectangle of recessed and paneled brick walls with a central hall and chapels on either side, a configuration such as will be found throughout Mesopotamia for the next two millennia. As at Eridu, the White Temple covers the remains of earlier shrines, but they are much more fragmentary. It must have been built in the Ubaid or the protoliterate period (Frankfort 1954:3 ff; Edwards et al. 1971:74 ff Liverani 1986:66 ff; Perkins 1977:110 ff). The later precinct on the site was dedicated to Anu—on that basis the assumption is usually made that the "White Temple" was also Anu's shrine. Certainly proto-dynastic Uruk, which at its height had 80,000 inhabitants living at the high density of 200 per acre, would qualify as a city nowadays—and that kind of density seems to have been quite usual in Mesopotamia. The first named "king" of Uruk, Gilgamesh, who is also the hero of the first epic poem, is now considered a historical figure who reigned some time between 2700 and 2600 BCE, about the time of the III Dynasty in Egypt.

Inana was the most impressive of other shrines at Uruk, approached as it was through an overwhelming portico of 9-ft diameter brick columns whose mud-plastered exterior was studded with glazed cone facing in a pattern of colored chevrons. They are the earliest freestanding columns found in Mesopotamia so far, and they announce the kind of finish elaborated on the ziggurats, which developed quickly from these tentative beginnings—every major city had one. They were known as mountains, condensations of earth and its power—and ascending them was a cultural act.

A small, perhaps ephemeral, pavilion crowned the summit on some occasions. It was called the "waiting room" and is considered by some to have been the location of a hierogamy—though the exact nature of the worship offered has never been clear. In fact Herodotus's account of the temple of Bel in Babylon remains the only eyewitness description of such a shrine. "In it, a great and well-covered couch is laid, and a golden table stands nearby. No image has been set up there, nor does anyone sleep there except one of the women of the place, chosen by the god" (I:138 ff). The only cuneiform text on temple building, called the "Esagil tablet," deals only with dimensions but Herodotus's description is confirmed by other Sumerian documents, such as the account of the wedding of Dumuzi and Inana in the Sumerian hymn of the moon god Nanna:

In your house on high, in your beloved home
I will come to live

O Nanna up above in your cedar-perfumed mountain . . .
O Nanna in your mansion of Ur
I will come to live
Lord! In the bed there I also
want to lie down. . . .   (Jakobsen 1976:126)

The Sumerian city-states coexisted with those of the Semitic-speaking Akkadians until they were overthrown by the empire-builder, Sargon of Akkad (reigned 2371-2316 BCE), and thereafter the Semitic-speaking Akkadians, Babylonians, and Assyrians dominated Mesopotamia. They took over Sumerian religious and civil practice, as well as the Sumerian system of writing. Powerful monarchs would claim to be lords of both Sumer and Akkad in the same way as the Pharaoh ruled over upper and lower Egypt.

While the Pharaohs had built their pyramids at the edge of the valley, and most were barely visible from the towns on the Eastern bank of the Nile, the ziggurats must have towered above Sumerian and later the Babylonian and Assyrian cities, which were built fairly low, with houses of two or three stories. Their surface was burnished by the colors of the glazed terracotta, similar to that of the early Inana temple at Warka, familiar to us in the reliefs of the Ishtar-gate from Babylon, restored by Robert Koldewey, now in the Pergamon Museum in Berlin. The shimmering, polychrome, and highly figured ziggurats were often attacked and rebuilt. Sargon of Akkad wrecked the ziggurat of Ur, and it was reglazed and rebuilt more than once, while the surface of the equally big ziggurat at Babylon was deliberately broken up by Sennacherib in 678 BCE—after which Nebuchadnezzar renewed the vast areas of glazed tiles on the walls and temples described by Herodotus. Everything was finally destroyed by Darius and Xerxes (521, 482–81 BCE).

The main Sumerian ziggurat-building towns were coastal—Eridu, Erech, and Ur. To their south lay the moving dunes of desert Arabia, and eastward the estuary marshes where a complex but impermanent form of reed building seems already to have been devised in an even remoter antiquity. It is commemorated in the painted and carved art of the Ubaid period. The population grew rapidly during the 4th millennium, and agricultural and rural settlements coalesced into larger and more complex units.

I therefore end by presenting you with an equation which seems insoluble—because it has too many unknowns. Two peoples occupy alluvial valleys and seem to have created analogous techniques, devices, and forms in very different circumstances. About the same time both built sacred artificial mountains, great feats of organization and financing, to be ostentatious markers to a collective identity and render tangible to themselves their new status as divinely authorized and guaranteed states. Much as the *idea* of pictorial syllabary writing may have originated in Mesopotamia, although there is no evidence that any particular sign migrated from Sumerian to Egyptian hieroglyphics, so the *idea* of a sacred mountain may have been first considered by the Sumerians on the Persian Gulf to assert a newly formulated statehood and the collective world-hypothesis which it enshrined, and had been adapted by the Egyptians for an analogous purpose. Their world-hypotheses were quite differently conceived.

The Sumerian stormy, torrential sky god mated with a motherly but turbulent earth; while the smooth female sky of the Egyptians overarched her male earth-consort and was fertilized by him. Inevitably the smooth pyramidal royal tomb which guaranteed the dead king his place between the rays of the sun-god had a different metaphoric context to the Sumerian she-mountain to whose summit a surrogate of the great mother would ascend to consummate her marriage with the god of the sky and the storm.

The later and further diffusion of the sacred mountain figure—to the Indian subcontinent and over the Silk Route to Southeast Asia and to China, and perhaps even to the New World by routes as yet unknown—has provided much material for speculation, some of it more fabulous than historical. Yet the insoluble problem remains as a great challenge to the historian and the prehistorian: the figure, the type I have been considering, however transmitted or mediated, can only be seeded in an intellectual and spiritual soil which will provide it with a matrix.

References

Amiet, Pierre, ed. *Naissance de l'Ecriture.* Paris: Éditions de la Réunion des Musées nationaux, 1982.

Andrae, Walter. *Die Ionische Säule: Bauform oder Symbol.* Berlin: Verlag für kunstwissenschaft, 1933.

Arnold, Dorothea, and Christine Ziegler, ed. *Egyptian Art in the Age of the Pyramids.* New York: Metropolitan Museum, 1999.

Badawy, Alexander. *The Architecture of Egypt and the Near East.* Cambridge, MA: MIT Press, 1966.

Crawford, Harriet. *Sumer and the Sumerians.* Cambridge: Cambridge University Press, 1991.

Diringer, David. *The Alphabet.* London: Hutchinson's Scientific and Technical Publications, 1968.

Edwards, I. E. S., C. J. Gadd, and N. G. L. Hammond, eds. *The Cambridge Ancient History.* 3rd ed. Vol. 1, pt. 2. Cambridge: Cambridge University Press, 1971:495 ff.

Emery, W. B. *Archaic Egypt.* Harmondsworth: Penguin, 1961.

Frankfort, Henri. *The Art and Architecture of the Ancient Orient.* Harmondsworth: Penguin, 1954.

———. "The Archetype in Analytical Psychology and the History of Religion." Reprinted in "Three Lectures." *Journal of the Warburg and Courtauld Institutes* 21(1958):168 ff.

———. *Ancient Egyptian Religion.* New York: Harper, 1961.

———. *Kingship and the Gods.* Chicago, IL: University of Chicago Press, 1978.

Giedion, Siegfried. *The Eternal Present: The Beginnings of Architecture.* London: Oxford University Press, 1964.

Hoffman, Michael A. *Egypt Before the Pharaohs.* New York: Knopf, 1984.

Jakobsen, Thorkild. *The Treasures of Darkness.* New Haven, CT: Yale University Press, 1976.

Koch, Klaus. *Geschichte der Egyptischen Religion.* Stuttgart: W. Kohlhammer, 1993.

Lévi-Strauss, Claude. "Introduction l'Oeuvre de Marcel Mauss." In *Sociologie et Anthropologie,* by Marcel Mauss. Paris: Presses Universitaires de France, 1950.

Liverani, Mario. *L'Origine delle Cittá.* Rome: Riuniti, 1986.

Lockyer, J. (Sir) Norman. *The Dawn of Astronomy.* Orig. pub. London, 1884. Cambridge, MA: MIT Press, 1964.

Marshack, Alexander. *The Roots of Civilization.* New York: McGraw-Hill, 1972.

Perkins, Ann Louise. *The Comparative Mythology of Early Mesopotamia.* Chicago, IL: University of Chicago Press, 1977.

Spencer, A. J. *Early Egypt: The Rise of Civilization in the Nile Valley.* London: British Museum Press, 1993.

Verner, Miroslav. *The Pyramids: Their Archaeology and History.* London: Atlantic, 2002.

Wales, H. G. Quaritch. *The Mountain of God.* London: B. Quaritch, 1953.

THE ONTOLOGICAL STRUCTURE OF MEDIANCE AS A GROUND OF MEANING IN ARCHITECTURE

Augustin Berque

The first reality of humanhood is that, standing on the earth with our feet, we tend to the sky with our heads. By doing so, we see the horizon, which links the earth to the sky; and this enables us to predicate the earth into a human world. Heidegger (1927) expressed this with the concept of *Horizontalität*, and more poetically by writing that "world and earth are essentially different of each other, yet never separate. The world is founded upon the earth, and the earth surges through the world" (1962:52).

This is not only phenomenology and the like. It is the factual condition of the species Homo. As André Leroi-Gourhan (1964) made clear, this species emerged in a triple process, which we can summarize with the following formula: hominization/anthropization/humanization, in which (a) hominization is the biophysical process through which a certain primate evolved into Homo; (b) anthropization is the physical transformation of their environment by humans; (c) humanization is the semantic transformation of this environment into a human world.

Each of these three aspects of the same process made possible, and was made possible by, the other two. The latter two amount to the development of technical systems (b) and of symbolic systems (c), which Leroi-Gourhan sees as the exteriorisation of a "social body" out of our "animal body." For example, the functions of our nails and teeth were exteriorized and developed into the use of pebble tools.

What is important here is that this exteriorisation was that of systems of functions, not of discrete material objects. A pebble is not a tooth, and a robot is not a hand; yet both express the development of human corporeality into wider functional systems. And these systems are a social body, invisible as such because they transcend the local definition of each of its physical components (our animal bodies as well as pebbles and robots). This is an essential difference with animals, which all possess, within each of their bodies, the total sum of their abilities. This is true even if they may have an *extended phenotype* (Dawkins 1999), e.g., nests or hives. This is why apes do not produce and keep tools, though they are able, like some other animals, to make use of certain objects as tools on particular occasions.

What Leroi-Gourhan has called our "social body" is nothing else than a positivistic illustration of that which Heidigger called "being outside of oneself" (*Ausser-sich-sein*), and Merleau-Ponty called "anthropological predicates." Human beings exist in the strong sense—that is, they are "standing" (*sistere*) "out" (*ex*) of themselves—because they have predicated their environment into a human world, which is their own social body. They stand outside of themselves, both technically and symbolically, as the systems of things which have exteriorized the functions of their animal bodies into what has become a human world (predicate).

Architecture, and human settlements in general, are a prominent expression of this predication, by human existence, of the earth into a world. And this is why they are, intimately, both technical and symbolic. Both matter and meaning, both subject and predicate, and both substance and sign.

TRAJECTION AND HUMAN EXISTENCE

Leroi-Gourhan figured the above exteriorization as a projection of human corporeality into the environment. I certainly agree that technical systems are a projection. For example, that which started as the function of our nails scratching the ground in search of more ants has been projected into robots scratching the surface of Mars in search of more knowledge. This is not a symbol. Symbols are that which makes it possible to speak of the robot on Mars, though it is not present here. They bring its presence on Mars back to our body here, in a mode which is not presence but representation.

Thus it appears that technical and symbolic systems are complementary to each other. Techniques project our body (*sôma*) into the environment as a world (*kosmos*), while symbols retroject the world into our body as a flesh ("chair" in Merleau-Ponty's vocabulary). This simultaneous process of projection/retrojection, cosmization/somatization, is what I call trajection. It makes our body an analogy of our world, and reciprocally (Berque 2000).

Cultural anthropology gives us plenty of examples of such correspondences (Lagopoulos 1995). Yet, caught within modern dualism, it sees them only as pure symbolical projections of human subjectiveness onto the environment. Such a one-way conception entails not only the arbitrariness of signs, which become pure fantasmatic connections between things and the human mind, but it separates the meaning of signs from our flesh. In that way, starting with Descartes' dualism, modernity has led to radically disconnecting mind, body, and things. Things have become discrete objects standing out there, devoid of any proper meaning; expressing this vacuity of meaning, signification (the work of signs) has ended in a pure game of floating signifiers.

But such a view cannot stand. Biophysics has shown that meaning and signs (the vectors of meaning) are coextensive to life. This has led to the development of biosemiotics (Hoffmeyer 1996). We can include Lakoff and Johnson's theses in this trend, inasmuch as they show that it is our living body which founds the meaning of our most elaborate thought (1999:58). Yet, in this way, we can understand only how matter predicates (subsumes) life, and life predicates (subsumes) mind; we can strictly not understand the reverse. This is because, in biosemiotics, the vector of meaning is material, e.g., hormones conveyed by the wind from one living body to another one. Meaning is physically present in the sign; whereas, in human symbolic systems, it is not. The meaning of the word "Mars" does not suppose that Mars is physically present—it supposes that it is represented in a human mind. And it can be represented, i.e., predicated by consciousness in our brain, because Mars is part of our world, and our world, while being retrojected in this way into our animal body, is no less a projection of this same animal body's physical abilities onto Mars by dint of our social body (e.g., Galileo's telescope as a technical system involving both Mars and Galileo's eye). And because of the physical disconnection of things and their representation, the predication here works the other way round than in biosemiotics. Here, it is not thought which is predicated by the body, and through it by the environment; it is thought which predicates the body into a person, and through it predicates the environment into a human milieu.

Thus predication works in two opposite directions, and what is the subject in one way (from our body to the world) is the predicate in the other way (from the world to our body). This trajection, by pro/retrojecting our bodyhood-worldhood, is the source of the meaning which the things have for us. Things are not objective, since, constituting our world, they are fraught with our body; but neither are they mere subjective representations. They are trajective, and this is why they have a meaning. And signs, which are the vectors of this meaning, far from being arbitrary, are embedded in that very pulsation, to and fro, of our existence.

I see trajection as the source of what Tetsuro Watsuji (1889–1960) defined as "the structural moment of human existence" (*ningen sonzai no kozo keiki*) and named *fudosei*, which I have translated as mediance (Watsuji 1979:3; Berque 1997). His conception of mediance, inspired by Heidegger's notion of *Ausser-sich-sein* (an essential motif of *Being and Time*), was a purely phenomenological one. It was, therefore, misunderstood by a wide majority of its Japanese readers, who generally take it in the sense of geographical determinism (i.e., culture as determined by the environment); whereas Watsuji, in the first lines of the book, explicitly rejects such an interpretation by stating that milieu (*fudo*) is not the natural environment (Berque 1992, 1996).

If we are aware of the trajection of things, mediance becomes much more substantial. It means that "half" (*medietas* in Latin, from which I coined mediance) of our being is within our animal body, while the other "half" is trajected into/from our environment, making it a human milieu (*fudo*); that is, our medial body. Watsuji opened the way to such a conception with his definition of *fudosei* as a "moment" (*keiki*). This word should be understood in the sense of the German philosophical (e.g., Hegel's) concept of *Moment,* which was derived from mechanics, i.e. the combination of two forces into one, causing a movement.

In my view, the unity of mediance is produced by the combination of two "halves" (or "forces"), which are the animal body on the one hand, the medial body on the other hand. "Medial" adds, to Leroi-Gourhan's notion of social body, the fact that this extension of our corporeality is not only technical and symbolic, but ecological as well, because human milieux, being a trajection of natural environments, necessarily suppose this base. And the total combination of all human milieux makes the ecumene (from the Greek *oikoumenê gê*, "inhabited earth"), which is the onto-geographical relationship of Humankind with the Earth. That is, ecumene is the abode of our existence.

Human settlements are ecumenal because they trajectively express our mediance. They are both the existential abode of our persons, and the substantial abode of our bodies. In this sense, they partake simultaneously of our world, and of the Earth.

THE MEDIANCE OF ARCHITECTURE

Trajection does not amount to a zero-sum game; in that case there would be no meaning at all. This is because a predicate can never entirely subsume its subject. Saying that "humans" (subject) "are mammals" (predicate) does not subsume entirely humanity in the category of mammals; because humanity includes a techno-symbolic body which other mammals do not have. In that way, the human subject exceeds its determination by the laws of nature. It is precisely that which made possible the emergence of human consciousness, the distinctive feature of which is to predicate contingently the reality of things one way or another. This higher degree of contingency makes the difference between human history (which is embodied in the ecumene) and natural history (which is embodied in the biosphere).

Yet, the substance of things can never entirely be reduced to its predication one way or the other: subject is not predicate, nor the reverse. This is why predicates can never be free-floating signifiers; they necessarily have a ground in their *hupokeimenon*. In these matters, we have to remind ourselves of Heidegger's notion of *Streit*, and pose the following: the Earth remains *hupokeimenê* (subject) in its very predication into a world; and by doing so, it gives a ground to the world. It gives a meaning to predicates, including signs, and especially to architectural ones, which are physically attached to the ground.

Modern dualism arose from the belief that the substance of things can be totally separated from that of human consciousness. This is impossible: things are trajective, and so is our consciousness. One of the main sources (the others are primarily Plato's metaphysics and Christianity) of dualism is Aristotelian logic: A is A, a thing is what it is and nothing else. Such a logic, that of the identity of the subject, cannot take into account symbolicity, in which A (a thing) is also non-A (a sign representing A through something else, e.g. a word). In this sense, neither can it take into account the essence of predication, in which the subject (i.e., A) becomes the predicate (i.e., non-A); that is, metaphor.

Modern dualism can neither take into account human existence nor the reality of things in a human world. Reality cannot be subsumed into a mere predication by human subjectiveness, i.e. to metaphor. Being trajective, reality is a combination of both logics above, the logic of the identity of the subject and the metaphoric "logic" of the predicate. Things are substances as predicated by human existence, including the reflexivity of consciousness. Mediance trajectively combines the two poles of things and consciousness.

Architecture, as we have seen, is fraught with mediance. Buildings are neither only objects standing out there, nor only the physical abode of our animal bodies; they also express our medial body, which means that they are a part of our own Being, and necessarily also that of other human beings, sharing that same medial body without which we would not exist as humans. This is the reason why architecture cannot do without ethics, because it concerns the very existence of others. Watsuji, who wrote extensively on art and architecture (e.g., in the last chapter of *Fudo*), included all these matters in his overall theory of ethics (*rinrigaku*) as "humanology" (*ningengaku*), i.e. "the study (*gaku*) of what is in between (*gen*, or *aida*) humans (*nin*, or *hito*)." Yet he did not elaborate a theory of architecture as project and practice. On the other hand, some important Japanese architects have introduced his notion of fudo in their own theories, such as Miyakawa Eiji in his 1979 book *Fudo to kenchiku* (Milieu and Architecture).

Modernity, and more so postmodern metabasism, could not take this into account. This is what we have to overcome, by taking into account the mediance of architecture, and of human settlements in general.

In architectural terms, "taking mediance into account," means to overcome creatively, case by case, the modern dichotomy between two antipodal attitudes: scrap and build on the one hand, or freeze (or copy) old forms on the other. Both attitudes stem from the same reduction of human settlements to discrete objects limited to the static identity of their *topos*. In his *Physics*, Aristotle defined the topos of a thing as the "immobile immediate limit of the envelope"

(*to tou periechontos peras akinêton prôton*) of that thing (212a). This definition is a corollary of the principle of the identity of the subject: the identity of A (the thing) cannot be non-A (i.e., exceed the physical limit of its *topos*). But this is not the reality of places in the ecumene, which are trajective. They are not only a topos, but also a *chôra*; that is, a set of ontological relations in which the identity of the thing and human existence imply each other, and which necessarily exceeds the topos of the thing. This can be related to Heidegger's (1958:170–93) distinction between *Stelle* and *Ort*. Stelle means the physical location of an object which might as well be located elsewhere; Ort means a place ontologically related with the thing which is there and with the "spaciation" (*Räumung*) emanating from that thing.

In this sense, places and things are alive. They are particular modes of human existence, and that is why, unless we have special reasons for doing so, we must neither scrap nor freeze them altogether. We must respect their mediance and display it creatively in our turn.

BUILDING IS NOT MERELY PREDICATION

Modernity, as we have seen, has tended to metabasism by disconnecting the substance of things from human subjectiveness. In the field of architecture, this has been expressed by a growing arbitrariness of architectural forms toward their ethical and ecological environment. This arbitrariness has consisted both in the modernist fashion, in repeating the same geometric forms everywhere, or, in the postmodernist fashion, in building any form anywhere. But that was not the only aspect of the question, and probably not the most important one. In the same movement, architecture has tended to disconnect world (i.e., the predicate) and earth (i.e., the subject,

8.2 Fondation Cartier by
Jean Nouvel, 1994. Paris.

hupokeimenon), jeopardizing the very ground of meaning, which lies in the trajective connection of the two. A symbolic expression of this tendency can be read, for example, in Niemeyer's use of V-shaped piles (*pilotis*), reducing the contact of architecture and earth to a single point.

A less anecdotal expression of this disconnection was the use of symbolically insubstantial structures and materials which tend to expel any terrestrial hupokeimenon out of architecture. Jean Nouvel's Fondation Cartier in Paris is a good example of this tendency. That which formerly was, like the other buildings of Boulevard Raspail, a substantial façade continuously connected to the ground (in the sense of both the soil and surrounding buildings), is here liberated from both, and has become a glass-and-metal structure through which the view and even vegetation make their way, like through the air itself. Birds, fooled by this "air," kept crashing upon the glass curtain. Images of their natural predators had to be engraved on it to keep them away.

Another expression of the same disconnection between earth and world, subject and predicate in modern architecture (including postmodernism and the like), is the use of materials

and forms which symbolize that the architectural object does not pertain to any earthly *chôra*; it
just happens to land there, on its purely physical *topos*. The archetype of this architecture is the
machine, more particularly so the airplane, or even better, the starship. A good example of such
E. T. (extraterrestrial) architecture can be seen in Shin Takamatsu's Syntax building in Kyoto,
which has much to do with a famous space robot of the time it was built, Great Mazinger, but
not with earthly concerns.

   As the meaning of things is structured through contrast and metonymy, the meaning of
E. T. architecture is that its environment amounts to intersidereal void, or, ontologically said, to
pure non-being. This is the essence of metabasism—pure predication. Airy architecture, like
that of Fondation Cartier, inasmuch as it pertains to the sky (=kosmos=world=predicate) rather
than to the earth, is of the same essence.

   This is certainly a problem, but we cannot say that such architecture is wrong altogether,
because, as we have seen, architecture is not only substantial, or terrestrial, or a subject
(*hupokeimenon*). Being trajective, it necessarily is also a predicate, airy or celestial to some
degree. The good question is then: to what degree can architecture be predicative, that is,
liberated from its earthly, i.e., social and environmental base?

   There can be no general answer to such a question, and therefore no ready-made
solution. The solution must be creatively devised case by case, precisely because it must respect
the mediance of the place and the circumstances of the building. To put it in a formula, the
architect must carefully balance his creation. There are cases when the subject, the earth, is more
important, for example when the historical or physical constraints of the site are particularly

evident. The architecture of the building must then be particularly modest, that is "tasting the earth" (*jimi* in Japanese). Yet there are other cases, in which the predicate must be stressed; that is, it must patently deliver a message. This is the essence of monumentality: a monument (from the Latin *monere*: advertize) must say something to the people. It must predicate something, by making use of signs.

The problem of modern, and particularly postmodern architecture, is that its metabasism has led to a loss of this necessary balance between subject and predicate. More and more buildings have tended to predicate; that is, to monumentality. Monumentality can have meaning only by contrast. If all buildings are monumental, meaning is lost, and by the same token the substance of human settlements (that is, dwelling on the Earth) disintegrates, because it cannot do without the ethical order of common predicates, meaningfully connected with a common ground into a common horizon. This common horizon cannot be but ethical and ecological. Purely predicative architecture is neither ethical nor ecological—it has no ground and it is not on the Earth, which lies under the sky. Living on the Earth under the sky is the condition of cosmicity, that is, a sense of truth and relevance emanating from our world. Purely predicative architecture has no cosmicity. By losing its *hupokeimenon*, it has also lost its *kosmos*.

Quoted in the *Asahi Evening News*, September 24, 2000, Frank Gehry defined a building as a "sculptural object . . . a spatial container, a space with light and air" (10). This is not the definition of a building—a terrestrial thing tending to the sky in a combination of earth and world, *topos* and *chôra*, subject and predicate. This definition is that of a pure monument, totally containing its identity within its *topos*, and free-floating in the air like a Derridian signifier. As Nishida would have put it, it holds itself in its very self-determination, *jiko gentei sono mono ni oite jiko jishin wo motsu* (1966:390).

I acknowledge that this quotation of Gehry's definition of a building was in fact made about a monument, namely his project of a World Aquarium in Panama, which, by the way, is full of ecological signs. But the problem is nonetheless that, if such a definition of buildings should become the rule, there would remain no ground at all.

REFERENCES

Berque, Augustin. *Écoumène. Introduction à l'étude des milieux humains* [Ecumene: Introduction to the study of human milieux]. Paris: Belin, 2000.

———. *Japan: Nature, Artifice and Japanese Culture*. Orig. pub. 1986. Yelvertoft Manor, Northamptonshire: Pilkington, 1997.

Dawkins, Richard. *The Extended Phenotype: The Long Reach of the Gene*. Oxford: Oxford University Press, 1999.

Gehry, Frank. "Gehry Project Could Revitalize Canal Zone." Interview in *Asahi Evening News*. September 24, 2000:10.

Heidegger, Martin. "Bauen, wohnen, denken" [Building, dwelling, thinking]. Orig. pub. 1951. In *Essais et conférences*. Paris: Gallimard, 1958, 170–93.

———. *Sein und Zeit* [Being and Time]. Tübingen: Niemeyer, 1927.

———. *Chemins qui ne mènent nulle part*. Paris: Gallimard, 1962.

Hoffmeyer, Jesper. *Signs of Meaning in the Universe*. Bloomington, IN: Indiana University Press, 1996.

Lagopoulos, Philippe. *Urbanisme et sémiotique dans les sociétés préindustrielles* [City Planning and Semiotics in Pre-industrial Societies]. Paris: Anthropos, 1995.

Lakoff, George, and Mark Johnson. *Philosophy in the Flesh: The Embodied Mind and Its Challenge to Western Thought*. New York: Basic Books, 1999.

Leroi-Gourhan, André. *La Geste et la parole* [Gesture and Speech], 2 vols. Paris: Albin Michel, 1964.

Miyakawa, Eiji. *Fudo to kenchiku* [Milieu and Architecture]. Tokyo: Shokokusha, 1979.

Nishida, Kitaro. "Bashoteki ronri to shuukyouteki sekaikan" [Logic of place and religious worldview], 1945. In *Nishida Kitarou zenshuu* [Complete Works of Nishida Kitaro], vol. 11. Tokyo: Iwanami Shoten, 1966.

Watsuji, Tetsuro. *Fudo. Ningengakuteki kousatsu* [Milieu: A Humanological Study]. Orig. pub. 1935. Tokyo: Iwanami Shoten, 1979, 3.

THREE GESTURES IN A POETICS OF PLACE

CHINESE SETTLEMENT AND DISRUPTION

9

Stephan Feuchtwang

This chapter will introduce three Chinese gestures: linking, centering, and gathering. I call them gestures because they are rhetorical, manifest graphic and verbal conventions. They are also the basic movements of a process that constructs place and story. The process is evident to both observer and participant on several spatial scales, from the interpersonal to the political to the cosmological. More from the observer's stance, there is also the temporal scale of historic change, and that will be the scale that frames my presentation of two case studies from post-Mao China. The two case studies will show how the three gestures accommodate and fashion intrusions and disruptions.

The places that the three movements make are both narrative and spatially internalizing. They establish a story in a landscape, a sacred landscape across which lines between centers are drawn. The centers are points for the gathering of influences from outside and at the same time they are an orientation to prior centers and to centers on an encompassing scale. Let me introduce them by reference to differing two-dimensional graphic perspectives for representing space.

CHINESE PERSPECTIVES OF SPACE

To begin a comparison between the perspective of Chinese landscape painting and cartography with their contemporary, late Renaissance European perspectives, Svetlana Alpers's book, *The Art of Describing* (1983), shows in great and illuminating detail how the Italians painted pictures considered as an object in the world, a framed window to which we bring our eyes. The book also shows how, on the contrary the Dutch painted a picture that took the place of the eye, leaving the frame and our location undefined (45). Italian painters used vanishing-point perspective to create illusional windows on the world, while Northern European painters such as Vermeer, using the same optical inventions, reproduced the effects of a camera obscura. In their paintings landscapes, interiors, and still-lives are descriptive assemblages of knowledge, like the contemporary maps, which often included townscapes in their margins.

Clunas (1997) points out that in China a dissociation between cartography and pictorial art began only in the Ming Dynasty, from the 14th century. Many Chinese scrolls have both foregrounds and aerial perspectives, like maps in both Holland and China. They are planimetric and at the same time shaded and pictorial; the viewer has to link these two and more perspectives while passing over the plane of the painting that unites them. The Dutch traced a single point along a line within the painting. On the contrary, if you look at a Chinese horizontal scroll the point changes along a river as you unroll it. In a hanging scroll there are also a number of points of perspective within the painting, marked by the tiny figures in the landscape, and there are others outside it, both above and beside the mountains. The passage through them is not retrieved into one viewpoint, either travelling within the painting as in Dutch painting or fixed outside it as in Italian painting. However, the viewer does follow a trail of perspective like that of Dutch painting.

The contrast with fixed-point perspective is subtle, since finally there is in both cases a fixing of an internal space *in* which and *to* which the surroundings are collected. However, there is a difference in the strategies of fixing boundaries, apparent when we turn from two to three dimensional art. Chinese gardens, built for their retirement by members of Chinese ruling society and painted or described in poems and calligraphy, can be compared with the estates painted by 18th century European painters for their owners. Both are internal worlds with an unfolding of views that are idealized disclosures of nature. But while the European estates and their paintings can be seen as displays, maps of an owned world, the view of a garden in China is an emblem of being well located in the world. By "well located" I mean both socially and appropriately, according to the suitabilities of view, sentiment, and time of year. The same might be said of an Italian or English garden, but the emphasis is placed differently. Chinese gardens are designed to relate sentiment inherent in the surroundings with the sentiment within the observer. There is an expected resonance between the viewer and surroundings in Chinese painting, writing about landscape, and the composition of gardens (see Fung in this volume for further discussion). In European gardens the sentiment aroused in the sensible viewer is not in the surrounding features so much as in some universal Nature.

There is a further difference in their representation as property to their owners. The European garden is an estate, a piece of contrived and owned nature for display and inheritance. The Chinese garden, separated from the outside world by walls, is a unified version of a larger scattering of pieces of land, of enterprise, and of high office. It is a locus of their dispersal and a focus of their reproduction. The garden is both the result and a resource of prosperity. Rather than a productive European estate, it is fruitful in precisely the non-staple products that are gathered and given as gifts in the establishing and maintenance of personal relations, in the making of links. It shows the capacity of a person to make and maintain social relations, as well as their refinement (Clunas 1996).

The various and overlapping principles of making and maintaining personal relationships, still very much alive in contemporary China, involve pointing up particulars without stating analytic categories of knowledge, leaving room for mutual and implicit understanding and the avoidance of open disagreement. Tacit space is maintained by this avoidance of conflict. Into tacit spaces, like the spaces in a painting of suggestive mists, the relationships being made can be projected and discussed on each side, with the expectations, obligations, and the uncertainties that they entail. Even today, the art of making relations or connections is named and formulated with great enjoyment in China (Yang 1994; Yan 1996; Kipnis 1997). In Western norms, formulations for building social relationships are either spoken or written about with pejorative humor or revealed in texts of scandalous sociology, as in books by Erving Goffman. Nowadays they have become a useful adjunct of working life or recreation or protest, called networking. As such they stand in contrast to the well-formulated ideals of spontaneous romantic relationships of friendship or love, or on the other hand purely contractual relationships. By contrast, Chinese formulations of making and maintaining personal relationships are honorable and central; the person is ideally an agent of relatedness (Chang 2004).

The principle of making links is also the work of the geomancer in choosing the best site for a dwelling. He looks at the potential site from several significant points around it, as well as viewing the same points from the site of the dwelling itself. In other words, the final chosen dwelling site is located in a landscape and linked to a place. The dweller is placed to maximum advantage, where advantage is an accumulation of material energies (*qi*) that flow through the raised forms and depressions of a topography. The dwelling—a house, a grave, a village, a town, or a city—becomes a center where the landscape is shaped, in order to gather the landscape's energies. It becomes a place centered on what the Chinese call a *xue*, sometimes translated as "lair," indicating where the dragon of the landscape dwells. It is the central space that focuses the surrounding perspectives and features for the inhabitants.

To summarize the contrast between these two modes of spatial rendering, the European from the Renaissance onward is an art of display, knowledge, and representation, whereas the Chinese is an art of location. Framing and linear alignment, from one or through a linear series of focal points, are the principles of the art of European visual representation. Linking, centering, and gathering are the principles of Chinese location, including its visual arts, until the introduction of fixed-point perspective in the 17th century. Thereafter, the two continued in parallel in China (Clunas 1997).

LINKING AND DISRUPTION

The construction of dwellings and gardens are not simply views upon the world, they are themselves versions of a world, idealizations, or utopic constructions of a seen and an unseen world. By unseen, I mean only that they are worlds that include both the dead and the living. The house goes beyond death because it contains a continuing social unit and it is able to be physically repaired and rebuilt. It represents a past and an aspiration—its inhabitants' social reproduction. In contrast to this long-term aspiration, dwellings and places on earth are linked in chains of unsettlement, as places of dislocation and movement to places of resettlement. At best, they recompose to form chains of places of origin, from which an ancestor has come.

In the cosmology of Chinese geomancy such disruption is conceived as the result of a disordering of the harmony of a universe of three powers, those of heaven, humans, and earth. Disorder in this conception is due to human lack of attendance to the principles of heavenly movement and earthly formation. Of the three powers, it is the responsibility of humans to locate and disclose the dynamic order of heaven and earth by ritual, a centering, ordering, and manifesting performance (Zito 1997). This concept is applied to any one place, as a centering of the universe upon the grave of a parent or on the dwelling of a family, and the line of descent or reproduction from each. *Fengshui*, Chinese geomancy, is the art of centering human microcosms. But when every place is a center of its own universe within the encompassing universe, those very universes can come into conflict. The encompassing location of settlement—village, city, kingdom—can be disrupted by the very operation of centering itself. It is a conflict of networks and their centers, each part of the surroundings for the other, each tapping almost the same landscape, each a rival center of the encompassing scale. Therefore, to be a place where every family can compose and preserve its reputation and its future, a tacit space must be maintained whose boundaries are not clear and throughout which there are sites of constant and creative maneuvering that can explode into conflict. When they do, there will be mediating appeals to encompassing harmony, by people commanding respect (having greater face), in order to recover the tacit space of maneuver. As a consequence, the art of centering and stories of geomantic operations abound in words for disruption as well as harmony. The main concern here will not be such internal disruptions and their resolution but large-scale disruption from the state. In particular I shall be looking at disruption by the Chinese state's modernizing projects, that is the equivalent of the introduction of fixed-point perspective into fengshui's spatial location.

Modernization and Clashes with Straight Lines

The project of modernity is spatially signified by a line that is the arrow of progress or development, not a center but pursuit of the vanishing point of abundance and infinity. As lived, the time and space of modernity remains a space, not a place. In the cosmology of Chinese geomancy, the project of modernity and its works are characterized by the straight line of roads and railways, or the digging of mines into the veins of the dragon. Whether undertaken by Western corporations or by Chinese part-state, part-private initiatives, every new project of a railway, road, mine, or multi-story construction such as the Bank of China building in Hong Kong could expect to be opposed on the grounds that it disrupted the harmony and depleted the resources of a centered space. Compensating measures were often demanded and granted.

The lines of the grid pattern of Chinese imperial cities were certainly straight, but they were broken by the walls, gates, and screen walls inside the entrances to their enclosures. They were the equivalent of the straight lines of the walls of rooms within a traditional domestic space. Not so the roads and straight verticals and horizontals of, for instance, contemporary Beijing. It is true that civil engineers and architects in Beijing as well as Hong Kong have consulted experts in fengshui for the sake of their clients, or in order to forestall suits from proprietors of buildings within view, but to the project of modernization, fengshui is out of date. The constitutionally atheist ruling party of the People's Republic of China or before it of the Republic of China both denounce fengshui practices as a mixture of fraud and superstition.

From the greater distance of an anthropologist, the understanding I offer is a condemnation of neither the disruptive project nor the defensive use of fengshui. It is to suggest that fengshui is an elaborate formulation and guide to the re-establishing of place and centricity after it has been disrupted.

The other principal effect of the project of modernization is the building of urban concentrations of dwelling and economic activity. It is a concentration of human settlement that must accompany the accelerating increase in population that accompanies capitalist economic growth and the scientific research and development that it spurs for increased productivity. It is the spreading of such concentrated settlements into the countryside, absorbing villages. One way of understanding this is as a conflict and a negotiation between the greater scale of the encroaching city and the place of a village. The tacit space of the village, maintained as a space for negotiation, is now at stake.

The forces of modernization are experienced much as any other forces according to whether the person experiencing them is (or thinks himself to be) an agent or a subject, a maker of history or a subject of fate. The arts of fengshui and of other strategies are here involved in adjustments to fate, and they can restore an element of agency. The rituals and processes by which fate can be tuned and adjusted, such as the reorientation of a grave, the rebuilding of a temple, or simply the rites of changing luck (*gaiyun*), can re-make a dwelling or a place by turning fate back to the genealogy of social reproduction and regeneration. In order to follow such re-making and how the gestures of centering, gathering, and linking are involved in it, I turn to two case studies.

CASE 1: DISRUPTION AND DISLOCATION IN DACHUAN

In his splendid book about the Kongs in Gansu, the anthropologist Jing Jun (1996) has described in the greatest possible detail a case of disruption and recovery of linkage in the re-making of place. I have selected from his book the salient details. It is one of many post revolutionary cases of seeking compensation, restoring genealogies, and rebuilding temples in northwest China. Restoration took place in a phase of opening after the closure of China that reached high pitches of xenophobia during the Cultural Revolution (1966–68), and the following years until Mao's death in 1976.

Kong is the family name of Confucius. The Kongs of Dachuan village in Gansu province trace their ancestry to him and to his birthplace, far to the east in the coastal province of Shandong, but their claims were not fully authenticated until 1937. In that year, as the eastern provinces were about to be invaded by Japanese armies, one of the Gansu Kongs, a rich merchant, travelled all the way to Confucius' birthplace to collect a genealogy that gave the Gansu clan recognition from the central clan. In this new genealogy their own Gansu register was included in the line of descent from Confucius issued by the central clan. The addition of the Gansu and of other Kong settlements throughout China was part of an attempt by the central Kong clan to resist a threat by the Nationalist government to nationalize their considerable estates, as part of the project of modernizing China. The merchant from Gansu had to return empty-handed, however, because the genealogy had not yet been printed, and very soon the war and Japanese occupation of the eastern provinces made printing and travel between Shandong and Gansu impossible. He was back again in Confucius' birthplace after the war, in 1948. This time he was able to collect a copy, but he left with it only a few hours before Communist forces arrived in the birthplace of Confucius and took it from the Nationalists. The birthplace, temple and mansions, were preserved as a national heritage but the privileges and estates of the Kong clan were removed and confiscated.

The establishing of an illustrious line was certainly subject to disruptions by both the main 20th century governments of China. These disruptions, plus invasion, civil war, and the Kong efforts to re-establish and maintain links, serve as background to a much worse disruption.

Dachuan village was the long-established rural center of the Gansu Kongs. In 1961, one of a number of hydropower projects on the Yellow River was completed nearby. These reservoir projects were themselves not only part of a vast program of reconstruction after civil war and occupation, they were projects of socialist modernization. The villagers had been mobilized to help build the dam. They had also been told to move to a designated new village site because the dam would create a lake that would flood their village. On the basis of previous, pre-Communist, failed or unfinishable projects the villagers did not take the warnings at face value that they should move further up the slopes of the valley. They were also reluctant to move onto more barren land. Finally they were forced to move only days before the village was flooded.

In their recalling of the event to Jing Jun, the worst fate to befall them was the drowning of their ancestors' tombs in part of the village cemetery and the building of the new village over the graves in the other part of the cemetery. They had only been able to remove the bones of the past three generations to new graves, leaving older graves behind or underneath. They had not been able to rebury with due ceremony even the bones they did save as this was considered reactionary in the new ideology of people's power and the speedy development of production.

The collectivization of land and labor had left the composition of the village mostly intact, including residential segments of the Dachuan Kong lineage. The villagers could have organized to remove the older ancestors' as well as the younger graves, but the Kong lineage organization had been destroyed. The villagers' regrets were vocal and poignant even thirty years later. Jing Jun heard endless stories and descriptions of the village as it had been, idealized but remarkable in their detail. In their stories the village's site had been selected by a founding father for his four sons who were its first settlers. The site was in a sinuous part of the valley that suggested a flying phoenix, protected by a range that suggested a dragon. Now it was under water. They talked about this freely, but the same people were reluctant to speak about the deserted tombs. That was too shameful and wounding a betrayal of their sense of place, with its roots in the graves of the ancestors.

1961 was also the year when the Great Leap Forward of collectivization and mass mobilization to increase production ended in famine. The survivors were too weak and lacking in food to have made the proper sacrifices, even if they had been allowed to conduct them. One old man who did bring himself out of his reluctance to recall their shame shook his head and said, "We knew the dead were tormented by the living, but nobody could get meat or any food to make sacrifices to comfort the deceased. At that time food was rationed and kept at the big collective dining halls. You cannot imagine how we were starving. Even the living had to eat grass roots." Another old man, using the language of neglected ancestors who become hungry ghosts to refer to himself and the other living skeletons, said: "In two days we relocated ten tombs and ate nothing. We had no appetite. We were too tired, too anxious. We looked like ghosts climbing out of the graves" (1996:82).

To restore themselves and to turn themselves back into human beings, they needed to grow crops and eat. They did that within a year after being allowed their own plots in 1961–2. They also had to do something about what they described to Jing Jun as a "shock to the ancestors," a "great affront," and a "deep disgrace" (1996:84). A major way by which they eventually reduced the shame and restored their sense of making their own history was to turn their new village into a place of which they could be proud as a lineage of Kongs. This could only happen after 1978's reforms when control of land and organization of labour were put back into the hands of households. This allowed a regrouping of the lineage organization, now including a number of members of the Communist Party with good connections in the county capital. The elders of the lineage organized collections of funds from fellow Kongs in Dachuan and other Kong villages of Gansu to build a temple to Confucius. There was an existing temple higher than the waters reached, but its land had been confiscated in 1953, cancelling the revenue that had funded the solemn rites that commemorated both Confucius and the Gansu Kong ancestors. The buildings were closed in 1958 and finally destroyed in 1974 during the campaign against Confucius and Lin Biao—Mao's chosen successor accused of having plotted to depose him.

The new temple is larger than the old one. Two geomancers selected the site, the ridgepole was raised with the appropriate ceremony and ritual safeguards, and tablets for the ancestors were installed and consecrated with the proper liturgy. The elders pieced together the rites from memory. On a large placard to one side of the temple's main entrance a memorial text reviews the previous buildings, destructions and rebuildings of the Dachuan Confucius temple. It mentions the latest destruction in the following sentence, translated by Jing Jun: "Damaged by the construction of the reservoir and destroyed in the Cultural Revolution, the Monumental Hall of Great Accomplishment suffered flooding, rotted in a salt marsh, and finally was dismantled during the Anti-Lin Biao and Confucius Campaign" (1996: 85–6). On its new site, Dachuan was by this means refocused and the other villages of the Gansu Kongs were linked to it as a centered place and as a story.

Case 2: Internalization of Tacit Space in Meifa

During the past 25 years in this latest opening-out phase of Chinese civilization but 2,000 km to the southeast of Dachuan, there has also been a movement to rebuild temples and restore genealogies. This involves not only fengshui but also festivals of procession and pilgrimage for local protector gods. In the village of Meifa in Fujian province, where my colleague Wang Mingming and I have conducted research, a former cadre led the restoration of his lineage organization and its focal buildings. He was also the local manager for a joint enterprise between the township government and an overseas Chinese investor (Feuchtwang and Wang 2001).

The restoration in Dachuan was a recovery of history and agency after a major change in the Chinese state. In the case of Meifa I want to focus on contemporary, post-Mao threats to the restoration of place. There, a new road was being built by the county along the bank of the river at a bend overlooked by the ruins of the ancestral hall. It ran between them and a great banyan tree that villagers called a Water-tail, symbolically and perhaps also in physical fact holding back the floodwaters of the river by supporting the bank.

The road would link sites for commercial and industrial enterprises in the nearby county town and the village. The main beneficiaries would be cadre-entrepreneurs. The former cadre was far more trusted by the villagers, even though he was a modernizing manager himself because he had already shown his dedication to the collective good of the villagers in 1962, when, risking his relatively high political position, he had supported the rebuilding of the ancestral hall destroyed in a flood of the river. After all the hard years of the famine, he felt sorry for the old men of the village who had nowhere to gather or be fed special foods on the days of honouring ancestors. The rebuilt hall was then destroyed by force during the Cultural Revolution in 1967. Now he was in charge of the rebuilding of the ancestral hall and the restoration of its rites for a second time.

In 1990 he employed a geomancer to diagnose the problems of the site on which the ancestral hall was to be rebuilt. The geomancer wrote a short essay for the reconstruction committee to consider. It makes no explicit mention of the road, whose raised foundations were being laid. But I think they are apparent in the following points from his essay: "At the center of beauty [of the site] there is a lack. At present the mound at the eastern angle of the southern position is too high, so [referring to the interaction of the five elements] Fire

prospers and overcomes Wood causing injury, stealing sunlight on the rock at the south-west side" (translation by Wang and Feuchtwang).

After listing other problems, it spells out the consequences of leaving matters as they are: "Winning promotion and entering high status will be frustrated. At the head, ear, and tail positions [of the dragon of the site] where Buddhists and Daoists should rise to illustrious heights, honour does not rise, there are no illustrious spirits. Disorder means that there will be no officials [born in the lineage], no involvement in public affairs. The soldier mound oppresses the host father, so there will be no offerings of respect. The mother temple rock is destructive. It attacks people."

Note that the problem is imbalance caused by the mound of the new road's foundation, and possibly also by a road bridge across the river just a little way beyond the site.

The ancestral hall, facing northwest, is at an angle to the river flowing from southwest to northeast, curving towards a confluence with another stream before turning round to flow southeastwards to the capital of the region, Quanzhou. A memorial about the re-opening of the hall states that it faces the mountain of Guanyin, the Goddess of Mercy, across the river and is shaded by a hill behind it. It goes on to celebrate the whole village coming together at the new building to establish the Land God in his place and to welcome the gods and spirits that would guard birth, long life and prosperity and complete the security and peace of the territory. The riverbank site and its frontal view is a "Four Waters Court that brings solid protection" according to the memorial printed in the genealogy compiled at the time of the hall's opening.

The geomancer recommended rebuilding the ancestral hall on a higher platform and digging a pool of water to cover the soldier rock. His essay introduced this in the cosmological conception of human action, namely that it was "for humans to build and for

9.2 View from the road onto the yard and front of the newly constructed ancestral hall.

9.3 View from the riverside in front of the ancestral hall across the water onto the mountains, as it should be were the road not to have partially obscured it.

heaven to change." The platform was raised, but the pool was not dug. And when the road was completed, it was even higher than when first envisaged by the geomancer. This troubled the former cadre when I spoke to him in 1995. Equally troubling is the fact that the road has a sharp bend just after it passes the hall and therefore appears from the entrance of the hall to be running straight at it.

9.4 The road, leading straight at the ancestral hall before bending sharply left along the riverbank. Note the small factories flanking the ancestral hall.

The hall is also now flanked by small factories that tell another story involving the former cadre. The villagers whose houses stood nearby had nearly come to blows with a team of cadres from the county government sent to appease them. They were protesting the low level of compensation they would receive for making way for this industrial development. Despite having an interest in one of the new factories, the former cadre was trusted enough by the villagers when he was called upon to sort things out, and he asked them to withdraw. Despite his having no official position at all, he persuaded them that the new development was to be welcomed because it would provide jobs. At the same time he warned the officials against lining their own pockets.

The same former cadre had overseen the rebuilding of the temple for Meifa's territorial protector gods and re-introduction of its annual festivals before he turned to the reconstruction of the ancestral hall. A story told by elderly villagers to Wang Mingming tell of how the temple and village appropriated the central area of fortune in the village. The land in front of the temple, providing for the upkeep of the building and the festivals of its gods, was small and infertile. In the other direction, the land behind was fertile and extensive but belonged to one, rich man. This inequality between private and communal land caused unrest among the villagers. They consulted the temple god through a spirit medium and the god's advice was to reverse the temple's orientation so that its front entrance faced onto the rich man's fields. They

9.5 Offerings of whole hogs
by the village representatives
at the entrance to the village
temple on the annual festival
of its protector god.

would automatically become temple land by virtue of the custom that the land in front of a temple is always communal. Overnight, so the story goes, the efficacious god himself produced the miracle of this reversal.

In the land reform of the early 1950s, the land in front of the temple was divided and redistributed to individual households. Subsequently it was turned into part of the collectively farmed land, and then redistributed again. The costs of rebuilding the temple and the holding of its annual festivals were all funded by donations, a standard amount from every village household, with some larger donations from wealthier residents or ex-residents living elsewhere. But the farmlands have been open to view from the immediate space in front of the temple. The immediate yard in front of the temple has to one side a permanent stage for operas performed on festival days.

Beyond, the green space remains as an essential extension of the yard. I asked the former cadre who had managed the rebuilding of the temple and the ancestral hall whether he thinks the fields in front of the temple could be turned into an industrial park. "Not while people feel as they do now—it would not be possible" (interview 2002). But as households gradually cease cultivating their plots in that expanse, it is threatened.

As the county road threatens the open space in front of the ancestral hall, the green space in front of the temple is threatened by encroaching urban and industrial projects.

Three kinds of property are juxtaposed in this tension. There is state investment in infrastructure and private investment in its exploitation, there is the real estate for the development of housing and apartment blocks for the expanding urban population and migrants, and there is the joint investment by subscription and donation in a building and its rituals that makes it a

9.6 Evening performance of opera at the village on the day of the annual festival of its protector god.

public property of those who live near or who trace their ancestry to this location. Commercial and real estate development threaten the village with disruption, dilution, and displacement.

This tension is surely apparent in all parts of the world. What I mean to draw attention to is both the tension and the specific motions or gestures by which place is re-made here and in other parts of China. It is a Chinese cosmology of accommodating and repairing, as it must, the intrusions and disruptions of the abstracting, alienating and straight-line project of modernity.

Now the space and the person in which negotiation of this tension could be worked out are under threat. On the road that now threatens the prosperity of the local lineage, the former cadre was himself knocked down and killed by a bus in 2003. One of the sources of his strength had been his four sons. Two of them became successful businessmen, and one of these had inherited enough of his father's sense of public duty to successfully stand for selection as the Party Secretary of the village. In this position he teamed up with the elected head of the village, a man who had been a close friend and partner of his father, the former cadre in the rebuilding of the temple and the hall. But when Wang Mingming and I spent an evening with them in 2004, the two men had a quite different view of the prospects for the green fields in front of the temple.

The village head himself ploughed a plot among the fields for growing rice, but he agreed with his new partner that it would be good for the village if the space were to be filled by new buildings. They disagreed only over whether they should be apartment blocks including some reserved as compensation for villagers or factories providing employment for villagers. The fertile land turned into real estate would become a profitable resource for the villagers individually, not collectively, and the open space would be filled in.

9.7 View from the temple onto what were green fields, with mountains in the background. Note the uncultivated land in the foreground.

9.8 The right side of the same open space in front of the temple. One strip of the fields is being ploughed in front of a traditional village house immediately behind which new village and city buildings loom.

They had successfully resisted the urging of the county government to turn over the whole village to urban registration, insisting instead that the village territory remain nominally rural. This kept it in their own jurisdiction and therefore also in the villagers' electoral powers. They knew they would be able to force any deal to provide jobs for villagers in the enterprises built on the land, by threatening to resign if they found that villagers were excluded. They knew their resignations would leave the village leaderless and the county and township governments would be left with a troubling disorder. So it was still a space of forceful negotiation, but it would be filled. Many people from elsewhere would also occupy it, probably outnumbering the villagers.

The nodal buildings of temple and hall will remain as a focus for the collective identity of villagers and for those who have left but still consider it to be home. But what will have happened to the tacit spaces that were the lineage and village "lairs?" They will have become confined to the nodal buildings themselves, while the village territory will have become part of the county city. Nearby structures will then cause attention to be focused much more on the internal space within the building and the spaces immediately in front of them. The village will have become a notional place, located by name and nodal buildings only. These in turn will have become features characterising the area. For newcomers the buildings will be a source of the place's story from an older past and negotiations over the place and its significance for locals will be through and about the internal spaces of these two buildings and the gathering yards in front of them. Tacit space will have been internalized.

THE STRATEGY OF THE THREE GESTURES AND TACIT SPACE

The Chinese strategy of location that I have singled out celebrates the name of a village or a line of descent that is also a set of links and social connections, not a single named donor or corporation as often seen in Victorian civic pride or North American campuses. The Chinese strategy is indirect. Powerful leaders and donors make their mark not by a building bearing their name but by combining their face with that of a locality through a significant ancestor or a temple where meetings, networks, and gossip are gathered. Together, the building and the open space in front of it constitute the *xue* of the place. The space and view are a gathering of material energies for the collective space within which each household has its own space and view. It is the tacit space in which conflicts arise and can be settled. The leader's gathering of a social network to himself and on behalf of the place is the equivalent of the material energies concentrated to rebuild the nodal buildings and to maintain them against outside disruptions. By contributions to and management of the focal buildings and the events that occur in the open space, donors and leaders are respected enough to be able to resolve internal disputes. Even more important, their management of and identification with the place give them the capacity and the responsibility to negotiate with agents and forces of intrusion and disruption.

These disruptions are now those of state and other projects of capitalist development, including that of urban real estate for apartments, and for commercial and production facilities. The result is an internalization of tacit space. I am suggesting that even as the geomantic description becomes a notional, rather than an actual view, the tacit space of gathering, linking, and centering continues to exist as a distinctive Chinese sense of public space.

REFERENCES

Alpers, Svetlana. *The Art of Describing; Dutch Art in the Seventeenth Century*. London: John Murray, 1983.

Chang, Xiangqun. Ph.D. dissertation, City University, London, 2004.

Clunas, Craig. *Fruitful Sites; Garden Culture in Ming Dynasty China*. London: Reaktion, 1996.

———. *Pictures and Visuality in Early Modern China*. London: Reaktion, 1997.

Feuchtwang, Stephan. *An Anthropological Analysis of Chinese Geomancy*. Bangkok: White Lotus, 2002.

———. *Popular Religion in China: The Imperial Metaphor.* Richmond, UK: Curzon, 2001.

Feuchtwang, Stephan, and Wang Mingming. *Grassroots Charisma: Four Local Leaders in China.* London: Routledge, 2001.

Jing, Jun. *The Temple of Memories: History, Power and Morality in a Chinese Village.* Palo Alto, CA: Stanford University Press, 1996.

———. "Villages Dammed, Villages Repossessed: A Memorial Movement in Northwest China." *American Ethnologist* 26,2(1999):324–43.

Kipnis, Andrew B. *Producing Guanxi Sentiment, Self, and Subculture in a North China Village.* Durham, NC: Duke University Press, 1997

Yan, Yunxiang. *The Flow of Gifts; Reciprocity and Social Networks in a Chinese Village.* Palo Alto, CA: Stanford University Press, 1996.

Yang, Mayfair Mei-hui. *Gifts, Favors, and Banquets: The Art of Social Relationships in China.* Ithaca, NY: Cornell University Press, 1994.

Zito, Angela. *Of Body and Brush: Grand Sacrifice as Text/Performance in Eighteenth Century China.* Chicago, IL: University of Chicago Press, 1997.

THE LANGUAGE OF CULTURAL MEMORY IN CHINESE GARDENS

IO

Stanislaus Fung

In the study of human settlements, it is a commonplace that traditional buildings and cities reflect not only practical indigencies but also symbolic meanings. The works of Mircea Eliade (1958) and Ananda Coomaraswamy (1977) have been my main guides in the study of architectural symbolism. In these works, the fundamental characteristics of space—point, extension, order, and enclosure—are the basic components of architectural symbolism. In the structuralist hermeneutics of Eliade, centrality and axiality in architecture are understood as part of a system of homologous symbols in traditional culture (Snodgrass 1985:1–10, Snodgrass 1990:8–62). Architectural structure and meaning are linked in a fixed relationship. However, the work of the anthropologist James A. Boon (1990) has evoked the idea that symbols that are homologous might nevertheless retain their specificity and are not necessarily substitutable with each other. In other words, architectural symbols of a seemingly universal character retain significant meanings derived from their situation and history (cf. Eliade 1965:208–11).

In my studies in the history of Chinese gardens, I gained the impression that the understanding of structure and meaning in Eliade and Coomaraswamy had little explanatory force in the study of Chinese gardens. The synchronic analysis of symbols seemed to belie the conspicuously historical understanding of space and time I found evident in Chinese gardens. Apart from the theme of the immortals' islands in early gardens, represented by three islands in a lake (Ledderose 1983, Cooper 1977), it was difficult to locate other instances in which spatial structure and religious meaning could be understood as a fixed relationship. In most contexts in which the theme of garden as paradise appears, it is not possible to delineate a clear relationship between the overall plan of a garden and the paradisiacal significance that its name may signify.

Gradually, Coomaraswamy's notion of a *philosophia perennis* gave way in my mind to the contrast of traditions in the field of comparative philosophy (see Neville 2000). The understanding of order in terms of one-many, part-whole relationships gave way to analysis in terms of a vaguely defined field with changing, pulsating foci (Hall and Ames 1998; Xu 2004). The function of walls in Chinese gardens is then understood not as the clear demarcation of inside and outside, profane and sacred, but as ambiguous boundaries. One encounters walls everywhere without necessarily being concerned with the wall that defined the garden in terms of inside and outside. I also began to see in textual sources on Chinese gardens how subject and object are not held in dualistic opposition. Key terms such as *yi* (appropriateness), *yin* (interdependence), and *jie* (borrowing) seem to be implicated in polar relationships modeled on the interplay of *yin* and *yang* (Fung 1997). My most recent work attempts to show how the apparently chaotic drift of a text on borrowing views might be understood as instantiating a peripatetic thinking circulating between self, scene, and action as three hubs of consideration

(Fung 2000). In another context, I made a close reading of several texts to show the interwoven nature of motion and stillness in the experience of Ming gardens. The *topos* of this discussion—winding paths, the remote heart, the overlaid appreciation of inner movement of *qi* (breath), and the outward movements of garden life—led me to question modernist assumptions of architectural space that had taken hold in studies of gardens (Fung 2003). In this chapter, I shall extend these explorations by considering two rather neglected Chinese texts relevant to the study of gardens: a Song dynasty "encyclopedia," *lei shu* (Xie 1992), and a Ming dynasty book of quotations (Tsukamoto 1928; Gôyama 1978).

My basic motivation is a dissatisfaction with the closure of meaning that seems usually to accompany the explication of Chinese gardens. In modern scholarship, the explication of literary references incorporated in Chinese gardens is accepted as a normal undertaking. These literary references have come to be understood as fixed and decipherable meanings of a garden. The two sources examined here will allow me the evocation of a more fluid and complex understanding of this matter.

My approach to reading these sources is derived from earlier studies of Chinese writings on gardens. In a previous study of the notion of "borrowing views," first elaborated in Chinese sources in the 17th century, I found a peripatetic thinking that shuttles between here-and-now and there-and-then (Fung 2000). The experience of a garden is not figured as a matter of enjoying an immediate scene but as two kinds of interpenetration, as follows:

1. The space of painting interpenetrates the space of cultural landscapes. In the *Xian qing ou ji* (Casual Expressions of Idle Feelings, 1671), by Li Yu (1611–80), a fan-shaped window of a boat cabin captures the landscape for travelers and invites them to consider the equivalence of painted landscapes (on folding fans) with the landscape outside the cabin (Li 1730:vol. 14, 4.16a–4.20a; Bray 1997:86 ff).

10.1 Boat with fan-shaped windows.

2. Another kind of interpenetration is that of textual memory and immediate scene. In Qi Biaojia's own account of his garden, entitled *Yu shan zhu* (Footnotes to Allegory Mountain), perhaps the most detailed text concerning a Chinese garden to be translated into English, scenic spots are discussed in relation to remembered texts that the author had memorized (Campbell 1999). For instance, Qi Biaojia tells us that his Bin Vegetable Plot yields one or two cartloads of sweet potatoes. He writes: "When eaten instead of grain, the harvest is enough to fill the bellies of a hundred people. I often find myself intoning those lines from Tao Qian's poem that go: 'Contentedly I sit/and pour the new spring wine,/Or go out to pluck/vegetables in my garden.' The atmosphere is very much akin to that found in the first poem of the 'Airs of Bin' section of the *Book of Songs* which speaks of 'boiling the mallow' and 'drying the dates,' and so I have named my vegetable plot, Bin" (Campbell 1999:259). Elsewhere, writing about "Water Bright Gallery," the owner tells us that the scene brings to mind a couplet of Du Fu's poem "Moon" (Campbell 1999:247).

A similar interpenetration of remembered text and immediate scene in the experience of gardens is conspicuous in the late Professor Chen Congzhou's study of Suzhou gardens, in which black and white photographs are paired with a quotation from Song dynasty song lyrics (Fung 1999).

These two kinds of interpenetration complicate our understanding of the imaginative engagement with gardens in Ming culture, and both depend on acculturation through the study of painting and poetry. In contrast to the ahistorical meaning of symbols revealed by the hermeneutics of Eliade and Coomaraswamy, it is striking to find in these texts a personal and

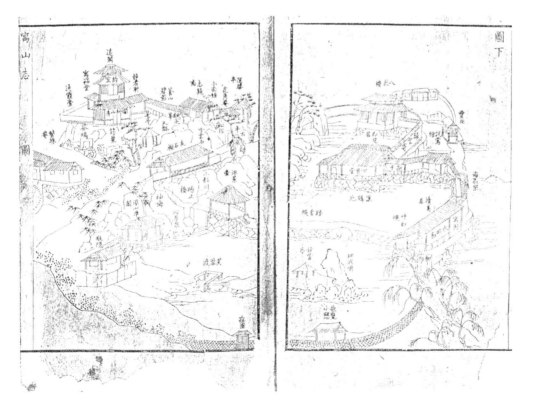

10.2 Qi Biaojia's Allegory Mountain (*Yu Shan*).

10.3 Chen Congzhou's *Suzhou yuanlin* (1956), showing the storied pavilion of "Viewing the Mountain" (*Jian Shan Lou*). The couplet below the photograph reads: Beyond the mist, fine blossoms light red/ Before the balustrade, piled-up rocks green and jagged.

open-ended encounter of place and meaning. They highlight the significance of textual recall in the experience of gardens. Two sources examined below in the following discussion are also caught up with this topic, and we shall see how they might enable a more historically layered understanding of the formation of textual recall and the experience of Chinese gardens.

A CHINESE ENCYCLOPEDIA

The first text is an encyclopedia or classificatory work, *Gu jin he bi shi lei bei yao* (Compendium of Things from the Past and Present Organized by Functional Similarity) (1257), compiled by Xie Weixin (1992). One section is devoted to gardens, with brief quotations to indicate the original context of the *topos* of gardens: poems from the *Book of Songs*, an entry from the *Shuo wen* dictionary, an excerpt from the Han dynastic history (referring to the story of how Dong Zhongshu, the Confucian, had lowered the blinds of his study and did not venture into his garden for three years). Literate readers would have memorized these sources either in their entirety or substantial parts of them, so only brief quotations are given in the encyclopedia. Writings from closer to the time of the compilation of the encyclopedia are transcribed at greater length, including the "Record of the Garden of Solitary Happiness," by Sima Guang (1019–86) and the colophon to the "Record of the Celebrated Gardens of Luoyang" by Li Gefei (fl. 1090). The section concludes with a series of quotations from poems.

The Chinese encyclopedia can be contextualized historically by considering the growth of printing (Chaffee 1995). Wood-block printing had been invented by Buddhists in or before the 8th century. In the 10th century, the government produced printed editions of the classics. Printing spread through China from the 10th century onward, generating an impact greatly different from the spread of printing in 15th and 16th century Europe. In Europe, the vernacular Bible and the Reformation are the main points of reference for early books, whereas in China the authoritative editions of the classics and the examination system for entry to officialdom serve as main foci for publications. The rise of the Chinese encyclopedia is related to the examination system (Elman 2000). Apart from writing a disquisition on political or philosophical topics and answering policy questions, the poetry candidates had to compose a poem and a rhapsody (Chaffee 1995:5). The encyclopedia contains material relevant to these requirements.

Incidentally and over time, the encyclopedia helped to formalize the range of texts and anecdotes that inform discourse on gardens, giving one layer of understanding for the literary recall that we see in later periods of Chinese history.

In philosophical terms, it should be noted that Chinese encyclopedias are not organized by "categories understood by appeal to shared essence or 'natural kinds,' but by a functional similarity or relationship that obtain among unique particulars" (Hall and Ames 1995:253). Distinguishing Chinese concerns from assumptions in Plato's and Aristotle's modes of classification, the Chinese encyclopedia gives examples and models, but not definitions. "In the absence of what we would take to be logically defined relationships, there is not much to discipline what appears to be a welter of disparate detail" (Hall and Ames 1995:253). One would say that the category "garden" is an aggregation rather than a matter of attributive identity (Rajchman 1991). This means that Chinese discourse on gardens is a situational discourse of concrete particulars rather than of abstract principles and concepts. Exemplary moments are positioned in a general pattern of cultural deference and allusive references. The new and fresh are cast as the old refreshed (Fung 2000:132–34). The literary resources circulated by the encyclopedia are part of a pattern of cultural development.

For example, the Garden of Artless Administration (Zhuo Zheng Yuan) in Suzhou has a storied pavilion called "Viewing the Mountain." From the upper story, one can see the mountains outside the city. The name of this pavilion alludes to a poem by Tao Qian (Davis 1983:1, 96). In Sima Guang's famous "Du Le Yuan ji" (Record of the Garden of Solitary Happiness) (1983), featured in the encyclopedia discussed here, there is a terrace, also called "Viewing the Mountain." The storied pavilion in Suzhou garden is therefore charged with the resonances of Sima Guang's garden and with Tao's poem. In this sense, the cultural memory of Chinese gardens is situational, episodic, local, and focal (and the foci may be acts of speech, fragments of texts, as well as actual gardens whether extant or not). The consolidation of historical instances in encyclopedias points to the cumulative nature of the tradition of Chinese gardens. However, it appears that this tradition is not just a "burden," but also the horizon of new experiences. A later book of quotations will take us directly to a discussion of this issue.

The Sweep of the Sword

In his preface to *Zhang wu zhi* (Treatise on Superfluous Things, ca. 1615–20), by Wen Zhenheng (1585–1645), the late Professor Chen Zhi mentioned a number of Ming texts relevant to the study of gardens (Wen 1984:2). Among these is a book of quotations compiled by Lu Shaoheng (fl.1624), called *Zui Gu Tang Jian sao* (The Sweep of the Sword from the Hall for Getting Drunk on Antiquity), written in 1624. Historians of Chinese gardens have been slow to explore the aphoristic literature from this period, and the contemporary scholar who has devoted most attention to it is the Japanese literary historian, Gôyama Kiwamu. I shall rely on his important work (1978) in what follows.

The Sweep of the Sword is divided into 12 sections, each distinguished by a single-character title. The presence of a section entitled "Scenery" might incline us to imagine that this is the reason why Professor Chen Zhi had mentioned this text as a source for Ming gardens. But after studying the text, it appeared that there might be more to it than that. The text is a disparate aggregation of suspended quotations citing fragments about personal relationships and outlook on life and about the appreciation of landscapes. We shall attempt to maintain the flavor of the aggregation and disjunction evident in the original work by adducing fragments, following a sequence of fragments with ad hoc comments to evoke a sense of consistency in spite of the variety of voices.

The compiler prefaces the first section, "Sobering Up," with these words:

> Those who take the wine of Zhongshan would lie intoxicated for a thousand days at a time. The present world is befuddled and harried. There is not a day that the world is not drunk and not a person who is not drunk. Those who seek after reputation are drunk at court. Those who seek after profits are drunk in the [political] wilderness. Those who are boisterous and ebullient are drunk with sounds, colors, carriages, and horses and the world has actually become a world in stupor. How can one get a dose of cool lucidity so that everyone would sober up? (Gôyama 1978:29)

The quotations are offered as a dose of "cool lucidity." There is a conspicuous tension between the sectional headings and the quotations themselves. Each quotation serves to focus attention and disposition. The general horizon is that of a corrective.

> Dwelling in the mountains is a fine affair, but with even a slight sense of attachment, it is the same as being in a market or at court. The connoisseurship of calligraphy and painting is an elegant affair, but with a little greed and obsession, one is just the same as merchants and dealers. Poetry and wine are pleasurable affairs, but once addicted to them, it can be just hell. Being hospitable is a liberal affair, but if one is caught up with vulgar fellows, it would feel the same as an ocean of suffering. (Gôyama 1978:34)

In the section on "Sentiments" we find quotations that deal with settings or scenarios that have a bearing on one's personal condition. In place of direct discussion of sentiments, we find oblique evocations of scene. The reader is often set in motion in search of a vantage point from which to consider the quotations. *The Sweep of The Sword* does not just offer flat declarations of principle or moral: "An evening of conversation with one person can be superior to ten years of reading. A piece of autumnal mountain can cure a patient. Half a cry from a spring bird can rouse a melancholic" (Gôyama 1978:49–50). The section on "Invigoration" is meant to enliven readers: "Peeking at an oriole beyond bamboos, peeking at water beyond trees, peeking at clouds beyond mountain peaks; it is hard to say whether I was being intentional or unintentional. Birds coming to peek at humans, the moon coming to take a peek at the wine, the snow coming to take a peek at the book; just see whether they have sentiments or not" (Gôyama 1978:52–53).

Here the mutuality of person and world seems to be highlighted as something that would perk up the frustrated reader: "When the leaves at the tip of a branch are about to fall, one loves the tree even more. Only when the wild bird in front of the eaves reaches death, only then can it leave the cage. This is how pitiful human existence is" (Gôyama 1978:54). This focus on transience and release seems to be aimed at everyday indifference.

The section entitled "Ling" seems to be about something noumenal, an indwelling, enlivening force. "Beyond the eaves of the thatched hut, one suddenly hears the bark of dogs and the crow of cocks, it seems like a world within clouds. Beneath a bamboo window, only with the murmuring of cicadas and the cawing of crows would one know the world of silence" (Gôyama 1978:59). Near the sounds of domestic animals, one retains a sense of a world beyond. In the sounds of nature lies our awareness of silence. The correlation of inside and outside is echoed in the following:

> Closing the door, the place becomes a deep mountain. Reading a book, the Pure Land is everywhere. . . .
>
> Searching for plum blossoms after the snow, visiting chrysanthemums before the frost, protecting the orchids during rain, listening to bamboos beyond the wind, these are surely the leisurely sentiments of rustics and truly the deep interest of literati. . . .
>
> One wishes to rise late during winter, early during summer. One wishes to sleep amply in spring and very little during the day. (Gôyama 1978:63–65)

In these quotations landscape appreciation is figured as a timely and particular matter. This is echoed elsewhere in the compilation; for instance:

> There is a place and a time for the appreciation of flowers. If one cannot be timely and wantonly command the guests, this would be an affront. Flowers of cold weather are suited to first snow, to clearing skies, to a new moon, to heated chambers. Flowers of warm weather are suited to sunny days, to slightly chilly weather, to grand halls. Flowers of summer are suited to the time just after rain, to brisk breezes, to the shade of fine trees, to the base of bamboos, and to storied pavilions over water. Flowers of cool weather are suited to invigorating moonlight, to the setting sun, to empty steps, to moss-lined streams, to withered vines next to rocks. If one disregarded the wind and the month, failed to select a fine spot, the qi and the spirit would be dissipated and seem entirely at odds to each other. How would this be different from the flowers in brothels and pubs? (Gôyama 1978:142)

The section on "Scenery" turns out to invite an exploration of the limits of intermodal equivalences between landscape, life, poetry, and painting. It is prefaced with the following words:

Making a hut among pine trees and bamboos, leisurely clouds seal the door. Leaning against the base of a green forest, pollens stain one's garments. Fragrant grasses fill the steps, several wafts of steam from [a cup of tea], the brightness of spring fills one's eyes, a yellow bird gives a cry. One can make a poem of this moment, or make a painting of it. One only fears that poetry would not express it exhaustively and painting would not exhaust its meaning. If a superior person or poet can exhaust it with fragmentary words or a few sentences, one can call it a poem, a painting, or a superior person or poet's poetry painting. (Gôyama 1978:87)

The section opens with a quotation that evokes movement through a landscape that seems eminently paintable:

Behind the door is a path, and the path should wind and turn. As the path turns there is a screen; the screen should be small. Passing behind the screen there are steps, the steps should be level. By the side of steps are flowers; the flowers should be fresh. Beyond the flowers is a wall; the wall should be low. In front of the wall are pine trees; the pine trees should be old. At the foot of the pine trees are rocks; the rocks should be strange. Facing the rocks is a pavilion; the pavilion should be plain. Behind the pavilion are bamboos; the bamboos should be sparsely planted. As the bamboos come to an end, there is a chamber; the chamber should be secluded. By the side of the chamber is a path; the path should branch out. As the paths meet up there is a bridge; the bridge should be precipitous. By the bridge are trees; the trees should be lofty. In the shade of the tree are grasses; the grasses should be green. Above the grasses is an irrigation channel; the channel should be narrow. The channel leads to a stream; the stream should turn into a waterfall. At the end of the stream is a mountain; the mountain should be deep. At the foot of the mountain is a dwelling; the dwelling should be square. At the corner of the dwelling is a vegetable garden; the garden should be broad. Within the garden are cranes; the cranes should dance. The cranes announce visitors; the visitors should not be vulgar. As the visitors arrive there is wine; the wine should not be declined. As the wine circulates there is a feeling of tipsiness; as one becomes tipsy one thinks of not returning home. (Gôyama 1978:88–90)

In another quotation delightful moments of experience are offered for poetic and/or painterly engagment:

In the midst of bamboos along three paths, the rays of the sun are watery; this is certainly a fine hour for rustics. Under a window, the sounds of wind and rain; this is also fine scenery for recluses. (Gôyama 1978:90–91)

There is a clear emphasis on an awareness of what might elude poets and painters, not as something absolutely beyond poets and painters but as something beyond certain persons on a specific occasion:

Those who paint snow cannot depict its purity. Those who paint the moon cannot depict its brightness. Those who paint flowers cannot depict their fragrance. Those who paint streams cannot depict their sounds. Those who paint people cannot depict their sentiments. (Gôyama 1978:96–97)

The point, then, is not that gardens are "like" poems or paintings. Rather, faced with a fine scene, "the superior person" can give expression to the moment in poetry or painting. Gardens and poems-paintings can be mutually generative via the involvement of a responsive artist.

In this section, and echoed elsewhere in the compilation, a thread of quotations also deals with the notion of contextual appropriateness:

Reading books is suited to storied pavilions. There are five delightful aspects to this. First delight, one would not be startled by a knock on the door. Second delight, one can look afar. Third delight, damp air would not invade one's bed. Fourth delight, at treetops and the tips of bamboos, one can converse with birds. Fifth delight, clouds and vapors reside among lofty eaves.

Windows are suited to the sounds of bamboos and rain. Pavilions are suited to the sound of autumnal winds. Benches are suited to the sounds of washing inkstones. Beds are suited to the sounds of turning the pages of a book. Moonlight is suited to the sounds of a lute. Snow is suited to the sounds of [making] tea. Spring is suited to the sounds of a zither. Autumn is suited to the sounds of a flute. The night is suited to the sounds of a washing block. (Gôyama 1978:97, 102)

We find in these quotations the notion that garden experiences are conjunctions of activities, of human time and seasonal time, and of sounds and settings. Gardens are momentarily focal rather than spatially bounded.

Gôyama Kiwamu has managed to identify some of the source texts of these quotations. They are mainly from the Song and Ming periods, and some of the authors involved are contemporary with the original compiler, Lu Shaoheng. But these suspended quotations are placed in a compilation that clearly presents them in a double register: (1) they are "things said" and (2) they point to future experiences and help bring them about. The quotations in *The Sweep of the Sword* weave history (the retrospective appearance of the past) and tradition (the prospective appearance of the past) in a strange temporality (Wu 1991:8). The present is dilated by recourse to things said in the past. This dilated or re-focused present then opens onto a future. As it opens up, it ushers in an event that unfolds to refresh person and world. The appearance of *The Sweep of the Sword*, according to Western historians, coincides with a time of social change in Ming China, in which gardens should be considered as property and conspicuous consumption (see Clunas 1996; Jackson 1999). *The Sweep of the Sword* can be seen as part of a broader pattern of the commodification of culture. Almanacs, encyclopedias, route books, collections of model essays, and books on the requisites of elegant living make available knowledges that were commonly acquired by experience or from personal and familial networks. By the late Ming period, various versions of these knowledges could be bought and sold in the form of printed books (Clunas 1991:118). I would argue though that the historical providence of a text such as *The Sweep of the Sword* should not be allowed to obscure the double register that I have identified, for the attractiveness of such a text for present-day students of landscape architecture lies precisely in its shuttling between present-dilating-toward-past (a gathering-up) and a sense of gathered moments opening towards a future.

I would like to gather the strands of the foregoing discussion into the form of a gesture. I have been exploring two layers of cultural memory in the history of Chinese gardens. The first of these, represented by the Song dynasty encyclopedia, formalizes a body of exemplary stories and texts of the Chinese tradition with regard to gardens. These function as ready-made discourses maintained in everyday usage in the same way as literary recall is maintained as an integral part of the experience of gardens. They are commonplaces that may be implicated in patterns of deference or difference. Outward movements in gardens become correlated with inward movements in recall and imagination.

The second layer of cultural memory is represented by *The Sweep of the Sword*. Here suspended quotations allow the words to be loosened from their original contexts; the reader is allowed to shuttle between prescription, suggestion, and evocation. This seems crucial to the capacity of the quotations to take on a significance for future experiences.

From the late Ming dynasty onward, these two layers of cultural memory operated together. The first maintains the specificity of historical orientation as allusion to exemplary events and personages that are integral to discourse on gardens. The second opened the tradition of "things said" to the scenarios of self-cultivation and social distinction. The crux is not simply remembering "who said what," but tuning oneself to a tradition and making one's way in a world of commodified knowledges in a social setting.

In the sources discussed above, the object of discourse is a tuning of personal disposition and not landscape as ideal object. In this sense, these texts can be construed in terms of virtuality, that is, as cultural objects that predispose cultural subjects to the experience of gardens. The texts do not consider this experience in (the overly definite) terms of the possible and the real, or in terms of the realization of possibilities. The texts are aimed at the evocation of experience and are not primarily directed at the circumscription of invention by an exemplary past. Both the literary citations of the Song encyclopedia and *The Sweep of the Sword* convey not just a past that is no more, or a future possibility that is not yet, meanings which seem over-invested in maintaining the volitional autonomy of the present. These texts harbor and help circulate virtualities that induce actualization through the tuning of dispositions. In this regard, contemporary discussions of virtuality in architecture and landscape architecture, which often turn away from notions of tradition in pursuit of new technological visions, can be sharply contrasted with the temporal horizons of the Chinese texts adduced here.

REFERENCES

Boon, James A. *Affinities and Extremes: Crisscrossing the Bittersweet Ethnology of East Indies History, Hindu-Balinese Culture, and Indo-European Allure.* Chicago, IL: University of Chicago Press, 1990.

Bray, Francesca. *Technology and Gender: Fabrics of Power in Late Imperial China.* Berkeley, CA: University of California Press, 1997.

Campbell, Duncan. "Qi Biaojia's 'Footnotes to Allegory Mountain': Introduction and Translation." *Studies in the History of Gardens & Designed Landscapes* 19(July–December 1999):243–75.

Chaffee, John W. *The Thorny Gates of Learning in Sung China: A Social History of Examinations*, 2nd ed. Albany, NY: SUNY Press, 1995.

Clunas, Craig. *Superfluous Things: Material Culture and Social Status in Early Modern China*. Cambridge: Polity Press, 1991.

———. *Fruitful Sites: Garden Culture in Ming Dynasty China*. London: Reaktion, 1996.

Coomaraswamy, Ananda K. *Coomaraswamy: Selected Papers. Volume 1, Traditional Art and Symbolism*, ed. Roger Lipsey. Princeton, NJ: Princeton University Press, 1977.

Cooper, J. C. "The Symbolism of the Taoist Garden." *Studies in Comparative Religion* (Autumn 1977):224–34.

Davis, A. R. *T'ao Yüan-ming (AD 365–427): His Works and Their Meaning*. 2 vols. Cambridge: Cambridge University Press, 1983.

Eliade, Mircea. *Patterns in Comparative Religion*. Trans. Rosemary Sheed. New York: Sheed and Ward, 1958.

———. *The Two and the One*. Trans. J. M. Cohen. Chicago, IL: University of Chicago Press, 1965.

Elman, Benjamin A. *A Cultural History of Civil Examinations in Late Imperial China*. Berkeley, CA: University of California Press, 2000.

Fung, Stanislaus. "Body and Appropriateness in *Yuan ye*." *Intersight* 4(1997):84–91.

———. "Longing and Belonging in Chinese Garden History." In *Perspectives on Garden Histories*, ed. Michel Conan. Washington, DC: Dumbarton Oaks, 1999, 207–21.

———. "Self, Scene and Action: The Final Chapter of *Yuan ye*." In *Landscapes of Memory and Experience*, ed. Jan Birksted. London: Spon, 2000, 133–40.

———. "Movement and Stillness in Ming Writings on Gardens." In *Landscape Design and the Experience of Motion*, ed. Michel Conan. Washington, DC: Dumbarton Oaks, 2003, 243–62.

Gôyama, Kiwamu. *Suikodô kensô*. Tokyo: Meitoku Shuppansha, 1978.

Hall, David L., and Roger T. Ames. "The Cosmological Setting of Chinese Gardens." *Studies in the History of Gardens & Designed Landscapes* 18,3(1998):175–86.

———. *Anticipating China: Thinking Through the Narratives of Chinese and Western Culture*. Albany, NY: SUNY Press, 1995.

Jackson, Mark. "Landscape/Representation/Text: Craig Clunas's *Fruitful Sites* (1996)." *Studies in the History of Gardens and Designed Landscapes* 19,3/4(1999):302–13.

Ledderose, Lothar. "The Earthly Paradise: Religious Elements in Chinese Landscape Art." In *Theories of the Arts in China*, ed. Susan Bush and Christian Murck. Princeton, NJ: Princeton University Press, 1983.

Li, Yu. *Liweng Yi jia yan quan ji*. 16 vols. China: Jie Zi Yuan, 1730.

Neville, Robert Cummings. *Boston Confucianism: Portable Tradition in the Late-Modern World*. Albany, NY: SUNY Press, 2000.

Rajchman, John. "On Not Being Any One." In *Anyone*, ed. Cynthia Davidson. New York: Rizzoli, 1991.

Sima, Guang. "Du Le Yuan ji." In *Zhongguo lidai mingyuanji xuanzhu*, ed. Chen Zhi and Zhang Gongshi. Hefei, Japan: Anhui kexue chubanshe, 1983.

Snodgrass, Adrian. *The Symbolism of the Stupa*. Ithaca, NY: South Asia Program, Cornell University, 1985.

———. *Architecture, Time and Eternity: Studies in the Stellar and Temporal Symbolism of Traditional Buildings.* 2 vols. New Delhi: International Academy of Indian Culture and Aditya Prakashan, 1990.

Tsukamoto, Tetsuzûo. *Suikodô kensô.* Tokyo: Yûhôdô, 1928.

Wen, Zengheng. *Zhang wu zhi jiao zhu*, ed. Chen Zhi and Yang Chaobo. Nanjing: Jiangsu kexue jishu chubanshe, 1984.

Wu, Kuang-ming. *History, Thinking, and Literature in Chinese Philosophy.* Sun Yat-Sen Institute for Social Sciences and Philosophy Monograph Series 7. Nankang, Taipei: n.p., 1991.

Xie, Weixin. *Gu jin he bi shi lei bei yao.* 3 vols. Shanghai: Shanghai guji chubaneshe, 1992.

Xu, Yinong. "Boundaries, Centres and Peripheries in Chinese Gardens: A Case of Suzhou in the Eleventh Century." *Studies in the History of Gardens and Designed Landscapes* 24,1(2004):21–37.

A Culture without a Temple

Ritual Landscape Sanctuaries and Female Superiority in State Religion in Ryukyu

Tsutomu Iyori

11

We usually take it as a matter of course: the existence of temple architecture in any culture. Temples stand in a sanctuary often located in such natural environments as mountains, forests, caves, groves, seashores, or riversides. If it survives as a temple, religious rituals in it or around it usually express a certain phenomenological significance corresponding to its origins. But in the case of a temple where customs or their documents are lost, we cannot recapture the initial ritual significance even if the physical structure or its traces remain. We must listen to the silent archaeological speech on the site of a supposed temple on the lost ritual (Miyamoto 1996, 1999; Hirose 1999; Okada 1999).

I make no theoretical presuppositions that any architecturalization of a sacred place is a sign of natural development or progress in the history of human settlements, as is the case of Laugier's (1979:ch. 1) idealistic primitive hut developing into a stone temple (Rykwert 1972:ch. 3). In some of the world's cultures, primitive or otherwise, architecture plays no role in a ritual context and there is no temple building as an object of worship.

In certain civilizations, temples were constructed in a natural sacred site as a result of human devotion to the supernatural. In another way these constructions were human representations of an environment. A temple could be a *simulacrum* of a sacred mountain (Lundquist 1993) or an embodiment of a sacred object or tree in a house temple, such as the Ise and Izumo shrines in Japan (Inagaki 1968). Inevitably, a temple is an artifact dedicated to a personalized divinity, with a great change in a ritual context before and after the creation of temple architecture (Rykwert 1972:ch. 6). Before the beginning of temple architecture, there was a long history of human sacred ritual practice. In order to understand the beginning of ritual practice in a sacred space compared to the physical beginning of temple architecture, we shall examine an Asian culture where, until the modern age, any temple architecture did not appear at either the state or provincial levels. The place is Okinawa, currently a prefecture of Japan.

OKINAWA, A CULTURE WITHOUT TEMPLES

In Okinawan religious culture, human devotion to ancestral or natural spirits through annual ritual performances was not accompanied by temple buildings. This absence could derive partly from the fact that female leadership in religious state institutions since the age of the Ryukyu Kingdom (1429–1879) played an important role in emphasizing ritual performances in sacred places rather than the architectural realization of sanctuaries. It could also be related to their conception of the divinities, which are not monotheistic, anthropomorphic, or personalized, but kinds of anima-like spirits: *Seji*, coming from heaven, *Obotsu*, and *Nirai-*

Kanai, from another paradise far beyond the horizon by invitation of hereditary priestesses during annual community rituals. During the days of the ritual performances, Okinawans believe that the spirits possess the priestesses who stay possessed until they leave at the finish of the rites. The possession rite in general is executed in the night in a sacred forest, with a limited group of priestesses or all female members of the community, from which men are excluded.

In 1966 William P. Lebra presented a general introduction to Okinawan contemporary religion. We shall examine three principal themes:

1. Females were superior in a spiritual capacity in ancient state religion. Chinese tribute status recognized the authenticity of royal rulership on the one hand and female benediction upon the king by newly installed state priestesses on the other.
2. Ritual pilgrimage in a sacred landscape in the state religion illustrated a principle of sanctity by making a tour of sanctuaries in divine nature.
3. Temple architecture in any sanctuary in Ryukyu tradition was absent. The royal castle was reorganized in the 18th century to make it the setting for a male monarch separated from female initiatives in the state religion.

A Brief History of the Ancient Ryukyu Kingdom

The Okinawan archipelago is located in the Eastern Chinese Sea off Fujian Province of China, about 600 km from Kyûshû, Japan. It was a significant participant in trade relations in Eastern Asia from the 14th century until the mid 16th century.

Before Okinawa Island became a kingdom in 1429, three provincial lords had begun a tribute relationship with China's Ming Dynasty in the 14th century. Each time a ruler changed in Ryukyu (the kingdom's name, which was altered from *Chuzan* in the 18th century), a Chinese diplomatic delegation came from Beijing via Fujian to legitimize the new Ryukyu king (Maehira 1988; Tomiwama 1992). The scene was recorded, for example, by the Chinese delegation of 1719, when an enthronement rite was held in a royal castle in Shuri (Hsu 1982:87–94; Maehira 1988:176–82). This relationship with China through the tribute system was maintained until the last Chinese enthronement rite was carried out in 1866.

In 1609, the Daimiate Satsuma of Kyûshû, Japan, occupied Ryukyu in punishment for the Ryukyu king's refusal to obey an order from the Tokugawa Shogunate to play a role in the negotiations with Ming China to reopen Japan-Chinese trade (Kamiya 1989:44–45). Since then, the Satsuma Daimiate and Tokugawa Shogunate controlled the succession of Ryukyu rulers, but left the kingdom its status as an independent state under the Chinese tribute system. On the occasion of the succession of the Ruler, Ryukyu was obliged to send its prince to report to the Shogunate in Edo (modern Tokyo) via Kagoshima (Yokoyama 1987:44–50).

Female Spiritual Superiority in State Religion

After 1609, the Ryukyu ruler was required to be diplomatically legitimized twice, once by a Chinese investiture delegation and second by the Edo (Tokyo) Shogunate. Internally, the ruler also needed to be authorized in a religious rite executed by the supreme priestesses, *Kikoe-o-kimi.* The same ritual was reenacted each time a new important state priestess was installed, including the supreme priestess herself, to give a benediction upon the ruler.

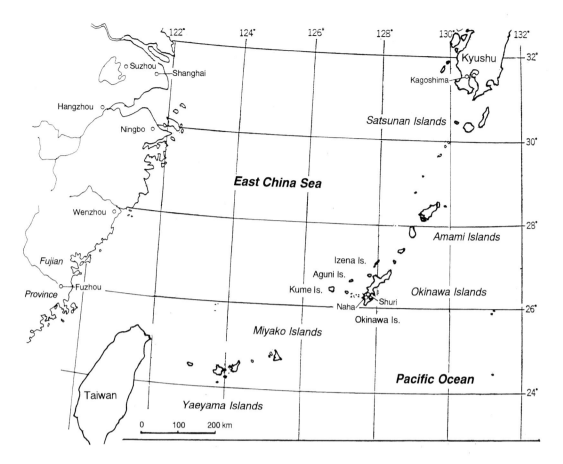

11.1 Ryukyu Archipelago.

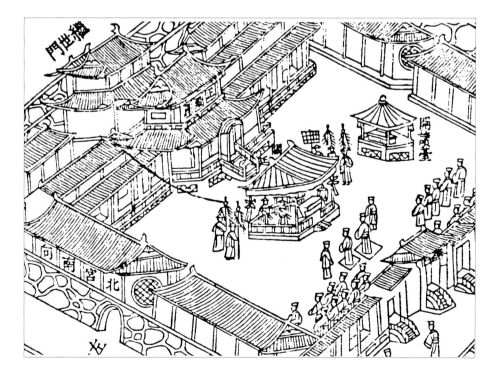

11.2 Chinese Enthronement Rite in the forecourt of the Shuri Castle.

TABLE 11.1 YEARS ELAPSED SINCE THE ACCESSION TO THE THRONE OF EACH KING UNTIL THE CHINESE ENTHRONEMENT RITE AND UNTIL THE *KIMI-TEZURI* RITE FOR THE KING

KING'S NAME	REIGN	YEARS ELAPSED UNTIL CHINESE ENTHRONEMENT	YEARS ELAPSED UNTIL KIMI-TEZURI RITE	DIVINE NAME OF KING
Sho-shin	1477-1526	3	1	Oguiyaka-moi
Sho-seiz	1527-1555	8	19	Tenitsugui-no-ajiosoi
—	—	—	23	—
—	—	—	[25]	—
Sho-gen	1556-1572	7	?*	Tedahajime-ajiosoi
Sho-ei	1573-1588	7	6	Wezoniyasue-ajiosoi
—	—	—	15	—
Sho-nei	1589-1620	18	19	Tedagasue-ajiosoi
Sho-hou	1621-1640	13	?**	Teniguiyasue-ajiosoi
Sho-ken	1641-1647	—	—	no divine name
Sho-shitsu	1648-1668	16	—	no divine name

There is no record to verify the execution of the Kimi-tezuri Rite in the reign of King Sho-gen. See Table 11.2.

** King Sho-hou had his divine name, but there is no record of the Kimi-tezuri Rite during his reign.

Table 11.1 shows that King Sho-sei (reign 1527–55) and Sho-ei (1573–88) twice received the benediction from their spirit protectors. We can find no record for King Sho-gen (1556–72), possibly because there was no succession of the supreme priestess during his reign (Hokama 1972:528; Ikemiya 1991:187–88). We can refer to the dates of the ritual in the collection of ritual sacred songs of the kingdom, *Omoro-sôshi*, which was compiled between 1531 and 1623, and to the life-data of each priestess in the genealogies of the nobilities and the gentries of the ancient kingdom (Naha City 1982).

Even today in Okinawa, when a succession of the hereditary priestess occurs, it is said that a divinity (*Kami*) is born, meaning that a priestess is ready to be possessed by the hereditary spirit of priestesses. Although the state religion disappeared along with the kingdom itself in 1879, the underlying structure of the religious system in the province survives on a community level because of voluntary hereditary priestesses.

On the level of family and kinship, and sometimes even on a community level where ritual traditions survive, we can observe the traditional belief that a male is protected by the spirit of his sister. Okinawans call these females Kami, with the spiritual capacity to protect them through both communal and household rituals.

In the state religion, the king was protected in the same manner, but by a pyramidal system of state priestesses, on the top of which Kikoe-o-kimi was situated with other high state priestesses such as *Aori-yae*, *Sasu-kasa*, and *Shuri-o-kimi*. The king was protected by many state priestesses, but in reality, they were his sisters and nieces or even his mother or aunt. In the case

EXECUTED YEAR/ MONTH OF THE RITE	GENERATION OF THE KIKOE-O-KIMI	REIGN OF THE KIKOE-O-KIMI	YEARS SINCE HER INSTALLATION	RELATIONSHIP TO KING	REIGN OF KING, WITH YEARS ELAPSED SINCE HIS ACCESSION TO THE THRONE	OTHER ACCOMPANYING PRIESTESSES OR SUCCEEDING STATE-PRIESTESSES (RELATIONSHIP WITH KING)
1477	?	?	?	?	Sho-shin, 0	?
?	Gessei (1st)	? - 1544?	—	sister	Sho-shin, ?	?
Aug. 1545	Bainan (2nd)	1545-1577	1	niece of elder brother	Sho-sei, 19	[Sasukasa(sister), Suri-o-kimi (daughter)]
Oct. 1549	id.		4	id.	Sho-sei, 23	Installation of Kimi-kanashi
	id.		6	id.	Sho-sei, 25	Installation of unknown state-priestess*
1556-72	id.	There is no record of Kimi-tezuri rite under the reign of King Sho-gen				
Oct. 1578	Baigaku (3rd)	1578-1605	1	mother	Sho-ei, 6	Aori-yae the 1st (aunt) / Installation of Sasukasa (daughter of predecessor) / Installation of Shuri-o-kimi (unidentified)
Oct. 1587	id.		9	id.	Sho-ei, 15	Installation of Sen-kimi (unidentified)
Oct. 1607	Getsurei (4th)	1607-1653	2	maternal cousin (Queen›s sister)	Sho-nei, 19	Installation of Aori-yae the 2nd (Queen) / Installation of Shimajiri-Sasukasa the 1st (mother-in-law) / Shuri-o-kimi (unidentified) / Installation of Sen-kimi (niece)
1609	Satsuma's conquest over Ryûkyû					
[After the compilation of sacred ritual songs, Omoro, in 1623, there was no record of Kimi-tezuri rites. However, several state priestesses remained and succeeded according to the genealogies]						
[1621-40]	(4th) stayed			cousin	[Sho-hou]	Kikoe-o-kimi, Aori-yae stayed / [Installation(?) of Shimajiri-Sasukasa the 2nd (sister)]
[1641-47]	(4th) stayed			great aunt	[Sho-ken]	
(There was no record of Kimi-tezuri, nor of the Chinese Enthronement rite for the King Sho-ken)						
1654**	name unknown (5th)	1654-1677	?	great aunt	[Sho-shitsu, 6]	[Installation(?) of Shimajiri-Sasukasa the 3rd (aunt)] / [Installation(?) Shuri-o-kimi the 3rd (aunt)]
1677.5.6.	Gesshin (6th)	1677-1703	1	queen***	Sho-tei, 9	Shimajiri-Sasukasa the 3rd stayed
	First installation rite (O-araori) record at Seefa Forest					Shuri-o-kimi the 3rd stayed
1677	Evacuation of a house for Kikoe-o-kimi in Kudaka Island					

An unknown state-priestess was installed [Chuzan Seikan, vol. 5].

** There is no record to verify the execution of Kimi-tezuri rite at this moment; however, the succession of the supreme-priestess and other state-priestesses, mentioned in the notes, is verified in the genealogies.

*** In 1667, the rank of Kikoe-o-kimi, hitherto superior to the Queen, was demoted under the Queen [Nyokan ososhi]. In addition, since 1677 the office of Kikoe-o-kimi was strictly attributed to the Queen [Kyuyo, vol.7].

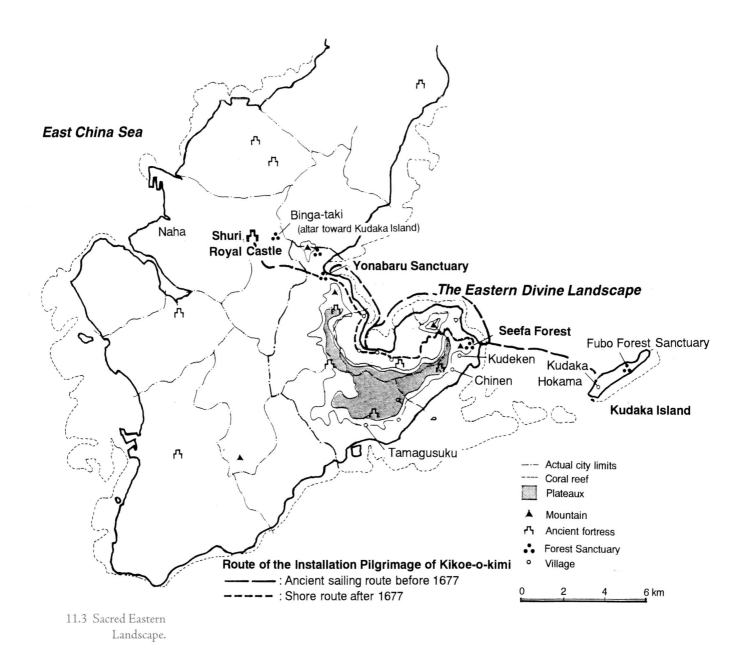

East China Sea

Naha

Shuri Royal Castle

Binga-taki
(altar toward Kudaka Island)

Yonabaru Sanctuary

The Eastern Divine Landscape

Seefa Forest

Fubo Forest Sanctuary

Kudeken

Kudaka

Chinen

Hokama

Kudaka Island

Tamagusuku

— · — Actual city limits
- - - Coral reef
▨ Plateaux
▲ Mountain
⌂ Ancient fortress
∴ Forest Sanctuary
° Village

Route of the Installation Pilgrimage of Kikoe-o-kimi
————— : Ancient sailing route before 1677
- - - - - : Shore route after 1677

0   2   4   6 km

11.3 Sacred Eastern
      Landscape.

of King Sho-nei (reign 1589–1620), he was protected by the queen, the sister of the queen, his mother-in-law, and finally by his very young niece. Together with other royal priestesses they have been called as a whole the "thirty three state-mistresses" (Nyokan Osôshi 1982:77–119).

The king was given a divine name, used only in the ritual by his protector priestesses, and a symbolic name expressing his spiritual nature, different from his Chinese name as Sho-sei, Sho-hou (Haneji 1962:58–59). The ninth King Sho-ken (reign 1641–47) died very young without having received a divine name, a Chinese enthronement rite, or a *Kimi-tezuri* rite by the priestesses. After him, Ryukyu kings did not receive a divine name (*Chûzan Seifu* 1962:116) indicating a decline of female initiatives in state religion that began with the occupation of Ryukyu in 1609 by the Satsuma Daimiate of Kyûshû.

Since before World War II, several pro-Japanese scholars such as Yanagita Kunio (1940), Origuchi Shinobu (1976), and Iha Fuyû (1938, 1939; as an Okinawan native scholar, he founded Okinawan Studies), regarded the tradition of female spiritual superiority in Okinawa as a remnant of ancient Japan's matriarchal stage. However, it should be compared not solely from a Japan-centric view but also in a global view of the history of female defeat in religious initiatives in society, as traced in an occidental context by Friedrich Engels in 1884. What is of further importance in the case of Okinawa is not a naive presumption that an archaic female superiority might have survived, but how and why this superiority was established as a social and religious role in the kingdom and was maintained until the modern age, while, on the other hand, a Confucian male political leadership was also adopted from Japan and China (Iyori 1995a).

RITUAL PILGRIMAGE IN A LANDSCAPE

According to two ritual summaries concerning state priestesses from 1706 (*Nyokan Osôshi*) and 1875 (*Ogishiki no Oshidai*), we know that from 1677 until the last installation rite in 1875, every succeeding supreme priestess of the kingdom made a tour to conduct a rite in order to receive her own sacred spirit. She followed a route from the royal castle in Shuri, stopping at an eastern seashore sanctuary called *Yonabaru* and finally arriving at midnight at the sacred forest known as *Seefa* on *Kudeken* Peninsula at the extreme eastern point of the main island.

The forest sanctuary Seefa was venerated for its sanctity to protect sailors. A ritual song *Omoro* in *Omoro Sôshi* commemorates a state ritual conducted there in 1500 before the royal navy set sail to conquer the southern islands of Yaeyama:

> Your Supreme Kikoe-o-kimi descend down here in Seefa forest
> Please be tranquil as you mind
> To protect and to favor our Lord
> So you descend here possessed with your spirit

11.4 Portrait, Ugui of King Sho-nei (reign 1589–1620).

By choosing a day of a good omen
Early in the Morning before the sun rise
Please make a prayer, O your Supreme Priestess,
To the Genius of the Forest
To invite a great spirit of conquest
Here on a cape representing all the sacred capes of the World.
(Royal Government of Ryukyu 1972:Vol. 1, 34)

Another prayer for the conquest seems to have been made after the procession returned to the royal castle in Shuri. The ritual song *Omoro* in the same volume tells us how and where it was done.

O Your Majesty, our Lord, please be present in a sacred forest in the Royal Palace
To execute an important ritual of our State
O Your Supreme Priestess Kikoe-o-kimi
Please reckon and possess great spirits to our soldiers
to fight for our State
O Kimihae, great priestess of Kume Island,
Go and prevail over Miyako Island
to lead the way to overcome the soldiers in Yaeyama Islands
Then your Supreme Priestess Kikoe-o-kimi,
with your Great Spirit, please prevail and protect the land. (Vol. 1, 36)

The pilgrimage rite would have ended with a final rite in the royal castle in Shuri, as in the example mentioned above. The installation rite for the supreme priestess would have been the Kimi-tezuri rite described below.

According to the ritual songs, *Omoro*, of Kimi-tezuri rite, recorded in the 4th, 6th, and 12th volumes of *Omoro-sôshi* compiled in 1623, there were five instances of the Kimi-tezuri rite conducted in 1545, 1549, 1578, 1587, and 1607 (Kadekaru 1988). The rite had two stages separated by several days. The first was held at midnight or very early in the morning, while the second was held during the day.

11.5 Sacred Seefa Forest viewed from the sea (1991): on the top of a hill in the center are two rocks which can be seen from the sea. They are the protector of the navigators in the Age of Kingdom, under the Seefa Forest.

In the case of October, 1607, five state priestesses appeared in the rite to give benedictions to King Sho-nei (reign 1589–1620). Quoted here is the one sung for the priestess Aori-yae (Queen, daughter of the former king):

O Eminent State Protector Aori-yae,
You descend to succeed your sacred Spirit.
(Here in a sanctuary of the Royal castle)
Please offer to our King
your Great Spirit, well known even in Heaven (Obotsu).
May King, descendant of the Great Sun with glorious longevity,
dominate the Land and prosper in Shuri Castle,
Forever as long as heavenly spirit and your Great Spirit protect him. (Royal Government of Ryukyu 1972:Vol.12, 742)

According to the ritual songs, the first stage was to be conducted in a sacred area, *Kyo-no-uchi*, in the royal castle (point 11 in Figure 11.7), where the spirits of newly succeeding priestesses were imagined to be descending from heaven to possess real priestesses. Being possessed, the priestesses got ready to protect the king and to give him the heavenly spirit of longevity. The first stage is the process of the spirit's possession of a new succeeding priestess.

The second stage took place a few days after the first, at noon in the case of August 25, 1545. The priestesses came from the sacred area into a feast court, *Una* (point 6 in Figure 11.7), which was the main forecourt of the royal castle, according to the report written by a monk, Taichû, who stayed in Ryukyu in 1603–05 (Taichû 1936). The priestesses accompanied the spirits from heaven who came to possess the king.

These two stages of the *Kimi-tezuri* rite are common even today in annual rites for visiting divinities in rural communities. The first stage of the arrival of spirits in a sacred forest is conducted in the evening or in the night, and the second on the next day during the daytime in a communal place in the village (Higa 1982; Hatakeyama 1981). In some cases, however, the

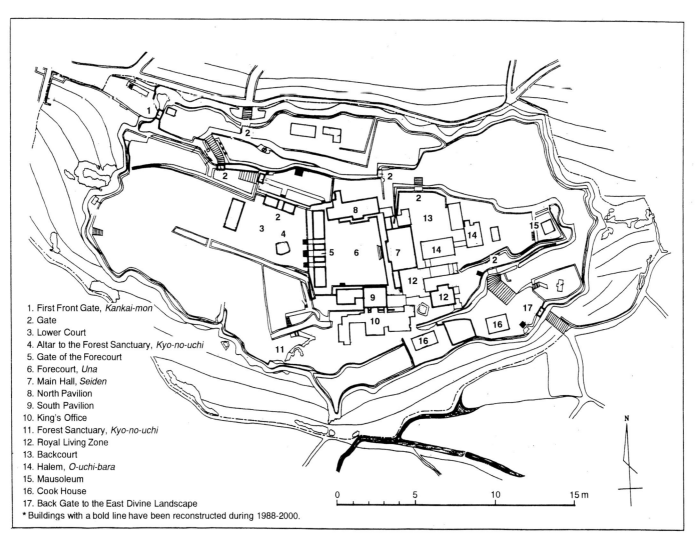

1. First Front Gate, *Kankai-mon*
2. Gate
3. Lower Court
4. Altar to the Forest Sanctuary, *Kyo-no-uchi*
5. Gate of the Forecourt
6. Forecourt, *Una*
7. Main Hall, *Seiden*
8. North Pavilion
9. South Pavilion
10. King's Office
11. Forest Sanctuary, *Kyo-no-uchi*
12. Royal Living Zone
13. Backcourt
14. Halem, *O-uchi-bara*
15. Mausoleum
16. Cook House
17. Back Gate to the East Divine Landscape
* Buildings with a bold line have been reconstructed during 1988-2000.

11.7 Plan of the Shuri
Royal Castle in the
19th century.

first secret stage, the rituals in a sacred forest during the night, have been lost and are simply indicated in ritual songs (Iyori 1989).

As for the cosmic spatiality expressed in the Kimi-tezuri ritual songs, we can observe a vertical axis from the feast court through the sacred forest and into the castle toward heaven, expressing a cosmic spatiality of the sacred forest from which the ritual procession of priestesses enters into a feast court of the royal castle on several occasions.

What is significant here is the lack of another cosmic horizontal axis toward the sea horizon, along which another spirit of the horizon had been invited. The lack must have been compensated for by a rite to invite the spirit from the horizon to make a pilgrimage toward the eastern sacred landscape.

The Kimi-tezuri rite held in the Shuri royal castle would have been in fact the last step in the progression of the installation pilgrimage rites for a newly succeeding supreme priestess, Kikoe-o-kimi, of the kingdom.

From 1677 to 1875 the supreme priestess attended her installation rite not in the royal castle but in the sacred forest in the most eastern peninsula of the main island (Royal Government of Ryukyu 1982). It is not known where and how the installation rite was performed before 1677 (Iyori 2003).

The forest sanctuary Seefa was a highly sacred ritual place of the kingdom since the beginning of the first Sho dynasty (1429–69) of Ryukyu (Haneji 1962). The eastern part of the main island around the peninsula, with the tiny island Kudaka five km to the east, was a sacred landscape where several state pilgrimage rites were performed by the king and his protector Kikoe-o-kimi. It was the place the royal family of the Sho dynasty commenced the conquest of the island, and was one of the places where, in the state myth, the creation of the land was begun, and where the five cereals were introduced into Ryukyu for the first time from the outside (Haneji 1962).

THE ORIGINAL ITINERARY OF RITUAL PILGRIMAGE

The Buddhist monk Taichû, who stayed in Ryukyu from 1603 to 1605, just before the Satsuma Daimiate's conquest of Ryukyu, and published *Ryûkyû shintô-ki* in 1648, witnessed an important aspect of the Kimi-tezuri rite. He described the fact that there had been a relationship between the installation rites of local priestesses called *Ara-kami* (newly installed priestess) and those of the central state priestesses. Local priestesses were installed in August and central state priestesses in October in the royal castle of Shuri, as reported in the ritual songs in *Omoro-sôshi* (Royal Government of Ryukyu 1972:Vol.12, 735–38, 740–45).

Further, in *Chûzan Seikan*, written in 1650 by Prince Haneji Chôshu, we find a further correlation with another series of state pilgrimage rites called *Miwoyadairi* which had possibly been conducted in the eastern divine landscape. Curiously, the names of state rituals were listed as if the author were describing a pantheon of the kingdom, perhaps indicating a ritual-centered tradition in the conception of the divinities in Ryukyu.

These state rites are as follows in the order of description:

1. The state rite of sailing to a sacred offshore island *Wau* (*Wau-no-miwoyadairi*), also called Ara-kami, which appears (the rite is conducted) every 30 or 50 years, possibly identifiable as an installation rite of Kikoe-o-kimi on Kudaka Island (Iha 1974; Iyori 1993).
2. State rite of sailing around a peninsula (*Ura-mawari-no-miwoyadairi*) identifiable with sailing around Kudeken peninsula.
3. State rite at *Yonabaru*, here described clearly as the place of the installation rite of the supreme priestess at Yonabaru on the eastern seashore.

These three state rituals, together with the Kimi-tezuri rite in Shuri royal castle, compose the pilgrimage itinerary of the installation rite for Kikoe-o-kimi, which would have been practiced until 1607 as noted above. The monk Taichû identified the Ara-kami rite with the Kimi-tezuri rite. That is, the Kimi-tezuri rite was not only a benediction rite for the king but also a last stage of the installation rite of a succeeding supreme priestess. With this analysis, we can understand why the forest Seefa had not been mentioned as a main place for the rite in any historical document before 1677, and even after 1677. These documents are *Ryûkyû Shintô-ki* (1648), *Chûzan Seikan* (1650), and, after 1677, *Ryûkyû-koku Yuraiki* (edited in 1713), a general survey of both state and local rituals and all the ritual places of the kingdom. The year 1677 is when it is certain for the first time that the installation rite for Kikoe-o-kimi was conducted only in the forest Seefa (Royal Government of Ryukyu 1982).

Sailing to an offshore sacred island, Izena or Tonaki Islands, for example, or making a pilgrimage to one of many sacred capes to refresh the spirits of a priestess and to invite spirits coming from the sea horizon, are rituals found in several places in Okinawa even today (Iha 1974; Iyori 1987, 1998a). In this sense, Kudaka Island was a sacred island off the eastern seashore in a divine landscape of the east, and the Seefa Forest was a sacred cape, when viewed from Shuri, the capital of Ryukyu Kingdom.

In my 1993 article, I reconstructed the original route (and roots) of the former pilgrimage installation rite with help from other evidence observed through annual rituals today in Kudaka Island and from the documents concerning the last installation rite in 1875 and its remaining ritual songs. Concerning the ancient royal pilgrimage, every two years until 1673, the king and his supreme state priestess used to visit Kudaka Island and the opposite side of the channel, Chinen and Tamagusuku, respectively, to perform a state agricultural rite for wheat (in Kudaka Island) and rice (in Chinen and Tamagusuku). The king's pilgrimage rite was stopped in 1673 when a religious reform commenced to simplify and to conceal female leadership in the state religion, as described below.

As a result of this analysis, we can reconstruct the original itinerary of the installation rite before 1677 as follows:

1. Start from the royal castle, followed by arrival at Yonabaru sanctuary, probably in August.
2. Perform the Yonabaru rite (on the seashore).

3. Sail around Kudeken peninsula (Sailing itself is a ritual).
4. Stop at Seefa Forest to make a prayer to the protector of navigation in the forest.
5. Sail further to Kudaka to perform the installation rite.
6. Return to the royal castle by the reverse route via Seefa Forest.
7. Perform Kimi-tezuri (benediction-giving) rite in the royal castle in October.

In fact, when Prince Haneji edited the royal genealogy to reorganize the Ryukyu pantheon (state-ritual organization), the king, along with his religious protector Kikoe-o-kimi, had been practicing the pilgrimage to Kudaka Island and the opposite part every two years. It is natural that before 1677, the installation rite of the supreme priestess was also held on Kudaka Island, the most sacred island in the east of the kingdom.

Suppression of State Religious Rituals

In 1672, only 22 years after his edition of the royal genealogy in which he advocated the traditional state rituals, Prince Haneji commenced religious reforms against the traditional practices he described in the genealogy (Takara 1989). He simplified the royal pilgrimage rites by eliminating the sailing procedure to Kudaka by the king, and replaced it with a royal envoy to the island (Tonaki 1988). He also arranged an altar near the royal palace in the capital Shuri to make a prayer toward the kingdom's sacred landscape of the east.

By the same logic he must have ordered simplification of the itinerary of the installation rite for Kikoe-o-kimi, to change the place of climax of the rite from Kudaka Island to the sacred Seefa Forest, an extreme eastern point of the kingdom, to receive a spirit of her own, being supported by other spirits from beyond the horizon. The Seefa Forest previously was a stopping point in the itinerary to make a prayer before and after sailing to Kudaka. It was not a final sanctuary in the pilgrimage. But after the change that Haneji ordered, the installation rite of Kikoe-o-kimi was held there ten times in total from 1677 until the last in 1875, just before the disappearance of the kingdom in 1879. In the same year, 1677, a palace on Kudaka Island was demolished, which might have served the king and Kikoe-o-kimi when they made an office there, but now served no use (Royal Government of Ryukyu 1974, vol. 7).

Curiously, there are traces of the ancient sailing process to Kudaka in ritual songs, particularly in volumes 13 and 19 of *Omoro-sôshi*, both compiled in 1623 before the reform (Iyori 1993:48–50). We can also find it in a document reporting the last installation rite in 1875 at Seefa Forest in several ritual songs sung in a climax of the installation rite at midnight and the next morning. The songs describe an illusionary sailing situation as if they were on Kudaka Island and were coming back from Kudaka. It could be a complementary ritual illusion that is often found in ritual literature in Okinawa even today.

Features of Okinawan Ritual Culture

I have closely examined the installation rite of the supreme priestess because it represents the essence of Ryukyuan female rituals, where architecture does not play a central role. What is important in this ritual-centered society is a phenomenal relationship between a secret place in a sacred area and a public open ritual place. In the case of the royal castle, the former is the sacred

forest of the castle and the latter is the central forecourt in front of the main hall. This relationship is expressed only by the execution of processional rituals and not by the physical construction of a temple or shrine, which would remain outside the ritual situation. In every village, even today, the rituals are performed without any temple architecture with priestesses participating under a tent, as is the case on Kudaka Island today (Iyori 1995b). In this sense, the performance of the processional rituals defines the sacred space in a landscape without a physical construction.

DISAPPEARANCE OF THE SACRED LANDSCAPE

Ritual performance had been so significant in state rituals of Ryukyu that a temple was never created that could be venerated as a permanent house temple of a personalized divinity. This is why a suppression of the pilgrimage rite by the Ryukyu king after 1673 could have easily weakened the significance of the sacred eastern landscape. After that, the sanctity was kept only by the practice of the installation rite, *O-ara-ori,* of the supreme priestess in the Seefa Forest (Royal Government of Ryukyu 1982a). Thus from the latter half of the 17th century, female leadership in the state ritual system in Ryukyu was weakened.

MALE BACKLASH

In contrast to the suppression of female state rituals in the royal castle of Shuri after 1670, the main court of the castle became a place for the manifestation of the power of the monarch by emphasizing the important relationship with China. An architectural device was invented at the beginning of the 18th century, with the permanent decoration of a Japanese-Chinese canopy, *Karahafu,* attached to the center of the main hall (Iyori 1998) where a royal seat was set for occasions of state administrative rites, thus expelling the ancient female religious rituals outside the forecourt into a peripheral sanctuary in the castle. In this sacred inner enclosure, Kyo-no-uchi, the ancient first step of the Kimi-tezuri rite had been performed—any men in the castle were excluded.

Moreover, the gate of the forecourt was renovated every time the Chinese investiture embassies came to legitimize the enthronement of the Ryukyu king. To prepare for the arrival of 1756, the gate was completely remodeled in 1754 in accordance with Chinese style. Along with political and religious reform from 1729 until 1752, and under the very strong leadership of the pro-Chinese chancellor Sai-on (a descendant of Chinese immigrants in the 14th century), the Shuri royal castle was extensively remodeled into a curiously Chinese, somewhat Japanese, and as a whole Ryukyu-styled castle (Iyori 1998b).

CONCLUSION

After the integration of the kingdom into Japanese territory in 1879, the castle lost its central political and religious functions. The Japanese government classified the main hall as a national treasure after a partial destruction in 1923 and altered it into a building to make prayers toward a Japanese state Shintô shrine inserted behind it. The castle was completely destroyed in 1945 at the end of World War II during American naval bombardment of Japanese positions. The Japanese government reconstructed the main part of the royal castle in 1990. The main hall, together with others around the ancient ritual court, reminds us of the days of royal sovereignty. The sacred landscape of the east behind the palace has yet to be restored.

We can read the changes suffered by the Shuri royal castle and its eastern sacred landscape through four centuries as a reminder of the struggle between the two leaderships—female religious superiority in state religion on the one hand, and male desire to express a Chinese monarchical system on the other. The latter, with its overwhelming administrative power, controlled traditional female rituals by its more modern conceptions of landscape, a *Feng-Shui* concept adopted from China (Kubo 1990), and land-measuring techniques introduced from Japan (Iyori 2000).

Both state levels of religion and administration disappeared altogether with the kingdom in 1879, but on a more basic ethnic level female leadership survives. Investigations done by anthropologists and ethnographers on female and male roles in Okinawan culture reveal many specific details from these histories that can be perceived here in overarching lines.

In contemporary times, the tradition of sacred places in every local level in Okinawa has encountered the drastic transformation of its landscape, where various networks of sanctuaries

11.10 Main Hall, Seiden, of the Shuri Royal Castle and the *Una* forecourt, reconstructed in 1992; center, Karahafu Canopy.

had been set for the routes of pilgrimage rites. Traditional community rituals are disappearing along with these landscapes, transformed by development and modern methods of construction. What we can learn from this history of a culture without temple but with pilgrimages in a landscape can possibly lead us to integrate the modern norms of land use planning or a sustainable land development plan with concepts of cultural landscapes and sacred places, even if the ancient rituals are forgotten.

References

Engels, Friedrich. *The Origin of the Family, Private Property and the State*. New York: Penguin, [1884] 1986.

Haneji, Chôshû (Sho, Jôken). *Chûzan Seikan* [Royal Genealogy]. In *Ryûkyû Shiryô Sôsho* [Collected Historical Documents on Ryukyu] 5. Tokyo: Inoue-Shobô, [1650] 1962.

Hatakeyama, Atsushi. "Hanjanashi" [A Rite of Visiting Divinities on Kudaka Island]. In *Okinawa-ken Kudaka-jima no Matsuri* [Annual Rituals on Kudaka Island, Okinawa], ed. Sakurai. Tokyo: Hakutei-sya, 1981.

———. "Aguni-jima no Yagang Orime" [A Visiting Divinity's Rite on Aguni Island, Okinawa]. *Nantô Bunka* 11(1989):45–108.

Higa, Masao. "Tokoyo-gami to Takai-kan" [Visiting Divinities and Their Cosmology]. In *Okinawa Minzokugaku no Houhou* [Methods in Okinawan Culture Studies]. Tokyo: Shinsen-sya, [1971] 1982.

Hirose, Kazuo. Shinden-ron Hihan heno Hanron [Reply to Mr. Okada's Critique on the Origin of a Shintô Temple]. *Quarterly of Archaeological Studies* 46,3(1999):1–5.

Hokama, Shuzen. "An Introduction to Omoro-sôshi." In *Omoro-sôshi*, ed. Saigoh and Hokama. Tokyo: Iwanami Shoten, 1972.

Hsu, Pao-kuang. *Zhong-shan chuan xin lu* [Chinese Investiture Ambassadors' Report on Their Stay in Ryukyu]. [1721] 1972. Tai-pei: Tai-wan yin hang; Japanese rpt. ed. translated by Harada. Tokyo: Gensô-sha, 1982 (references are to Japanese edition).

Iha, Fuyû. "Koryûkyû no Seiji" [Politics in Archaic Ryûkyû]. In *Iha Fuyû Zenshû* [Collected Works] 1. Tokyo: Heibon-sha, [1922] 1974.

———. "Wonari Kami no Shima" [Island of Wonari-kami, Men Protecting Sisters]. In *Iha Fuyû Zenshû* [Collected Works] 5. Tokyo: Heibon-sha, [1938] 1974.

———. "Kin-mamon no Raihô" [Divinity Arriving from the Horizon]. In *Iha Fuyû Zenshû* [Collected Works] 5. Tokyo: Heibon-sha, [1939] 1974.

Ikemiya, Masaharu. "Ou to Ouken no Shûhen" [On the Religious Authenticity of the Rulership of Ryukyu]. In *Shin Ryûkyû-shi* [New Ryukyu History], ed. Ikemiya et al. Naha: Ryûkyû Shinpô-Sha, 1991.

Inagaki, Eizo. "Honden Keishiki no Kigen" [The Origin of the Main Building's Shrine Style]. In *Jinja to Reibyo* [Shrines and Mausoleums] 16. Tokyo: Shogaku-kan, 1968.

Iyori, Tsutomu. "Oku, Shisha no Shima" [Profoundness of the Religious Spatiality in Okinawa: An Island of the Dead]. In *Kûkan no Genkei* [Archetypes of Sacred Spaces], ed. Ueda et al. Tokyo: Chikuma-Shobô, 1983.

———. "Two Modes of Spatiality in Okinawan Religious Landscape: A Case Study of the Annual

Cycle of Rituals in Izena Island, Okinawa Japan." *Kikan Jinruigaku* [Quarterly of Anthropology] 18,2(1987):3–106.

———. "On the Spatio-Temporal Nature of Harvest Ritual Sites in Kume-shima of Ryukyu." *Jinbun* 63(1989):143–62.

———. "Formation of a Ryukyu Kingdom's Sacred Island off its Eastern Coast." *Human and Environmental Studies* 2(1993):23–55.

———. "Red Cloth Canopy and White Tent in the Feast Court: Remains of Royal Ritual Settings in Annual Feasts of Kudaka Island, Okinawa Japan." *Bulletin of Japanese Studies* 12(1995b):121–57.

———. "Images of Life-Environment Expressed Through Annual Rituals & Feasts in the Villages of the Southern Part of the Main Island of Okinawa." *Journal of Okinawan Folklore Studies* 19(1998a):27–75.

———. "Karahafu Canopy of the Ryukyu Kingdom's Royal Court: The Origin and Changes of Features in the Course of the 18th Century." *Journal of the Society of Architectural Historians of Japan* 31(1998b):2–37.

———. "Accuracy of the Old Map of Shuri, Made in the Beginning of the 18th Century." In *Chizu to Rekishi Kûkan* [Historical Spaces Read through the Maps]. Tokyo: Taimei-dô, 2000.

———. "Reconsideration upon the Enthronement Rite, O-ara-ori, or Initial Visit to her Fief, Executed by the Supreme Priestess, Kikoe-o-kimi, of the Ryukyu Kingdom."

Kadekaru, Chizuko. "Omoro-sôshi Shinnyo Kô" [On Priestesses Appearing in Omoro-sôshi]. *Okinawa Bunka Kenkyû* 14(1988):267–328.

Kamiya, Nobuyuki. "Satsuma no Ryûkyû Shinnyû" [Satsuma's Invasion into Ryukyu Kingdom in 1609]. *Shin Ryûkyû-shi* [New Ryukyu History], ed. Ikemiya et al. Naha: Ryûkyû Shinpô-sha, 1989.

Kojima, Yoshiyuki. "Shuri-jô" [Shuri Royal Castle]. In *Nihon no Kamigami* [Divinities in Japan] 13, ed. Tanigawa. Tokyo: Hakusui-sha, 1987.

Koyama, Kazuyuki. "Omoro-sôshi ni miru Obotsu Shinnyo Shûdan" [Presence of Priestesses Serving for the Heaven (Obotsu) in Omoro-sôshi]. *Okinawa Bunka Kenkyû* 19:313–55.

Kubo, Noritada, ed. *Okinawa no Fùsui* [Feng-Shui in Okinawa]. Tokyo: Hirakawa Shuppansya, 1990.

Laugier, Marc-Antoine. *Essai sur l'architecture.* Brussels: Pierre-Mardaga, [1755] 1979.

Lebra, William P. *Okinawan Religion: Belief, Ritual, and Social Structure.* Honolulu, HI: University of Hawaii Press, 1966.

Lundquist, John M. *The Temple: Meeting Place of Heaven and Earth.* New York: Thames and Hudson, 1993.

Maehira, Bôshô. "Ryûkyû Kokuô no Sappo Girei ni tsuite" [Chinese Enthronement Rite of Ryukyu King]. In *Okinawa no Shûkyô to Minzoku* [Okinawan Religion and Folk Customs]. Tokyo: Daiichi Shobô, 1988.

Miyamoto, Nagajiro. *Nihon Genshi Kodai no Jûkyo Kenchiku* [Houses in Antiquity Japan]. Tokyo: Chûou-Kôron Bijutsu Shuppan, 1996.

———. "Jingû Honden Keishiki no Seiritsu" [Beginning of Ise Temple Style]. *Mizugaki* [Journal on Shintô Studies] 183(1999):10–18.

Naha City. "*Kafu Shiryô: Shuri*" [Collection of Genealogies of Ancient Nobilities in Shuri]. History of Naha City Series 1,7. Naha: Shishi Hensyu-shitsu, 1982.

Okada, Seishi. "Jinja Kentiku no Genryû" [Origin of Proto-Shintô Temple Architecture]. *Quarterly of Archaeological Studies* 46,2:36–52.

Origuchi, Shinobu. "Okinawa ni sonsuru waga Kodai Shinkô no Zanshi" [Remains of Archaic Japanese

Religion in Okinawa]. In *Origuchi Shinobu Zenshû* [Collected Works] 16. Tokyo:Chûô Kôron, [c. 1924] 1976.

Royal Government of Ryukyu, Bureau of State-Priestesses, *Omoro-sôshi* [Compilation of Ritual Sacred Songs of the Ryukyu Kingdom] 22 vols. compiled in 1531 (vol. 1), 1613 (vol. 2), 1623 (all vols. except 11, 14, 17, and 22). Reprint, ed. Saigoh and Hokama. Tokyo: Iwanami Shoten, 1972 (song references are to Iwanami reprint edition).

———. Bureau of State-Priestesses. *Nyokan Osôshi* [Summary on Successions and Rituals of the State-Priestesses before 1706]. In *Shintô Taikei* [Compiled Historical Documents on Shintô Religion] 52, ed. Kojima. Tokyo: Shintô Taikei Hensan-kai, 1982.

———. *Ryûkyû-koku Yuraiki* [General Survey of State and Local Rituals and Ritual Places of the Ryukyu Kingdom]. In *Ryukyu Shiryô Sôsho* [Collection of Ryukyu Historical Documents] 1 & 2. Tokyo: Inoue-Shoten, [1713] 1962.

———. *Kyûyô* [Official Chronicle of the Ryukyu Kingdom]. Tokyo: Kadokawa Shoten, [1745-1876] 1974.

———. Ohsato Prefecture [Majiri]. *Oaraori Nikki* [Preparation Record for the Installation Rite of Kikoe-o-kimi in 1840 at Yonabaru site]. In *Shintô Taikei* 52. Tokyo: Shintô Taikei Hensan-kai, [1840] 1982a.

———. "Kikoe-o-kimi Goten narabini Ogusuku Ogishiki no Oshidai" [Summary of Annual Rituals in the Palace of Kikoe-o-kimi and the Royal Castle of Shuri]. In *Shintô Taikei* 52. Tokyo: Shintô Taikei Hensan-kai, [1875] 1982b.

Rykwert, Joseph. *On Adam's House in Paradise: The Idea of the Primitive Hut in Architectural History.* New York: Museum of Modern Art, 1972.

Saitaku, ed. "*Chûzan Seifu*" [Royal Genealogy of the Ryukyu Kings]. In *Ryukyu Shiryô Sôsho* [Collection of Ryukyu Historical Documents] 4, 5, ed. Iha et al. Tokyo: Inoue-Shoten, [1701] 1962.

Taichû. *Ryûkyû Shintô-ki* [Report on Ryukyu Religions], with notes by Yokoyama. Tokyo: Okayama Shoten, [1648] 1936.

Takara, Kurayoshi. "Shô Jôken no Ronri" [Logic in the Pro-Japonist policy by Shô Jôken in the Age of Kingdom]. In *Shin Ryûkyû-shi* [New Ryukyu History], ed. Ikemiya et al. Naha: Ryûkyû Shinpô-sha, 1989.

Tanabe, Yasushi. *Ryûkyû Kenchiku* [Architecture in Ryukyu]. Tokyo: Zayûhô-kankôkai, 1972.

Tanigawa, and Y. Higa. *Kamigami no Shima* [Islands of Deities]. Tokyo: Heibon Sha, 1979.

Tomiyama, Kazuyuki. "Ryûkyû no Ouken Girei" [Ryukyu Ruler's Sovereignty Rituals]. In *Ouken no Kisô he* [Toward a Root of Royal Sovereignty], ed. Akasaka. Tokyo: Shinyô-sha, 1992.

Tonaki, Akira. "Ryûkyû Ouken-ron no Ichi Kadai" [An Inquiry into Ryukyu Ruler's Religious Sovereignty]. In *Okinawa no Shûkyô to Minzoku* [Okinawan Religion and Folk Customs]. Tokyo: Daiichi Shobô, 1988.

Yanagita, Kunio. "Imo no chikara" [Female Superiority in Folk Religion]. In *Teihon Yanagita Kunio Shû* [Collected Works] 9. Tokyo: Chikuma Shobô, [1940] 1969.

Yokoyama, Manabu. *Ryûkyû-koku Shisetsu Torai no Kenkyû* [Studies on the Arrival of Ryukyu Envoys in Edo]. Tokyo: Yoshikawa Kôbunkan, 1987.

Etruscan Boundaries and Prophecy

Larissa Bonfante

12

From the 19th century on, the history and function of national and ethnic boundaries have been subjects of discussion. In the 20th century, frontier studies came into their own, with frontiers understood as places of interchange as much as boundaries to be defended. Human settlements have at all times depended on the presence of boundaries to define their borders and thus their real identity in space, time, and history. Spatial boundaries determine their area, temporal boundaries, political reality, and their existence in religious space. Recent scholarship has focused on the function of geographical, political, ethnic, and linguistic boundaries in antiquity (Cifani 2003:23–25). We shall deal here with metaphorical, abstract, religious boundaries and the place of boundaries in the world view of the Etruscans.

Boundaries, both physical and ritual, were of prime importance for this people whose culture almost united Italy before the Romans. The importance of property boundaries has been further confirmed by the recent discovery of one of the longest Etruscan inscriptions, a bronze tablet recording a property transaction (Agostiniani and Nicosia 2000). I will attempt to trace the evidence for their belief in the sacred quality of boundaries, a belief reflecting the deep hold of their religion in all aspects of their life. Their practice informed their own rituals, which in turn became a powerful influence on long-lasting rituals of the Romans.

Archaeology reveals the Etruscans in central Italy, between the Arno and the Tiber Rivers, in the period of their greatest glory, ca. 800–500 BCE, as the most civilized of the inhabitants of Italy, along with the Greek colonies in the south. Theirs was a culture of an aristocratic society of wealthy, sophisticated citydwellers, with great families who marked their status with luxuriously decorated and furnished private houses and princely tombs.

Each city-state had its own peculiar character. Like the ancient Greek cities or the cities of Renaissance Italy—it is no coincidence that the Renaissance started in this region—they had developed *in situ* as independent, autonomous entities. Although their language was different from any other, there is no sign of their having come from anywhere else. Their hill sites were continuously occupied since at least 1000 BCE, and their settlements soon had two out of three of Clyde Kluckhohn's signs of civilization: 5,000 inhabitants, a written language, and a monumental center. When the Greeks came soon after 800 BCE, attracted westward by the magnet of Etruscan mineral wealth, the idea of the city-state was perhaps already present in Italy. The Greeks brought to Italy the alphabet, monumental architecture, Greek mythology, and other innovations and social models. But the Etruscans kept to their own language, religion, beliefs, and traditions, as did the Romans, their neighbors across the Tiber, to whom the Etruscans passed on many Greek aspects of civilization. Roman religion also absorbed and long preserved aspects of Etruscan religion, though they always distinguished these from their own native rituals and cults. No doubt this absorption was encouraged by the aristocratic Etruscan priests who felt more akin to the Roman upper classes than to Etruscan-speaking slaves and freedmen (Momigliano 1975:15).

The Etruscans were thus a ranking civilization that played an important part in the history of the world, both in their own time and place and through their influence on Rome and in Europe. But unlike the Greeks and Romans, whom we seem to know best through their writings, their literature is lost to us. This loss has made it difficult to understand their history and their beliefs. It has also made it difficult to evaluate their achievements and their influence. Yet we have a good deal of other evidence—the archaeological remains of Etruscan cities and necropoleis, their art and inscriptions, and scattered accounts by their neighbors, rivals, and enemies, the Greeks and Romans. In fact, Latin literature preserved traditions and colorful stories of early Rome in the 7th and 6th centuries BCE and of the time when an Etruscan dynasty ruled. We can therefore learn something about their ideals and ideas, including the importance of Etruscan boundaries in their world view.

Rome preserved much technical know-how of the Etruscans, who taught them to build roads, bridges, and sewers, to trace the boundaries of towns and temples, and to measure land. At the end of the 6th century BCE the Etruscan artist Vulca, from Veii, was called to Rome to build the temple of Jupiter Optimus Maximus on the Capitoline Hill. The remains of that great temple, one of the largest in the Mediterranean at that time, show that it was made in the Etruscan style, probably by Etruscan builders and craftsmen who settled in the nearby area later called the Etruscan Quarter, the *vicus Tuscus*. The Romans likewise appreciated and appropriated Etruscan rituals and crafts connected with divination, the tracing of boundaries, and the purification of the army along the route of the triumph. They had enormous respect for the Etruscan ability to read the will of the gods from a variety of signs such as lightning bolts and the entrails of sacrificial animals.

In *The Idea of a Town* (1988) Joseph Rykwert describes and illustrates the importance of Etruscan ideas and rituals concerning boundaries and their influence, interpreting archaeological and literary evidence. The inspiration for this chapter derives from his work. I will note here only a few examples of the kinds of material available, some conclusions that can be drawn, and some avenues currently being explored (Bonfante 1998, 1999). Subjects will include cosmic boundaries and earthly boundaries, the *saecula* or boundaries of time, the route of the triumph, and, in the funerary sphere, grave markers and the boundaries to be crossed by the dead on their long journey to the Underworld.

Some 13,000 or so Etruscan inscriptions have come down to us—a number of these are on boundary stones, often bearing the Etruscan word for boundary, *tular*. Several of these boundary stones found in Carthage, where they were probably set by colonists after the third Punic War (146–49 BCE), are dedicated to Tinia, or Jupiter, the god of the day or sky (Rix *ET* Af 8.1–8.8; Bonfante and Bonfante 2002:183–85). This is not surprising, since Etruscan *termini* or boundaries were under the protection of the sky god. Boundary stones (Lambrechts 1970; Morandi 1991a; Aigner-Foresti 1994) are in the province of the sky, as Rykwert notes, citing the words of the prophecy of the nymph Vegoia. Knowing the greed of men, when taking over the land of Etruria, Jupiter ordered that visible boundary stones should be set out in the fields and publicly acknowledged. This prophecy, dating to ca. 90 BCE, is important for the Etruscans' concept of the sacred quality of boundaries and limits in the Etruscan scheme of the relations between gods and men (Dobrowolski 1991:1213–30).

Scias mare ex aethera remotum. Cum autem Iuppiter terram Aetruriae sibi vindicavit, constituit iussitque metiri campos signarique agros. Sciens hominum avaritiam vel terrenum cupidinem, terminis omnia scita esse voluit. Quos quandoque quis ob avaritiam prope novissimi octavi saecula data sibi [...] homines malo dolo violabunt contingentque atque movebunt. Sed qui contigerit moveritque, possessionem promovendo scelus damnabitur a diis. (Lachmann 1848–52:348–50)

[Know you that the sea has been separated from the sky. When Jupiter chose the land of Etruria for his own, he established and ordered that the level lands be measured and the fields be defined. Knowing man's greed and hunger for land, he decreed that everything should be determined with boundary markers. Because of the greed found at the end of the eighth saeculum, men will willfully and with evil intent violate and touch and move these boundary markers. But whoever will touch them and move them, enlarging his own property and diminishing the other man's, because of this crime he will be cursed by the gods.] (Harris 1971:31–40; Bonfante 1998)

The prophecy has been used by scholars as a document proving the deep division in Etruscan society between the *domini* and the *servi*, because it goes on to stipulate the various punishments for servi and domini who move the boundary stones: the servi will fall into a worse slavery, the families of the domini will die out, there will be plagues, famines, scourges, discontent, and revolution among the people.

Prophecies, portents, and the answers of the Etruscan *haruspices*—soothsayers or diviners—known to us from Roman literature date from the great crisis of the civil wars of the 1st century BCE (Sordi 1972). They show that while the Romans cared deeply about their own religious rites, they also depended on the specialized Etruscan techniques which could help them preserve the *pax deorum*. This recognition of each others' religion, or at least of what the Romans took and made their own, evidently contributed to the unity of Italy. But most important for this unity seems to have been the concept of *terra Etruria* and eventually of *terra Italia* as a geographical expression (Sordi 1992:125–27, 1995:24–27). The Etruscan idea of boundaries sanctified by Jupiter brought in the idea of a geographical area—rather than religion or language—as providing a people with its identity.

There are boundaries between men and gods, though communications are allowed between them. The gods send messages: humans must learn to read them. The Roman author Seneca describes the turn of mind that made the Etruscans particularly adept at this skill: "The difference between us and the Etruscans is . . . that, while we believe that lightning is released as a result of the collision of clouds, they believe that clouds collide so as to cause lightning. For since they attribute everything to the gods' will, they believe, not that things have a meaning insofar as they occur, but rather that they happen because they *must* have a meaning" (*Quaestiones Naturales* 32.2).

And not surprisingly in a polytheistic religion, boundaries existed between gods in the divine society. A peculiar monument, a life-size bronze model of a sheep's liver, found at Piacenza in north Italy, is a visual record of the boundaries existing between gods (Van der Meer 1987). The liver is marked off into 42 sections, each of which contains the Etruscan name of a god. These correspond to the regions of the actual sacrificial liver being read by the priest

12.1 Etruscan bronze model of a sheep's liver from Piacenza. 2nd century BCE.

and also to the regions of the sky that were under the protection of that god. The emphasis on boundaries in the functions of gods recorded on the liver is impressive. The names of several gods are repeated more than once. The name of Tin, or Tinia, originally a divinity of the day and identified with Zeus and Jupiter, appears five times: Tin was a protector of boundaries. Inscriptions on the eight boundary stones found in Tunisia (2nd or 1st century BCE) dedicated them to Tin. Selva, the Roman god Silvanus, whose name appears on the liver, was also in charge of boundaries, as shown by a bronze statuette of a youth, dedicated to the god as *selvas tularias*, "Selvans of the Boundaries" (Morandi 1987–88:85–86; Bonfante 1991). The word for boundaries, *tul*, which appears on the liver, actually appears on a number of boundary stones— one, from Cortona, bears the inscription *tular rasnal*, "the boundaries of Etruria." Modern Todi, ancient Tuder, a city in the region of Umbria on the border of Etruscan territory, derives its name from this Etruscan word for boundary.

There was a mystic correlation between the parts of a sacred area, like the sky, and the surface of the liver of a ritually sacrificed animal. A teaching device, the model liver was used by the Etruscan priest for his divinatory practice of reading the entrails of animals, as shown by a number of representations of priests holding such a liver. The Etruscans were particularly skilled in *haruspicina*, the science of reading omens, and the Romans respected, hired, and imitated them. The liver from Piacenza was perhaps once used by a haruspex connected with the Roman army.

The story of Tanaquil, as told by the Roman historian Livy (1.34), shows the Etruscan queen reading the will of the gods in the divisions of the sky in a manner similar to that of the priest reading the liver. Tarquin, son of the Corinthian Demaratus, emigrated from Tarquinia to Rome with his ambitious Etruscan wife, Tanaquil (Bonghi Iovino and Treré 1997). The couple had stopped on the Janiculum hill, within sight of the city, when a bird suddenly plummeted down upon them, snatched Tarquin's hat, and took it up into the sky. Then, just as suddenly, it swooped down again and put it back. Tanaquil interpreted this on the spot as an omen of her husband's future kingship: she noted the kind of bird, the quarter of the sky it came from, and the place from where it returned. "The Etruscans were particularly good at divination," Livy explains.

The Romans attributed a number of rituals to Romulus, Rome's founder and first king, including many that were of Etruscan origin. Plutarch credits Romulus with having traced the city's original boundary in 753 BCE by ploughing a furrow around it, in accordance with Etruscan ritual (*Life of Romulus* 11). In fact a bronze image of a ploughman, part of the decoration of an early Etruscan ritual cart of the 8th century BCE, seems to illustrate such a ceremony (Carandini 1997:250–62; 2000:passim; Cornell 1995:57–62). Romulus was also credited with having celebrated the first triumph. The religious ceremony of the triumph included a primitive purification ceremony, a ritual procession tracing a magical line around the city. This was an ancient rite that seems to have preceded Etruscan influence in Rome. When the armies returned from a war, they had to be purified before they could be allowed to reenter the city, or they would pollute it with their blood guilt. At the time of the most solemn ceremony of the triumph the army, having marched around the ancient Palatine in this ancient purification ceremony, followed the victorious general as he brought the booty that had been vowed to the god—then, and then only, being allowed by law to cross the boundaries of the city with the army in full array and fully armed.

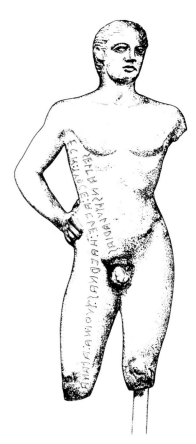

12.2 Bronze statuette of an Etruscan youth, dedicated to "Selvans of the Boundaries." 4th century BCE.

12.3 Bronze image of a ploughman, part of the decoration of a ritual cart from Binsenzio, Olmo Bello necropolis. 750–700 BCE.

12.4 Etruscan red-figure cup
with Admetus and Alcestis.
4th century BCE.

Once a king, Tarquin was credited with having celebrated a great triumph in Rome. Indeed, we can now see that it was the Etruscans who first brought the pomp and luxury of the triumph to the city, adding to the primitive ritual of the *circumambulatio*. We can imagine Tarquin in his chariot leading the army in the ritual, purificatory procession up to the Capitoline Hill, to bring the trophies and spoils of the campaign to the newly built temple of Jupiter Optimus Maximus. The triumph was the greatest honor a Roman could achieve, and Cicero yearned in vain all his life for one, unaware or underplaying its basic function as a purification ritual for blood shed (Bonfante 1970:49–66).

One of the most important Etruscan boundaries was that between the living and the dead. Grave markers placed outside the grave marked this boundary and represented the deceased inside the family tomb. We see not only a boundary but a distinction between man and woman, who in the aristocratic art of Etruria are regularly represented as equal, as a couple, representative of the family unit. At the most frequented necropolis of Cerveteri, the grave markers placed outside the grave show this distinction in the form of a house for a woman and of a phallus-shaped pillar for the man. Such grave markers are also depicted in Etruscan art. They are shown on a 4th century vase with a representation of Alcestis, about to die for her husband Admetus, where they surely signify the approach of Death (Beazley 1947:166–67, 303, pl. 37). A similar pair of gender-distinct markers is shown by Heracles and Juno, flanking the enthroned Tinia (Jupiter) on an engraved bronze mirror (Bonfante 1998). These are remarkably sexually explicit: the male symbol next to Heracles is a realistic phallus, while the female herm next to

Juno is a representation of the female sexual organs. Rykwert's reconstruction of the cults of Terminus (male) and Juventas (female) in his description of the temple of Jupiter Capitoline, and of the Roman mundus as feminine and pomoerium as masculine (Rykwert 1996:511–12; 1988:126–27), has a surprising parallel in the representations of these herm-like sexual organs represented next to Heracles and Juno.

Scholars have long traced the geography of the Etruscan Underworld, as well as the routes and rituals that brought the deceased beyond its gates. The Greek Underworld of Homer's *Odyssey*, perhaps by way of Polygnotus's 5th century painting of the *Nekyia* at Delphi, is frequently illustrated on Etruscan wall paintings from Tarquinia of the 4th century BCE. But some aspects of the afterlife of dead souls seem to be specifically Etruscan, among them the appearance of the demons, Vanth and Charu, who accompany the dead on their journey to the Underworld, and who are regularly added to pictorial representations of Greek myths after the 5th century BCE.

Most relevant to our topic is the emphasis on the physical boundaries between the world of the living and the world of the dead. Artists represented the fortified walls of the Underworld (Krauskopf forthcoming). They even represented the stone marking the threshold of the Underworld, sometimes shown as the stone of Sisyphus. In Etruscan myth his sacrilegious crime consists of moving this boundary from its appointed place, and he is shown several times, once in the Tomb of Orcus, at Tarquinia, with an inscription near his head, *tupi sispes*, "the crime [or punishment?] of Sisyphus." In the François Tomb from Vulci he appears bearing the huge boulder on his shoulder; on it perches a winged female demon, perhaps the personification of his crime, guilt, or punishment (Buranelli 1987:180–81; Roncalli 1996:37–54, 1997:37–54, 2001:249–72).

12.5 Engraved Etruscan bronze mirror with Jupiter, Juno, and Hercules. Ca. 300 BCE.

This traditional religious lore was well known to Etruscan priests and their Roman neighbors. In the 4th century, Roman aristocrats were sending their sons to Cerveteri, ancient Caere, to learn "letters," just as they would later send them to Athens in the late Republic and Empire (Livy 9.36). The literature these upper-class Roman youths studied was most probably not poetry or drama but omen-reading, in which the Etruscan priests were recognized experts. Roman consuls and generals needed to have these skills in order to carry out their duties.

The *etrusca disciplina* included works on the interpretation of thunder and lightning, on the reading of the gods' will from the livers of sacrificed animals, and on other signs sent by the gods to men. According to their doctrine, a certain number of saecula or phases of history have been allotted to each people. This teaching foresaw a total life span of a 1,000-year period for the Etruscans, divided into ten eras of unequal length. Like all the doctrines of the etrusca disciplina, it had been revealed by seers or prophets, and it is known to us because the Romans held this Etruscan learning in great honor. They preserved the books in which they were written, translated them, and incorporated much of the techniques for learning about the will of the gods into their own religious rituals. From what remains of these texts we learn that there was some controversy about the length of the total period (1000 or 900 years) of Etruscan history, and also about the number of eras (ten, nine, or eight).

There was no doubt, however, about the length of each era, and therefore of the whole Etruscan life span, because the end of each era was announced by a particular sign or prodigy. A terrifying trumpet blast, out of a clear sky, marked the end of the 8th saeculum in 88 BCE (Plutarch, *Life of Sulla*, 7.4 ff). This era seems to have started around 200 BCE. The 9th was

12.6 Etruscan wall-painting (copy), from the François Tomb, Vulci. Sisyphus and Amphiaraos. 4th century BCE.

very short: it lasted from 88 to 44 BCE, when a comet marked its end, in the turbulent period following Caesar's death. In 19 CE a final trumpet blast sounded the end of the last saeculum, and of the thousand-year history of the Etruscan people (Dio Cassius 57.18.3–5) (Sordi 1972; Hall 1986). Their belief in such limits or boundaries of time eventually turned out to be a self-fulfilling prophecy, marking the end of the Etruscans as a people: they became Romans.

Thus ended, according to their own calculations, and in reality, a group of people who predicted their own end and then saw it happen. The Etruscans' concept of their own identity was radically different from that of the Romans. According to the same Etruscan prophecy, the allotted length of time for the Romans was 12 saecula. The Romans listened with awe at such Etruscan prophecies of divine destruction and punishment, which were current in this period. But they chose to hear the prophecy, spoken by Jupiter, that their rule would have no end or boundary: "I have given you rule without end or boundary" (imperium sine fine dedi) (Vergil, *Aeneid.* 1.297).

Conclusion

The Etruscans were distinguished by the importance of boundaries in all areas of their life and religion: spatial, temporal, social, religious, geographic, actual and ideal, political and ritual. These boundaries were clearly marked and visually represented. In spite of the loss of their literature, archaeology provides much evidence about this aspect of their system of beliefs, as well as the form and wealth of their necropoleis, their temples, sanctuaries, and cities. Etruscan inscriptions and art reflect this aristocratic society's concern to maintain the stability of their world and the harmony between men and the gods in the cosmos. The doctrine of the saecula set forth the ages that had been allotted to the Etruscan people. On the model liver from Piacenza were incised the areas ruled by the various gods: this microcosm, which reflected the macrocosm, and allowed the priest to read the messages the gods sent to mankind. This was a revealed religion. Its prophets included the child-like, earth-born Tages, and the nymph Vegoia, whose prophetic warning against upsetting boundary stones was circulated by the Romans during the time of their civil wars. One of the few words we are sure of in the Etruscan language (only two hundred or so can be understood) is tular, "boundary." The Romans, who valued the etrusca disciplina and admired the skill of their priests, preserved traditions, rituals and techniques involving such ideas. Rome's sacred boundaries were laid out by Romulus—traditionally in 753 BCE—according to Etruscan ritual; and much of the form of the triumph, the most central of Roman symbols, was of Etruscan origin. And finally, the idea that a geographical area could determine national identity, rather than religion, language, or ethnicity, made possible the universality of the Roman empire.

References

Agostiniani, Luciano, and Francesco Nicosia. *Tabula Cortonensis*. Rome: L'Erma di Bretschneider, 2000.

Aigner-Foresti, Luciana. "La Lega etrusca." In *Federazioni e federalismo nell'Europa antica*. Milan: Università Cattolica del Sacro Cuore, 1994.

Beazley, J. D. *Etruscan Vase Painting*. Oxford: Oxford University Press, 1947.

Bonfante, G., and L. Bonfante. *The Etruscan Language. An Introduction*. Manchester: Manchester University Press 1983; rev. ed. 2002.

Bonfante, Larissa. "Roman Triumphs and Etruscan Kings: The Changing Face of the Triumph." *JRS* 60(1970):49–66.

———. "Un bronzetto da Bolsena(?)." *Miscellanea Etrusca e Italica in onore di Massimo Pallottino. Archeologia Classica* 43(1991):835–44.

———. *Etruscan Mirrors*. Corpus Speculorum Etruscorum 3. Metropolitan Museum of Art, New York. Rome: L'Erma di Bretschneider, 1997.

———. "Il destino degli Etruschi." In *Libertà o necessità? L'idea del destino nelle culture umane*, eds. A. Bongioanni and E. Comba. Turin: Ananke, 1998.

———. "Fama nominis Etruriae." *Continuità e discontinuità nella storia d'Italia. Analecta Romana* 26(1999):167–71.

Bonghi Iovino, Maria, and Cristina Chiaramonte Treré. "Tarquinia." *Testimonianze archeologiche e ricostruzione storica. Scavi sistematici nell'abitato* (Campagne 1982–1988). Rome: L'Erma di Bretschneider, 1997.

Brown, Frank E. "Of Huts and Houses." In *In Memoriam Otto J. Brendel*, eds. L. Bonfante and H. von Heintze. Mainz: Philipp von Zabern, 1976.

Buranelli, Francesco. *La tomba François di Vulci*. Rome: Quasar, 1987.

Carandini, Andrea. *La nascita di Roma. Dei, lari, eroi e uomini all'alba di una civiltà*. Turin: Einaudi, 1997.

———. *Roma, Romolo, Remo e la fondazione della civiltà.* Catalogue of exhibit. Rome: Electa, 2000.

Cifrani, Gabriele. *Storia di una frontiera. Dinamiche territoriali e gruppi etnici nella media Valle Tiberina dalla prima età del Ferro alla conquista romana.* Rome: Libreria dello Stato, 2003.

Citarella, Armand O. "Cursus Triumphalis and Sulcus Primigenius." In *Parola del Passato* 35(1980):401–14.

Cornell, T. J. *The Beginnings of Rome.* London: Routledge, 1995.

de Grummond, Nancy T. "Mirrors and *Manteia*: Themes of Prophecy on Etruscan and Praenestine Mirrors." In *Aspetti e problemi della produzione degli specchi etruschi figurati*, ed. Antonia Rallo. Rome: Aracne, 2000.

———. "Some Unusual Landscape Conventions in Etruscan Art." *Antike Kunst* 25(1982):3–14.

Dilke, O. A. W. *The Roman Land Surveyors: An Introduction to the Agrimensores.* Amsterdam: A. M. Hakkert, 1992.

Dobrowolski, Witold. "Il mito di Prometeo: il limite tra il cielo e la terra nell'arte etrusca." In *Miscellanea etrusca e italica in onore di Massimo Pallottino.* *Archaelogia Classica* 43(1991):1213–30.

ET = Rix, Helmut. *Etruskische Texte I-II. Editio Minor.* Tübingen: G. Narr 1991.

Foster, B. O. *Livy.* Books 1–2. Cambridge, MA: Harvard University Press, 1919.

Fugazzola Delpino, Maria Antonietta. *La cultura villanoviana: guida ai materiali della prima Età del ferro nel Museo di Villa Giulia.* Rome: Edizioni dell'Ateneo, 1984.

Hall, John. "The *saeculum novum* of Augustus and Its Etruscan Antecedents." *ANRW* 2.16.3(1986):2564–89.

Harari, Maurizio. "Les Gardiens du paradis. Iconographie funéraire dans la céramique étrusque." *Quaderni Ticinesi* 17(1988):169–93.

Harris, W. V. *Rome in Etruria and Umbria.* Oxford: Oxford University Press, 1971.

Krauskopf, Ingrid. In *The Religion of the Etruscans,* ed. Nancy de Grummond. Austin, TX: forthcoming.

Lachmann, C., ed. *Gromatici veteres.* Diagrammata edidit Adolfus Rudorfius. Berlin: G. Reimer, 1848–52.

Lambrechts, Roger. *Les inscriptions avec le mot ëtularí et les bornages étrusques.* Florence: Biblioteca di Studi Etruschi, 1970.

Momigliano, Arnaldo. *Alien Wisdom. The Limits of Hellenization.* Cambridge: Cambridge University Press, 1975.

Morandi, Alessandro. "Cortona e la questione dei confini etruschi." *AnnCortona* 23(1987–88):7–37.

———. *Epigrafia di Bolsena etrusca.* Rome: L'Erma di Bretschneider, 1990.

———. *Nuovi lineamenti di lingua etrusca.* Rome: Erre Emme, 1991.

Ogilvie, R. M. *A Commentary on Livy, Books 1–5.* Oxford: Oxford University Press, 1965.

Rojas, Felipe. "From Etruria to Latium. Etrusca divinatio et agrimensura romana." Paper presented in the Ancient Civilization Seminar, Classics Department, New York University, Fall 2000.

Rix, Helmut. See *ET*.

Roncalli, Francesco. "Laris Pulenas and Sisyphus: Mortals, Heroes and Demons in the Etruscan Underworld." *Etruscan Studies* 3(1996):45–64.

———. "Iconographie funéraire et topographie de l'au-delà en Etrurie." In *Les Etrusques, les plus religieux des homes*, eds. Françoise Gaultier and Dominique Briquel. Paris: La Documentation Française, 1997.

———. "Spazio reale e luogo simbolico: alcune soluzioni nell'arte funeraria etrusca." *Acta Hyperborea* 8(2001):249–72.

Rykwert, Joseph. *The Idea of a Town: The Anthropology of Urban Form in Rome, Italy, and the Ancient World*, rev. ed. Cambridge, MA: MIT Press, 1988.

———. *The Dancing Column: On Order in Architecture.* Cambridge, MA: MIT Press, 1996.

Seneca. *Naturales questiones*, ed. and trans. T. H. Corcoran. Cambridge, MA: Harvard University Press, 1971–72.

Sordi, Marta. "L'idea di crisi e rinnovamento nella concezione romano-etrusca della storia." *ANRW* 1.2(1972):781–93.

———. "Storiografia e cultura etrusca nell'imperio romano." In *Atti del II Congresso Internazionale Erusco. Firenze, 1985.* Florence: Istituto di Studi Etruschi, 1989, I: 41–51.

———. "Il problema storico della presenza etrusca nell'Italia settentrionale." In *Etrusker Nördlich von Etrurien*, ed. Luciana Aigner-Foresti. Conference, Vienna, 1989. Vienna: Österreichische Akademie der Wissenschaften, 1992.

Van der Meer, L. B. *The Bronze Liver of Piacenza.* Amsterdam: Gieben, 1987.

van Gennep, Arnold. *The Rites of Passage.* Chicago, IL: University of Chicago Press, 1960 [1908].

Razing the Roof
The Imperative of Building Destruction in Danhomè (Dahomey)

Suzanne P. Blier

rchitecture has often been identified as a paradigmatic creative art, but it is also, and equally importantly, an art of unique violence, as seen in terms not only of the processes of building construction, but also the variety of architectural forms and landscape features which must be razed in order for new buildings to be erected in their stead. Whether as a result of war, the planned leveling of earlier community edifices (and the displacement of associated peoples), or as structures built in "virgin" landscape, new architecture only emerges through the destruction of earlier forms—built or natural. Architectural vision and practice thus are poignantly contradictory phenomena that reveal *a priori* the inherent ambiguities of the individuals and cultures that construct and inhabit them. While architects and architectural historians have often paid close attention to the creative aspects of architecture and planning (as well as an array of larger social, economic, and symbolic concerns), relatively little scholarship has focused on the equally powerful forces of building destruction (or processes of "unbuilding") which are a vital part of the larger architectural process.

This chapter examines aspects of architectural destruction in the kingdom of Danhomè (Danxome, Dahomey), situated in the modern Republic of Benin in West Africa. In other West African cultures, such as the rural Batammaliba, elements of architectural destruction also have clear-cut symbolic and religious roots, even though coming from quite different architectural traditions (Blier 1987). The Danhomè kingdom, founded in the 17th century, expanded rapidly over the course of time under a series of powerful (often bellicose) monarchs, and it drew both architectural prototypes and mythic features from the various cultures that came under its military control. Rather than identifying with a holistic creative myth—as did many African kingdoms, such as the Yoruba—the Danhomè kingdom defined itself through a narrative of political dominance replete with architectural signification.

The Post

The Danhomè account of dynastic origins speaks not of gods or human creation as such, but rather of the founding ruler Hwegbaja who, angered by a neighbor named Dan (and desirous of his land), took a pole (known locally as *kpatin*) and skewered it through Dan's stomach, killing him. The fledgling Danhomè ruler then built a new palace on the corpse of the unfortunate man. The name Danhomè, "in the stomach of Dan" (Dan, *xo*-stomach, *me*-in), derives from this horrible act, a story recounted in nearly every Danhomè history for this reason (Le Herissé 1911). Today this name appears prominently on the palace facade of Danhomè's

13.1 The palace of King
Gbehanzin (1889–93).

early King, Akaba (1685–1705) because land originally identified with Dan was later integrated
into Akaba's palace terrain. Dan's descendants still live today in a family compound nearby. The
account of Dan's murder became a charter of sorts for the Danhomè monarchy, a justification for
the expansionist drives of its early rulers, and a vivid exemplar of the punishment afforded those
who did not submit to Danhomè desires. Poles, partly for this reason, feature prominently in
palace altars. The royal mantra, "always make Danhomè bigger," is evinced in this story, an idiom
that is a central component of the Danhomè palace complex as well. The palace complex was the
work of ten monarchs, as each king built a new part of the complex adjacent to the palace of his
predecessor. When the monarch died, he was commemorated in his own palace section.

The account of Danhomè origins cited above is clearly a very different narrative (and myth of
building inception) than that of many other African cultures, reflecting the often violent dynastic
history of Danhomè, a kingdom which came to power as a key participant in the tragic era of
the international slave trade. Interestingly, the Danhomè god who is said to have taught humans
architecture, is also the god of war, Gu. According to Mercier (1954), "Gu [iron god] brought
down to earth by Mawu—he cut down trees and taught men how to build shelters and instructed
them how to dig the ground" (223). The icon of this god is an iron machete, an image displayed
prominently on the façades of several palaces. The kingdom's main myth of origin in turn features
a leopard whose bloodthirstiness often is depicted in related wall paintings and bas reliefs.

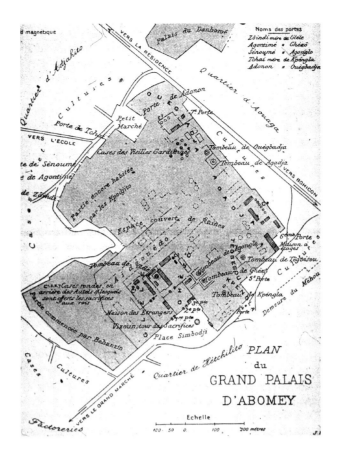

The kpatin pole said to have been positioned in the body of Dan also figures centrally in everyday Danhomè architectural practice. Indeed, the primary act of building a house in this region historically has consisted of a rite in which a kpatin branch is planted in the earth—the first support for what will be a living fence (the base of a freshly cut kpatin branch will root) demarcating the boundary of the house land. In addition to this post Roberto Pazzi (1976) suggests, "To clear a new field, especially if one must take it from a forest, one must do a rite of propitiation which addresses the ancestors and the invisible forces that inhabit it. One raises a mound for them, where one makes offering as part of the harvest" (208). Like the kpatin fence, which defines the property boundaries of the new house, four kpatin trees also historically are secured in the earth to define the perimeters of a new tomb. The planting of the kpatin and subsequent trees of this species to create a fence serves in essence to reserve (and protect) the space. We can liken this to urban centers in the West, where the first real architectural act is generally the building of a fence around the building site to be followed by the razing of the previous structure and the removing of the debris and earth where one wants to build.

At the same time, the planting of the kpatin in the body of Dan functioned in part to guard the secret of the origins of the state in Hwegbaja's appropriation of the property from its rightful owners, in this case the indigenous populations and rulers who had been living on the Abomey plateau long before this dynasty came to dominate here. The link between secrecy and fences is imbedded in local language as well. When one wishes to reveal a secret, one says *ede kpa*, "he removed the fence."

Reflecting the architectural and iconic importance of the fence in the Danhomè account of dynastic origins, Danhomè palaces are noteworthy as much for their properties of walled enclosures as for the structures built inside. The English traveler Dalzel, who visited the nearby Danhomè town of Cana during the reign of the 18th century monarch Tegbesu, noted: "The king has several palaces, each occupying an air of terrain of nearly a square mile. The description of that of Calmina will serve for all the others. This palace . . . is surrounded by a great rampart of clay in square form, of a height of around 20 feet" (Pazzi 1976:xiii). The local Fongbe (Danhomè) term for palace, *xon, xonme,* is drawn from the word "door" (*hon*), the means of access (and denial of access) through a fence/wall (Pazzi 1976:193). Each king and queen mother creates his or her own door into the palace as part of the enthronement process. As such, the door refers not only to the mat or plank that historically closed the point of entry into the structure or space but also to the vital symbol of power and the authority of

13.4 Royal gong players, singing in front of the main entry to the palace of King Gbehanzin during annual ceremonies.

the person residing inside. In part for this reason, during the annual *Hwetanu* ceremonies, royal *kpaligan* (gong) players sing accolades to the deceased kingdom rulers in front of their palace doors.

The principal building form in the Danhomè area for both royal and non-royal residences is a structure of laterite rich bright red earth (today often mixed with or plastered with cement), of rectilinear design usually with a single door and one or perhaps two small square windows. Roofs, which in the past were thatched, are now of corrugated metal. Other structures appear to have been largely circular (though of the same red earth walls and roofs of thatch). Today round buildings figure prominently as royal temples, shrines, and tombs, in the royal precinct and elsewhere.

As with the prominence of the kpatin pole/tree in the Danhomè account of dynastic origin, the house in turn is generally accepted as a vital symbol of the state. The royal priest Mivede suggested to me that in the kingdom of Danhomè, the image of the house often serves as a political metaphor: "Abomey is the house; Danhomè is the house. Thus no harm will come

to the house. Even if one puts fire to the house it will not burn. The enemies will not be able to take it away" (personal communication 1986). Local historian Nondichao explained to me similarly that "the kingdom is like a room" (personal communication 1986). Royal greetings reference houses. Whereas in Fongbe, the local language, one ordinarily greets people by saying *a fon gangia*, "did you awaken well?" to the king one says instead *n'kan hwegbio* "I have come to ask after the house." The king, in this sense, is the ultimate house owner and housekeeper of the nation. Like royal greetings, local language also offers insight into the role of the kpatin post in fencing the first Danhomè palace. The stomach (*xo*), that part of the body of Dan where the post was inserted, in turn is believed to be the seat of one's emotions. *Xomesin* ("the stomach is attached, tied up") is the local term for anger (see Blier 1995a:141). By suggesting that Hwegbaja built his palace in the stomach of Dan underscores not only the hostility of this act but also the wellspring of anger potentially still felt by Dan's family and other local residents through the act of being dispossessed.

There are other important architectural-anthropomorphic references in Danhomè building practice. As in many other parts of Africa, key features of these buildings are identified with the body. The roof (*xo-ta*) refers literally to the head of the house. The heads of defeated enemies were often positioned on the palace roof, where they were a visible reminder of war victims. The main courtyard of the family and palace compound in turn is called *agbonu* "mouth of the wall." The "stomach of the house" (*xofome*) refers to the house floor (Pazzi 1976:163, 191, 207, 235, 287). The placenta is buried behind the house, and it is here where the mother takes her bath. It also is behind the house where the toilet is located, the term being "one goes behind the house" (*e yi xo-gudo*). The house floor is where the fullness of the house—its inhabitants and its wealth—is safeguarded. That the new Danhomè palace was said to have been built in the stomach of Dan in this way too makes reference to various ideas of loss.

The Python

While the architectonic violence implicated in King Hwegbaja's act of killing Dan and marking his stomach with an upright pole is an image that is no worse than many of the gruesome ontological features of early European state-building contexts, for example in London or ancient Rome, the story of Dan after whom the Danhomè kingdom was named is far more complex and provocative than even the above-discussed features of this narrative suggest. The term "Danhomè" has another etymological source that is also rich in architectural meaning. In the Danhomè language, Dan (Dangbe) is also the word for the powerful local python god who is held to be responsible for ocean currents, the wind, wealth, and change more generally. Symbol of the ancestors, the python is a potent icon of life and regeneration. To utter the name of the kingdom, Danhomè, i.e., "in the stomach of Dan," is also to state that Danhomè inhabitants (and their monarchs) reside in the middle (within the encircling circle) of the powerful python god, Dan/Dangbe. Representations of this god are frequently seen in architecture (both palace and religious) and other forms.

13.6 Royal bas-relief of Dangbe the python deity.

The very center (middle, stomach) of the palace accordingly incorporates a ritual area named for this python, *Ayido Hwedo*, as the serpent Dan in rainbow form is called. Here historically important sacrifices were made, the wealth and moisture bringing properties of the ritual are particularly well appreciated. The moat and wall that surround the capital are similarly identified with this python deity (Blier 1998). Like the moat, the python god is said to surround the earth with its undulating body, propelling the ocean's strong currents, and other forms of movement. Shown biting its tail in many of its royal and religious portrayals, the python deity also alludes to the shared consumptive (destructive) and creative (life promoting) properties of the Danhomè kingdom and its powerful rulers and gods. Accordingly, in addition to bringing wealth, the python also is thought to bring death to its enemies (in nature by constricting then devouring its prey). Like the door (and palace), called *xon/hon* that plays the role of funnel or catch-basin of the kingdom's wealth, the city's dry moat served not only to safeguard the city from enemy attack but also to keep the vitality and wealth which was amassed in the center through war and trade from fleeing. In this way the dry moat and adjacent wall, which was designed by Hwegbaja's son King Agaja (1708–32), helped to protect the city (and its monarch) from internal theft. Here too its reference to the sacred python is apt.

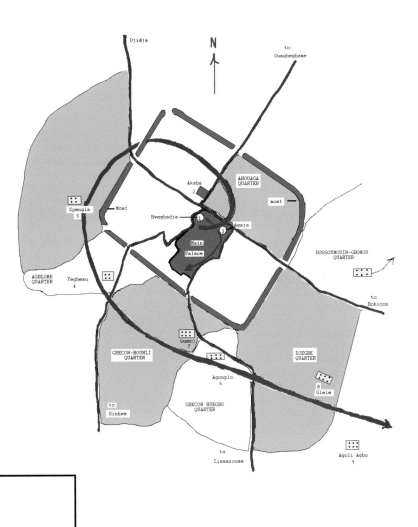

The historic process of urban renewal in the Danhomè capital of Abomey (Agbome), beginning with the killing of Dan in the early years of the kingdom, subscribed to a similar serpentine spiral form. As each ruler came to power he not only increased the size of the central palace (the interior, the stomach, of the python), but he also built for himself—his family, ministers, priests, artists, and servants—a princely palace with sometimes vast parcels of adjacent land for his family, courtiers, servants, and ministers. This space was appropriated from the indigenous inhabitants, a process which forced local residents whose properties were being annexed to move farther and farther from the center. Appropriating and building on these earlier settlements in a counterclockwise spiral pattern, the striking visual (and conceptual) parallels between architectural change over time (and space) and the spiral form tail-consuming python god Dan is strikingly evidenced. A team of local ethno-historians (Houseman et al. 1986) first documented the spiral pattern of royal expansion, but during my 1985–86 fieldwork I was able to further document this pattern while also linking it specifically to the python god Dan. The prominent spiral form of the capital's spatial conception suggests that King Agaja and the city's early designers designated at the outset both a specific plan for the city and a certain pattern of change through urban renewal. Interestingly, the disposition of palace areas

13.9 Spiral placement of ritual "houses" dedicated to past family members set up during the memorial ceremonies for Daxo. Hwawe.

identified with Danhomè's many kings follows a similar spiral form in this case moving in a clockwise fashion as each king built a new entry or door. During the memorial rites for the ancient priest-king Daxo from the earlier adjacent kingdom at Hwawe (Blier 1995b), small ephemeral houses were set up in a similar spiral fashion in honor of deceased members of this important royal family.

In the preceding pages I have suggested two strikingly different and yet complementary meanings of the kingdom's name, Danhomè, each with vital architectonic significance. One version is focused on Hwegbaja's neighbor, Dan, who lived on land that the new king hoped to use for his own needs and whose death made sacred the new kingdom. The other version refers to the powerful python god, Dan, who brings moisture, wealth, and well-being to its worshipers as well as impoverishment and sometimes death to those who opposed its tenets.

It appears that it was the founding King Hwegbaja's grandson, King Agaja (1708–32), who designed the first plan for the fledgling capital in the early 18th century following his successful military campaign to the coastal area around Ouidah and what was then the Savi Kingdom. In honor of this military victory, and his early conquest of Allada which lies midway between the two, Agaja is said also to have introduced the first annual "custom" rites (*Xwetanu*). Court songs and local oral traditions that I collected reaffirm that Agaja's architectural vision for the new dynasty at Abomey entailed four key elements. The first three features were relatively standard in urban planning around the globe: (1) the designation of a center; (2) establishing the principal avenues leading from and to this point; (3) marking the city's exterior border with a massive dry moat and adjacent interior rampart wall of earth. In reference to this latter feature, the new city was named or renamed Agbome (Abomey), i.e., "inside the moat." The fourth element in the Agbome city plan is more unusual and constitutes the creation of the spiral-form plan discussed above, which is the basis for royal and urban growth and renewal.

Each of these elements worked together to make the city what it would become. Before deciding on the dimensions of the dry moat that would give Abomey its name and form, King Agaja had to select a center for the plan, a point from which key measurements would be taken. Agaja's choice of a center was the small house next to his own palace that had belonged to his father, Hwegbaja, prior to appropriating the land of Dan. It was here where the four main roads leading into the capital along the cardinal directions would join together. Thus the notion of center had at once architectural, historical, and political significance. Directly opposite the house of Hwegbaja, a new market was founded, assuring the center would have economic vitality. One of the city's most sacred precincts was established diagonal to Hwegbaja's ancient home. In reference to the latter, Pazzi explains (1979): "For the Fon, this city represented the central point, the *vodun* (or blood) of the universe" (119). Abomey for this reason also was sometimes called Hun, a term referring to the hotter, sacrificial aspects of the Vodun worshiped by the religious forces in this area (Blier 1995a).

Significantly, the idea of a moat or walled city was not new in this part of Africa, the 13th–15th century CE capital of Ife in nearby Nigeria, or the coeval Togo site of Tado being among the most important examples. The coastal town of Savi whose ruler, Huffon, King Agaja had defeated is also said to have had a moat (Norman and Kelly 2004). These earlier moats, however, are generally circular. According to Skertchly (1974), during the reign of Agaja the city came under attack but after "being repulsed, [they] filled this ditch with their dead bodies." The plan created by King Agaja is roughly square. The reasons for this shape are not clear. Perhaps the role of the rectilinear kpatin fence enclosure in the kingdom's founding was a factor. There is also a vital cosmological association of this shape. Bernard Maupoil (1981) in his analysis of Danhomè geomancy traditions, suggests that "the square form of nearly all the houses in lower Danhomè responded to a desire to propitiate the four great Vodun resting at the cardinal points" (546). These included most importantly Mawu the sun god (in the east), Lisa the lunar deity (in the west), Sagbata and the earth gods (in the north), and Hu and Hevioso the water gods (in the south). Maupoil notes: "The square symbolizes the domain of that which is knowable, the earth." The circle, in contrast "represents the domain of the unknowable or the sky" (546). The local term for cosmos (*weke*) integrates the two. A circled square or cross-embedded circle is an important royal icon that appears prominently in thrones, drums, and other arts. Square shapes are also important in contexts of royal divination signs (Blier 1990, 1991a). That both rectilinear and circular buildings distinguish the palace precinct serves in this way to make visible the kingdom's control over both the knowable and unknowable worlds.

As the Danhomè monarchy expanded, the question of control became even more important. Hence at the same time as the resisting communities outside of Abomey were leveled by the invading Danhomè troops, key markers, ranging from boulders and saplings to religious structures and whole markets, were brought back and set up in the capital. With each new victory, Danhomè's capital became richer and more varied. Le Herissé (1911) notes accordingly of King Ganyeheso that "he killed the king of Zakpo [and] brought back the fetish of their market. At the time of this transfer, Aho [Hwegbaja], son of Dako, planted the trees that still shade the market of Bohicon" (283). The importance of these foreign forms also figured into the sometimes strict local sumptuary rules. According to these rules, Forbes (1851) explains "no man [other than the king] must alter the construction of his house, sit upon a chair, be carried on a hammock" (34). That King Guezo (1818–58) designed his palace entry in the style of the two story houses of the wealthy Brazilian slave traders living on the coast is noteworthy. Local rules meant that other elites could not follow suit.

A closer look at the type of pole that was said to have been forced through Dan's stomach suggests a similar feature of demise and growth. As noted above, the particular tree species in question, the kpatin fence tree (*ceiba pentadra, bombaceame*) (Brand 1981:20) self-roots when it is planted. When one cuts a branch of the tree (hence killing it) and places it in the ground, it becomes a new living tree. Hence it carries key qualities of a tree of life, a symbolism underscored by the fact that even in extreme cases of drought on this often water-depleted plateau, the kpatin will survive where certain other trees will die.

Architectural Death

Processes of architectural construction also reinforce this co-joined destruction-regeneration theme. The use of cord called *kan* is particularly important in this regard. Not only were lengths of cord used here when measuring land (Pazzi 1976), but because nails historically were not employed in this culture, key parts of building construction (roofs, fences, doors) were realized by tying together various parts with cords. Particularly when braided, cords serve as icons of family succession, that which ties one generation to another. Yet cords are also and equally importantly symbols of slavery (see Blier 1985). Indeed *kannumon* "thing in cords," is the Danhomè word for slave. Because Danhomè dynastic expansion dovetailed closely with the bloodshed of slavery raids, the associations with binding were particularly poignant.

The basic building measure, a bamboo pole, was similarly linked to military power. In the words of Le Herissé (1911): "After conquering the whole country, Agaja [the creator of Abomey's plan] wanted to know the dimensions of his kingdom towards the south. He commanded someone to measure the distance from the Danhomè palace to the beach of Ouidah—a distance of 23,502 bamboos. The bamboo that was used for this still existed when the French entered Abomey [in 1892]. It measured 4.5 to 5 m" (298). Because the creation of the new city plan followed directly on Agaja's extraordinary military victory over the coastal town of Savi (hence control of the port and affiliated Western trade), the means of measurement (control and building) seems to be linked closely with the history of his conquest as well.

King Agaja's extraordinary military success against the Savi kingdom of Huffon (particularly for a kingdom then of little renown) was marked architecturally in other ways as well. Here too, Le Herissé's (1911) history offers important examples. He writes: "During [Agaja's] reign, a king from near Porto Novo [a town on the coast], Ataki of Bozoume, pushed his warriors toward Abomey. He was conquered and taken prisoner. Our king [Agaja] put him in charge of sweeping the front of his palace each day" (298). One still calls this vast area where Ataki carried out his punishment, Ataki-ba-ya "Ataki looks for the earth." Seeing the defeated King Ataki hunched over each day sweeping this space, an act historically associated

13.10 The area in front
of the palace entry
of King Guezo known as
Atakinbaya.

with women and children, would have been a sight that few forgot. This act of denigration is recalled still today in the name of the area in front of the main palace portal, which is referred to as Atakinbaya.

Like the defeated king, Ataki, sweeper of the palace front, many of the palace builders and laborers in Danhomè appear to have been slaves or prisoners of war. Adandojan, the palace engineer, was in charge of one of the largest prisons. It was he, as Skertchly (1874) explains, who had the "authority over the men who are employed in building and repairing the palace walls and sheds" (120). Not all the laborers were bound workers, however, for as Skertchly also noted: "The masons, carpenters, and other workmen who were engaged in building the Jegbe palace [the princely palace of Glele, 1858–89] were [paid] . . . cowries, cotton cloths, [and] oranges" (376). These men also presumably played an important role in constructing many of the auxiliary palaces that the Danhomè monarchs constructed in this broader region.

Architectural "decoration" also carried the weight of the creative-destructive ethos. King Agaja, for example, is said to have decorated his palace walls with long strands of cowrie shells that hung down from the upper timbers. Cowries represent traditional currency here, a reference in part to the influx of wealth into the capital that came with Agaja's capture of the Atlantic coastal area around Savi and Ouidah, and even more importantly, the Euro-American markets which lay across the sea. But cowries also incorporate deeply imbedded associations with slavery, as one of the forms of capital that figured in the acquisition of slaves.

Other, more direct references to violence are found in Danhomè palace decoration, in particular enemy crania. According to a 1724 letter written by a British prisoner of King Agaja (Pazzi 1979) it is said that this king "has already paved the area of his two principal palaces with the skulls of those he beat in war" (274). His successor King Tegbesu, the British traveler Norris (1773) informs us, lived in "a simple room isolated from the court which surrounds it by a wall, high as the chest and whose summit is garnished with a row of human jaws. The small area around the room is paved with skulls, those of neighboring kings and other distinguished persons who fell prisoner during the course of wars" (148). Tegbesu's grandson, the 18th century ruler Agonglo, after defeating a town "called Agonkpa [brought back] the head of this king . . . to ornament the walls of the [princely] palace at Bekon-Huegbo" (Le Herissé 1911:309–310).

The spirit houses called *djexo* associated with the souls of the late kings are similarly linked to violence. The earth out of which these walls were made are said to have been composed of a combination of sacrificial blood and imported alcohol. Their form enhances the deathly association of these buildings. So low are they, and their entries so small, that one necessarily rubs against the blood and earthen walls on entering and exiting, with vital properties of death rubbing off as one goes through the threshold.

It was well-established practice in turn that each king was to expand the territory beyond the limits he had inherited, so as to assure that his own name would not be forgotten or disappear. While this is a noble, indeed vital, goal in any individual or culture, in African civilizations such as Danhomè, architecture played a particularly central part in retaining the memory of past individuals. Demolishing an individual's ancestral homestead is seen to be a deeply troubling event. Interestingly, the term most frequently used in reference to military destruction is to "break" a town, i.e., to break [deny] it of its people, its goods, its future, and its past. This complements in striking ways the idea of planting a kpatin branch to establish a new house or kingdom.

The disappearance of identity implicit in the notion of breaking the house of another could be experienced at any level of society. Skertchly describes what happened to the once extensive compound of the de Souza family in coastal Ouidah during the reign of the late 19th century Danhomè King Glele. De Souza, a wealthy Brazilian slave trader, met his end, according to Skertchly (1874), by being "poisoned by the fetish people for giving information to a [British anti-slavery] man-of-war of the loading of a slave ship. As such an offence is high treason, the property of the aggressor [here de Souza] becomes confiscated to the [King]. The valuables are removed by a corps of soldiers, called the Donpwe, sort of state spies, and the house broken [destroyed]. It afterwards passed into the hands of the African company, but is now deserted and in ruins" (48).

It is noteworthy that the Donpwe royal spies whose task it was to break the houses of those found guilty of treason or other similar acts, are also responsible for carrying out key death rites during the funerals of residents throughout Danhomè. Death, impoverishment, and the decimation of individual and family identity are strikingly co-joined here.

Nowhere is this link between disempowerment and architectural death more clearly reflected than in the example of Danhomè's King Adandozan (1789–1818) who was forcibly removed from power by his brother, King Guezo, purportedly for pressing for an end to the slavery trade as a major source of state revenue. Not only was Adandozan's name removed from the royal histories, but his section of the main palace was reclaimed and renamed and his larger princely palace was left to fall into ruin. This contrasts in vital ways with the treatment of the palace of Daxo, the ancient monarch of adjacent Hwawe, who appears to have acquiesced to the emerging presence of Danhomè King Hwegbaja in the early 17th century (Blier 1995a). Daxo's palace is carefully maintained to this day, its once vast interior spaces and bright red lateritic though slowly crumbling walls are lovingly preserved and are a focus of key state rituals.

The theme of capture and display is also evoked in striking ways in one of the most important and distinctive forms of Danhomè palace architecture, the *ajalala*. It was in this structure where the king sat in state during principal court sessions. It was here too where important foreigners came to meet with the monarch. Like many other historic Danhomè buildings, the *ajalala* reception hall displayed an array of militaristic themes, represented in this case through richly painted bas-reliefs—scenes of battle, various weapons, and the strong animals of kings, among other things. Additional *ajalala* bas-reliefs mocked the leaders of enemy states, in essence encouraging further military action, a key source of the kingdom's wealth. In one such image from the *ajalala* of King Guezo we see a monkey holding a piece of corn in one hand while trying to grasp another ear of corn with the other. Describing this image, Maurice Ahanhanzo Glélé (1974) notes: "This greedy and insatiable monkey represents the king of Oyo . . . against whom the King Adandozan repelled himself to disengage from the suzerainty of Oyo to whom Agbome payed annually an important tribute. Adandozan sent to the king of Oyo, instead of a tribute, a parasol on which was designed a monkey" (17). While military might and co-joined themes of demise and regeneration are amply demonstrated in the decorative program of the *ajalala*, other features of this building form convey the theme as well.

The very term for this building, *ajalala*, refers to a cage, trap, or fishnet (*aja*) (Le Herissé 1911:358). Like the name of the kingdom's founder Hwegbaja, whose name means "the fish escaped the cage (*aja*)," the *ajalala* building or "great cage" of the palace evokes the dual identities of traps with both promoting death and bringing beneficence. Perhaps nowhere is this idea more saliently revealed than in the extraordinary interest in new architectural form displayed each year during the dry season ceremonial period and Hwetanu. In conjunction with this rite, not only were older palace and city buildings such as residences and religious

13.12 *Adjalala* of King
Glélé during annual
ceremonies with ministers
aligned in front.

buildings generally rethatched, repaired, and rebuilt, but key palace structures were wrapped for the occasion in richly colored applique cloths. Enormous applique tents also were set up in front of the palace on this occasion. Dozens of other new structures, both temporary and permanent, were built around the capital in conjunction with this celebration as well.

The polychrome cloth appliques which were applied to tents and major palace structures during these ceremonies have their own war-linked history, particularly as associated with espionage. Spies of the king in Danhomè are referred to as *agbajigbeto* ("hunter of the veranda"), a tradition of special saliency in light of the above discussed account of the Brazilian slave trader de Souza. According to Paul Hazoumé (1956:24), as one of the most important state officials, the *agbadjigbeto* had a role in keeping the state's enemies at bay by positioning ritually empowered protective objects both in foundation holes and in related buildings to hold the enemies back.

PRESERVING THE ARCHITECTURAL PAST

There are implications in this tradition of architectural destruction and creation as well for local practices of renovation and preservation. Part of the ancient Danhomè palace complex in Abomey today comprises a museum, one of the earliest African architectural complexes placed on the UNESCO list of protected sites. In the 1970s and 1980s, the palace *adjalala* buildings of the 19th century Kings Guezo and Glele with their magnificent polychrome bas-reliefs were in dire need of financial support for basic repairs. The corrugated iron roofs added by the French decades earlier (Blier 1991b) had gaping holes, and the buildings' extraordinary bas-relief tableaux were being destroyed by rain as a result of the replacement of the buildings' low, steep slanting (and wall-protecting) thatch roof with a higher, shallow roof which left much of the wall area open to the elements. The buildings had been carefully studied and meticulously drawn. With Maurice Ahanhanzo Glélé, one of King Glélé's descendants, a key administrator at UNESCO, lovers of architectural preservation had reason to be hopeful that the long needed repairs would be soon underway. The target date was 1989 when activities associated with the centennial of the death of King Glélé were to take place.

A very different story unfolded. In the year preceding the highly anticipated Glélé centennial, the main palace buildings to be restored, the bas-relief decorated earthen *adjalala* buildings of Kings Glélé and Guezo, were knocked to the ground to make way for "new" palace structures based on the historic exemplars. In the palace at this time was a still nameless German tourist who happened to be visiting the area. Using a bicycle chain and helped presumably by some of the palace employees, he was able to remove a few of the bas-reliefs before they were pulverized in the destructive mayhem of the renovation-rebuilding project. Most of the bas-reliefs were lost, and the few that remained were in very bad shape. The Getty Conservation Institute, which had just prior to the destruction, signed on to help with the palace preservation project, arrived to find a very different situation than they had anticipated (Piqué et al. 1999). The team of preservation experts moved the dislodged early bas-reliefs that could be preserved and secured them in a special structure within the palace museum after undertaking whatever restoration could be done on them. At the same time, one of the city's best-known contemporary artists, Cyprien Tokundagba (a temple painter by early avocation who had risen to international fame in the recent Paris exhibition, *Les Magiciens de la Terre*) had been hired to replicate the original 19th century bas-relief tableaux in the new palace structures.

The replacement edifices were much smaller than the originals because the walls had been raised largely within the footprint of the original walls, rather than removing the piled earth that had amassed. This made the "replica" buildings somewhat impractical for display of some key museum objects as had been intended. There were rumors of possible corruption as well, since one of the Glélé family leaders owned the local cement factory and would have profited from the new building project. The destruction of these buildings is considered by African architectural historians and others to be an immense loss, on par with the loss of McKim

Mead and White's Pennsylvania Railroad Station in New York. In some ways the Danhomè palace destruction is even worse since there are so few such buildings extant in Africa that have survived periods of violence and colonial disinterest, and there is an ongoing lack of local and other funds for restoration. That this happened while the buildings were on UNESCO's watch was particularly sad.

But there is more to this tragedy than first meets the eye. This is a story not only about a lack of effective oversight. It is also an example of the complexities of cultural identity and preservation as seen through architecture, and the paradoxical factors of creativity and destruction—of loss as a critical part of building innovation and change. As noted at the outset, in constructing something new, other buildings, landscape features, and critical open spaces necessarily are destroyed. In the kingdom of Danhomè (and indeed in much of Africa) where innovation in art and architecture is highly privileged, the balance between preservation and creativity historically has tended to be strongly skewed toward the latter.

Indeed, if a royal centennial had occurred when the kingdom was still a powerful independent state, I believe that much the same thing would have happened, i.e., as part of the celebration honoring a past king, key ancient palace buildings associated with him (as well as probably those of his predecessors) would have been demolished and new modern structures would have been raised in their stead. The difference between then and now is that the new palace buildings, rather than being copies of earlier models as occurred in this case, would have been bold new forms in keeping with the most recent architectural practices both in Danhomè and in the larger (known) world. There is a long history of such architectural renovations in Danhomè, with buildings associated with earlier monarchs being rebuilt or redecorated in the course of celebrations that honor these kings in later eras. As Joseph Adande (1976–77) has suggested: "permitting artists to redo artistic origins [and] permanent historical reconstruction . . . in the Agbome [Abomey] kingdom has foundations which are cultural" (54). As he goes on to explain: "That which a son does, that which a descendant inaugurates, he always does it in the memory of his father, or on the path of this latter one." Ideas of old and new in this sense are integrally linked. "Even the early kings want to be up-to-date," it was suggested to me in one interview by the court historian Nondicao (personal communication 1986).

King Glélé accordingly named the entry to his new palace area *hwehundji*, "entry of mirrors," most likely after Versailles, the famous French palace which no doubt was known to him through travelers' descriptions. Key shrines and princely palace structures also were remodeled in conjunction with important rites such as the annual "Customs" (Hwetanu). As suggested below, many of the most strikingly modern buildings in West Africa are created in conjunction with death.

By way of conclusion, it is important to turn briefly to related traditions of contemporary architecture in this area. Bold, new residences of cement today often stand out in both the urban and rural landscape of southern Benin. Commissioned by wealthy individuals in the middle and late years of their lives as living memorials, these buildings serve as handsome spirit houses through which the memories of individuals will be evoked long after their deaths. That many such buildings are constructed in rural areas alongside rustic structures of earth and corrugated iron, make the unique appearance of these bold structures particularly striking. Thus, according to Le Herissé (1911), "the dominant idea of the social regime of the Danhomè [inhabitants] to perpetuate one's name is the unique preoccupation of the family chief, who sees in this the assurance that after his death, he will not be forgotten. . . . All individuals who have built a house, create there [a new structure] . . . the memory of which is tied, always to his name. The conservation of one assures the perpetuity of the other. In consequence, successive generations will be responsible for keeping up the dwelling of the deceased and the rebuilding of it" (252–53).

Today some of these buildings are rented out for steep prices to wealthy visitors; in other cases these structures serve as family homesteads. Irrespective of use, such buildings speak to the primacy of death and regeneration in architectural practice. Like the kpatin fencepost linked both to death and the foundation of the kingdom, as well as the spiral python form of Abomey's urban renewal plan, these buildings reflect not only the competing productive and destructive idioms of human existence but also the vital imperative of death in various contexts of architectural innovation and creativity.

As with this tradition of architectural memorials, what should be emphasized in the end is that much of our experience of architecture and landscape in Danhomè—as is often the case elsewhere—involves processes of mourning, as both consciously and unconsciously the built environment conveys the deep loss witnessed as a result of ongoing architectural change. Our experience of architecture necessarily manifests subtle and not-so-subtle features of trauma that such loss necessarily entails. If there is any lesson for modern urban planners in Africa or elsewhere in the Danhomè traditions examined here, it is that these vital issues of loss and memory need to be recognized as a fundamental human need in every community, likened in many ways to sunlight, grocery stores, and parks. One's first encounter with many urban centers the world over is with the city's refuse heap, recycling centers, water reprocessing plants, and cemeteries. This is both appropriate and positive, for such signs of death and transformation are deeply potent if somewhat pungent references to the inherent links between demise, death, and architectural creativity.

References

Adande, C. E. "Les grandes tentures et les bas-reliefs du Musée d'Agbome." *Mémoire de Maîtrise d'Histoire*. Université Nationale du Benin, 1976–77.

Blier, Suzanne Preston. *The Anatomy of Architecture: Ontology and Metaphor in Batammaliba Architectural Expression*. Chicago, IL: University of Chicago Press, 1987.

———. "King Glélé of Danhomè: Divination Portraits of a Lion King and Man of Iron (Part I)." *African Arts* 23,4(1990):42–53, 93–94.

———. "King Glélé of Danhomè: Dynasty and Destiny." *African Arts* 23,4(1991a):44–55, 101–103.

———. "The Musée Historique in Abomey: Art Politics, and the Creation of an African Museum." *Arte in Africa*, vol. 2 of *Quaderni Poro*. Milan: Centro Studi di Storia delle Arti, 1991b.

———. *African Vodun: Art, Psychology and Power*. Chicago, IL: University of Chicago Press, 1995a.

———. "The Path of the Leopard: Motherhood and Majesty in Early Danhomè." *Journal of African History* 26,3(1995b):391–417.

———. *The Royal Arts of Africa: The Majesty of Form*. New York: Abrams, 1998.

———. *Butabu: Adobe Architecture of West Africa*. Photographs by James Morris. Princeton, NJ: Princeton University Press, 2003.

Brand, Roger-Bernard. "Rites de naissance et réactualisation matérielle des signes de naissance à la mort chez les Wéménou (Bénou/Dahomey)." In *Naître, Vivre et Mourrir*. Neuchâtel, Switzerland: Musée d'Ethnographie, 1981.

Dalzel, Archibald. *The History of Dahomy: An Inland Kingdom of Africa*. London: Frank Cass [1793] 1967.

Forbes, Frederick Edwyn. *Dahomey and Dahomans: Being the Journals of Two Missions to the King of Dahomey and Residence at His Capital*. London: Frank Cass, 1851.

Glélé, Maurice Ahanhanzo. *Le Danxomè: Du Pouvoir Aja à la nation Fon*. Paris: Nubia, 1974.

Hazoumé, Paul. "Le Pacte de Sang au Dahomey." *Trauvaux et Mémoires de l'Institut d'Ethnologie* 25(1956). Paris: Institute d'Ethnologie.

Houseman, Michael, et al. "Note sur la structure evolutive d'une ville historique, l'exemple d'Abomey." *Cahiers d'etudes africaines* 26,4(1986):527–46.

Herissé, A. Le. *L'ancien royaume du Dahomey: Moeurs, religion, histoire*. Paris: Emile Larose, 1911.

Maupoil, Bernard. *La géomancie à l'ancienne Côte des Esclaves. Institut d'Ethnologie* 42. Paris: Musée de l'Homme, 1981.

Mercier, Paul. "The Fon of Dahomey." In *African Worlds: Studies in the Cosmological Ideas and Surreal Values of African Peoples*, ed. Daryll Forde. London: Oxford University Press, 1954.

Norman, Neil, and Kenneth Kelly. "Landscape Politics: the Serpent Ditch and the Rainbow in West Africa." *American Anthropologist* 106,1(2004):98–110.

Norris, Robert. *Memoirs of the Reign of Bossa Ahadee, King of Dahomy*. London: Frank Cass, 1789.

Pazzi, Roberto. "L'Homme eve, aja, gen, fon et son univers: Dictionnaire." Lomé, Togo. Mimeograph, 1976.

———. *Introduction à l'Histoire de l'aire culturelle Ajatado*. Études et Documents des Sciences Humaines, Université du Benin, ser. A, no. 1, 1979.

Piqué, Francesca, et al. *Palace Sculptures of Abomey: History Told on Walls*. Los Angeles, CA: Getty Conservation Institute, 1999.

Quénum, Maximilien J. *Au pays des Fons: us et coutumes du Dahomey,* 2nd ed. Paris: Larose, 1938.

Skertchly, J. A. *Dahomey as It Is*. London: Chapman and Hall, 1874.

Waterlot, G. *Les Bas-Reliefs des Bâtiments royaux d'Abomey (Dahomey)*. Paris: Institut d'Ethnologie, 1926.

SIGNS OF THE ANCESTORS
AN ARCHAEOLOGY OF MESA VILLAGES
OF THE PUEBLO REVOLT

T. J. Ferguson and Robert Preucel

14

In 1680, after 140 years of Spanish exploration and colonization of New Mexico, the Pueblo Indians united in an armed revolt to drive the Spaniards from their land. Roman Catholic priests and Hispanic settlers were executed, missions and haciendas were burned, and Pueblo warriors laid siege to the Spanish capital of Santa Fe. The Hispanic settlers who survived this onslaught fled to El Paso, where they temporarily reestablished their Spanish colony 400 km (250 mi) south of its original location. The Pueblo Revolt of 1680 was the first successful insurrection along the northern Spanish frontier, and, for a time, the Pueblo Indians once again exercised sovereignty over their homelands.

The Pueblo Revolt was a tumultuous and pivotal period in the history of the Pueblo people, and the Pueblo world after the rebellion was strikingly different than what it had been prior to the uprising. When the Spaniards first entered the region in 1540, there were more than 75 pueblos in an area extending from the Rio Grande in the east to the Hopi Mesas in the west. After the second revolt ended in 1696, Pueblo peoples were reduced to occupying 26 pueblos.

During the 16 years of resistance, Pueblo leaders engaged in a constantly shifting network of political and social alliances. Pueblo cultural values were reasserted to displace the religious teachings of Catholic missionaries. The occupation of many villages was disrupted by warfare, and some Pueblo tribes became extinct. There were dramatic changes in the location and formal structure of many Pueblo settlements. In several instances, new villages were constructed in defensive locations on high mesa tops, incorporating people from different home villages and ethnic groups into new, briefly occupied communities. With the return of Spanish rule, all of the Pueblos except Acoma and Hopi gradually moved back down to reoccupy their mission villages, where they live today. Pueblo Revolt mesa villages thus embody important developments in Pueblo social organization and community identity and link the modern villages to their immediate past.

Archaeology provides a valuable means to further our understanding of what transpired during the period of Pueblo resistance (Preucel 2003). Although a written history of the rebellion was documented by the Spaniards engaged in the reconquest of their colony, this history remains silent about many aspects of Pueblo life. The study of the archaeological record offers a view of history that is independent of Spanish chronicles, and this consequently allows us to more fully comprehend the lives of the Pueblo ancestors who lived during this turbulent period.

In this chapter, we examine the structure and meaning of ten mesa villages occupied after the Pueblo Revolt of 1680. We analyze the range of variation in the architectural form and spatial organization of these villages, and we explore the social meanings of these settlements using semiotics, the study of how meaning is produced by sign-systems (Preucel and Bauer 2001).

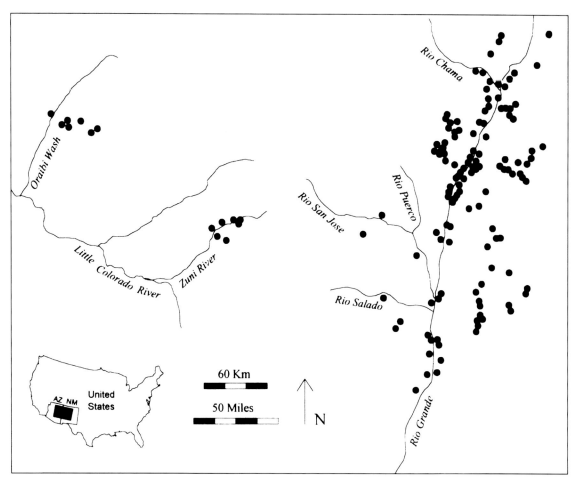

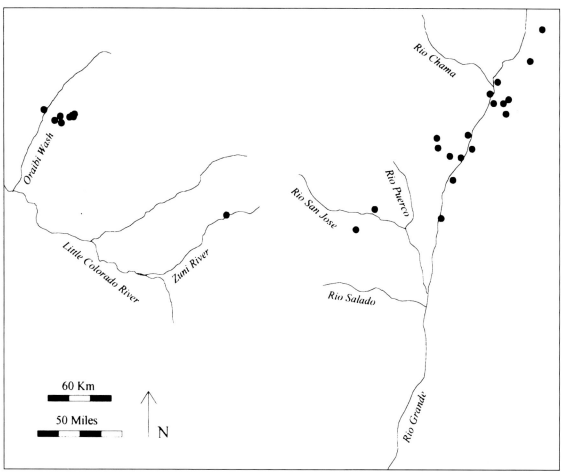

14.1 Pueblo villages before
(top) and after (bottom)
the Pueblo Revolt.

The architecture of mesa villages provides important information about the transformation of Pueblo society that occurred during the Pueblo Revolt.

Pre-Revolt Pueblo Settlement Patterns

When the Spaniards arrived in 1540, the settlement pattern of the Pueblo peoples entailed the occupation of densely packed clusters of large, plaza-oriented pueblos (Schroeder 1979). These clusters were defined in part by a mosaic of peoples speaking different languages. The cultural landscape was richly interwoven along the Rio Grande such that there were Tiwa-speaking people at Taos and Picuris in the north, and Tiwa-speaking people at Sandia and Isleta in the south. Similarly, Towa-speakers occupied Pecos Pueblo in the east and a cluster of villages in the Jemez district to the west. Keresan-speaking peoples were clustered along the Rio Grande and at Acoma and Laguna along the Rio San Jose. Clusters of Zuni- and Hopi-speaking pueblos lay to the west of the continental divide. The languages spoken in different settlement clusters formed a key basis for political and social alliances between otherwise autonomous villages.

The pueblos in these clusters were generally located on or near the valley bottoms, in proximity to the best agricultural land in the region. There is a substantial amount of variation in settlement plans within and among these clusters, but virtually all of the pueblo villages were oriented around one or more plazas and kivas used in the performance of ceremonial activities.

Between 1540 and the Pueblo Revolt of 1680, there was a substantial, tragic decline in population and an attrition in the total number of villages. These demographic changes were caused by the introduction of new diseases in the Southwest, the implementation of Spanish

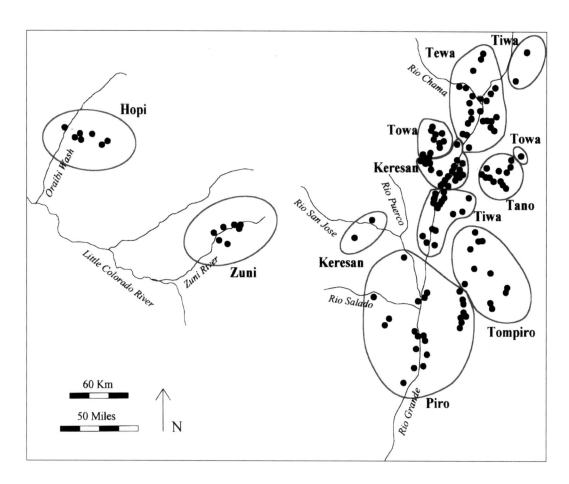

colonial policies, and the appropriation of land and resources by Hispanics. After 1609, the Spanish government was committed to supporting New Mexico as a mission field, and mission churches and conventos were established at the major Pueblo villages, administered by Franciscan priests.

A Brief History of the Pueblo Revolt

The Pueblo Revolt of 1680 was instigated by a coalition of tribes acting under the leadership of Popé, a Tewa Indian from San Juan Pueblo (Knaut 1995:167–80). In a meeting of medicine men at the Tiwa village of Taos Pueblo, Popé and other leaders preached a form of revivalism involving the renouncement of Spanish beliefs and customs, ritual purification, performance of traditional ceremonies, and an armed insurrection to destroy the Catholic missions and retake Pueblo land from the Hispanic colonists (Preucel 2000). The rebellion began on August 10, 1680, and the Hispanic colonists who survived the initial onslaught sought refuge in their colonial capital, Santa Fe. By late August, Santa Fe was under siege by 2,500 Pueblo warriors. After the Pueblo forces cut off Santa Fe's water supply, the Hispanics had no recourse but to retreat southward to El Paso. The Pueblos, acting in unity, had prevailed.

The Spaniards immediately began a series of military campaigns to retake their colony (Bailey 1940:1–8; Hackett and Shelby 1942). In 1681, Juan Antonio de Otermín, the Spanish governor in exile, led a failed attempt at reconquest. After recapturing the southern Tiwa village of Isleta, Otermín's forces advanced north but were ultimately forced to retreat, and little

was accomplished other than burning and sacking ten unoccupied pueblos. Otermín's successor as governor, Pedro Reneros de Posada, led another attempt at reconquest in 1687. Posada made it as far as the Keresan pueblo of Santa Ana, but his attack only succeeded in capturing a few horses and sheep. The next governor, Domingo Jironza de Cruzate, led an expedition to the Keresan pueblo of Zia in 1689. Here a fierce battle was fought and hundreds of Pueblo men and women were killed. Cruzate then turned his attention to an investigation of quicksilver mines, and retreated back to El Paso with no further attempts at reconquest.

In 1692, Diego de Vargas was appointed governor of New Mexico, and he began a series of campaigns to reclaim the colony (Espinosa 1940; Kessell and Hendricks 1992; Kessell et al. 1995). After 12 years, the political unity of the Pueblo tribes had dissolved, and the Pueblos were subjected to increasing attacks from the surrounding Navajo, Apache, and Ute tribes. In 1692, Vargas led a seemingly triumphant expedition to Santa Fe, meeting with little armed resistance and achieving an essentially ritual repossession of the colony. Vargas then returned to El Paso to prepare his Hispanic subjects for recolonization the following year.

Upon his return to New Mexico in 1693, however, Vargas found the Pueblo Indians once again ready to defend their land. Arriving at Santa Fe, which the Pueblo Indians now occupied, Vargas was forced to attack and retake the settlement in a pitched battle. Military forays against resisting pueblos continued into 1694, when several of the villages discussed in this chapter were attacked and destroyed. The mesa village of Kotyiti, for instance, built by Keresan-speaking people from Cochiti Pueblo, was attacked and burned on April 17, 1694. Three months later, the mesa village of Astialakwa, occupied by Jemez people and their allies, was defeated after a fierce battle.

In 1696, violence again erupted, but Vargas soon extinguished this second Pueblo Revolt. Some armed hostility continued, and in 1703 the Zuni Indians punished the egregious misbehavior of a number of Spanish soldiers stationed at their pueblo by executing them. After this final incident, the Pueblos came to a new accommodation with the Spanish colonists, and in the 18th century became the military allies of the Spaniards in a series of campaigns against the Navajo, Apache, and other tribes raiding the Pueblo and Hispanic settlements of New Mexico.

PUEBLO SETTLEMENT PATTERNS DURING THE REVOLT

The documentary record provides a substantial amount of information about Pueblo settlement patterns during the rebellion. The aborted attempt at reconquest in 1681, during which hundreds of Indians perished, left no doubt among the Pueblo peoples that the Spaniards would wage a bitter military struggle to regain their colony. In response to this threat, a number of Pueblo communities established mesa villages as military redoubts. These mesa villages were constructed on defensible high ground and were fortified with walls and bulwarks at the mesa edge where Pueblo warriors could resist Spanish attacks.

14.5 Defensive wall along edge of mesa near Bolesakwa.

TABLE 14.1 PUEBLO VILLAGES DOCUMENTED BY VARGAS

	1692	1693	EARLY 1694	LATE 1694	1696
Acoma	O	—	—	—	O
Astialakwa	—	—	O	U	—
Awatovi	O	—	O	—	—
Black Mesa	—	—	O	U	O
Boletsakwa	O	—	—	O	U
Cerro Colorado	—	O	—	—	—
Chimayo	—	—	—	—	O
Cochiti	U	U	U	—	U
Cuyamungue	O	—	U	O	U
Dowa Yalanne	O	—	O	—	O
Galisteo	U	—	U	—	—
Jacona	O	—	U	O	U
Jemez	U	U	—	—	—
Kotyiti	O	O	O	U	—
La Cienguilla	—	U	—	—	—
Los Pedernales	—	—	—	—	O
Mishongnovi	O	—	—	—	—
Nambe	O	O	U	O	U
Old San Felipe	—	O	O	U	O
Patowka	—	—	U	O	O
Pecos	—	O	O	O	O
Picuris	O	O	U	—	U
Pojoaque	O	—	U	O	U
San Cristobal	O	O	U	O	U
San Felipe	U	U	-	O	-
San Ildefonso	O	O	U	O	U
San Juan	O	O	U	O	U
San Lazaro	O	O	U	O	U
San Marcos	U	U	—	—	—
Santa Ana	U	O	O	O	O
Santa Clara	O	—	U	O	U
Santa Fe	O	O	O	—	—
Santo Domingo	U	U	U	O	U
Senecu	U	O	—	—	—
Shongopavi	O	—	—	—	—
Taos	U	O	U	—	U
Tesuque	—	O	U	O	O
Walpi	O	—	—	—	—
Zia	U	U	O	O	O

Mesa Villages in italics; O = occupied, U = Unoccupied, — = no information

Spanish records document that many of these mesa communities were multiethnic communities, where people from different villages banded together to form military and socio-cultural alliances. Kotyiti, for instance, was occupied in 1692 by people from the three Keresan villages—Cochiti, San Felipe, and San Marcos (Preucel 2000:12–13). A year later, the San Felipe residents had withdrawn and established their own mesa village at Old San Felipe, overlooking the banks of the Rio Grande. Other examples of mesa villages with multiethnic populations include Boletsakwa on San Juan Mesa, where Keresan and Jemez people lived together, and the village of Dowa Yalanne in the Zuni district, which included several families from Tano and Tewa pueblos in 1696 (Kessell et al. 1998:236, 328, 968–70).

At the same time mesa villages were established, some pueblo villages on the valley bottoms continued to be occupied. Spanish chronicles of the revolt demonstrate that these valley pueblos were periodically vacated when they were threatened by Spanish soldiers. There was thus a complex ebb and flow of people into and out of valley bottom and mesa top pueblos in response to changing political and military circumstances.

FORMAL ATTRIBUTES OF PUEBLO REVOLT PERIOD MESA VILLAGES

Sufficient data exists to analyze ten of the Pueblo Revolt mesa villages. These include Kotyiti, LA 84, Old San Felipe, and Canjilon Pueblo (Old Santa Ana) located on mesas overlooking the Rio Grande Valley (Bandelier 1892; Logsdon 1993:133–34; Nelson n.d.; Preucel 1998, 2000); Boletsakwa, Astialakwa, Patokwa, and Cerro Colorado in the Jemez

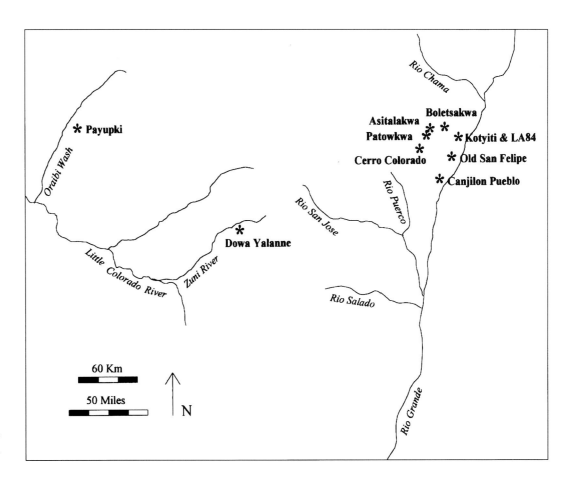

14.6 Locations of Pueblo Revolt mesa pueblos.

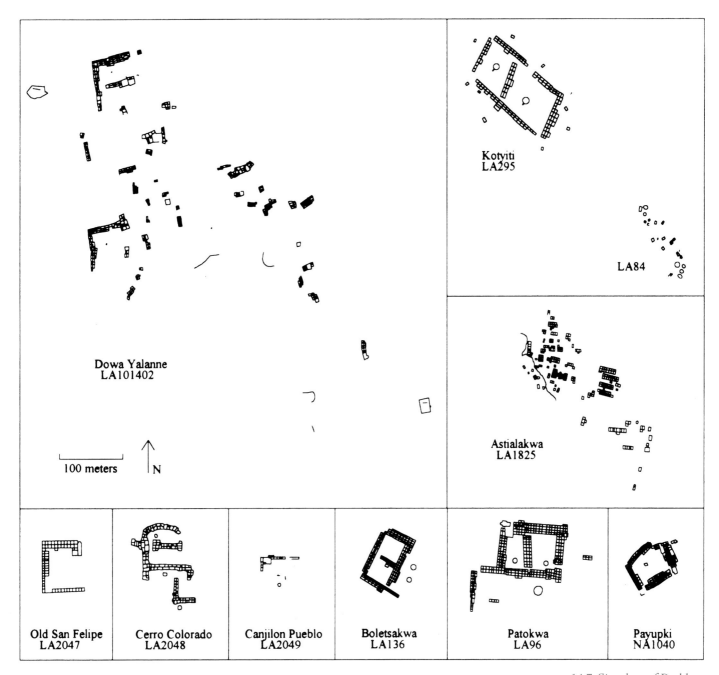

Kotyiti
LA295

LA84

Dowa Yalanne
LA101402

100 meters   ↑ N

Astialakwa
LA1825

| Old San Felipe LA2047 | Cerro Colorado LA2048 | Canjilon Pueblo LA2049 | Boletsakwa LA136 | Patokwa LA96 | Payupki NA1040 |

14.7 Site plans of Pueblo Revolt mesa villages.

mountains (Dougherty 1980; Holmes 1905); Dowa Yalanne on a mesa near Zuni Pueblo (Mindeleff 1891:89, Ferguson 1996:47–55); and Payupki, a village on the Hopi Mesas founded by Tiwa immigrants from the Rio Grande toward the end of the Pueblo Revolt (Mindeleff 1891:59–60, Brandt 1997).

All of these mesa villages were constructed and occupied for relatively brief periods of time, so their architectural plans are not obscured by earlier or later occupations, as is the case at Acoma Pueblo, the Hopi village of Walpi, and other sites. The generally good preservation of the Pueblo Revolt mesa villages and the absence of subsequent settlement make it possible to investigate the variety of social responses that Pueblo peoples implemented during a momentous period of political and cultural stress.

TABLE 14.2 FORMAL ATTRIBUTES OF PUEBLO REVOLT VILLAGE SITE PLANS

Site No.	Name	Formal Plaza	L-shaped Unit	Curvilinear Unit	Parallel Units	Dispersed Units	Plaza Kiva	External Kiva	External Great Kiva	Corner Gate	Center Gate	Catholic Church
LA2049	Canjilon Pueblo	—	•	—	—	—	—	•	—	—	—	—
LA84	LA84	—	—	—	—	•	—	—	—	—	—	—
LA2047	Old San Felipe	—	•	—	—	—	—	—	—	—	—	•
LA295	Kotyiti	•	•	—	—	•	•	—	—	•	•	—
LA2048	Cerro Colorado	•	•	•	—	—	•	•	—	—	—	—
LA136	Boletsakwa	•	—	—	—	—	—	•	—	•	—	—
NA1040	Payupki	•	—	—	—	—	•	—	—	•	—	—
LA1825	Astialakwa	—	—	—	•	•	—	—	—	—	—	—
LA96	Patokwa	•	—	—	—	—	•	—	•	•	—	•
LA101402	Dowa Yalanne	—	•	—	—	•	—	—	—	—	—	—

Examination of the site plans of the ten Pueblo Revolt mesa villages at the same scale and orientation reveals a number of interesting formal attributes. There is substantial variation in layout and size. Five of the villages include formal plazas, defined as open areas delineated by architectural units on four sides. Three of these sites—Kotyiti, Patokwa, and Boletsakwa—have distinctive double plaza plans. Other sites have curvilinear, L-shaped, or parallel architectural units. Several sites, such as Astialakwa, Dowa Yalanne, and LA 84, have ranchería plans, in which buildings are dispersed in space with a less formal layout than the plaza-oriented villages. Two sites—Dowa Yalanne and Kotyiti/LA 84—include both large, formal pueblos and ranchería-style buildings. Some villages have identifiable ceremonial architecture (i.e., one or more kivas, either within plazas or outside the pueblo), while other sites lack these ritual features.

The number of architectural units composing the villages, defined as a mass of contiguous architecture completely surrounded by open space, varies from one at Old San Felipe to 49 at Astialakwa. The size of architectural units at Pueblo Revolt villages, measured as the number of ground story rooms they contain, varies from one at Canjilon Pueblo to 134 at Patokwa. The total site size varies from 17 rooms at Canjilon Pueblo to 433 ground story rooms at Dowa Yalanne. In total, the ten villages include 1,775 ground story rooms. Many of these villages incorporated multistoried architecture, so the total number of rooms is actually much greater. At Dowa Yalanne, for instance, where the preservation of architecture and differences in the height of rubble in ruined buildings were studied, 127 second story rooms were identified at the two largest room blocks, an increase of about 30% in the total number of rooms (Ferguson 1996:47–55). Other Pueblo Revolt mesa villages also contained multistoried architecture, but the total number of rooms at these cannot be quantified using existing data.

STRUCTURAL ANALYSIS OF PUEBLO REVOLT MESA VILLAGES

The analytical techniques of space syntax are used to investigate structural differences in the use of open space at the Pueblo Revolt villages. The method and theory of space syntax was developed by Bill Hillier (1996; Hillier and Hanson 1984) and Julienne Hanson (1998) as a means to objectively quantify the spatial relations entailed in the way that architecture structures movement, and hence social interaction, within buildings and settlements. Space syntax involves the reduction of settlement plans to graphs whose spatial properties can then be quantified to enable the comparison of sites of varying sizes and configurations

Beginning with a site plan, the open space within a settlement is divided into the fewest possible convex spaces, i.e., areas in which no tangent drawn on the perimeter passes through the space. A person standing in a convex space thus has a clear and unobstructed view of the entire area. Next, a series of axial lines are drawn through convex spaces by inscribing the longest straight line that can be drawn through the open space structure, and then continuing until all convex spaces have been crossed. In an axial space, a person is able to see, move along, and interact with other people through the entire route of the line. Using these techniques produces axial graphs whose spatial properties can be quantified.

In our analysis, we concentrate on "Integration" (Hillier and Hanson 1984:108–109), the syntactical measure that quantifies the depth each axial space is from every other space in a site plan. Integration measures how many steps are entailed in moving from one space to another, and then compares that to all the spaces in a settlement. This measure is then standardized to enable the comparison of axial systems of different sizes. High Integration values indicate an axial space is well-connected to other spaces in a settlement; low values indicate spatial segregation, i.e., relatively isolated axial spaces.

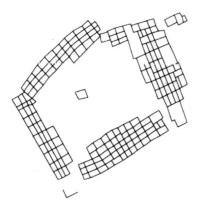

Step 1 - site plan

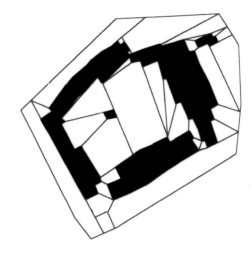

Step 2 - convex space map

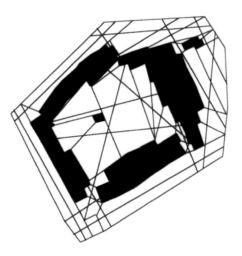

Step 3 - axial space map

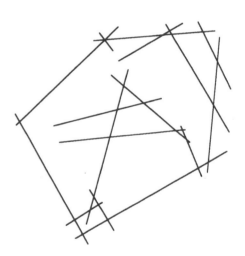

Step 4 - axial space graph

The distribution of Integration values for the ten Pueblo Revolt villages are depicted as notched box plots. These box plots illustrate the range of Integration values for each site, along with the median value (at the center of the notch) and the confidence intervals of the distribution (defined by the edges of the notch). An analysis of variance (Kruskal-Wallis One Way Analysis of Variance statistic = 111.117, probability = 0.000) indicates there are statistically significant differences in the spatial structure of many of the Pueblo Revolt mesa villages. The notched box plots can be used to determine which sites are different. Where the notches of box plots overlap, the distributions are statistically similar; where notches do not overlap, the distributions are statistically different.

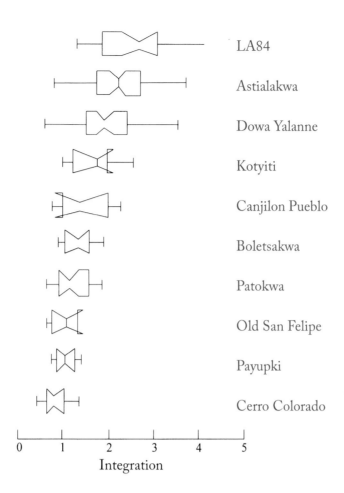

LA84

Astialakwa

Dowa Yalanne

Kotyiti

Canjilon Pueblo

Boletsakwa

Patokwa

Old San Felipe

Payupki

Cerro Colorado

0   1   2   3   4   5

Integration

14.10 Notched box plots of Integration values for Pueblo Revolt mesa villages.

Our analysis confirms that the three sites with ranchería plans—LA 84, Astialakwa, and Dowa Yalanne—have higher mean integration values than those of the other villages. The well-integrated spatial structure of these sites indicates their defensibility came from their location on top of high, steep-sided mesas rather than from any fortress-like configuration of their architecture. After one gained access to the mesa tops, it was easy to enter and move around the villages.

Dowa Yalanne presents an interesting case because its spatial integration is similar to both the ranchería plan of Astialakwa and the plaza-oriented plan of Kotyiti (labeled as Old Cochiti in the box plots). Kotyiti, in turn, has a structural similarity to the other plaza-oriented pueblos of Boletsakwa, Patowka, and Payupki that are significantly less integrated than Dowa Yalanne. To determine whether the similarity between Dowa Yalanne and Kotyiti was due to the nine isolated rooms that surround the dual plaza pueblo, the main room blocks at Kotyiti were analyzed with and without these outliers. This analysis reveals that the two configurations of Kotyiti are statistically similar to each other and to Dowa Yalanne. Although their plans appear very different, Dowa Yalanne and Kotyiti exhibit similarities in the integration of their spatial structure. We think this similarity is due to the presence of the two large L-shaped residential units at Dowa Yalanne and the influence these have on the overall spatial structure of the site.

In thinking about the highly integrated ranchería settlements and the more spatially segregated plaza-oriented pueblos, we are intrigued by the fact that Astialakwa and Dowa

TABLE 14.3 SIZE OF GROUND STORY BUILDING PLANS AT PUEBLO REVOLT VILLAGES
(Measured as number of rooms)

SITE	NO. ROOM BLOCKS	MIN. SIZE ROOM BLOCK	MAX. SIZE ROOM BLOCK	MEAN SIZE OF ROOM BLOCKS	TOTAL NO. ROOMS
Canjilon Pueblo	2	1	16	8.50	17
LA84	20	1	2	1.15	23
Old San Felipe	1	64	64	64.00	64
Old Cochiti	13	1	45	11.23	146
Cerro Colorado	3	28	84	48.67	146
Boletsakwa	3	33	99	56.67	170
Payupki	3	3	127	61.33	184
Astialakwa	49	1	34	5.08	249
Patokwa	6	4	134	57.17	343
Dowa Yalanne	39	1	75	11.03	433
TOTAL	**139**	**1**	**134**	**12.77**	**1775**

Yalanne were both multiethnic settlements. It would have been much easier for immigrant social groups to construct architectural units in the open spatial structures of ranchería settlements than in highly planned pueblos. At Kotyiti, the outlying rooms of the plaza pueblo and the adjacent ranchería settlement at LA 84 may also denote the presence of immigrants.

Movement through settlements with well-integrated spatial structures would have been relatively unrestricted, with political and social activities carried on in public. This plan appears to be associated in villages where there was less social control by a central authority or well-established traditional theocracy. The spatial orientation of ranchería settlements was toward the community as a whole rather than the more highly segregated spaces associated with religious activities in plaza-oriented pueblos. At Dowa Yalanne, the diversity in the number and size of buildings as well as its open structure appear to represent the social experimentation that was going on during the Pueblo Revolt, as multiple villages coalesced into a single settlement (Ferguson 1996:145). This process entailed the realignment of families, clans, and villages into entirely new social units. Other processes involving social fragmentation were at work as well. At Kotyiti, for instance, the newly formed community quickly split apart, and groups of people left to join a series of different villages.

The villages with low integration values seem to be associated with the converse. They appear to have had greater social control exercised by a centralized decision-making authority such as a cacique or council of religious leaders. The segregation of space in the plaza-oriented pueblos meant that access within the settlements was restricted such that movement was along particular pathways governed by gateways. The architecture thus physically channeled social interaction and segregated specific areas of the pueblo associated with particular social groups. This suggests that some religious and political activities were carried on in secret, as they had been in the home villages occupied before the revolt.

Payupki, the settlement constructed by Tiwa immigrants from Sandia Pueblo to the Hopi Mesas, exemplifies the highly segregated spatial structure that stands in marked contrast to

TABLE 14.4 CROSS-TABULATION OF SIMILARITIES AND DIFFERENCES
IN SPATIAL INTEGRATION

INTEG.		LA84	ASTIALAKWA	DOWA YALANNE	KOTYITI	CANJILON PUEBLO	BOLETSAKWA	PATOKWA	OLD SAN FELIPE	PAYUPKI	CERRO COLORADO
2.585	LA84		yes	no	no	no	no	no	no	no	no
2.280	Astialakwa	yes	—	yes	no	no	no	no	no	no	no
2.015	Dowa Yalanne	no	yes	—	yes	yes	no	no	no	no	no
1.731	Kotyiti	no	no	yes	—	yes	yes	yes	yes	yes	no
1.488	Canjilon Pueblo	no	no	yes	yes	—	yes	yes	yes	yes	yes
1.390	Boletsakwa	no	no	no	yes	yes	—	yes	yes	yes	no
1.343	Old San Felipe	no	no	no	yes	yes	yes	yes	—	yes	yes
1.275	Patokwa	no	no	no	yes	yes	yes	—	yes	yes	yes
1.108	Payupki	no	no	no	yes	yes	yes	yes	yes	—	yes
0.887	Cerro Colorado	no	no	no	no	yes	no	yes	yes	yes	—

Mean Integration for all sites = 1.792

the spatial integration of ranchería settlements. The architectural plan of Payupki has a clear internal focus that physically separated its residents from their hosts at the neighboring Hopi villages. We think the fact that the spatial integration of Payupki is similar to that of Kotyiti is due to the plaza orientation of both pueblos.

THE MEANING OF PUEBLO REVOLT ARCHITECTURE

The Pueblo Revolt mesa villages were clearly established for defensive purposes. The construction of these villages on high mesas created formidable strongholds against the reduction campaigns of the Spaniards, as well as providing protection from the increasingly frequent raids of the Apache, Navaho, and Ute. Beyond the geometry of space syntax that structures social interaction, these mesa villages also have important ideological meaning, and this can be read in terms of their role in mediating modes of spacetime, which we identify as "ancestral space" and "lived space." For Pueblo people, mesas (along with mountains, hills, lakes, and rivers) were and are the homes of specific supernatural beings. The shrines located in these areas were and are used by religious practitioners during specific times of the year to insure the well-being of the community.

When Popé and the other leaders of the Pueblo Revolt held an inspection tour of the pueblos in the fall of 1680, they preached a nativist and revivalist agenda that admonished people to abandon Spanish customs and live in accordance with the ways of their ancestors (Preucel 2000). According to Pedro Naranjo, a San Felipe ritual leader, Popé told the Pueblo people that "living thus in accordance with the law of their ancestors, they would harvest a great deal of maize, many beans, a great abundance of cotton, calabashes, and very large watermelons and cantaloupes." He then went on to say that "they could *erect their houses* and enjoy abundant health and leisure [emphasis added]" (Hackett and Shelby 1942:248). In this statement, the architecture of the mesa villages is linked directly to revivalism and the idea of living a traditional Pueblo life.

It seems significant that many of the new Pueblo Revolt mesa villages were founded on the site of, or adjacent to, the ruins of earlier villages. It can thus be argued that in these cases the Pueblo people were quite literally living with their ancestors. In addition, mesas are metaphorically linked to clouds, rain, lakes, and various supernatural deities. For example, one translation of the name Kotyiti is "Cochiti in the clouds" (*Henati Kotyiti*).

The diverse composition of these mesa villages, which often included people from different language groups, has already been noted. Kotyiti, Boletsakwa, Cerro Colorado, Black Mesa, and Dowa Yalanne all incorporated immigrants from various Rio Grande villages. These multiethnic villages are testimony to the emergence of new political alliances. The social processes entailed in these villages facilitated the popular, pan-Pueblo discourse advocating cultural revitalization (Forbes 1960, Preucel 2000).

We think the intriguing variability in the architectural layouts of the Pueblo Revolt mesa villages, including both highly segregated plaza-oriented pueblos and highly integrated ranchería plans, is related to the different ways that language and material culture were actively used during the Pueblo Revolt to mediate community and social identity. The formal plaza-oriented villages are of special interest because their site plans embody elaborately coded intentional design.

In evaluating what the architectural plans of Pueblo Revolt mesa villages mean, it is important to keep in mind that meaning is not a thing in and of itself, but an ever-shifting relation between an object (which exists in the world), a sign (a thing that represents the object), and an interpretant (an idea produced in the mind by the sign). The production of meaning is thus intimately associated with human cognition, conceived as the study of the logic of signs. This characterization of meaning is, of course, the one proposed by the philosopher Charles Sanders Peirce, one of the founders of semiotics. Peirce grounded his theory of semiotics in logic, mathematics, and the sciences. In this approach, signs are not arbitrary because they include icons and indices, that is, signs that have definite relations to their referents. Over time, however, the meanings of signs may change.

Richard Parmentier has successfully applied Peirce's theory of semiotics to a number of anthropological questions. He has drawn attention to the centrality of cultural categories of historical time and, at the same time, cautioned us to avoid imposing our own analytical distinctions and conceptualizations upon other cultures (Parmentier 1985:133–34). For Parmentier, the "cultural coding of eventfullness" is a semiotic process with multiple temporal modalities expressed through both language and material culture. He draws an important distinction between two categories of signs—"signs in history" and "signs of history." The former refers to value-laden objects implicated in social strategies that focus attention on specific historical processes and events. As such, "signs in history" are the loci of historical intentionality. In contrast, "signs of history" signify the particular ways in which a society objectifies its past.

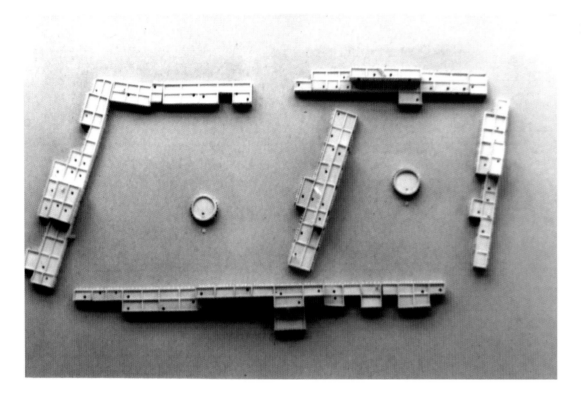

"Signs of history" are used in the discourses of the past, and play a particularly important role in how historical knowledge is recorded and transmitted. The relationships between these two types of signs are complex, and he notes that in traditional, oral societies "signs in history" are often simultaneously "signs of history."

Pueblo society following the Revolt of 1680 can be interpreted as a semiotic system where political and social meaning was established and reproduced through the mediation of different modes of spacetime. We identify "ancestral or mythic spacetime" as the dangerous space occupied by supernatural deities and beings, and "lived space" as the spacetime that people inhabit in the course of their daily lives. These modes are linked together by the ceremonial calendar and transformed through ritual practice. When katcinas dance in the plaza of a Keresan pueblo, for instance, they recall the primordial time when people and katcinas lived together in harmony at an ancestral village known as White House, occupied just after the emergence of the people from the underworld. The katcinas are interpreted by Pueblo people as a way of restoring world harmony and balance, and ancestral and lived spacetime merge during their performance.

Pueblo Revolt mesa villages can be read both as "signs in history" and "signs of history." All of the mesa villages are, in fact, signs in history because they are the result of pragmatic decisions to vacate mission villages and take up residence at new, defensible mesa top locations. They are an indication of a commonality of purpose that transcended individual village and united people across ethnic lines. The need to vacate the mission villages was likely caused by the violence that took place in them at the time of the Pueblo Revolt of 1680. In fact, the death of the missionaries and destruction of the churches and conventos may have "polluted" the mission village and made it an inhospitable site for the revival of traditional religious practices.

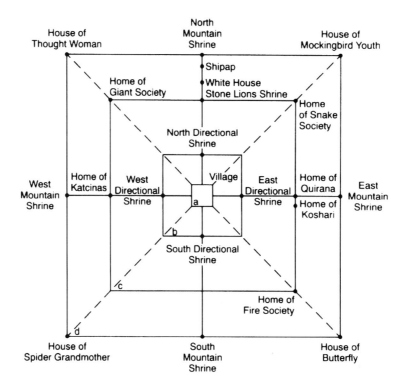

Key: a=village and plaza shrines; b=directional shrines; c=society shrines; d=mountain shrines.

Another "sign in history" is provided by the plaza-oriented mesa villages and contemporaneous ranchería settlements at Kotyiti/LA 84 and Patokwa/Astialakwa. Here the contrast is between the dual plaza pueblos built to embody the Pueblo worldview and the ranchería settlements that appear to have been built with more immediate, practical concerns in mind. The absence of ceremonial kiva architecture at the ranchería villages indicates the people who resided at these sites were not socially positioned to create a sacred landscape thus they would have had to modify their traditional religious practices. LA 84 is adjacent to Kotyiti and Astialakwa is near the plaza pueblo of Patokwa, and we think that residents of the ranchería sites probably participated in religious activities at the nearby plaza pueblos. Because there is a close connection between ritual and power in Pueblo society, the lack of religious architecture at the ranchería villages implies political dependence.

Some of the mesa villages can also be interpreted as "signs of history," that is as structures consciously built to embody a group's history. Preucel has argued that Kotyiti functioned as an indexical icon of Keresan cosmology (Snead and Preucel 1999). The Keres world is conceptualized as a series of nested, but interrelated, regions containing mountains, hills, lakes, springs, hunting grounds, agricultural fields, and mineral resources—all of which are focused on a central village (White 1962). Supernatural beings inhabit the places at the edge of the world, and the regions extending into the pueblo are associated with the deities of medicine societies and shrines. The Keres world is divided in half along gender lines, with the deities of the west

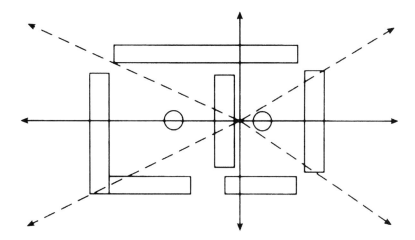

14.13 Schematic plan of
Kotyiti showing some
indexical and iconic relations
between architecture and
aspects of the
Keres worldview.

being female (Thought Woman and Spider Grandmother), and those of the east being male
(Mockingbird Youth and Butterfly).

Some of the formal, plaza-oriented attributes of Kotyiti appear to iconically represent
important aspects of the Keresan universe as recorded ethnographically. Three of the four
corner gateways point to the corners of the world and likely establish relations with the deities
dwelling there. The fourth gateway, present when Vargas visited the site, was filled in with
residential rooms late in the site's occupation. The fifth or center gateway, positioned between
the northern room blocks, likely gave access to Shipap, the place of emergence from the
underworld. Shipap is typically invoked at multiple levels in pueblo villages, for example in the
floor of kivas and at plaza shrines. The double plaza plan of Kotyiti and other mesa villages may
attest to the renewed importance of the traditional moiety organization in establishing social
and political balance. We think that the architecture of Kotyiti, as an icon, legitimized the
political agenda favored by some of the leaders of the Pueblo Revolt, including Alonzo Catiti,
Antonio Malacate, and El Zepe.

We believe that the high degree of semiotic coding of Kotyiti is consistent with its
metaphorical linkage to the proto-ancestral village White House referenced in traditional
Keresan oral history (Benedict 1931). This idea cannot be demonstrated but it finds some
support in a story recorded by Matilda Coxe Stevenson (1894) in the late 19th century that
recounts how a Zia village was founded in the image of White House:

> During the journey of the Sia from the white-house in the north they built many villages.
> Those villages were close together, as the Sia did not wish to travel far at any one time. Finally,
> having concluded that they had about reached the center of the earth, they determined to
> build a permanent home. The ti'ämoni desiring that it should be an exact model of their
> house of white stone in the north, held a council, that he might gain information regarding
> the construction, etc., of the white village. "I wish," said the ti'ämoni, "to build a village
> here, after our white-house of the north, but I cannot remember clearly the construction

14.14 The mesa of Dowa Yalanne, home to a Pueblo Revolt village and several Zuni shrines, looms over Zuni Pueblo, providing a "sign of history" that helps constitute Zuni social identity.

of the house," and no one could be found in the group to give a detailed account of the plan. The council was held during the night and the ti'ämoni said, "Tomorrow I shall have someone return to the white-house, and carefully examine it. I think that the Si'sika [swallow] is a good man; he has a good head; and I think I will send him to the white-house" and calling the Si'sika he said: "Listen attentively; I wish you to go and study the structure of the white-house in the north; learn all about it, and bring me all the details of the buildings; how one house joins another." The Si'sika replied, "Very well, father; I will go early in the morning." Though the distance was great, the Si'sika visited the white-house, and returned to the ti'ämoni a little after the sun had eaten [noon]. "Father," said the Si'sika, "I have examined the white-house in the north carefully, flying all over it and about it. I examined it well and can tell you all about it." The ti'ämoni was pleased, for he had thought much concerning the white-house, which was very beautiful. He at once ordered all hands to work, great labor being required in the construction of the village after the plan laid down by the Si'sika. Upon the completion of this village, the ti'ämoni named it Kóasaia. It is located at the ruin some 2 1/2 miles north of the present site of Sia. (57–58)

While there is no way to know with certainty whether this account was created as part of the Revolt Period discourse, it shows the relationships between religious teachings and the architecture of some Keresan villages.

In addition to being an icon of ancestral form, the plan of Kotyiti is indexical because its gateways and openings channeled the movement of people through the village in ways that would remind people of the differences between this new village and the street layouts of their recently vacated mission pueblo. This interpretation is consistent with the results of our space syntax analysis, which indicates a high degree of spatial segregation and relatively isolated axial spaces.

Finally it is interesting to note that the Spaniards themselves recognized the symbolic significance of some of these villages. Catholic churches were built at two of the mesa pueblos—Patokwa and Old San Felipe—before their occupation ceased. These missions represented both the reimposition of Catholicism with its rich tradition of meanings and practices and the reinstatement of the Spanish colonial government at the end of the Pueblo Revolt.

Conclusion

Although the Pueblo Revolt mesa villages are no longer currently occupied, they have not been abandoned and forgotten. They remain powerful signs of history for the Pueblo peoples whose ancestors resided in them. The mesas where these villages are found are the location of many important shrines, and, in fact, many of the mesa villages themselves are considered sacred sites. These mesa villages, and the history they embody, continue to play an important role in the cultural discourse of Pueblo people.

The mesa villages of the Pueblo Revolt have much to teach us about the diverse strategies Pueblo peoples implemented in a period of remarkable social and political stress. The differences in the spatial structure of plaza-oriented pueblos and ranchería settlements indicate that Pueblo peoples responded in a variety of ways as they formed alliances with each other to defend themselves from Spanish retribution. The rich semiotic meanings read from the site plan of Kotyiti and potentially from other mesa villages represent an exciting advance in archaeological study that takes us beyond processual approaches to the past into a new and richer intellectual territory.

References

Bailey, Jessie Bromilow. *Diego De Vargas and the Reconquest of New Mexico.* Albuquerque, NM: University of New Mexico Press, 1940.

Bandelier, Adolph F. *Final Report of Investigation Among the Indians of the Southwestern United States, Carried on Mainly in the Years from 1880 to 1885, Part II.* Papers of the Archaeological Institute of America, American Series 4. Cambridge: Cambridge University Press, 1892.

Benedict, Ruth. *Tales of the Cochiti Indians*. Bulletin of American Ethnology 98. Washington, DC: USGPO, 1931.

Brandt, Elizabeth. *Pueblo Missions National Monument Cultural Affiliation Study*. National Park Service Applied Ethnography Program, Southwest Systems Support Office, Santa Fe, NM: National Park Service, 1997.

Dougherty, Julia D. *Refugee Pueblos on the Santa Fe National Forest*. Cultural Resources Report 2. Santa Fe, NM: Santa Fe National Forest, 1980.

Espinsosa, J. Manuel. *First Expedition of Vargas into New Mexico, 1692*. Albuquerque, NM: University of New Mexico Press, 1940.

———. *The Pueblo Indian Revolt of 1696 and the Franciscan Missions in New Mexico*. Norman, OK: University of Oklahoma Press, 1988.

Ferguson, T. J. *Historic Zuni Architecture and Society, An Archaeological Application of Space Syntax*. Anthropological Papers of the University of Arizona 60. Tucson, AZ: University of Arizona Press, 1996.

Forbes, Jack D. *Apache, Navaho and Spaniard*. Norman, OK: University of Oklahoma Press, 1966.

Hackett, Charles W., ed., and Charmion C. Shelby, trans. *Revolt of the Pueblo Indians of New Mexico and Otermín's Attempted Reconquest, 1680–1682*. Albuquerque, NM: University of New Mexico Press, 1942.

Hanson, Julienne. *Decoding Homes and Houses*. Cambridge: Cambridge University Press, 1998.

Hillier, Bill. *Space is the Machine*. Cambridge: Cambridge University Press, 1996.

Hillier, Bill, and Julienne Hanson. *The Social Logic of Space*. Cambridge: Cambridge University Press, 1984.

Holmes, William H. "Notes on the Antiquities of the Jemez Valley, New Mexico." *American Anthropologist* 7(1905):198–212.

Kessell, John L., and Rick Hendricks. *By Force of Arms, The Journals of Don Diego de Vargas, 1691–1693*. Albuquerque, NM: University of New Mexico Press, 1992.

Kessell, John L., Rick Hendricks, and Meredith Dodge. *To the Royal Crown Restored, The Journals of Don Diego De Vargas, New Mexico, 1692–1694*. Albuquerque, NM: University of New Mexico Press, 1995.

———. *Blood on the Boulders, The Journals of Don Diego De Vargas, New Mexico, 1694–97*. Albuquerque, NM: University of New Mexico Press, 1998.

Knaut, Andrew L. *The Pueblo Revolt of 1680, Conquest and Resistance in Seventeenth-Century New Mexico*. Norman, OK: University of Oklahoma Press, 1995.

Logsdon, Paul. *Ancient Land, Ancestral Places*. Santa Fe, NM: Museum of New Mexico Press, 1993.

Mindeleff, Victor. "A Study of Pueblo Architecture in Tusayan and Cibola." In *Eighth Annual Report of the Bureau of American Ethnology for the Years 1886–1887*. Washington, DC: USGPO, 1891.

Nelson, Nels C. "Excavations of Pueblo Kotyiti, New Mexico." Unpublished manuscript. New York: Archives of the American Museum of Natural History, n.d.

Parmentier, Richard J. "Times of the Signs: Modalities of History and Levels of Social Structure in Belau." In *Semiotic Mediation: Sociocultural and Psychological Perspectives*, ed. Elizabeth Mertz and Richard J. Parmentier. New York: Academic Press, 1985.

———. *The Sacred Remains: Myth, History, and Polity in Belau*. Chicago, IL: University of Chicago Press, 1987.

———. *Signs in Society: Studies in Semiotic Anthropology.* Bloomington, IN: Indiana University Press, 1994.

Preucel, Robert W. "The Kotyiti Research Project, Report of the 1996 Field Season." Report Prepared for the Pueblo of Cochiti and the USDA Forest Service, Santa Fe, 1998.

———. "Living on the Mesa: Hanat Kotyiti, A Post-Revolt Cochiti Community in Northern New Mexico." *Expedition* 42(2000):8–17.

Preucel, Robert W., ed. *Archaeologies of the Pueblo Revolt.* Albuquerque, NM: University of New Mexico Press, 2003.

Preucel, Robert W., and Alexander Bauer. "Archaeological Pragmatics." *Norwegian Archaeological Review* 34(2001):85–96.

Schroeder, Albert H. "Pueblos Abandoned in Historic Times." In *Handbook of North American Indians* 9, ed. Alfonso Ortiz. Washington, DC: Smithsonian Institution, 1979.

Snead, James E., and Robert W. Preucel. "The Ideology of Settlement: Ancestral Keres Landscapes in the Northern Rio Grande." In *Archaeologies of Landscapes: Contemporary Approaches*, ed. Wendy Ashmore and A. Bernard Knapp. Oxford: Blackwell, 1999.

Stevenson, Matilda Coxe. *The Sia.* Bureau of American Ethnology, 11th Annual Report. Washington, DC: Smithsonian Institution, 1894.

White, Leslie. *The Pueblo of Sia, New Mexico.* Bureau of American Ethnology Bulletin 184. Washington, DC: Smithsonian Institution, 1962.

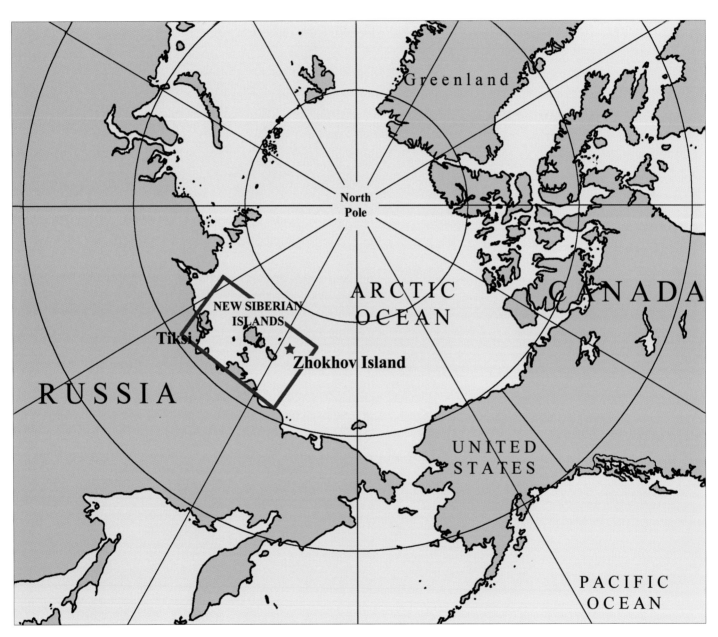

Greenland

North
Pole

ARCTIC
OCEAN

CANADA

NEW SIBERIAN
ISLANDS

Tiksi

Zhokhov Island

RUSSIA

UNITED
STATES

PACIFIC
OCEAN

15.1 Part of the
northern hemisphere

IMAGING THE PAST

Edmund Carpenter

15

Z hokhov Island, on the central Siberian coast 700 miles northeast of Tiksi, contains an archaeological site where every seed, insect, hair, pollen, dropping, hide, and wooden tool has remained preserved in ice, essentially as it was when the last occupant walked away, 8,000 years ago (Pitul'ko 1993; Pitul'ko and Kasparov 1996). Zhokhov was then part of the mainland, warmer, the tree line closer, with plants and insects not found there today. Still, it was tundra, barren and unyielding.

Today's landscape conveys the impression of absolute permanence and detachment. It is not hostile. It's simply there—untouched, silent, complete. It's very lonely. Why would anyone live there?

Food. In the High Arctic, early hunters let game multiply, then swept in, harvested, moved on. Zhokhov offered additional assets: polar bear hides for trade, driftwood for houses.

Those tiny houses brought back memories. In 1951–52, in the Canadian Arctic, I wintered in such a hut, larger than these, but still very crowded. It wasn't easy for me. Unlike my hosts,

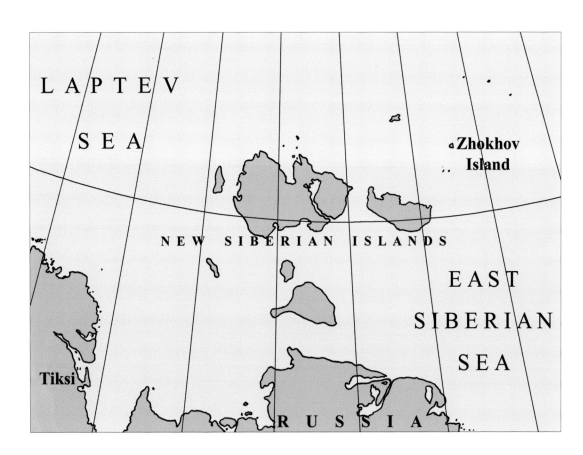

15.2 New Siberian Islands.

15.3 The site, looking south
toward the beach, about half
a mile away.

15.4 The site, looking north.
The ridge (originally higher)
offered some protection from
winds from the north.

15.5 Houses were built of wood. Frost splintered many logs and turned them upward. Some protruded above the surface, disclosing the site.

15.6 The ice resisted reflectors, even microwave, and we fell back on chisels.

I couldn't turn off my mind. They virtually hibernated. Perhaps their metabolism slowed. They seldom moved. Their eyes glazed over. They ignored conversation.

How does one turn off a mind? Not easy for a literate person. Tolstoy and his brother formed a club: initiation required standing in a corner for 20 minutes, not thinking of a white bear. British prisoners of war, finding idleness unbearable, faked passports, counterfeited money, wove civilian clothing.

Not so my Eskimo hosts. They switched off. They stopped thinking. Yet, before my eyes, an inchoate mass became a formidable hunter, then returned to his previous state. Even in sleep, they differed. They slept lightly. Roused by an emergency, they moved quickly, collectively, no matter how tightly packed that dwelling.

I cannot exaggerate how small those quarters were. I once saw vapor rising from flat snow, beside a protruding mast. A family of three, with stone lamp, lived in a snow cocoon. The mast prevented the snow from collapsing.

Years later, circumstances took me back to the spot where I'd wintered. By then, the site resembled an ancient ruin. My former companions were dead. Their descendants lived modern lives. Only memory remained.

Today when I find myself back in the Arctic, looking down at tent rings or house ruins, I try to imagine the lives and hearts of those who once lived there. Archaeologists frown on this, but we all do this secretly, so let me now do it openly, reconstructing the past through personal experience.

When you live tightly packed, day after day, week after week, going outside only to hunt, and then only the men, it is best to mute individualism. Eskimos avoid the first person pronoun. They don't say, "I'm getting angry," but "This igloo may witness anger"; not "I killed a bear," but "One's harpoon chanced to embed itself in a mangy bear."

Muted speech alone cannot guarantee peace. Eskimo murder is known. But, compared to Europeans in isolated outposts, Eskimos remain models of restraint. The environment helps. When temperatures exceed -50°F and gusts of wind reach 60 mph, the smallest, most crowded dwelling offers warmth, companionship.

Westerners often comment on the leniency of Eskimo parents. The real taskmaster is the environment. Accept it, study it, or die. Let me offer one example. On the polar ice, when snow or fog fills the air, the horizon disappears and you are suddenly blind white, in a seamless balloon, no up, no down, no point of reference, nothing the eye can cling to.

It can be very dangerous. I recently read of two young Eskimos caught in that situation, without even wind to guide them. One set off blindly, relying on memory. The other devised a string and float; whenever he came to open water, he tested the current, knowing the spring runoff flowed offshore. His companion rejoined him. Both reached land.

I recall traveling in fog along a dangerous coastline. Visibility was zero, yet we never slowed. My companions listened to the surf and to the cries of birds nesting on promontories; they smelled the shore and surf, felt the wind and spray, and read, through their buttocks, wave patterns created by the interplay of wind and swell. They were not lost without sight.

In the High Arctic, atmosphere can distort. Before your eyes, a coastline disappears. Dog becomes bear-sized; bear, dog-sized. What first seemed a stable landscape becomes, as you watch, something else.

Long periods of light and dark alternate annually. White ice replaces dark water. Great ice barriers turn turquoise, then disappear. Aurora Borealis, crackling with electricity, fills the sky, in every color. Yet, in this changing landscape, Eskimo maps proved so accurate, so detailed, only aerial photography replaced them.

One Eskimo map covers half of Baffin Island. Others span coastlines for hundreds of miles. Many are so detailed, so correctly proportioned, we have a right to ask: what special gifts set Eskimos apart as cartographers?

They start with the whole, then delimit the particular. They shun any single point of view. When handed a photograph upside down, they examine it as given. They view maps from any direction. The case system in their language favors space, not time.

Mapping begins with place-names. Most are visually descriptive. Some are acoustically memorable. All are mnemonic devices, songs sung like roll calls as one paddles along a coast, either in fact or memory. Travel coordinates come from the prevailing wind. The dominant wind rose serves as compass.

The story I like best about Eskimo maps concerns Charles Hall, a journalist/explorer who mapped southeast Baffin Island in 1860. First he asked a local hunter, Koojesse, to draw Frobisher Bay from memory. The next year he set out in a whaleboat, himself at the rudder; Koojesse in the bow, sketching; and Eskimo women, rowing.

From this came three more maps. Koojesse's second map, though detailed, suffered from Hall's interference. Hall drew his own map, connecting fixes. At the end of the trip, a rower volunteered her map.

Of these four maps, Koojesse's first effort, from memory, is excellent. His second map, though more detailed, lacks balance. Hall's map, except for the fixes, is unusable. The anonymous rower wins. Her map superbly matches aerial photographs.

Did Zhokhov's residents sketch in the snow, the way Eskimos do? We'll never know. No question, the earliest known art is highly realistic. This may be changed as further discoveries are made, but, at the moment, it suddenly bursts forth. We know little about early man's sensory profile, that is, how he used his senses, but one thing is certain: survival required keen familiarity with the land. Surely it's no coincidence that optical realism in art first appears in what was then a northern setting, and continued in the north, intermittently, until recently.

Otherwise, optical realism is rare in tribal arts. Until the rise of the city-states, Euclidean space, the beginning of science, etc., tribal art was almost everywhere, except in the Far North, more symbolic than optical. Its appearance at the very beginning of art, in Paleolithic times, took two forms: sculpture and painting. In both, animal representation is so precise that we can identify species. In Eskimo sculpture, we can tell a Common Loon from a Red-throated Loon and recognize postures characteristic of each.

15.8 A combination of ice, water, and mud.

15.9 Even during the warmest months, snow flurries were common.

Paleolithic cave painting sometimes included shading, depth. A bovine figure in Lascaux has two heads. Illuminated by flickering oil lamp, we see it in profile. Shift the lamp: the head turns toward us. I'm reminded of 19th century optical toys where still images come to life and move.

Add humor. One Paleolithic spear-thrower depicts an ibex defecating, with a bird pecking seeds from the emerging turd. Humor remained a recurring feature of northern art, especially as visual pun.

15.10 Eskimo tents.
Drawing by Enooesweetok,
1913-14.

In Mesolithic times, circa 7–8,000 years ago in northern Europe with much later survivals, of course, realism gave way to schematic representation, especially genealogical representation. Similar designs occurred in Paleolithic times, coexisting with optical realism. However, in Mesolithic art, schematic art took over, while realism, except in the North, faded (Schuster 1986:88–91).

What do these schematic designs represent? Fortunately, they're still made by modern tribesmen. They tell us these designs represent the tribe's two moieties, each divided into two clans. They say this four-fold division reflects a kinship system based on cross-cousin marriage, with matrilineal descent. Such a system balances power equally between moieties and sexes.

No credible evidence exists of matriarchy, anywhere, ever. But cross-cousin marriage, combined with matrilineal descent, certainly favors gender equality. It may once have characterized many, perhaps most, early groups.

Evidence for this survives in the centers of Mesolithic culture, say the Maglemose of northwest Europe. I doubt, though, that it characterized Mesolithic hunting bands in northern Siberia. Arctic conditions there favored male leadership. Among Arctic peoples, young women have few rights. But, as they age, they acquire some, assume others, and relations tend to balance out.

Do any clues, vestiges, survive, no matter how remote, about the lore and religious beliefs of those who once lived in this lonely camp? Driftwood then littered the beach, carried downstream by the Lena from Siberia's interior. Canadian Eskimos in the High Arctic, having never seen a living tree, believed driftwood grew like seaweed, at the bottom of the ocean. Did that lore originate in Siberia?

We know that Zhokhov residents practiced scapulimancy, divination designed to reveal distant or future events. In this divination, a scapula is scorched, then "read" in terms of the resulting cracks—an ancient tradition, certainly Paleolithic. Hunters use it to decide where to pursue caribou. And we can reasonably guess that they accorded polar bears, which they took in great numbers, an elevated status.

I imagine they had part-time shamans. Shamanistic performances I've witnessed always remind me of my dentist: the costume, the assistant laying out equipment, the negotiated fee, etc. Like scapulimancy, shamanism is ritual, not religion.

Do any clues survive concerning Zhokhov's religion? A legitimate place to look would be among distant descendants. Zhokhov's inhabitants belonged to the land-based, marginally maritime, micro-blade culture of mainland Siberia. They had sleds, presumably dog drawn. No evidence of watercraft has been recognized. Few bones from the sea occur in its middens. Mesolithic peoples in Siberia lived primarily from the land.

Emigrants carried their culture to Arctic America, then Greenland. Over millennia, with many modifications, principally maritime adaptations, it became, ultimately, Eskimo culture as we know it.

I see Zhokhov's residents as proto-Eskimo. If so, vestiges of their religious beliefs may survive today among living Eskimos. Central to Eskimo religion is a mythic woman sacrificed by the community to save itself. They never asked that the universe be this way. But, "*ayornamut*" [It cannot be otherwise]; they accept life on its own terms.

They do more than accept: they take upon themselves the responsibility for the fact that life is the way it is. They give Sedna the power of life and death over them. Sedna was an orphan or woman thrown from an *umiak* or skin boat, who clung to the gunwale, where her stepfather cut off her successive fingers. These became the seals and walrus the Eskimo now depend upon for survival. Sedna sends them forth to hunters who respect them. Those who were forced to abandon her now place themselves in her power, dependent upon her good will, her respect for all life (Carpenter 1973:210–17).

Supporting evidence comes from "Paleolithic Venuses." These tiny figurines were worn suspended from their ankles. Inversion symbolized death. I think they represented ancestors, dead people guarding the living while they awaited rebirth (Schuster and Carpenter 1996:268–77).

Over two dozen such figurines were uncovered at Malta, a late Paleolithic site near Lake Baikal, in central Siberia. That tradition continued elsewhere, in various areas, especially Canada and Greenland (Carpenter 1990).

No such figurine has been found on Zhokhov. No tale of sacrifice survives. Still, I think it likely that acceptance of life, sacrifice of an innocent, and rebirth of all life were basic beliefs to those who once lived in this lonely camp.

Not too many years ago, archaeology was essentially loot. You dug up the enemy or those for whom you had little respect. As science expanded, archaeology became data. We now have close to a dozen dating techniques. At Zhokhov, we can tell the season, even the month, a caribou or bear died, from the teeth alone. In a canine coprolite, we found two distinct worms, plus their eggs, plus two microbes, neither of which was or is friendly to humans.

A grave of an adult female, plus newborn infant, was marked by two feathers gracefully bound by split quill. A comparable grave of mother and child, in distant Denmark (same date, same tool kit, same lifestyle), lay on a bed of swan pelts, presumably to carry them to limbo and rebirth.

References

Carpenter, Edmund. *Eskimo Realities*. New York: Holt, Rinehart and Winston, 1973.

———. "How an Upside-Down Lady Became an Upside-Down Bird." *Festschrift, Renée Boser*. Basel, Switzerland: Museum für Völkerkunde, 1990.

Carpenter, Edmund, ed. *Enooesweetok's Drawings*. Originally published as *Drawings by Enooesweetok of the Sikosilingmint Tribe of Eskimo, Fox Land, Baffin Island*, by Robert J. Flaherty, Toronto, 1915. New York: Rock Foundation, 2001.

Pitul'ko, Vladimir V. "An Early Holocene Site in the Siberian High Arctic." *Arctic Anthropology* 30,1(1993):13–21.

Pitul'ko, Vladimir, and Alcksey K. Kasparov. "Ancient Hunters: Material Cultural and Survival Strategy." *Arctic Anthropology* 33,1(1996):1–36.

Schuster, Carl. *Social Symbolism in Ancient & Tribal Art*. New York: Rock Foundation, 1986.

Schuster, Carl, and Edmund Carpenter. *Patterns that Connect*. New York: Abrams, 1996.

The Oasis Model
Pietro Laureano

Oasis communities show that humankind has not only trod the path of enormous, powerful empires, but has also carved out small and self-sufficient communities. Gigantic, far-flung empires require more and more energy and resources in order to stave off catastrophe, creating a situation that becomes more terrifying with the passage of time. This is what is happening in the Nile Valley at the moment, and in many other areas of the Mediterranean and of Arabia, where enormous growth rates are underpinned by major dams, by overuse of deep water tables, by costly desalination plants, or by huge projects that use ever more remote resources.

An alternative model is the oasis community that has allowed human life and society to continue even after the collapse of great empires. Oasis societies have been able to hand down collective knowledge and rules for peaceful coexistence that are indispensable for their survival. They are able to live in harmony with the surrounding environment and to make use of its resources without depleting them. The underlying philosophy is the transformation of what seem to be environmental disadvantages into renewable resources. The lag in modern development that left the archaic landscape and settlements intact has given us a viable alternative of great value for the future. The combination of oasis paleo-technology and new

16.1 The cyclical creation of an oasis: a slight depression collects humidity; the palm tree flourishes and provides shade and biological material which attract the other organisms; the humus produced enables other cultivation.

appropriate technologies could set in motion a true cultural recovery: we could safeguard the remnants of the past and revitalize them as models of how to save our planet, which is an oasis in the cosmos.

An oasis is a human settlement in a harsh geographical situation. It uses rare resources available locally in order to set off a rising amplification of positive interactions that creates a fertile, self-sustaining environmental niche in direct contrast to its unfavorable surroundings.

The vital niches of oases are the result of humanity's work and knowledge that is suited to the environment and handed down from generation to generation; they are the result of local genius and knowledge. The date palm, an indispensable oasis plant, does not grow spontaneously but is the result of domestication and cultivation. In the desert every palm grove has been planted, cultivated, and irrigated. In oases, water resources also are carefully managed and distributed, and they depend on successful catchment techniques.

Water Techniques and Types of Oases

Oases differ based on geography and on the techniques used. There are a number of different types of oases. According to the hydraulic and geomorphologic system, it is possible to make a distinction between the following: *wadi* oases use the large river bed of a dried-up river; *erg* dune desert oases are situated in the very heart of the sandy desert; and *sebkha* oases are created around the depression of a great salt lake (Laureano 1985, 1986).

Wadi oases are situated along the upper reaches of a water network where watercourses carve deep canyons out of sedimentary sandstone or out of calcareous rock. Because they are close to mountain peaks or highlands, sometimes these oases can benefit from permanent, meager water supplies, though often these exist as underground flows or as short floods from

16.2 The oasis of Taghit, in the Algerian Sahara, and the adobe fortified habitat. At the foot of the dunes, the oasis is fed with waters filtrating below the Great Western Erg.

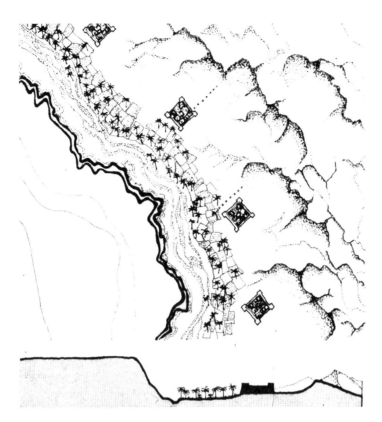

16.3 The *wadi* oases are a linear system along the fossil riverbed. Water for cultivation is drawn up by dams and wells.

annual rainfall. These oases take the form of long ribbons of vegetation running between steep cliffs. Palm groves cover the entire riverbeds because they will be occasionally flooded. Only in the deepest stretches of the bed is there a narrow, bare strip where a small creek might run. Deep dikes built perpendicular to the *wadi* bed block the underground flows, retain the soil, and transform the watercourse into a succession of embankments that can hold arable fields. Other land suitable for farming might be obtained along the slopes of the banks, organizing them into terraces that can be irrigated by means of an ingenious technique that uses gravity flow. Canals branch off from upstream water intakes following the land slope for the fields to be irrigated. They are higher than the riverbed, thus enabling irrigation by the force of gravity and cultivations at a higher level than the natural bottom.

The water supply changes according to the *wadi*'s carrying capacity. It may only be available in deposits in the subsoil. In this case, water collection is made from embankments using intakes situated at the bottom to drain the water gathered in the deposits upstream from the dike. When this system does not work, water is obtained by wells that, by means of sunken dams, collect the humidity kept in the subsoil. Water buckets are lifted by a long rocker arm fitted with a balance weight and placed on two high adobe (unfired brick) vertical rods, a technique illustrated on an Akkadian cylinder, dating back to the 3rd millenium BCE.

Erg oases are established deep in the sandy wastes of the dune desert as a protection against the most implacable and difficult terrain. It provides survival potential for those aware of desert ecology. Dune desert formation is based on the direction of winds and the shapes of rock reliefs. Each grain of wind-borne sand moves continuously. The dune forms when wind comes up against an obstacle and grains of sand are dropped. The largest grains of sand bounce

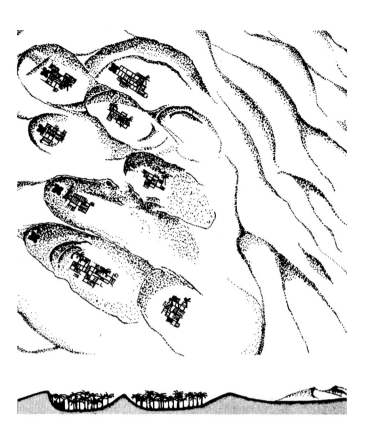

16.4 *Erg* oases are established deep in the sand. The shape of the *erg* is moulded by the palm trees which form a barrier to protect the cultivation.

and drop successively lower on the hard rocky surfaces. Once there has been a scattering of sand grains, the accumulation grows steadily larger because the grains no longer bounce off the sand. Both reliefs situated at enormous distance and more microscopic obstacles to the flow of sands can be responsible for formation of the dune and the morphology of the *erg*.

The horizontal component of the wind action causes the dunes to move, although only the isolated ones having a crescent shape (called *barkhane*) actually travel. The single sand grains on the surface of other types of dunes move continuously, but the general shape does not change. For this reason, it is possible to see an oasis situated at the foot of a large dune that is apparently ready to sweep it away, while in actuality the oasis has been living in balance with the dune for centuries. Although the front of the *erg* is continuously moving like the coastal settlements of the sea, it is dangerous only after catastrophic events or devastating actions.

Erg oases follow the laws regulating the formation of the great ocean of sand and use those laws to set up protective dune barriers. They are not based on a geomorphologic structure or on a well-defined hydrological system because the relief is covered with sand. In some cases *erg* oases depend on shallow, underground water that the root of the palm trees can reach directly in the subsoil. Such palm groves are called *bur*, which means, "not irrigated." The farmer has a hard task to accomplish, which consists of preventing the sands from sweeping away the isles of palm groves. Consequently, the farmer starts to excavate a ditch to enable the palm trees to be closer to the humid area of the soil. Dry palm leaves are placed around the ditch as windbreaks and cause the sand to be released. In accordance with the mechanism of successive and continuous accumulation, protective manmade dunes are created, which are called *afreg*. Over the course of time, these dunes grow higher and the oasis starts to look like a sand crater with a tilled bed. The canopies of the palm trees close off the top of these funnels and in this

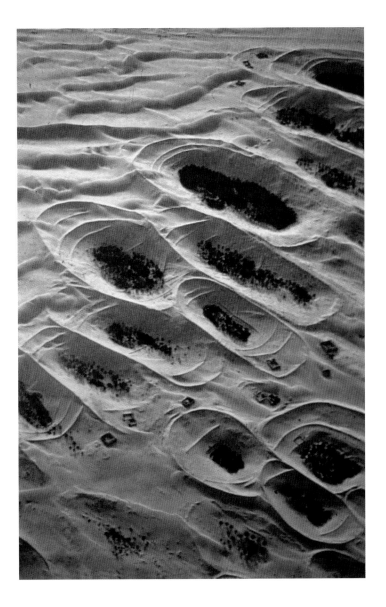

16.5 *Erg* oases in the Algerian Souf region with the artificial craters (*bur*) that are dug out and protected by barriers of leaves.

16.6 The formation of artificial sandy dunes called *afreg* in the Sahara Desert. An adobe ribbon creates the first accumulation of sand on the soil. As time goes by, formations reaching up to 100 m of height generate beautiful pyramidal artificial dunes such as the one seen here.

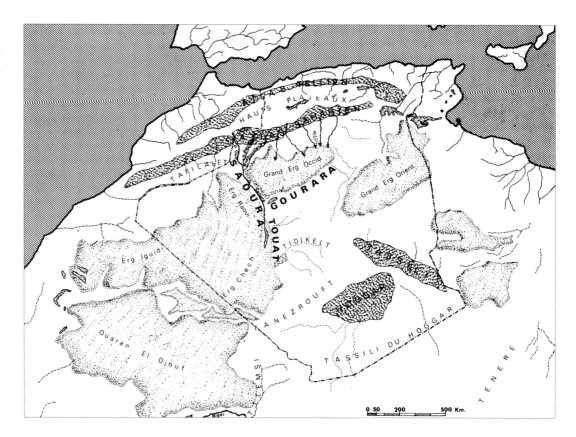

16.7 Geographical locations of places cited in the text.

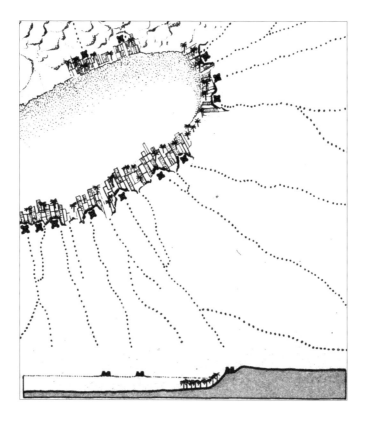

16.8 *Sebkha* oases form a lenticular system along the edges of deep dry basins. Water is frequently intercepted by means of a series of spread-out drainage tunnels (*foggaras*).

16.9 The ribbon of artificial dunes (on the right) protects the palm grove, which slopes down the deep depression of the *sebkha* from the rock of the citadel, where drainage tunnels run down the highland flow. Oasis of Ighzer at the margins of the *sebkha* of Timimoun, Algeria.

way sustain a microclimate inside. In Eastern Algeria, in the Souf region of the Great Eastern Erg, these carved-out depressions in the sand create an extraordinary landscape where the continuous movements of the *erg* undulate single-file along the dunes, thanks to hundreds and hundreds of craters. These craters look as if they are floating on the sand, which could submerge them at any moment, whereas in reality the *erg* favors the oasis, which absorbs moisture from it, and protects itself from the wind and the heat. A monumental task is accomplished: to live constantly in the continuously changing dune sea by controlling its movements and shaping its landscape.

Sebkha oases are situated along the margins of major depressions. They have an elliptic shape with a side against the front of the *erg* and the other free of sand. The oases, as coastal settlements of a lake, surround the *sebkha*, using strategies of both the *erg* oasis and the *wadi* oasis. Their specificity is due to the type of water supply that is based on huge hydraulic works. The oases exploit the particular morphology of the *sebkha* where the flows converge. The oases make it possible to survive deep inside the Sahara, which can be rendered fertile even though there is no surface running water and no precipitation.

WATER MINES

Rare water resources are sometimes caught by means of underground drainage tunnels, which are locally called *foggara*. This method dates back thousands of years and was used over a vast area ranging from China through Persia and Spain to Latin America (Goblot 1979). The *foggara* of the Sahara Desert are more or less the same, making allowances for local differences, as the *qanat* or *kariz* of Persia, the *falaj* of Arabia, the *khottara* of Morocco and the *madjirat* of Andalusia. Similar water works have been found in Peru and in Mexico in pre-Columbian farm units called *hoyas*. It is difficult to establish exactly whether these systems come from

16.10 The interior of a drainage tunnel, called *foggara*, dug out of the calcareous rock that is able to catch the water inside the porous soil. Oasis of Timimoun, Algerian Sahara.

knowledge dissemination or from opportunistic processes in areas having the same physical and climatological characteristics. The construction of the most ancient towns was based on the building of these systems.

These ancient methods of water production are still used in the regions of Gourara and Touat of the Algerian Sahara desert. The system is composed of about a thousand *foggaras*, of which half are still working, extending in an underground network totalling 3,000–6,000 km. A number of wells on the surface can be recognized by their characteristic raised rims resulting from excavation and are useful for identifying the location of the tunnels. Shafts dug about 8 to 10 m apart ensure ventilation during the underground digging; they are also used for maintenance work. However, they do not reach down to the level of the water. *Foggara* excavation starts from the settlement site going up to the edges of the alluvial cones of the dried-up *wadi*. Unlike a feeding canal, the *foggaras* do not convey water from the springs or underground ponds to the place where it is used. However, because of their underground pathway, they catch the microflows seeping through the rocks and create surface water by

STRUCTURE AND MEANING IN HUMAN SETTLEMENTS

tapping moisture from the soil; thus they act as production systems or water mines. The tunnel, which is dug parallel to the ground, does not go down as far as the water table, but where possible, it drains off the upper soils without causing the lowering of the aquifer. In fact, it allows the absorption of water necessary for the maintenance of the aquifer. The subsoil area for water supply looks like a big rocky sponge rather than an underground basin; it is fed with microflows conveyed to the *sebkha*.

Water is supplied via surface condensation, called hidden precipitation. Hidden precipitation allows gazelles to drink by licking the night dew off stones that are steeped in moisture; lizards and scarabs get the water they need for survival just from the water contained in the air.

The whole *foggara* network, with its huge quantity of vertical pipes and drainage tunnels, is an aquifer maintenance system which ensures the soaking of the soil by means of the exchange with atmospheric moisture. Al Karagi's 11th century treatise lists three origins of *qanat* water supplies. Because of the heat differential, during the night humidity is released into the sand; from there it flows down to the underground canals until it reaches the fields. The *foggaras* foster this process by acting as pumps that attract the vapor-laden air. During the night, cold air sinks to the ground and humidity seeps into the *foggaras*. After sunrise, the entire process is reversed. As the ground heats up, the air in the *foggara* rises as it is expelled through the air shafts that are exposed to the burning temperatures of the desert. The air circulation in the underground tunnel operates by suctioning the air from the lower part of the shaded area of the palm grove. The humidity is thus sucked out and recondensed on the walls and on the ground before the air can exit from the shafts. Water is preserved in the pores of the soil, which becomes more and more steeped in water; gravity pulls the water down to the underground canal and to the opening that feeds the oasis.

The Sahara desert is rich in prehistoric structures made up of barrows and underground rooms which can be interpreted as humidity and dew collection systems. Underground chambers or mounds of stones favor the process of condensation and water conservation. The so-called solar tombs made up of concentric circles around the barrow are ancient methods for the collection of moisture and dew and could have belonged to cults devoted to the practice of water harvesting. The long lines of stones which sometimes radiate out from the circle are actually water collectors. They are open toward the slope and converge in the underground chamber. They were used to canalize and divert the humidity collected on the condensation surfaces. The origin of the *foggara* is likely the result of the development of this condensation chamber technique. In the marshy environment of Saharan prehistory, pure drinking water was produced through percolation in caves. As desertification developed and the water supplies of underground rooms depleted, man likely tried to widen the excavation to follow the direction of the flows, thus creating a tunnel that lengthened the condensation chamber and expanded the drainage area. This is actually the technique of the *foggaras*, which has the characteristic of using all the different principles of water production: catchment, percolation, and condensation.

The Structure of the Oasis

The structure of a *sebkha* oasis is comprised of a *foggara* 4 to 8 km long which runs from the border of the depression upstream to the highlands, of a fortification situated along

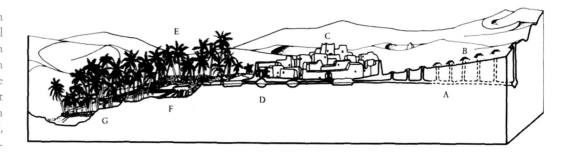

16.11 The water produced in the *foggara* underground tunnel (A) and recognizable through the surface excavation shafts (B), flows beneath the adobe habitat (C), where it is collected in decantation tanks (D) useful for food, ablutions, and the maintenance of cool temperature inside the houses. Water is conveyed in open-air channels by means of *kesria* (F), whose function is to measure and distribute the water flow, to irrigate the palmgrove (E), which is shared in tilled parcels by means of mud walls (G).

a rocky edge, and of a strip of palm groves extending downstream from the *sebkha* as deep as the *foggara's* carrying capacity allows. The amount of arable land that can be captured from the desert depends on the water resources of the drainage tunnel. The open-air ditches called *seguia*, which flow throughout the entire tilled areas, follow paths marked by earthen walls; they flow beneath the walls or along them. Irrigation by continuous runoff is necessary for a constant washout of the soil since the concentration of salts is higher in the areas closest to the *sebkha*. However, this method does not fit the cultivations of orchards and would require a large quantity of water. Therefore, irregular irrigation can be adopted by harvesting water in single small rectangular basins with rounded edges called *majen*. The overall water supply is divided by capillaries to these small final reservoirs, each having a minimum storage and distribution capacity, which supply the tilled parcel.

Because of the runoff, oases have a humidity rate as high as 80%, even though desert climates have humidity rates as low as 5%. The water that evaporates from the running water in the open-air ditches contributes to the overall cycle that makes up the oasis effect. Even a single plant can trigger a whole vital system: the moisture it gathers, the shadow, the dried vegetable remains, and the protection from the wind produce the humus and create a biological niche used by the other organisms which, in their turn, bring their contribution to the system. Water loss that would otherwise take place because of biomass transpiration is kept to a minimum because of the canopy of the palm groves that also serve to attract and accumulate moisture.

Flow measurement is carried out by blocking the water in the main canal with a perforated copper sheet known as *hallafa*, whose tiny holes are plugged with clay. The next step is to unstop the holes progressively until the water flows consistently. The set of holes thus obtained, which represents the overall flow, is then divided according to each ownership share. By the same method, the size of the holes to be drilled in the comb-shaped stone that is used as a dividing wall is determined.

It is interesting to note that the smallest quantity of measure, as big as the tip of the little finger, is called *habba*, a term applied to the barley seed and related to the measure of gold. It is not possible to say whether the diameter of the hole was made according to the diameter of the barley seed, but there is a clear relationship between the barley seed and a precise quantity of gold. There is, therefore, a significant relationship between the measure of water, cereals, and gold. Since all the *foggaras* have the same runoff rate—controlled to avoid erosion and the lowering of the canal slope—the volume of a *habba* can be defined.

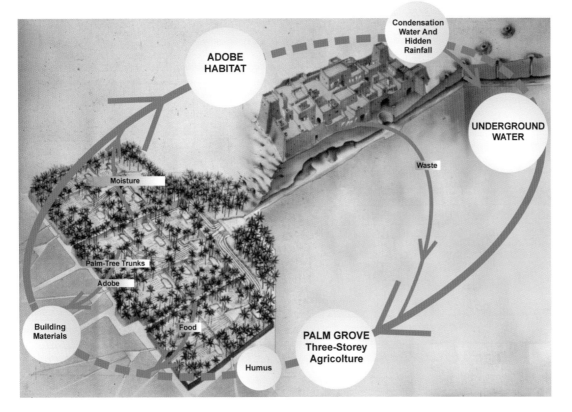

Condensation
Water And
Hidden
Rainfall

ADOBE
HABITAT

UNDERGROUND
WATER

Moisture

Waste

Palm-Tree Trunks

Adobe

Building
Materials

Food

PALM GROVE
Three-Storey
Agricolture

Humus

16.12 The traditional complex system (the Oasis Model). The oasis is a self-catalytic system in which the first supply of water condensation and moisture is increased by the installation of palm trees which produce shade, attract organisms, and form humus.

16.13 A water master of the Algerian oasis of Adrar showing the perforated sheet (*hallafa*) used for measuring the flows at the outlet of the big *foggara*.

Hydric Genealogy

Legal succession, marriage, and the sale of property are responsible for the ongoing system of breaking down and building up an intricate series of systems of stone water sharing (called *kesria*), links, and bridges. The bridges are necessary where one or more ditches cross over in order to avoid having the waters mix. A framework of water that registers passing generations, family ties, and family property in a system of kinship is physically represented by the network of ditches (Marouf 1980). Like a garden full of memories, an oasis reveals its own history through the flowing of its precious liquid.

Water is the life blood that is distributed among families. The jewel, the symbol of fertility that Berber women wear round their necks, is the stylization in different shapes of the water repartition system. Also the Egyptian hieroglyphic *mes*, meaning to be born, has the same shape, which confirms the close links between the oasis culture and the most ancient civilizations of the desert. The same motif is reproduced in carpet patterns, women's hairstyles, and in women's tattoos (Laureano 1987).

16.14 Oasis of Timimoun (Algerian Sahara), *kesria,* a water quota sharing system.

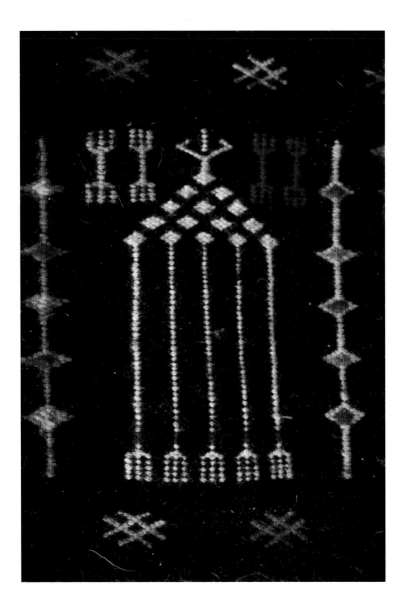

Hairstyles mark the different phases of women's growth, linking them to the farming practices and to the genesis of the oasis. At birth, the head, which usually has no hair, represents the original cosmic space. During childhood, girls' heads are shaved, with only one lock left in the middle of their heads, a symbol of the original land. During puberty the only part of the hair shaven is a narrow strip surrounding the head under the hair grown in the central part of the head; it is the symbol of the salted and sterile ocean surrounding the earth which is not yet farmed but is ready for being tilled. As time goes by, the part of the hair that is shaved is divided into locks by a median line that reproduces the central canal of the irrigation systems. When a girl is ready for marriage, her hair, which is no longer shaved but is divided into lines and small plaits, represents the tilled land where the water flows through the irrigation canals. Married women let their hair grow and braid it into thick plaits to represent their fertility like that of the oasis. Women's hairstyles reveal their stories, which are identified with those of the entire system. The water that fertilizes the fields is shared among properties; it is inherited, and it is the life blood of a fertile union that founds the family and perpetuates the community.

16.16 Women's hairstyles.

The relationship between the ego and the world sets up a pact between culture and nature; the symbol and the tradition are witnesses and guardians of this pact which ensures the maintenance of universal harmony. It is this solid relationship in which man can find consolation for the temporary nature of his existence and space becomes full of the holiness which is necessary for its safeguard and protection. The strict link between human actions and nature's harmony imposes a set of proscriptions, bonds, and prescriptions since even the simplest actions can contribute to the maintenance of universal balance. Therefore, in the oasis, the constant relationship between microcosm and macrocosm is not a metaphysical idea, but it is an ethical principle based on specific material needs.

THE OASIS MODEL ENLARGED

These ecological and spiritual aspects of oases are typical of settlements in the deserts of the Sahara and Arabia and are widespread throughout the Near East, on Mediterranean islands (Malta, Crete, Sardinia, Sicily, Lipari, Cyprus, Egadi, Balearic) and peninsulas, and in a number of geographical areas. The features they share are geomorphological harshness, arid climates, and low humidity conditions. Oasis systems are *autopoietic* and self-sustaining in a range of conditions: adobe oasis cities such as those along dry river beds in Yemen, which use the inhabitants' organic waste to fertilize the sterile sand, rendering it suitable for use in bold architectural designs; stone oases which, from prehistoric times onwards, have been dug out of the tufa stone of the Sassi of Matera and in the Gravine and Lame of Apulia where the water necessary for survival is condensed in the caves and on adobe constructions; religious oases carved out of the erosion valleys in Cappadocia, in Palestine, in Thebaid, and in Ethiopia organized in the form of hermitages and walled gardens irrigated by drainage tunnels, cisterns, and ditches; sea oases spread throughout the arid islands of the Mediterranean and the Red Sea supplied by airborne sources of water; and even oases of humid forests where, due to the special karst environments, no surface water courses can form, which makes the settlements completely dependent upon atmospheric water collection and conservation, such as the *chultun*, typical of Mayas in Yucatan, Mexico.

OASIS CITIES: SHIBAM, YEMEN

Shibam, a city in Yemen, is constructed entirely of adobe. Very high towers are made of unfired bricks that have been left out in the sun to dry. Using adobe means enormous energy savings; adobe is also an excellent heat insulator in buildings. The city is situated in the middle of a large *wadi* valley, the dry bed of a river that is filled with water only sporadically, typical of desert areas. Unusual flooding could completely overwhelm and destroy the city. At the end of the 1980s, a proposal was put forward to protect the city with a reinforced concrete structure. This would have meant a massive switch to concrete for a culture that up until now has only used adobe and has maintained a state of energy and economic self sufficiency by doing so. This is a city that has existed for ages and, in the course of its history, has survived a number of floods. How then did Shibam protect itself and avoid complete destruction?

The city protected its hinterland by making a resource out of something that could actually be considered a force of destruction (Laureano 1995). The floods were dammed upstream and

16.17 The Hadramaut Valley and the ancient walled town of Shibam, Yemen, are surrounded by the embankments and channels of the traditional system for flood sharing and farming, now largely abandoned.

broken up along the slopes and tributaries of the long riverbed. The watercourse of the river was transformed into a continual system of deflecting weirs and ditches that broadened the floodable area and dissipated the force of the water out over an enormous surface that was thus made suitable for agriculture. Great depressions in the ground were dug around the city to collect and absorb water, creating artificial sand craters that could be tilled and which were protected along their rims by earthfill and shaded by palms. The city's organic wastes were dumped into depressions that, together with the water, made fertile soil of the sterile sand of the loess.

The very existence of the city of Shibam, with its supply of organic waste matter, made the palm trees and farming possible in a continuous, positive feedback cycle. Not only do foodstuffs feed the population and eventually return to the soil as fertilizer, but the entire city, with its forms and architecture, is founded upon the eternal principle of complete reuse of resources. The adobe bricks come from the garden soil. Humus was continuously created and dug up in the craters, giving the soil its colloidal quality and binders that in turn permitted the bold architecture and solidly constructed buildings. The buildings followed a town plan and an architectural structure that were in harmony with the need to collect precious organic waste. All the tower houses had a façade giving onto a dead end street. Toilet drains situated on each floor of the buildings deposited waste matter. The excrement was retrieved in woven straw baskets that were kept at the bottom of the façades where the excrement dropped through trap doors. All of this was possible because liquid waste was kept quite separate from solid waste, because liquid waste can damage adobe buildings. The solid waste dried quickly due to the dry climate and was transported to the farm craters. The separation of liquid and solid waste was carried out via toilets that were in use for centuries before the water closet cabinet came into use. The clever thing about Shibam's toilets was that this separation of liquid and solid

16.18 The sewage disposal system: (a) organization of a blind alley to discharge the solid and liquid waste dropping from the houses; (b) the two-outlet toilet which allows the separation of liquid and solid excrement; (c) the façade of a building equipped with sewage shafts and droppings collection baskets. Shibam, Yemen.

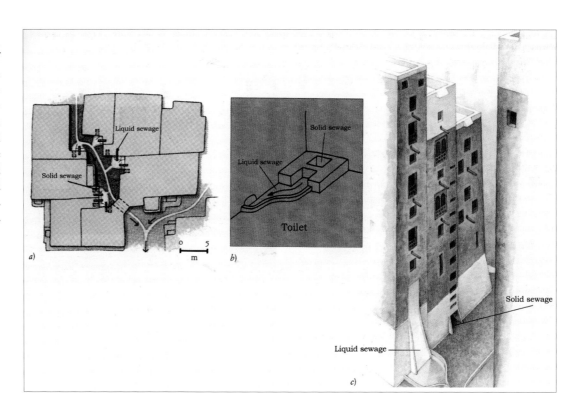

16.19 The complex tradition system (the ecosystem of Shibam). At Shibam habitation is important for the fertilization of the fields with which it interacts in an indissoluble cycle of careful utilization of resources. Human excrement, collected and dried in the sun, is converted by impounded floodwater into humus and colloidal material essential to making the desert tillable. It is also used for building and periodic renovations of the high adobe houses.

excrement happened right at the beginning. The toilets had two outlets: a front outlet for liquid waste and a back outlet for solid waste. Both were carried by gravity down to the collection baskets on the street. The buildings were constructed so they leaned slightly outwards the higher they went, like an upside-down ziggurat, so each water closet could let its contents fall down to the base of the building.

Shibam is a city whose entire town plan and architecture can at least partially be explained by its toilets. This approach reveals an understanding allowing for the organization and management of all energy exchanges from basic biological needs to the most expensive resources—in a closed cycle where all resources are used and reused over and over again.

Stone Oases: The Sassi of Matera, Italy, and Petra, Jordan

The Sassi of Matera in southern Italy are a prime example of how archaic societies lived and managed resources throughout the karst areas of Lucania, Apulia, and Sicily, which are still to this day unappreciated and unknown. The Sassi of Matera are a complex system of cave dwellings and buildings made of blocks of tufa stone obtained by digging long passageways underneath the steep slopes of a deep gorge, the Gravina. In the 1950s, the Sassi of Matera were officially declared "the shame of Italy," given the cave-like nature of their dwellings and the lack of hygienic facilities, and the entire population of the Sassi was relocated. Today, the Sassi have been acknowledged by UNESCO as being part of humankind's heritage and as an area of exceptional interest because of the brilliant solutions contained in the construction of an ecosystem that have been handed down from prehistoric times (Laureano 1993, 1994). Thanks to their new interpretation as stone oasis and man-made ecosystem, the Sassi of Matera have become a prestigious destination on an international scale. Today, they are almost wholly restored and about 5,000 inhabitants came back to live in the grotto-houses.

Since the Neolithic age, a number of techniques were developed for digging on the calcareous highland and for collecting water. These techniques have lasted in the Sassi down to the modern age. Bell-shaped cisterns, huts, and small canals were enclosed in deep ditches, forming circles or ellipses, and were therefore called entrenched villages. It is likely that the ditches were not for defense purposes but rather were used in Neolithic times for animal husbandry and farming. An analysis of aerial photographs showing where vegetation grew more thickly also shows drainage systems (Leuci 1991) used for water collection or humus collection, and mazes of corrals for agricultural and animal management. Animals were kept in enclosures and herded through passageways so they could be counted, milked, or sheared, which might explain a number of enigmatic paintings that show cows crossing thresholds. Though the customary explanation is that these were symbolic depictions of rituals they were probably rather mundane depictions of daily life as livestock herders. It is interesting to note that even today, the herders of the *Murge*—the dry highlands of the area—fence in their pasturelands in a similar manner, using more or less the same archaic shapes as did their Neolithic forebears.

The Age of Metals provided new implements that made it easier to excavate caves and pits. As the environment deteriorated, these caves became ever more attractive as human dwellings. As a matter of fact, the progressive disappearance of the plant cover left the surface villages without shelter and the land unprotected and was the cause of a shortage of wood for building and heating. The climate ranges from freezing winters to broiling summers. Water

16.20 The Sasso Barisano, one of the two large depressions forming the ancient town of Matera.

was not to be found at all in rivers or water tables; the only water was provided by torrential rainfall so it was absolutely necessary to use the techniques of collecting rainwater and storing it underground.

An increasingly popular form of courtyard dwelling around a well shaft was developed during the Neolithic age subsequent to the development of excavation techniques where tunnels radiated out from a central shaft. This dwelling model also arose in remote areas such as Matmata in Tunisia and on the dry plains of China. It was the origin of the courtyard dwelling used by the Sumerians, the Egyptians, and in the Roman and Islamic world. Indeed, an arrangement of courtyard dwellings is actually only the equivalent in buildings of what can be observed from cave dwellings. A house near the Neolithic site of Murgia Timone—across from the Sassi of Matera—proves just how effective this type of construction is. The house is rectangular in shape like the megaron of Crete and is divided into three spaces of two open rooms and a third room underground. The courtyard acts as an impluvium for water and provides a protected, open air, sunny space for the preparation of food. At the opposite end is a garden used for waste and as a compost heap that has been carved out of the rock. Very similar cultivation constructions have been found near Petra, in the Jordanian desert. The caves keep a constant temperature year round and are ideal shelters for human beings and for animals, for the storage of grain and water. After the Murgia Timone structure was discovered and freed of sediment, the underground cistern soon filled with water, even though there had been no rainfall. In other words, the device started working again, using capillary infiltration and condensation.

Even the barrows of the Bronze Age took their shape from functional and ritual water collection practices. The barrows were basically a double circle through which ran a corridor with a room excavated down the center. The structures were inserted along the excavation of archaic Neolithic walls that had been abandoned when the buildings were constructed, but were still capable of attracting moisture. What has been found in Matera is quite similar to prehistoric structures made up of barrows and underground buildings in the Sahara desert.

In Matera, original Neolithic techniques were used to create a habitat system that was adapted to the combined use of a number of different water production techniques: purification, distillation, and condensation. During the torrential rainfalls, the terracing and the water collection systems protect the slopes from erosion, and gravity pulls the water down toward the cisterns in the caves. During dry spells, the caves at night suck out the moisture in the air; the moisture condenses in the lowest underground cistern, which is always full even if it is not connected to outside canals. Multitudes of underground stories are topped by long tunnels that slope downward underground. Their slope is oriented to allow the sun's rays to penetrate down to the bottom when heat is most necessary, especially during the winter, when the sun's rays are more oblique and can penetrate the underground areas. During the warm season, when the sun is at its zenith, it shines only on the entrance to the underground caverns, which thus remain fresh and humid. Up to ten stories of caves have been discovered, one on top of another, with dozens of bell-shaped cisterns, all connected to each other by means of canals and water filter systems. A number of giant bottle-shaped caverns, with a diameter that goes from 15 to 30 m, are often found side by side and allow the water to be progressively purified as it flows.

The Sassi of Matera are the result of the evolution and urban saturation of the water collection systems of the archaic society of farmers and herders. Blocks of calcareous stones were dug out of the caves; the caves were extended outward and tended to close up in a

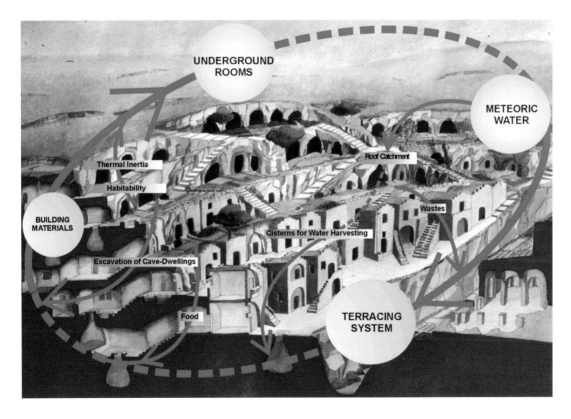

16.21 The traditional complex system (the eco-system of Matera). In the Sassi of Matera the dugout caves drain the slope and the inside of the rock, making the cavities useful and providing water storage for the inhabitants and terrace cultivations.

horseshoe shape around a terraced clearing that created a protected area, a communal courtyard called a *vicinato*. The original irrigated vegetable garden became a collective courtyard with a cistern underneath that collected the water running off the roofs. An overhang became a rooftop garden. The sideways flow of water turned into stairs and vertical connections of the urban complex. The whole arrangement of small streets and paths was formed by following the canal system, which is why the streets are so maze-like. It only looks chaotic—actually the streets follow the ancient water system. Thus, the Sassi of Matera are the result of an ingenious technology which while exploiting resources was at the same time able to preserve the environment and stave off erosion. The fact that these techniques have lasted down to the modern age allows us to understand how other "stone oases" managed to survive, even when all that is left of them are a few archeological remnants. Understanding the techniques allows us to safeguard them.

The archaeological city of Petra, Jordan, was carved out of the desert canyon by nomad tribes thousands of years ago. It is now a UNESCO World Heritage site and an endangered site. Petra's environment is undergoing a dynamic transformation. The erosion of the sandstone walls is part and parcel of geological and meteorological processes. Since Petra was abandoned from the 6th to the 8th century BCE, the crumbling of its surface has speeded up and is now proceeding at a catastrophic rate (Assante di Panzillo, et al. 1993). The presence of human beings kept the stones of Petra from crumbling. The Nabatean peoples of Petra were able to make use of the rare rainfalls that, when they came, were sudden and violent, in order to create gardens and tilled land out of the desert canyon. The so-called Nabatean farms are exemplary in terms of water production by hydrogenesis, according to water condensation methods mentioned in the Bible (Mayerson 1959), and which are now being used again in trying to till the Negev desert (Negev Institute for Arid Zone Research) (Evenari, Shanan, and Tadmor 1971). As described in ancient writings, Petra was a city of canals, basins, fountains, and gardens (Strabo, *Geography* 16.4.21; Diodorus the Sicilian, *Historical Library* 19.94). This could not be more unlike what remains of Petra, now windswept and sandblown. An urban microclimate was created by means of what might be misconstrued as aesthetic devices such as waterfalls, water lilies, and gardens, but which actually were the best protection possible for the buildings carved out of he sandstone. The plants slowed the wind; the wind no longer carried silicate sand, which acts as a harsh abrasive. The whole system of eaves and canals collected the rainwater and protected the monuments.

If Petra is to be saved, then we must think according to ancient logic and reconstruct the entire ecosystem. The UNESCO project aims at reconstructing a system of canals, terraced overhangs, and cultivated gardens in an area close to Petra, the *wadi* Al Mataha. The Nabatean system whereby the high cisterns distributed the water to basins and fountains for the irrigation of fields and gardens will be reinstated. This is an integrated project that proposes the archaeological restoration of an ecosystem so that ancient water production and cultivation systems can be made viable. Local inhabitants will be called upon to become involved both socially and economically to manage the cultivated fields and make use of the water resources. A new area of Petra that is hardly ever visited by tourists will be opened up to tourism. This project makes use of culture as a tool to protect the environment while at the same time promoting the regional economy.

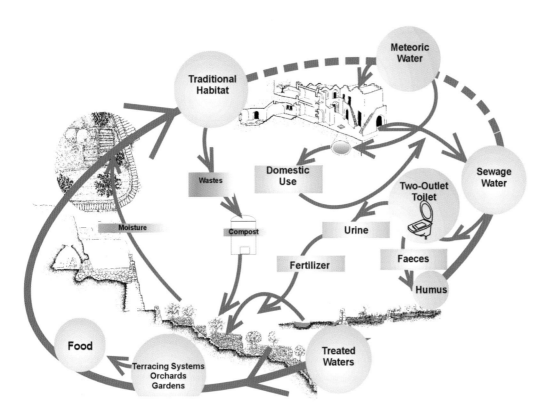

16.22 The traditional model for a new technological paradigm. Each traditional technique, remembered and safeguarded, is an exceptional heritage of experiences and knowledge which is today in danger of being lost. It is not a question of reproducing exactly the solutions in each context but rather of adopting the logic with which they operate by using advanced technologies. The cycles of nature interact with traditional urban ecosystems and demonstrate processes based on an appropriate use of resources, including the production of wastes which are not a problem, but rather materials that support the other components of the cycle.

The Oasis Model for a New Technological Paradigm

Oasis systems such as Shibam, the Sassi of Matera, and Petra show how archaic societies developed within a resource-scarce economy and survived thanks to the very innovative, prudent, and frugal management of natural resources. The reason why such cities are so aesthetically pleasing is they lived in harmony with their environment over long stretches of time. When the balance between resources and their productive use—painstakingly maintained over the centuries—is lost, then the ecosystem collapses and sets off a process of deterioration. In the Mediterranean basin and in its islands and peninsulas, in Syria, Lebanon, Mesopotamia, Palestine, Arabia, and northern Africa, the sites of the most ancient civilizations, where archeological excavations bring to light cities once surrounded by immense greenery, with fertile fields and thriving gardens, are now abandoned and buried in sand. For more than three thousand years, the process of desertification marched onward relentlessly; it worsened during the industrial age and reached catastrophic proportions since the mid-20th century.

This continuous deterioration is not due to natural and climatic conditions, but rather to indiscriminate pressures being brought to bear on natural resources. In developed countries, the traditional models of life, of production, and consumption have been cast aside in favor of a system that depletes local resources (Laureano 2001). This fosters overgrowth of the developed areas by means of massive recourse to external resources, first from the hinterland and then from more and more remote areas.

The entire planet is involved in this mechanism, which destroys our plant heritage and our landscapes. The chain of transmission of knowledge about how to deal with our environment, handed down from generation to generation over thousands of years, has been broken. The loss of this knowledge is why we are at the end of our capability to maintain and govern lands whose balance and harmony are the fruit of labor and culture. Today the natural balance of the entire planet is endangered. It is therefore necessary to plan interventions that reintegrate our cultural and historical memory of how the environment was sustained because it constitutes a strategy for the survival of all humankind.

REFERENCES

Assante di Panzillo, C., B. Bousquet, C. Jouffray, B. Lane, P. Laureano, A. Ohannessian-Charpin, J. Rewerski, and F. Zayadine. *Petra Archaeological & Natural Park-Management.* Paris: UNESCO, 1993.

Diodorus the Sicilian. *Biblioteca Storica* [Historical Library]. Palermo: Sellerio Editore, 1986.

Evenari, Michael, Leslie Shanan, and Naphtali Tadmor. *The Negev: The Challenge of a Desert.* Cambridge, MA: Harvard University Press, 1971.

Goblot, Henri. *Les Qanats, une technique d'acquisition de l'eau* [The Qanats, a technique for water collection]. Paris: Mouton, 1979.

Laureano, Pietro. "Wadi Villages and Sebkha Villages in the Saharan Ecosystem." *Environmental Design* 2(1985):16–25.

———. "The Oasis. The Origin of the Garden." *Environmental Design* 1 (1986):65–71.

———. "Les ksour du Sahara Algérien: Un exemple d'architecture globale" [The oases of the Algerian Sahara: An example of global architecture]. *ICOMOS Information* 3(July–September 1987):24–35.

———. *Giardini di Pietra, i Sassi di Matera e la civiltà mediterranea* [Stone gardens, the Sassi of Matera and Mediterranean civilization]. Torino: Bollati Boringhieri, 1993.

———. "Le complexe trogloditique des Sassi de Matera" [The troglodyte complex of the Sassi of Matera]. *Actes du Symposium International consacré au patrimoine souterrain creusé* [Proceedings of the international symposium on the carved underground heritage], ed. J. Rewerski. Saumur: CEPPSC, UNESCO, 1993, 1994.

———. *La piramide rovesciata. Il modello dell'oasi per il pianeta Terra* [The upturned pyramid. The oasis model for the Earth]. Torino: Bollati Boringhieri, 1995.

———. *Atlante d'acqua. Conoscenze tradizionali per la lotta alla desertificazione* [The Water Atlas. Traditional knowledge to combat desertification]. Torino: Bollati Boringhieri, 2001. English version ed. by UNESCO. Barcelona: Laia Libros, 2004.

Leuci, Giuseppe. "Ancora sulle opere neolitiche a Passo di Corvo (Foggia)" [Again on the works of the Neolithic Age at Passo di Corvo-Foggia]. *L'appennino meridionale* [The southern Appennines]. Naples: Annuario del Club Alpino Italiano sezione di Napoli, 1991.

Marouf, Nadir. *Lecture de l'espace oasien* [Reading of the oasis space]. Paris: Sindbad, 1980.

Mayerson, Philip. "Ancient Agricultural Remains in the Central Negev." *BASOR* 153(1959):19–31.

Strabo. *The Geography of Strabo,* trans. H. L. Jones. Cambridge, MA: Harvard University Press, 1982.

The Evolution of Settlement
Fieldwork at Zuni Pueblo 1995–97

Tony Atkin

The Zuni are indigenous people who live in the high desert region of the southwest United States along the Arizona and New Mexico border. Over the centuries they have evolved a culture and architecture that reveal the reasons and relations of their natural and communal world. These relationships are embodied in the physical form and material of their land and pueblo, the "Middle Place" of their creation and origin narratives. To a great extent, the Zuni have maintained and passed on their traditions. Their religion is still strong and viable and has been passed down with great care over the centuries. Almost all tribal members speak the Zuni language, which is now taught in the public schools, and participate in an extremely active ritual calendar. The human experience, expression, symbolism, and values of the Zuni are revealed in the physical form of the pueblo, and comprise a significant cultural resource.

Although relatively stable and strong, Zuni culture is threatened by the surrounding dominant culture as well as social and material problems within the pueblo. With the advent of the automobile and federally funded housing on adjacent land, the settlement has suburbanized, resulting in the depopulation and gradual erosion of the historic core. New housing, largely paid for by the U.S. Department of Housing and Urban Development, has been built as freestanding single-family units in subdivisions that spread out from the historic pueblo, or in the relatively new town of Black Rock, five miles away. Many Zuni would like to revitalize the center and rehabilitate the old pueblo, find culturally appropriate methods of new construction, and conserve their natural landscape and tribal resources.

The Zuni culture survives in many of its original forms, perhaps because of the tribe's remote location, somewhat autonomous economy, and the religious and political conservatism of its leaders. It seems that the architectural form of the pueblo has never been static—in fact, the contrary. The evidence is that the Zuni have continually reconstructed their pueblo. Since photographic records, surveys, and measured drawings were made beginning in the mid-19th century, the pueblo's form has evolved through many changes of materials, density, occupation, and social relations while keeping the same general plan and pattern of settlement. The loss of the need to defend themselves, along with the overwhelming technological forces of the 20th century—including automobiles, electricity, and plumbing (installed in 1961)—have dramatically altered the outline, massing, and form of the habitation structures. However, the locations of the six *kivas* (clan-affiliated ceremonial rooms), dance plazas, and religious pathways have maintained their integrity and positions to a remarkable degree over time.

The surrounding terrain of buttes, arroyos, and distant mountains has greatly influenced Zuni life. The mark of prior human habitation can be very slight in the Southwest; built forms

17.1 Zuni waffle gardens
and village beyond, from an
historic photograph.

grow out of and are continuous with the natural forms and materials of the region. The present
pueblos are thought to be the descendents of great prehistoric sites of tremendous sophistication
such as the Chaco Culture complex in northwestern New Mexico, which reached its zenith in
the 13th century—perhaps Pueblo Bonito or some other Chacoan great house is the "great
white house" of the Keres origin narrative described by Alfonso Ortiz (1969), the eminent
Southwestern anthropologist from San Juan Pueblo. Methods of masonry construction similar
to those at Chaco are in plentiful evidence at Zuni.

After Chaco Canyon and other northern New Mexico sites were abandoned, pueblo
societies developed along the Rio Grande and farther west in New Mexico and Arizona.
Agricultural methods were mostly designed to maximize food production in a very dry climate.
Rain, or its absence, is a major focus of pueblo ritual. Large-scale irrigation has been used since
at least the time of Chaco, but at Zuni there was also a unique development called a "waffle"
garden, which describes a grid of little cells made of 5- or 6-in high earthen walls surrounding
a planting bed about 20 in^2. Each cell provided sustenance and protection for a single plant
and made irrigation with a water jug relatively easy. Besides holding the irrigation water, the
little earthen walls capture dew at night and prevent the desiccation of the young plant from
the wind. In traditional Zuni building, there is great continuity in the materials and form of
the architecture, landscape, and site. Many photographs taken in the early 20th century show
the stepped housing blocks with earthen roofs; a middle ground of corrals, gardens, enclosed
workspaces, courtyards, and pathways; and finally the larger landscape beyond.

The roofs of the Zuni are justly famous. They are flat, habitable, earth-covered platforms
that were used for everything from food preparation and drying to doubling as an amphitheater
for observation of ritual ceremonies in the plazas. Many of the roofs contain woodpiles and

hornos, the domed ovens introduced by the Spanish that became a ubiquitous feature of the pueblo. Each family has at least one of these outdoor ovens. On feast days, the combined aromas of baking bread and the juniper bough brooms used to clean out the ovens are pungent and memorable.

The 20th century brought great changes to the pueblo. The original Zuni construction method for walls used gathered ledge stones that were sorted and set in mud mortar with a mud plaster finish and sometimes a kind of whitewash covering made of *kechipa*, a material composed of fine silicates. In the late 1920s, St. Anthony's Mission was established north of Zuni in another attempt to convert the Zuni to Roman Catholicism. Two Italian masons were brought in to build the mission and taught some of the Zuni how to quarry, dress, and lay up the local stone in the "Italian" manner. This resulted in walls of dressed stone here and there throughout the pueblo with arched windows and mud or lime mortar joints. This type of construction became the norm in the 1930s and 40s and is now considered by many Zunis to be a traditional Zuni masonry technique. The Zuni were never completely converted to

17.3 A new gable and
tarpaper roof on
an old house.

17.4 Early 20th century
masonry, now considered
traditional.

Catholicism. As recently as the 1960s, the Catholic Church within the village was in ruins. Then, the tribe accepted an offer from the U.S. Park Service to restore and stabilize the structure. Currently, no Roman Catholic services are performed there and the interior has been painted with murals of Zuni gods and ceremonies.

Developments in the 20th century were not kind to the pueblo form. Several of the six remaining *kivas* are falling in, with two having collapsed completely and one abandoned. Some have been closed because the roofs are unsafe. It seems the preferred conveyance for contemporary Zuni is a brightly colored pickup truck, and cars and trucks are driven everywhere, including throughout the old pueblo, contributing to its structural instability and deterioration.

17.5 Contemporary Zuni (1996) including (right) traditional stone and earth walls, extended *vigas* and roof projections, along with (left) picture windows, T-111 siding, and the ubiquitous shiny pickup truck.

17.6 Zuni *ad hoc* construction. Each family in the village has an outdoor oven (*horno*) like the two on the right.

Many industrialized materials are now used in repairs and reconstruction, including concrete block, Portland cement, manufactured doors, and aluminum-frame picture windows. There is a lot of *ad hoc* construction—for example, old *vigas*, the traditional pine or fir roof beams, supported by a new concrete block wall.

The flat roofs of Zuni have been very useful but difficult to maintain over the centuries, and they have greatly deteriorated since the Zuni discontinued their traditional ritual maintenance. Many of the buildings have a new gabled tarpaper roof simply placed on top of the old flat roof, which remains inside. The austere pueblo interior seen in early photographs has become filled with televisions, couches, and pictures of the grandchildren, but may still contain ritual

objects and pottery. Tourism and stylistic promotion have in some cases overwhelmed the ancient cultural practices of the area. Under the auspices of the office of Housing and Urban Development, the United States government has subsidized culturally inappropriate and poor-quality frame housing built in a suburban Levittown pattern.

THE SURVEY

In 1995, 1996, and 1997, the Department of Architecture at the University of Pennsylvania joined Cornerstones Community Partnerships, a New Mexico–based community preservation organization, and Zuni tribal members in a project to document the most historic part of Zuni Pueblo. Ed Crocker, Cornerstones' technical director, and his assistants had been involved since 1990 with the preservation of some of the pueblo buildings at the request of the Zuni tribal council. The joint documentation project offered the hope of finding the cause of and proposing solutions for the many structural and material problems that were in evidence in the old pueblo at the time. In the process of this assessment, a record was made of the pueblo's form and condition in the late 20th century, which can be compared to prior surveys, descriptions, and drawings such as those by Mindeleff (1891), Kroeber (1917), Stubbs (1950), and Ohio State University for the Historic American Buildings Survey (1972).

During the course of the survey, many aspects of the pueblo's unique spatial and temporal aggregation were revealed. These attributes demonstrate the continuation of certain settlement configurations that tie the Pueblo to its extraordinary site and embody Zuni history and culture.

Halona:wa, site of the present Zuni village, is a very important archaeological site, but the top layer is still occupied and forms the center of Zuni life and identity. Since the mid-19th century the Zuni Pueblo has been extensively photographed, and examination of these records reveals that the surface structures and elements have constantly been remodeled. However, the contemporary pueblo physically rests on the ancient structure and spatial typologies, and the pueblo form continues as the locus of Zuni cultural memory and practice.

The Zuni village of Hawikku, about 20 mi to the southwest of the contemporary Zuni Pueblo, was the site of the first European contact with the Pueblo Indians in the Southwest, but was abandoned sometime before 1680. In the survey drawings by Hodge (1937), one can see the settlement pattern later established at Halona:wa, the present central Zuni village. Halona:wa was occupied at least by 1540, when the Spanish came to the Southwest. Then, however, it was probably a much smaller place, an outlier of the major village at Hawikku. After the Pueblo Revolt of 1680–90 (see Ferguson and Preucel, Chapter 14 in this volume), the whole tribe of six villages consolidated into a single pueblo at Halona:wa. At this time the settlement greatly expanded and surrounded the Catholic church, which was constructed originally at the edge of the village in 1629–30.

The United States government began mapping Zuni lands during the Mexican-American War in the 1840s. In 1857 a survey party run by Edward Beale brought the first wagons and even camels to the Southwest to test their suitability as a method of transport in the American desert. After a series of wars and military actions, the neighboring Navajo were subjugated in 1868. The Zuni and other pueblos assisted the U.S. government because the Navajo had long been their traditional enemy. The first comprehensive mapping of Zuni, done by Victor and Cosmos Mindeleff, two Russian brothers, was completed in 1881 and published in 1891 by the newly established U.S. Bureau of Ethnology. They used a compass and tape to show the aggregated housing blocks in plan. They made no elevations, but the lighter shading on their plan indicates the upper levels of what was then a five- or six-story complex. They also surveyed and drew many of the details of Zuni and Hopi construction.

The year 1879 was the beginning of the era of the great ethnological gold rush at Zuni. Frank Hamilton Cushing (1857–1900), a member of the first Smithsonian expedition, moved into the Zuni governor's house and eventually became a Bow Priest. Cushing wrote many of

17.8 Contemporary Pueblo interior.

17.9 Mindeleff's plan of
Zuni published in 1891.
Lighter shading represents
upper levels.

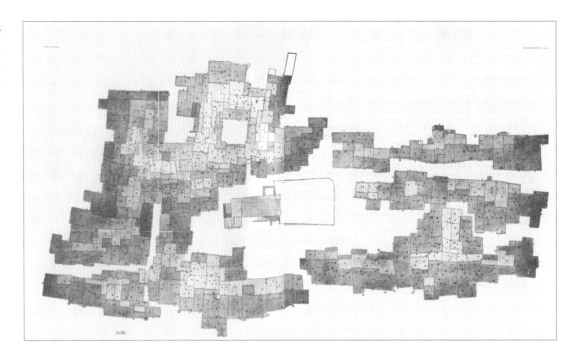

the most informative reports about Zuni and publicized his expereinces with the tribe in widely circulated American popular magazines in the late 19th century. Posthumous publications (1920, 1941, 1988) continue to form the basis of comparison for the study of Zuni history, though the Zunis seem conflicted about Cushing today and question some of his statements and aggressive behavior.

In 1915 and 1916, the anthropologist A. L. Kroeber spent two summers of fieldwork at Zuni Pueblo. As a part of his study, he surveyed and produced a new plot of the pueblo because it had changed substantially since the Mindeleffs' 1881 plan. He stated, "the town has altered in too many respects since 1881 to make Mindeleff's excellent plot of that date serviceable at present" (Kroeber 1917). In fact, Kroeber noted, three *kivas* had changed their location.

Kroeber's work was first published in "Zuni Kin and Clan" in 1917. He concluded that while the outlines of the house blocks bore remarkable similarity to the survey done thirty-five years before, almost every house in the pueblo (at least those visible on the exterior) had been reconstructed. New houses, or parts of new houses, had been built with larger rooms and somewhat higher ceilings. Many of the uppermost rooms seen on the Mindeleff plan had been dismantled or had collapsed. Construction practices were not made to support the five- and six-story buildings recorded by Mindeleff, and were unstable at this height.

Although Kroeber said it "would have been of the greatest interest to know the interior" (e.g., stories under the roofs) he was not allowed to enter. "The Zuni regard their roofs as public highways, and were entirely indifferent to a survey being made. Their homes, on the other hand, they feel to be private, and any attempt to enter all the inner and lower chambers at will would be impossible" (Kroeber 1917:189 90). He states that many of the stone walls were "curvilinear," from their covering with many layers of mud plaster and a general lack of concern with skilled masonry. He describes the major "K'ochina plaza," which is still in use, as being "filled in," about 28 ft above his benchmark at the southwest side of the pueblo near the Zuni River. "This court is said by the [Zuni] to be well above ground level. When the houses that formerly occupied this area were abandoned and pulled down, their lower two stories, or possibly three, were filled in [creating the present level of the plaza]."

Kroeber continues: "It is likely that this was an old procedure. The streets and courts of the town gradually rose from the accumulation of refuse, the wash from the earth roofs and mud plaster walls, and the blow of sand and dust until chambers that originally were level with the ground became partly or wholly subterranean. New stories were raised upon the old walls and the lowest floors filled in" (194). Kroeber goes on to say that between July 19 and August 8, 1915, after some unusually heavy rains, at least half a dozen houses had fallen in or been torn down.

This constant reconstruction was not a situation solely related to lack of structural integrity or the use of earthen materials. Kroeber cites the Zuni custom of improving and if possible rebuilding one's house after being "designated one of the hosts of a Shalako god in the great December ritual." *Shalako* is the Zuni ritual performed near the winter solstice, when the gods return to the village to bless it. Typically, eight houses are built or rebuilt each year, to precise specifications, including the kitchen location and the provision of a large room for ceremonial dancing. This room is built without a floor to accommodate the 10' tall height of the *Shalako*, and, one suspects, to connect the ceremony directly to the earth. After the ceremony, the floor is filled in and the space becomes the family's living room. The *Shalako* god enters the new building to the chants and prayers of the inhabitants, and dances until dawn.

I attended this remarkable two-day ceremony in December 1994. The new houses constructed for the ceremony were all made of concrete block and were located a mile or two from the old village, but the surpassing beauty and mystery of the ceremony still have great power. The Zuni spectators seated in the great, long room looked on with quiet attention as a mixture of corn meal and ground turquoise was placed in the corners of the room. Long monotonous chants were punctuated by a flurry of activity and the sharp clack of the God's beak, as well as visits by the mudheads (*Koyemshi*), warriors (*Salimobiya*), and others representing the Gods. Costumes included rabbit pelts and pine boughs, masks and elaborate headresses. Steaming bowls of lamb and *posole* corn stew were served to everyone about 1 a.m., including outsiders who were allowed to observe the ceremony through the windows or through a slot in the kitchen wall. I felt after the long night of dancing and chanting that even this new construction of industrialized materials had become spiritually embedded in the Middle Place.

At least two subsequent surveys documented the evolution of the pueblo. Stanley Stubbs (1950) took aerial photographs in 1948, when the suburbanization of the village really began. By this time, the multi-story housing blocks were no longer in the central core, and many of the inhabitants had moved to surrounding locations. The old pueblo was still surrounded by gardens and pens for livestock. A survey was conducted in 1972 by Ohio State University for the Historic American Buildings Survey, using photogrammetric mapping techniques (Borchers 1972). This survey was used as a base drawing and a comparison for our survey work in the 1990s.

Eighty years after Kroeber, we were able to verify some of his speculations. Because as architects we were expected to know something about structures and materials, we were allowed into the interior of one of the oldest house blocks when a retreat room in the interior collapsed. The Zuni trainees made emergency repairs, and the tribal administration decided to pursue a complete survey of this entire section of the village to see what might be done to stop the further collapse of the old floors and walls. The Lieutenant Governor of the pueblo took us around and introduced us to the resident families, who allowed us to survey and measure all but a few rooms that were said

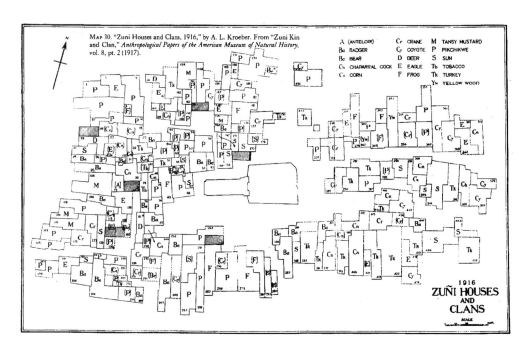

17.10 Kroeber's plan of
Zuni showing clans and Kiva
locations first published
in 1917.

17.11 Aerial photograph of
Zuni in 1949.

to contain religious materials. Ownership of the houses in the old village is matrilineal, and it was invariably a mother or grandmother who gave us permission to do the measurements.

We worked with Zuni mentors and young trainees, using measuring tapes to triangulate the exterior spaces, a straight edge with a telescopic sight and plane table called an alidade, and a water level (a method of establishing elevations in blind situations) for measuring heights and

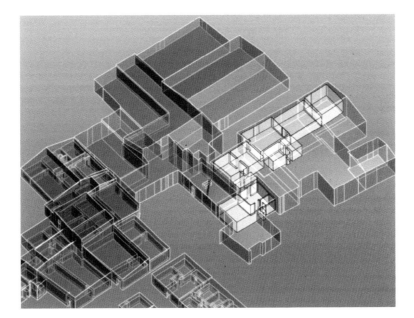

the interior elevations of the rooms. Students made both a cardboard model and a computer model of the parts of the pueblo that we studied.

The housing blocks we surveyed are made up of aggregated and, in many cases, interconnected rooms. These modules of Zuni building are somewhere around 12 or 14 ft wide by about 15 or 16 ft across, dimensions based on the technology of the stone and earthen walls and span of the wooden beams (*vigas*) that support the roofs. The modules vary within these physical limits (recent rooms are larger) and are also combined in a variety of ways. Individual families occupy an interconnected collection of rooms, some with multiple levels that wind around and through the form of the pueblo.

17.14 Survey drawings
(1995–97) of plans of
northeast housing blocks.

Our survey area surrounded the primary plaza, which is a remarkable architectural space. From the surrounding roofs, one is on the rim of a concave space that connects to the ground and to the center of the plaza. Looking up, on the horizon is Dowa Yalanne, the sacred corn mountain, which, even though a great distance away, forms the enclosing fourth wall of the plaza. At the time of the survey, many of the buildings surrounding the plaza were in poor condition, but they are transformed into a community amphitheater during rituals and dances that regularly occur there with all the observers sitting and standing on the roofs. We were told that the plaza area is the place in the Zuni origin narrative where the great water spider (who had a leg in each of the oceans) touched its breast to the ground and showed the Zuni where to establish their village.

The survey team was able to test the idea reported by Kroeber that there were two or three levels of buried houses under the plaza at Zuni. We were allowed to drill small core samples in three locations, confirming that contemporary Zuni is on a tell, a mound built up over centuries, that is made of the materials of former dwellings. It is, to my knowledge, the most extensive site of this kind in North America. Parts of some of the Hopi villages have no doubt been constructed in the same way. At Acoma Pueblo, some of the housing blocks near the edge of the mesa rest on lower rooms, and the St. Esteban del Rey Church stands on the pre-contact village that was destroyed and leveled by the Spanish in the 16th century. Our core samples at Zuni indicated that the present housing blocks to the northwest of the church sit on layers of older habitations between 16 and 32 ft deep.

We found that rooms on the outer layer of the housing blocks had been completely rebuilt in recent decades, some of them as recently as the early 1990s. However, some of the inner rooms have been maintained. They are quite old, the heart of the pueblo. The contemporary pueblo surrounds and rests on these ancient rooms.

As part of our survey work, we were admitted into some of these interior rooms. A dendrochronological analysis by the University of Arizona Tree-Ring Research Lab in

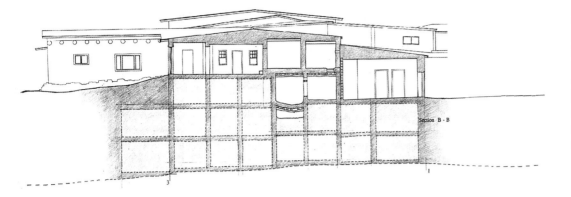

November 1987 from the *vigas* in one of these interior rooms west of the plaza gives harvest dates ranging from 1665 to 1699, about the time the Zuni came down off Dowa Yalanne, where they lived during the Pueblo Revolt, and when all the separate Zuni communities joined at the present site of Halona:wa. According to these tree ring dates, the room containing these *vigas* was probably built in the late 1600s.

We entered the housing block from the plaza through a new room, the living room of one of the families. Beyond was the room that was dated by dendrochronology, subdivided by a thin juniper post and mud plaster (*jacal*) wall. We went farther in to a third room, where the floor had partially collapsed, and a room below that, partially filled with earth, could be entered through a worn stone hatch. Apparently many of the rooms below the present grade were collapsed and built over as Kroeber stated, but at least in this case the lower room remained accessible.

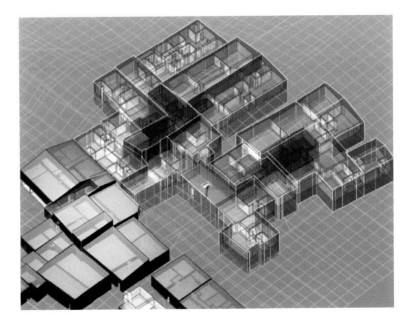

17.16 Computer rendering of northeast housing blocks showing central and lower areas of remaining ancient rooms (shaded red) surrounded by modern construction.

17.17 View of plaza looking north in 1996.

The Design Studio

In addition to the survey, our design work involved us in several Zuni, Cornerstones, and federally sponsored youth training programs. The students were able to join in, to quarry and lay up stone walls, to make adobe pressed blocks, and to prepare and apply mud plaster finishes. We helped the Zuni build several walls in the manner taught by the Italian masons from the 1920s and also completed some demonstration adobe walls.

To build these walls we used a machine that makes pressed-block "adobes." The earth is tossed into a large hopper and the machine compresses it into a cohesive brick, producing five to ten bricks per minute. The pressed block does not have to dry in the sun like a traditional adobe. It can be put immediately in the wall, which saves a great deal of time in construction.

We tested certain modern systems for their compatibility with traditional materials and methods. We tried EPDM composite rubber roofing under a packed earth cover to see if we could fix the difficulties with the flat roofs. This worked well enough in demonstration, but we were unable to apply it on an actual roof in the pueblo. We tested different kinds of mud plaster additives to make the surface plaster stronger. We also built a new waffle garden for one of the Zuni grandmothers. After she chose the site, we made a large adobe wall on the north with a stone coping as a heat sink to help extend the growing season and a traditional coyote fence on the west to moderate the wind. It included a little stone seat on which to rest in the sun.

Finally, the students made some proposals for rebuilding within the old village and designs for new housing outside it. Among other projects, they proposed an alternative development to the HUD-sponsored subdivisions, consisting of six housing units along an arroyo near Black Rock. After interviewing several families scheduled for new houses, we proposed that the new units be made out of native materials—adobe walls with stone foundations—but with a modern service core for electricity and water. The automobile traffic is kept to one side, and on the other we proposed to reestablish some of the community gardens and work space that were

17.18 View of plaza roofs looking north in 2000. Plywood door at bottom right is same as plywood door at plaza on left of Figure 17.17. Top two stories are new construction.

once a part of the old pueblo. We also tried to imagine ways to use the land so the buildings would fit with the topography and work with the hydrology of the soil in beneficial ways. The Zuni we worked with were excited by the proposal but it was not accepted by the local HUD administrator at the time.

The experience of working with contemporary Zuni was extraordinary. Some of the young Zuni came to Philadelphia and saw Zuni tribal objects on display and in the storage rooms of the University of Pennsylvania Museum of Archaeology and Anthropology, which has an extensive collection. They also visited the studio at Penn and worked with the students on their projects. At the end of each of the three years of the study we went back to the Zuni Pueblo and presented the students' work to the community. It was a significant educational experience for the students to receive the Zuni's response to their work. The students found the study to be particularly meaningful in their own self-identification and maturation, through direct interaction with a venerable native culture and its evolving relationship to a unique site.

I re-visited the village in the spring of 2000 and 2004. Exterior parts of some of the housing blocks had again been rebuilt. The new rooms were constructed of conventional 2x6 framing with stone veneer, quarried, and laid up by many of the Zuni trainees and mentors with whom we had worked on the documentation and training project. Applied (non-structural) beam ends, representing *vigas*, indicate the ceiling and floor levels. An architect from Albuquerque provided drawings for this "pueblo-style" reconstruction, the most recent in a long and continuous process of rebuilding the pueblo exterior. Although these recent remodelings might be seen as a nostalgic image of historic Zuni, they were accomplished by Zuni workers using local stone, a marked improvement over building practices in 1994. So far as could be seen, the older interior rooms we measured had not been affected. However, at least one house that contained an interesting historic fireplace and stone floors had been remodeled with new vinyl floors, drywall ceilings, and electrical wiring.

17.19 Project for new affordable housing designed by University of Pennsylvania students Patrick Eeley and Gabriella Seca.

In this regard, Zuni makes a striking contrast to other historic sites in the Southwest that have been meticulously restored and frozen in time. Contemporary Zuni sits on and around its ancient site, and the tribe continues to inhabit, modify, and constantly rebuild the topmost and exterior layers of their settlement, as they have done for many centuries.

References

Cushing, Frank Hamilton. *Zuni Breadstuff*. New York: Museum of the American Indian, 1920.

———. *My Adventures in Zuni*. Santa Fe, NM: Peripatetic Press, 1941.

———. *The Mythic World of the Zuni*, ed. and ill. Barton Wright. Albuquerque, NM: University of New Mexico Press, 1988.

Ferguson, T. J., and Richard E. Hart. *A Zuni Atlas*. Norman, OK: University of Oklahoma Press, 1985.

Hodge, Frederick Webb. *History of the Hawikuh, New Mexico: One of the So-Called Cities of Cibola*. Los Angeles, CA: Ward Ritchie Press, 1937.

Kroeber, A. L. "Zuni Kin and Clan." *Anthropological Papers of the American Museum of Natural History* 8,2(1917):39–204.

Mindeleff, Victor. "A Study of Pueblo Architecture." *Eighth Annual Report of the Bureau of Ethnology*, Washington, DC: USGPO, 1891.

Stubbs, Stanley A. *Bird's Eye View of the Pueblos*. Norman, OK: University of Oklahoma Press, 1950.

Webb, William, and Robert A. Weinstein. *Dwellers at the Source: Southwestern Indian Photographs of A. C. Vroman 1895–1904*. Albuquerque, NM: University of New Mexico Press, 1973.

The Primitive Origins of Modern Architecture

Le Corbusier's Voyage to the East

M. Christine Boyer

18

Charles-Edouard Jeanneret, known to us now as Le Corbusier, made what has been called a reversed grand tour, leaving from Berlin in 1911. Instead of going to Rome first, he went to Istanbul. His travel articles, letters to his mentor and friend William Ritter, with further recollections added between 1914 and 1916, were assembled into a small square book entitled *Le Voyage d'Orient*, published posthumously at the beginning of 1966 and in English as *Journey to the East* in 1989. Le Corbusier was a good storyteller, and, as Vladimir Propp suggested, all quests start with the central character missing a specific attribute, whether he or she recognizes it or not. The hero sets off in search for what is missing, and the quest propels the narrative forward. Defined as a rite of passage, the journey becomes a testing ground full of struggles in which the hero is transformed and finally achieves a new status. The hero, Jeanneret, must end up in a different place from where he begins and must solve the enigma at the heart of the tale. The voyage between is uncertain and full of tension and unexpected surprises. The unwinding of the journey becomes the space of his story, and it is rich in meaning. This chapter will offer only a brief outline of some of the point plots around which Jeanneret's narrative unfolds.

"Prayer on the Acropolis"

As recollections of his youthful travels at the end of his life, the reversed tour (Vogt 1987) is an idea that Jeanneret may have borrowed from Ernest Rénan's "Prayer on the Acropolis" (1883), a chapter in a small booklet that he purchased in Athens in 1911 (Turner 1977). A late 19th century Oriental philologist, Rénan cherished the power of science and men of action. In his later years, after the events of the world ceased to absorb his whole being, Rénan had many memories that he presented in *Recollections of My Youth* (1883), including his "Prayer on the Acropolis." At Athens, in 1865, he first experienced a strong impulse to look behind him. What was this backward impulse that Rénan expressed, this reversed tour across his lifetime back to a place where, at least for Rénan, perfection in art, literature, and philosophy existed? The Acropolis defied comparison; it was absolute space, something that existed only once as a constant referent. His prayer on the Acropolis was recognition that its perfection had been a point of departure and focal point for the work of his entire life. Progress, he argued, took its point of departure from a "profound respect for the past"; hence his adherence to the lessons of his youth had made him a free and independent spirit (Chadbourne 1968:125, 136). Had Rénan successfully achieved his goal of absolute honesty? Had he kept an ideal vision alive?

His prayer, which he imagined he created on the Acropolis when he had succeeded in understanding its perfect beauty, its absolute truth, was probably sketched in Athens in 1865, then completed 11 years later in 1876. As his powerful maxim proclaimed: "What we say of ourselves is always poetry" (Chadbourne 1968:125). Rénan willfully wrote his life less factual than imagined as an exemplary fiction worthy of being emulated in the future. He envisioned his ideal life as whole, its purpose to create a higher harmony out of discords and opposites, to preserve intact a dualistic nature combining rational intellect with emotional instincts, childlike sensibility and candor with mature somber struggles and wisdom.

As Rénan created his truth of being through writing, so Jeanneret forged his own autobiographical myth. He too would ask at the end of his life, as Le Corbusier, if the words of his lifetime had been truthful and precise communications—like the Parthenon, the perfect poem written in stone. Had they moved you?

H. Allen Brooks claims in *Le Corbusier's Formative Years* (1997) that this voyage of self-discovery to the East remained a vivid experience in Jeanneret's mind, a central trope mentioned in each of his future books, because during this trip his ideals were shaped. He returned from this rite of passage, as Brooks argues, mature and whole, his past integrated with his present. But Jeanneret was a mere 24 years of age at the time of the trip, still with much to learn and many inversions and fictitious inventions to make. It seems that Jeanneret remained politically unaware throughout his trip to the East. He chose not to discuss the political tensions wracking the Balkans or the territorial disintegration of the Ottoman Empire as Austria-Hungary and Italy annexed some of its lands. These tensions would erupt into the first Balkan War in 1912, a war that pitted Greece, Montenegro, Bulgaria, and Serbia against the weakened Ottoman Empire. While the voyage to the East may have been an informative journey of self-discovery, care needs to be taken about what was discovered and what may have been invented.

The Orient on the Map of Europe

Jeanneret stayed in Istanbul 51 days. Most of his articles concern his journey down the Danube and through the Balkans, and his experiences in Istanbul. In contrast, the ritual of the Grand Tour, which by the end of the 17th century had become obligatory for the elite of northern Europe, usually consisted of a trip across the Alps and through upper and central Italy to study monuments and landscapes. Its ultimate goal was a prolonged stay in Rome. The Grand Tour was an ascent to lofty regions, the natural heights of the mountains and the cultural heights of Italy and Rome. It was a journey of contrasts and comparisons: lands of rainy weather/sunny weather, of wealth/poverty, past/present, progress/backwardness. Although the requisite Grand Tour was a thing of the past by the early 20th century, still Jeanneret would experience the same set of contrasts even though his journey was reversed. He traveled from folk art to classical art, through the plains of Eastern Europe to the heights of Mount Athos and the Acropolis, from being a painter to being an architect.

During the difficult time he had spent in Berlin and Munich in 1910–11, Jeanneret longed to take a soothing voyage of escape, where he could study in a paradoxical manner both folk art and the origins of classical art. He had a romantic desire to study what more advanced civilizations had left behind. He was influenced by the writings of Alexandre Cingria-Vaneyre, who recommended travel to Greece and the area around Constantinople in order to study

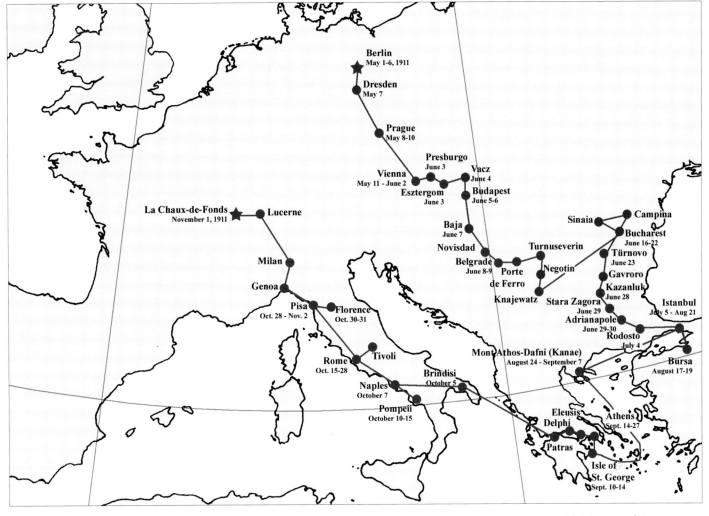

18.1 Jeanneret's journey.

those mountainous landscapes with their architecture of simplified geometric shapes and right-angled universal forms with large unbroken wall surfaces. When color was applied it was in natural earthy tones of olive green and ochres offset by white walls of marble and whitewash, and it was this architecture and these colors that Cingria-Vaneyre advocated for the Suisse-Romande (Turner 1977:237).

Nevertheless, in a long letter to his teacher, L'Éplattenier, Jeanneret continued to write of his desire to visit Rome, to study classical architecture and "to create *volumes which play under the light* in rhythms based on geometrical shapes; joy of form rediscovered for a feast of the eyes" (Brooks 1997:245). Travel to the East was condoned neither by L'Éplattenier nor Jeanneret's father, and thus marked a defiant gesture of independence on Jeanneret's part

Jeanneret had by this time also met his great mentor, William Ritter, a prolific novelist and biographer who was also an art and music critic for several European journals. A friend of Cingria-Vaneyre, he too was interested in re-examining the roots of classical tradition and the myths of ancient Greece. Ritter was an enthusiastic adventurer who traveled throughout Eastern Europe and the Balkans, and in 1910 he published a romantic novel of peasant life in Slovakia, *L'Entêtement Slovaque* [Slavic Infatuation]. No doubt this anthropological account stressing the simple Slavic houses that seemed to spring naturally from the soil added to Jeanneret's interest to experience for himself the lands and people of the exotic East (Brooks 1997:218, 501; Gresleri 1987:349–50). By 1910, it was generally accepted among historians that European civilization had its origin not in Greece or Rome but in the far older civilizations of Egypt, Judea, Babylonia, and Assyria, and this may have added intrigue to Jeanneret's quest for physical difference and cultural displacement.

The East or Orient was still an empty place on the map that Europeans drew; it had yet to be reshaped in the image of the West or annexed by colonial empires. A late 19th century concept, the Orient was used specifically to designate the Ottoman Empire, depicting it as an apathetic empire of negligent rulers and sluggish people. All regions once ruled by the Turks, such as the Balkans and Greece, were considered contaminated by Oriental influences and stuck in a primitive stage of development. As non-European "others" they would be excised from the map of the West in the Balkan wars of 1912–13. Whatever the West was, the East was the opposite. If the West was self-characterized by a penchant for rationality, an enlightened land of democracy and economic dynamism, industry, and culture, then the East was a quasi-mythological obscure place of marvels and mysteries, a land of despots, economic stagnation, and folklore as Jeanneret marked on his map (Lewis and Wigen 1997).

Meanwhile Jeanneret had also met his lifelong friend, August Klipstein, who was writing a doctoral dissertation on "El Greco" and was interested in studying the influences of Byzantine icons on the iconography of the painter (Gresleri 1987:216). The two young men decided to travel together, taking the Balkan route to the East. Klipstein and Jeanneret departed on May 25, 1911, for a five-month trip through the Balkans to Constantinople, Mount Athos, and Athens. Jeanneret would experience both rapturous surrender and an invasive alien power, and he would in the end perceive a crucial difference between Stamboul and Athens.

Learning to Write

Architectural historians pay selective attention to Jeanneret's writings and rhetorical style, placing more emphasis on their architectural and sometimes urban references. They tend to quote at random from his writings without analyzing the development of ideas from one book to another. They seem confused by his paradoxical mode of reasoning that combines supposedly incompatible themes such as folk art and classical art, the primitive and the technological. In particular they have not placed much emphasis on the fact that Jeanneret undertook this voyage as a painter, opening himself to the sensuous influence of pottery and local fabrics. He saw things in colors—the bright elaborate pinks, ochres, azure blues of the Balkans, or the gold and bronze tones, the reds, blacks, and dark greens of Byzantine icons. He was fascinated by the hand-made curves of Syrian pots and the feminine mystery of women in veils. And he wanted to commit these visual impressions to words. Only in 1914–16 in La Chaux-de-Fonds did Jeanneret consider himself to be an architect, or a builder, at which time he inserted his Greek recollections into the text.

At the end of *Journey to the East*, on October 10, 1911, Jeanneret added an epilogue in the form of a confession:

> I have finished at last! I wanted "to commit myself," to be obliged to pursue it to the very end. I thought it would be nice to have living memories of this journey. These

notes are lifeless; the beauties I have seen always break down under my pen; there were murderous repetitions. That would bore me and torment me for hours, disheartening hours of vexation, of despair. . . . During my hours of gold, ivory, and crystal, there were flaws, stains, and cracks—because of these notes that I so wanted to write! I didn't know my own language, I have never studied it! (266)

It is clear that Jeanneret wanted to be a writer, to communicate to others his thoughts, impressions, and experiences throughout his lifetime. Thus the more than 45 books he wrote should be treated as literary endeavors worthy of analysis in their own right. Le Corbusier would finish his final piece of writing, a little book entitled *Mise au Point* [Bringing into Focus] in July 1965, the same month that he corrected the French manuscript of *Journey to the East*. Mise au Point opens: "Nothing is transmissible but thought. Over the years a man gradually acquires, through his struggles, his work, his inner combat, a certain capital, his own individual and personal conquest. But all the passionate questions of the individual, all that capital, that experience so dearly paid for, will disappear. The law of life: death. Nature shuts off all activity by death. Thought alone, the fruit of labor, is transmissible" (Le Corbusier 1997:83). Toward the end of the book he noted that after rereading *Le Voyage d'Orient,* he found "that the line of conduct of little Charles-Edouard Jeanneret at the time of *Le Voyage d'Orient* was the same as that of Père Corbu" (1997:100).

Le Corbusier's attempt in the beginning and in the end of his life was to transmit thought through words, no matter how limited or inaccurate they might be (Le Corbusier 1997:60, 74). His French identity card from the time he became a nationalized citizen in 1930 gave his profession as "Homme de Lettres." He did not declare himself to be either an architect or a painter. Writing was a lifelong endeavor, another mode of expression that occupied him like painting, architecture, photography, and cinema. The travel journals that Jeanneret kept on his trip to the East were his testing ground as a writer. They contain a mélange of different writing styles, for he borrowed from *The Art of Building Cities*, written by the Viennese architectural historian Camillo Sitte in 1889, a method of writing in sharp contrasts, juxtaposing cities and places that he disliked against those he liked. He drew great inspiration from the flowery picture-writings of Ritter's colorful depictions of peasant life, handcrafts, simple houses, and landscape settings (Brooks 1997:237). But most important of all was the influence of the fin-de-siècle Turkophile, travel writer, and novelist, Pierre Loti, who wrote *Aziyadé* (1879), *Le Marriage de Loti: Fantôme d'Orient* (1892), and *Les Désenchantées* (1910), among others.

Loti was actually Julien Viaud, a French naval officer and diplomat. His double, however, was immersed in the sensuous East, especially Turkey, adopting the local dress, habits, and language and exploiting the women in every port of call. His discourse was a tapestry of autobiographical accounts, travel lessons, and journal notes. His tone was nostalgic, his passion articulated in somber refrains, for he mourned the lost of an "authentic" East as it falsely mimicked the West and adopted a façade of modernity. Jeanneret appears to have taken on Loti's mantle, completely absorbed in the perfume and intoxicating charm of the East. He wished to see the white vertical columns of marble in their ruinous form lying parallel to the horizontal lines of the sea, but these dreams would be greatly embellished with a variety of apparitions.

For example, Jeanneret finally arrives at his destination: He has come to worship the Constantinople that Loti so vividly described, a city he already knew to be beautiful. To mark

18.2 Watercolor by Jeanneret
of the mosques of Istanbul,
July 1911.

his entrance, Jeanneret repeats a Lotian motif, describing a postcard photograph almost exactly: cypress trees in the foreground, the silhouette of the Golden Horn beyond, the minarets and cupolas of the mosques puncturing the starry sky, and a crescent moon suspended above. But he wants reality to puncture this dream. He calls out the three districts of the city. "Pera, Stamboul, Scutari: a trinity . . . there is something sacred about it" (Le Corbusier 1989:83).

Confused, he returns to the Oriental dream: the hour is full of madness, he is surrounded by suffocating fragrances, the sky is a pool of fire as in an icon, the night trickles with gold, his imagination wanders. Something is not right with the Oriental hallucination bathed all in gold. Is it a sense of déjà vu or the exhausted repetition of a cliché? This suspended judgment, the use of another's expressions, makes Jeanneret shift his pronouns from "I" to "we." He wanted enchanted Stamboul to be pure—or so he wrote:

> to sit upon her Golden Horn all white, as raw as chalk, and I want light to screech on the surface of domes which swell the heap of milk cubes, and minarets should thrust upwards, and the sky must be blue. Then we would be free of all this depraved yellow, this cursed gold. Under the bright light, I want a city all white, but the green cypresses must be there to punctuate it. And the blue of the sea shall reflect the blue of the sky. (85)

His heart is heavy for reality appears to be worse than the mirage. Constantinople is an enormous city of disarray and disorder and not a primitive landscape. It is better to return to illusion and trompe-l'oeil (88). Is he literally mimicking Loti, who was likewise upset by the modernization of Istanbul during his own visit in August of 1910 and by the oppressive spectacle of fires in 1911 that destroyed more than 10,000 houses? Both men's obsession engenders fear as well as empathy, their passion born on a somber note mixing love with death, eros with thanatos (Lafont 1993; Quella-Villéger 1992; de Saint-Leger 1996). Jeanneret comments that the imperially corrupt Byzantium had died, that its spirit could not be roused from the stones that remained. The color yellow pervades his view as it would in the aging pages of a photographic album—melancholic and mournful.

In another chapter, entitled "She's and He's," Jeanneret worships the little donkeys and young women of Stamboul—a quixotic juxtaposition of exotica. From the first moment, the donkeys won him over for he began with simple things. But he hated the women for the first

18.3 Watercolor by Jeanneret of the Suleymaniye Mosque, as seen from Pera, Istanbul, July 1911.

three weeks—all the time in which his heart was heavy with failed expectations. In spite of this, Loti had taught him how to delve into the realm of the inaccessible, and so one day he found these women "charming in their mysterious black veils, their disquieting anonymity of identical silks, their hidden treasures all alike. Now it seems to me they are ravishing despite and also because of that second skirt flung over their heads, that makes an impenetrable veil. You will find real coquettes underneath.... After all, these veils conceal a penetrable mystery" (1989:129–30).

He wrote a postcard to Madame L'Éplattenier, the wife of his teacher, noting that "here one does not touch lightly upon the subject of women. But just yesterday ... a young Turkish girl, so exquisite I'd say (though it makes me bite my tongue) one á la Loti, spoke to me. Then all the walls caved in, and here I am sending greetings to all women—friendly, adoring, loving, ecstatic, and who knows! And here is my proof. Affectionately yours, C-Ed. Jeanneret" (1989:257,n.6).

Here we have all the Lotian clichés repeated, for Loti considered Stamboul and Oriental women one and the same. They represented the Turkish secret and are used to gain insight and entry into the Orient in order to fuse with its landscape. Loti wrote in *Les Désenchantées* (1910): "But at this hour, he loved all this Stamboul passionately, whose thousands of evening lights began to be reflected in the sea; something attached him there desperately, he didn't define it well, something which floated in the air above the immense and diverse city, doubtless an emanation of feminine souls—because in the end, it is almost always that which attaches us to places or objects— the feminine souls which he had loved and which mingled together" (Szyliowicz 1988:105).

Following Loti, Jeanneret's exotic East becomes erotic, a city enveloped in mystery and enchantment which he came to love. He writes, "We left a conquered and adored city" (1989:149).

After a 24-hour quarantine at the mouth of the Black Sea, his ship passed Constantinople again. Melancholy struck him at the site where Asia, in an unforgettable spectacle, abruptly withdraws from Europe. He writes: "I don't believe I shall ever again see such *Unity*! . . . We passed by rapidly. I only wanted to look into the glaucous sea, where the boat's shadow marks immeasurable depths. For me it was as if the veil of my little temple had also been torn away!" (152).

There follows a melancholic flashback to a strange spectacle of fire—cafes were crowded, idlers stood gawking, street vendors sold lemonade and ice cream—utilizing another scenographic Lotian metaphor. Fires puncture the harmony of Loti's stories, erupting and eradicating the past, leaving dark empty holes where there are no memories. And the Turks do nothing about them. In *Aziyadé*, Loti used the motif of fire as catharsis: it woke him from his Turkish idyll and allowed him to regain his lost equilibrium and leave Stamboul before it was too late (de Saint-Leger 1996:168–70). So, too, the fire of Stamboul is the finest spectacle of Jeanneret's *Journey*, a tableau of Oriental golds and blacks devouring his dream of a million and one nights. He can describe his passion in words and try to draw and paint it, but it is the fire itself that finally offers him the grandeur and magic of the Orient:

> It seems like an intermission at a theater where a great, extraordinary spectacle is performed, but whose audience is blasé because they know it all and nothing more can interest them. For Stamboul has been burning like this for centuries. . . . The fantastic plume of the fire swells to full size and then begins to subside. There we stand before this spectacle that is beyond understanding and leaves us stupid, overcome by a great melancholy. Looking anguished at the thrashings of this enraged dragon, we repeat over and over: It's horrible, it's horrible! (156, 158)

Then there are only recollections and regrets to be made. He blames his writing: "It's over, and yet I haven't said a thing! Not even a word about Turkish life—a word! It would take a book. Our meager seven weeks did not suffice to give us a glance of it. For this reason, I've held my tongue on this subject. . . . To speak of Stamboul and not to describe its life is to remove the soul from those things I have spoken of. . . . I saw the twilight of Constantinople" (160).

And he colors it purple—violet mixed with black, the last color on the spectrum before colors become extinct.

Learning to See

Jeanneret was also learning to see, to acquire knowledge through appearances and to record these images in words and in drawings, watercolors, and photographs. His painterly eye drew quick fragmentary sketches, stopping suddenly to frame and record direct impressions. He often drew in bold black outlines and made watercolors in bright splashes of color. He used his camera eye to travel through space, across a landscape, focusing in and withdrawing to afar, enclosing the spectator within his panoramic gaze. Bringing the horizontal line into focus sets up a cinematic experience—redoubled as writing-in-movement. Jeanneret writes across a continuous line of flickering images that appear, disappear, and reappear, that interject the past in the present and move between opposites of desire and fulfillment, expectations and projections.

The landscape through which Jeanneret travels becomes a melodic flow of fantastical images in which the following refrain repeats itself: climbing the heights of a citadel, taking a long shot toward the horizon, panning across the plains below. For example: they travel from Vác to Budapest by train, a forewarning that industry has invaded the terrain and Jeanneret will not like this city. He calls it "a leprous sore on the body of a goddess" (39). The musical refrains that he had learned to read from the womanly curves of the landscape and the soothing calm that it instilled within him were destroyed by harsh insertions of mechanical noise, music from a saxophone or a French horn. From its citadel, the Buda castle, one had a panoramic view of the damage: the endlessly open sweep to the horizon, squeezed together, limited and enclosed within the boundaries of the city.

> One is surrounded by a vibrant organism of palpitating mountains. A generous outpouring of nacreous fluid rises up slowly from the plain. The Danube encircles the mountains, condensing them into a powerful body that faces the boundless expanses of the plain. But over this plain there spreads a dull black smoke into which the network of streets disappears. Eight hundred thousand inhabitants have rushed here in the last fifty years. And disorder in pompously deceitful forms has rendered this city suspect. (40)

THE ENIGMA AT THE HEART OF THE TALE

Between 1914 and 1916, while living in La Chaux-de-Fonds, yet hoping to escape to Paris, the center of modern intellectual life, Jeanneret inserted two chapters—"Recollections of Mount Athos" and "The Parthenon"—into his serialized letters, reorganizing them into a book that he hoped would be published. By this time, however, Turkey was the recognized ally of Germany and thus was the enemy of France, because France and Germany were at war. In these additional chapters Jeanneret loses some of his Lotian style and emphasizes another, borrowed from Ernest Rénan. He has solved the enigma at the heart of his tale, and finds himself in a different position. Now Jeanneret is also an architect, a builder, and no longer the self-proclaimed painter and romantic writer of the earlier chapters. He would keep the faith of the builder of temples and erect structures based on simple truths and clear statements, and they would move the spectator as the Acropolis had moved the young Jeanneret.

He opens his recollections of Mount Athos with a series of misperceptions that need to be corrected: we mis-estimate the present, our intellectual pursuits are misguided by a hodgepodge of antiquated ideas, we are mis-focused, petrified in stone by having looked too long behind us. We need to be purified in order to take up the task of the present! As an architect he searches for those few primitive forms that will generate an infinite number of expressions. He is learning to bracket, to strip the object under architectural analysis of all magico-religious attributes: "The obsession for symbols that lies deep inside me is like a yearning for a language limited to only a few words. My vocation may be the reason for this: the organization of stone and timber, of volumes, of solids and voids, has given me, perhaps, a too general understanding of the vertical and the horizontal, and of the sense of length, depth, and height as well" (176).

Yet visions from epic times still affect him, and even though he knows that Byzantium is as empty as an echoless chasm, it still moves him. He wants to flee from Mount Athos because he still feels the pull of the Orient, but he cannot. He has to find the reason why this strange attraction compels him. Is it because the church of Athos provides a concise model? "The powerful unity of its language is so sober that it confers to this impression [in its clearly articulated plan and section] the purity of a diamond. Hard and solid, it is the crystallization of a Hellenic clarity, mysteriously combined with indefinable Asiatic evocations" (197).

Then there is the arrival in Athens and the first view of the Acropolis and its pearl, the Parthenon. The essence of this noble and serene work of art lay in its inscrutable nature. It was the meeting point of antagonisms, where the rational and the emotional resided. The experience of this encounter was quite terrifying for Jeanneret: the bewilderment of reason combined with states of frenzied rapture. Its strangeness caused suffering, a tortuous machine that dominated yet enthralled. He addressed the experience with a set of questions and subsequently a lifelong dedication to achieving the same perfection, truthfulness, and clarity it revealed to him. He too would become a master craftsman, an artist possessed with privileged powers, for he had seen the Acropolis and been inspired. He wrote:

18.4 Drawing by Jeanneret of Simonos Petras, one of the many monasteries perched "like eagle eyries at the top of steep, inaccessible rocks" of Athos.

> To see the Acropolis is a dream one treasures without even dreaming to realize it. I don't really know why this hill harbors the essence of artistic thought. I can appreciate the perfection of these temples and realize that nowhere else are they so extraordinary; and a long time ago I accepted the fact that this place should be like a repository of a sacred standard, the basis for all measurement in art. Why this architecture and no other? I can well accept that according to logic, everything here is resolved in accordance with an unsurpassable formula, but why is it the taste—or rather the heart that guides people and dictates their beliefs despite their tendency to ignore it at times—why is it still drawn to the Acropolis, to the foot of the temples? This is in my case an inexplicable problem. . . . Yet why must I, like so many others, name the Parthenon the undeniable Master, as it looms up from its stone base, and yield, even with anger, to its supremacy? . . . Those who, while practicing the art of architecture, find themselves at a moment in their career somewhat empty-headed, their confidence depleted by doubt before that task of giving a living form to inert matter, will understand the melancholy of my soliloquies amid ruins— and my chilling dialogues with silent stones. Very often, I left the Acropolis burdened by a heavy premonition, not daring to imagine that one day I would have to create. (216, 217, 232, 234)

Istanbul would represent for Le Corbusier a confession of love: the dense accumulation of life and dilapidated buildings, of people and their resignation to take life as it comes. This love, this richness, this aesthetic were juxtaposed against the call of duty, the clarity, the purity that the Parthenon represented. This struggle between Istanbul and Athens was finished only during WWI when the Parthenon won out: and only then would the power of that monument become an obsession and an ideal (Passanti 1987:58).

During the five years that Jeanneret was living in La Chaux-de-Fonds, after his return from the East and before his final move to Paris in the winter of 1917, he was enveloped by uncertainty and depression. His letters to Ritter are full of complaints about his bad moods, the cultural limitations of his colleagues and teacher, the pettiness of his clients and merchants, and the provincialness of the town. His only solace was to climb the mountains and look westward towards Paris (FLC R3-18-257 6-4-1912). He makes constant reference to his "stories" from

18.5 Charles-Edouard Jeanneret on the Acropolis, September 1911.

18.6 Drawing by Jeanneret of temples on the Acropolis, September 1911.

18.7 Drawing by Jeanneret of the Parthenon as seen from the Propylae, September 1911.

64

18.8 Watercolor by Jeanneret of the northwest side of the Parthenon, September 1911.

Stamboul, which always allowed him to speak of his innermost self (FLC R3-18-144 5-12-1911). He cries out, "Eleusis, Patras, Brousia," and closing his eyes he can make their images appear. Ritter had told him "to make them remember you have gone to the Acropolis" but this only brings more wrath from his colleagues and a greater sense of isolation. Jeanneret fears he will not have the faith of the builders of temples and be able to act. Everything seems to be a question for him: should he stay and attend to his responsibilities to his parents, his teacher, his colleagues, or should he flee to Adrianopolis, Paris, or Chicago (FLC R3-18-163 5-3-1912; R3-18-197 24-8-1912; R3-18-265 9-5-1913)?

A year after returning from the East, he promises Ritter that he will begin to write about and paint Adrianopolis, Athos, and the Acropolis—places which have remained up to now only in his memory. The lands of the sun obsess and rule over him and he must submit to paper the reasons why they possess him (FLC R3-18-233 26-1-1912; R3-18-254 6-4-1912). More than a year passes and he still complains that his Athos with its bit of poetry is not accessible in the atmosphere of La Chaux-de-Fonds. He is more and more convinced that architecture is the art of an organism preceding from within and opening without, linking inward spirit to outward action. And yet an "unhealthy hesitation creates suffering each time that it is necessary to work and a paralysis seizes me when, some orders having been given me, it is necessary to realize them. Because in each volume, detail and ensemble the possibility of making a Parthenon is there, or at least [making] something perfectly beautiful. Then impotency grips you and you contract without the possibility of release" (FLC R3-18-329 24-3-1914).

Finally in June of 1914, he has finished writing the chapter on Athos and will send it to Ritter for comment. He confesses that it was difficult to write since he had to overcome a reproach that constantly held him back and yet he wonders if the framework of a story about incidents from one's youth was not a sufficient skeleton on which the drama of an entire lifetime might unfold (FLC R3-18-341 17-6-1914). Just as he finished writing this chapter, the blackness of war intervened, and it would not be until February of 1916 that the draft of his memories of the Acropolis were added to those of Athos. He describes these two chapters as an account of skies of gold on icons, of marbles with the clamor of bells, and the overwhelming inhuman machine of the Parthenon (FLC R3-19-10 16-2-1916).

Since we do not know how much Le Corbusier corrected the texts of his *Journey to the East* or what the editor, Jean Petit, might have added when he published the work, as charged, after Le Corbusier's death, it is helpful to turn to a letter that Jeanneret wrote to Ritter from Pisa on November 11, 1911. It is a strange letter prescient of the utopian schemes Le Corbusier would develop in the 1920s and full of implicit references to Descartes's *Discours de la Méthode*. He complains that depression grips him, that he feels caught in a circle of restraint, and yet he calls himself a soldier of battle who is engaged in a struggle within himself, a constant discourse of "moi." His credo has become: "we will do better." He claims he will escape to Egypt, to Asia. These places are useful for the present because it is necessary to whiten the world, to eat, drink, and taste the goods of the earth, to love the body and the heart, and to be thrown stones at in public after putting up a good resistance. It is necessary to accept a new dogma and to whip those who do not want it. He writes all of the above after his proclamation:

> I will obey my destiny . . . at all cost. . . . I stammer over elementary geometry with the eagerness of knowledge and of being able to construct one day. In their crazy race, red, blue, and yellow all become white. I am crazy for the color white, the cube, the sphere, the cylinder, the pyramid . . . all a single color and a great empty void. Prisms stand up erect, balanced, rhythmically marching, having a black dragon which undulates on the horizon. . . . They have only a blue sky above them, placed on a polished marble dais, a monolith stippled by no other color. At noon, the light reduces the cubes to a surface, at evening, the rainbow appears. . . . In the morning they are materialized with shadows and lights, clear as a working drawing. One perceives their base, top and sides. Night is more than ever white and black.

Then he asks rhetorically:

> Do you see revealed an architecture of a tragedy? . . . Some straight roads with windows like a checkerboard on façades. No ornament. A single color, a single material in the entire city. Some autos roll by, some airplanes pass without anyone paying them attention. There will be some streets on the roofs, in the midst of flowers and trees, one will mount them on great staircases and one will pass over bridges. Then one will descend a well made staircase that can give you the air of an emperor and fill the heart with generosity. . . . Here and there will be a temple, a cylinder, a half-sphere, a cube, a polyhedron. And empty spaces in which to breathe.

He concludes the letter after discussing bourgeois responsibilities to marry, have children, and work plus his own obligation to teach under L'Éplattenier's direction at the École de l'Art: "Yes, I can only desire what is my duty. You know well what is my destiny. . . . I feel myself done for. You say risk-taker. You do not like that I have the head of a Russian pope on his deathbed, hard and sharp as a knife. You see certainly that my pen makes me as transparent as glass" (FLC R3-18-128 1-11-1911).

Perhaps we should not make much of this letter, which appears dreamlike, combining consciousness of his own thoughts, a strenuous process of detachment and emptying, along with his tragic vision of future cities and his stubborn call for a new dogma. Is the dragon on the horizon a reminder of the catharsis of fire and the need for new beginnings that he experienced in Stamboul? He is returning as a "condemned man" to endure years of suffering and isolation in La Chaux-de-Fonds; he is not escaping as he wished.

But Jeanneret is also revealing mental images that will become fixed and recurrent themes. It appears that he has been studying geometry seriously, making references to n-dimensional space. He follows the path of the sun as it shines light on an empty Cartesian plane, knowing that the city is a complex entity and any understanding of it will pass through successive phases of time. This city of his dreams is mobile; it cannot be seen all at once, but only with movement from different points of perspective do its volumes rise up, recede, and return. When the sun is at the meridian a cube is reduced to a flat surface. With less light the two-dimensional square is dragged in the opposite direction until it projects into a three-dimensional cube with height, breadth, and depth. At night the surface may be all black and white, like a checkerboard—the ultimate Cartesian grid. This space of Jeanneret's is in our minds—it can have the analytic precision of a working drawing or simultaneously it can be filled with arbitrary constructions, hypercubes whose top, sides, and bottom are seen all at once. It is above all projective of things to come.

Jeanneret is revealing ideas that will dominate his architecture and urbanism in the 1920s. First of all, architecture is for Jeanneret an intellectual activity based on a geometry of ideal solids absolutely invariable yet entirely mental. He writes in the series of articles collected as *Urbanisme* in 1925 (1971) that in great cities, the glory of the mind triumphs. It follows the logical conclusions of simple reasoning and develops well-conceived plans with clear intentions. Antiquity has left a demonstration of these facts: "Egyptian temples, the rectilinear cities of North Africa (e.g. Kairouan), the sacred cities of India, the Roman cities of the Empire, or those built in the great tradition: Pompeii, Aaigues-Mortes, Monpazier" (Le Corbusier 1971:93). When cities struggle forward following policies of chance, disorder, drift, and idleness, their death will surely be the end result. But when they strive toward order and respond to the appeal of geometry that speaks directly to the mind, they create a "crystallization of pure forms" as the material support for their beauty. "If only the question is minutely studied in the light of reason, and is touched with some poetical feeling, the replanning of a great city should give results which are as practical as they are eminently architecture" (1971:104).

REFERENCES

Brooks, H. Allen. *Le Corbusier's Formative Years*. Chicago, IL: University of Chicago Press, 1997.

Chadbourne, Richard M. *Ernest Rénan*. New York: Twayne, 1968.

de Saint-Leger, Marie-Paule. *Pierre Loti l'insaissisable*. Paris: L'Harmattan, 1996.

FLC=Fondation Le Corbusier, Villa Jeanneret, 8–10 Square du Docteur Blanche, 75016 Paris, France.

Gresleri, Giuliano. *Le Corbusier, une encyclopédie*. Paris: Éditions du Centre Georges Pompidou, 1987.

Lafont, Suzanne. *Suprêmes Clichés de Loti*. Toulouse: Presses Universitaires du Mirail, 1993.

Le Corbusier. *Journey to the East*. Trans. Ivan Žaknić. Cambridge, MA: MIT Press, 1989.

———. *The Final Testament of Père Corbu: A Translation and Interpretation of Mise au point*, trans. Ivan Žaknić. New Haven, CT: Yale University Press, 1997.

———. "The City of Tomorrow and Its Planning." In *Urbanisme*, 8th ed., trans. Frederick Etchells. Cambridge, MA: MIT Press, 1971.

Lewis, Martin W., and Karen E. Wigen. *The Myth of Continents: A Critique of Metageography*. Berkeley, CA: University of California Press, 1997.

Passanti, Francesco. "The Skyscrapers of the Ville Contemporaine." *Assemblage* 4(1987):58.

Quella-Villéger, Alain. *La Politique Méditerranéene de la France 1870–1923: Un Témoin: Pierre Loti*. Paris: Éditions Harmattan, 1992.

Rénan, Ernest. "Prayer on the Acropolis." In *Recollections of My Youth*. New York: G. P. Putnam's Sons, 1883.

Szyliowicz, Irene L. *Pierre Loti and the Oriental Woman*. New York: St. Martin's, 1988.

Turner, Paul Venable. *The Education of Le Corbusier*. New York: Garland, 1977.

Vogt, Adolf Max. "Remarks on the 'Reversed' Grand Tour of Le Corbusier and Auguste Klipstein." *Assemblage* 4(1987):38–51.

SYMBOLIC SETTLEMENTS
THE AMERICAN IDEOLOGICAL TENSION BETWEEN PRIVATE HOMES AND PUBLIC HOUSING

19

Lawrence J. Vale

As the 21st century continues, two forms of domestic settlement in American cities stand as polar opposites. At one extreme is the vast plaid of the residential streetscape, the full flowering of the traditional American ideological emphasis on the middle-class single-family home. At the other end of the domestic spectrum is the public project housing the nation's poorest populations in vilified superblocks of low modernist urbanism. This chapter examines the relationship between these two forms of settlement, emphasizing their shared cultural origins and ongoing tensions (Vale 2000). The housing project and the single-family home are more than mere opposites; they are twin products of a shared cultural system.

When the early large housing projects were built—from the 1930s through the 1950s—architects and policymakers wished to maximize the aesthetic distance from the dark tenements and alleys they intended this housing to replace. Supporters also intended the new housing projects to manifest certain virtues associated with the single-family home and the shared public realm of an idealized village. They designed these settlements as part of a reward system for the worthy working-class poor, a selective collective of carefully vetted nuclear families judged to be deserving of temporary government assistance.

By the mid-1950s, however, public housing had lost its cachet. An initial tenant population selected precisely to comprise those most likely to be upwardly mobile did indeed move on, aided by all manner of government subsidies supporting home mortgages and suburban growth. As fewer and fewer upwardly mobile families applied for public housing, both the structure and the meaning of public housing began to change.

Neighborhood by neighborhood, public housing projects shifted from rewards to sustain worthy families—waystations along the road to homeownership—into holding stations for coping with the society's least-advantaged members. Simultaneously, from the mid-1950s onward, promoters of large public housing construction relinquished all attempts to make its forms consistent with the ideals of the single-family home. This is epitomized by the vast districts of highrises built in Chicago, but also by building complexes in cities such as St. Louis, Philadelphia, and Baltimore. Only in the 1980s and, especially, in the late 1990s under HUD's HOPE VI program—a $5 billion effort to demolish and replace some of the nation's most notorious housing projects—did public housing design attempt to regain its formal and ideological connections to the ideals of the single-family home. Significantly, designers returned to the symbolic settlement landscapes of the single-family home at precisely the moment policymakers sought to re-tenant the projects with the sort of upwardly mobile residents that they attracted a half-century before.

Before tracing the way that public housing projects have functioned as forms of settlement, it is worth stepping back to consider the multiple ways in which the meaning of such places may be constructed.

How Does Public Housing Convey Meaning?

Housing projects are projections of meaning, and these meanings are themselves constructed in diverse ways by a broad range of individuals and groups. To interpret the range of such meanings entails understanding not only the views of those most directly involved but also, as cultural psychologist Jerome Bruner (1990) suggests, understanding "the structure and coherence of the larger contexts in which specific meanings are created and transmitted" (65).

Housing projects convey meaning in a variety of ways, and it is not enough to ask *what* they mean; the prior question is *how* such meaning is conveyed. Drawing on a typology established by constructivist philosopher Nelson Goodman, it seems possible to distinguish among several different kinds of architecturally grounded meanings. A project may convey meaning literally by denotation, signs calling attention to the fact that the buildings are "Housing Authority Property" or by evidence of graffiti and vandalism. Housing projects also express meaning through their site plans, materials, and building massing by exemplifying their unique properties through the use of design techniques such as repetition and regularity. At the same time, the housing project may invite metaphorical interpretation, through allusions to institutional settings such as prisons or hospitals—places that may make similar (and equally non-homelike) use of shared entrances, perimeter fencing, and exalted placement of management personnel. Finally, the physical form of a project may convey meaning in mediated ways, becoming equated with broad concepts and stereotypes such as underclass, drug market, gang turf, or welfare queen (Goodman 1988:33–44).

As such broader meanings become attached to places, the links to the specific formal qualities of the built environment tend to blur. The meaning of public housing (even to those who actually live within it) becomes a blending of personal experience with newspaper accounts, television reports, and film portrayals. The housing project means by virtue (or by vice) of what demonstrably happened there (*that* murder in *that* courtyard on *that* date) but also by more generalizable notions about the sorts of things that *could* be expected to transpire in *that* sort of place, often generated by media stories.

The names of public housing projects have become useful locational devices, not only for suggesting where some undesirable aspect of contemporary urban reality may lurk, but for allowing those in more affluent areas to continue to believe that poverty and its associated dangers are somehow carefully bounded and labeled and that personal security remains possible elsewhere. In 1989, during the investigation of Boston's internationally notorious Stuart murder case, for example, white suburbanite Charles Stuart pinned blame for the inner city shooting death of his pregnant wife on a black male. Most of the media and police who interrogated residents of the nearby Mission Hill public housing project were only too willing to believe this explanation, at least until Stuart himself became implicated in the killing. Similarly, when there is a drug raid at a public housing development, it is usually reported as a drug raid *on* that development, as if all residents were potentially culpable. As was the case with the slum neighborhoods that preceded it, there is guilt by physical association with the place even in the absence of social association with the perpetrators. In most newspaper accounts of neighborhood crime, reporters convey the location by providing a street name. When such problems occur in (or near) public housing, by contrast, often the reports simply provide the name of the housing project, using this identifier as a stand-in for both neighborhood and street.

The Ideological Origins of American Public Housing

In probing the interplay between structure and meaning in public housing projects, what seems most fascinating is the extent to which both structures and meanings have evolved, even as the term *public housing* has remained constant. The meanings of public housing projects have shifted in all of the dimensions just outlined. Certainly, the literal meanings have changed, exemplified by the transformation of signage from authority-promulgated requests to "Keep off the Grass" to gang-disseminated spraypaint graffiti. Similarly, the architectural forms have changed, from the initial courtyard-oriented housing schemes of the 1930s to the premium placed on open space in the postwar superblock projects, which minimized the penetration of streets in order to protect pedestrians from traffic, to the return of street orientation in more recent incarnations (Franck and Mostoller 1995; Franck 1998). More culturally revealing than these kinds of shifts in meaning, however, are the transformations that have occurred in terms of metaphor and broader mediated references. Built to allude to idealized village forms, the most common metaphors used to characterize later projects included terms such as *no man's land* or *prison*, appellations used not only by commentators but by residents themselves. At the same time, "the projects" came to stand as a metonym for all manner of urban policy failure and personal irresponsibility.

The structure and meaning of public housing projects are each inextricably tied to broader questions of moral judgment and moral surveillance. The origins of American public housing cannot be understood apart from the broader cultural context of ideological support for the moral advantages of single-family homes and homeownership. The tension between the early promoters of public housing and the highly resistant leaders of the private real estate industry forms demonstrates the overriding importance of this link.

Even earlier, however, the nation's major tenement reformers viewed housing reform as an act of domestic purification, the replacement of one unhealthy form of settlement by another form judged more truly American and wholly Christian.

From Tenements to Homes

In their efforts to eliminate the slums of Lower Manhattan, Jacob Riis and Lawrence Veiller carried the ideal of the individual home into the heart of the nation's largest city, port of entry for the greatest number of impoverished immigrants. Riis, the Danish immigrant police station reporter turned photojournalist, and Veiller, the author of much of New York's early housing legislation, worked together to expose the evils of Manhattan's slums to the rest of the nation. Both men wished to transform tenement house districts into neighborhoods of private homes. Each believed that good American citizenship could only come with life in a single-family dwelling, and each wished to eliminate the high-density American city. Veiller pursued tenement reform through legislation intended to let light into the interiors of buildings and to create open space between buildings, allowing the city to take on a less urban appearance, while Riis—a missionary with a camera—saw enlightenment in Christian terms, exposing corruption with the aid of explosive flash spots.

In *A Ten Years' War* (1900), Riis's account of his fight for the home in the 1890s, he insisted: "the home, the family are the rallying points of civilization. But long since the tenements of New York earned for it the ominous name of 'the homeless city.'" He claimed that "the tenement itself, with its crowds, its lack of privacy, is the greatest destroyer of individuality, of character. As its numbers increase, so does the element that becomes criminal for lack of individuality and the self-respect that comes with it." For Riis, the good home must be "separate, decent and desirable." So, too, he warned that government should not provide these homes to the impoverished; they must be the reward for hard work. "Any charity scheme merely turns him into a pauper, however it may be disguised, and drowns him hopelessly in the mire out of which it proposed to pull him." For Riis, the solution to New York's (and America's) housing ills required not more laws but more Christian homes. In *The Peril and the Preservation of the Home* (1903), he revealed his true ambition: "Put back the family altar and let there be written over it the old stout challenge to the devil and his hordes: 'As for me and my house, we will serve the Lord;' and even the slum tenement shall seek to attack it in vain." His classic photo essay, *How the Other Half Lives* (1890), featured biblically inspired chapter titles such as "Genesis of the Tenement" and "The Awakening" and described his goal of destroying existing tenements so as to "let in more light."

Lawrence Veiller's writings carried little of Riis's emotional appeal but instead promulgated a regulatory framework for tenements that, between 1901 and 1920, would be extended well beyond New York City. Veiller phrased his housing reform as a system of constraints intended to free the dense, multi-story brick tenements from unhealthy conditions through progressively restricting the percentage of a lot that a tenement-house could occupy. He sought to maximize space behind and on the side of a tenement so as to admit more light but, significantly, saw no particular use value for this open space he so craved. He called these spaces "yards" but defined them simply as "open unoccupied space on the same lot with a tenement house." Veiller, like Riis, distrusted many of the people he professed to assist. He believed that any attempt to make use of the empty public areas would be in vain. As for gardens, he suggests that the immigrant poor would use them only as "the gathering place for the waste material of family existence." Such undefined provision of open outdoor public space became an unwitting prototype for the desecrated and desolate plazas of many mid-20th century public housing projects (Veiller 1910:15; 1920:27; as quoted in Handlin 1979:213).

Critics applauded Veiller's 1914 Model Housing Law because it united the specifications for all types of dwellings in a single document. Its true effect, however, was to endow the single-family house with a preferential legal status, while revealing Veiller's distaste for all "multiple dwellings." Like Riis, Veiller ultimately wished to phase out the multiple dwelling completely. He categorized dwellings into three "classes": (1) private dwellings, (2) two-family dwellings, and (3) multiple dwellings—clearly implying that only single-family homes are "private." His broader aim was to eliminate multiple dwellings completely. With his plethora of rules, regulations, and restrictions, he wished to make such housing economically unfeasible to build: "By means of this plan of classification it is possible to encourage the construction of private dwellings and two-family houses and to discourage the erection of tenement houses and other forms of multiple dwellings by making the provisions relative to the latter more stringent than those affecting the former classes. . . . The effect of these more stringent requirements in increasing the cost of construction may, however, so discourage the construction of buildings of this kind as to practically stop their erection." In seeking to eliminate the multiple dwelling, Veiller (1920) joined with many others in touting the single-family home as the goal of every American family.

Promoting Single-Family Homes

The ideas and images promulgated by the real estate industry and by a variety of home-oriented magazines beginning in the 1920s reveal a great deal about the social and cultural expectations regarding class and gender that, then as now, have colored American approaches to housing provision. This ideological emphasis on the moral superiority of the single-family owned home (strongly supported by the federal government beginning in the 1920s) thus greatly conditioned the emergence of any subsequent government-sponsored alternative.

Throughout the 1920s, various private developers—with full federal approval—took the lead in promoting the ideological aims and political benefits of enhanced homeownership (Weiss 1988:3–5). The chief propaganda effort of the National Association of Real Estate Boards in 1922, entitled *A Home of Your Own*, couched its strongest plea in the language of the independent yeoman. This 20-page booklet (Folsom 1922) impugned the moral and sexual inadequacy of renters by noting that homeownership "puts the MAN back in MANHOOD" and enabled one to be "completely self-reliant and dominant." Conversely, continued tenancy suggested an inability "to be your own man" since it entailed "[turning] over to others the control of the place that is the center of your whole personal and family life." NAREB thought that women could benefit from homeownership as well: "To install your wife in a home of her own is a convincing demonstration of your affection and consideration for her comfort and happiness." Suitably installed, this wife would gain "the joy of possession that relieves housework of its monotony."

Renting was "anti-family," whereas homeownership conferred "moral muscle" and "better citizenship." "Millions of fine boys and girls" had "gone wrong," NAREB opined, because their parents "failed to provide their growing sons and daughters with the wholesome surroundings and interests of owned homes, thereby forcing them to turn to the artificial pleasures of 'down town' for their amusement." The single-family home served to keep children "off the streets" by making their home and yard "their center of interest." Such districts of homes permitted "lasting friendships among worth-while neighbors," while sparing contact with "rented houses in which many families of unknown habits have lived." These private homes promised protection from "the unwholesome and not infrequently contaminating ideas of the floating classes that predominate in the close-in rental districts."

NAREB's booklet warned against other problems of city life in rental areas, since "the conditions are all against the safety of life and limb." "The traffic dangers from playing in the streets, and in going to and from school, are constant. Each day takes its toll." NAREB challenged parents to get a home "as far away from business and the fever and sham of transient life as possible."

In short, the propaganda of the home-building industry and its many allies in government constantly reiterated the moral superiority of owned homes over rented apartments. In equating

neighborhood stability with the psychological and economic stability of individuals and families, the home promoters insisted that stability required total spatial and class segregation from the dangers and temptation of streetlife and transient persons. NAREB's booklet even referred to the home as a personal "Mecca," treating the home and its environs as sacred space, safely distant from "unwholesome" and "contaminating" influences. Secure in the family castle, the sturdy individualist homeowner and his nurturant spouse needed no particular housing assistance from government. As the mass residential foreclosures of the Great Depression soon made clear, however, government mortgage guarantees were an essential pillar supporting this entire ideology of idealized domesticity. For Franklin Roosevelt, as for Herbert Hoover, such support for single-family homes seemed wholly justified, an investment in domestic tranquility cloaked in patriotism.

The Great Depression also made it obvious that most Americans could not yet afford to purchase and maintain such homes, prompting the government at long last to consider federally subsidized low-income housing projects. Initially touting public housing as a means to restore employment in the building trades and to promote slum clearance, supporters of such public housing programs in the 1930s also viewed the new projects as rewards for upwardly mobile members of the working class. Like the new mechanisms for securing and expanding the availability of home mortgages, the early public housing efforts endeavored to shore up the domestic fortunes of worthy citizens and to protect them from less reputable neighbors.

The Owned Home is Necessary to the Welfare of the Child.
The owned home, and the family stability and permanency that it helps to create, does more than any other thing to promote the physical, mental, and moral well-being of children.
It lessens the dangers from sickness and accident.
It shelters youthful innocence against moral dangers.
It creates a right attitude toward life in the growing mind.
It provides wholesome interests and lessens the attraction of outside excitements.
It makes childhood happier.
Every Child Has the Right to a Home of Its Own
The rearing of a child is a serious and difficult matter. It is the business of the home—the chief business of life.
Few parents succeed in meeting the responsibilities of child training to their own complete satisfaction. No parent, therefore, can afford to overlook a means that will greatly lighten this responsibility and aid him in mastering many of its most important and delicate details.
The permanent family home is such a means. It is the greatest of all aids in the rearing of children. A large part of the failures in after life can be traced directly to its absence.
It establishes a permanent condition and influence in their lives that averts many of the worst dangers, both physical and moral, to childhood; molds their ideas and ideals of life and creates a powerful influence for success throughout their lives.
The child's danger from sickness is far less in the owned home than in the rented house in which many families of unknown habits have lived.
In old houses and neighborhoods, hidden sources of infection are many and are difficult to locate until too late. There is less of sunshine in the closely built-up sections and in the vicinity of the higher buildings. The circulation of fresh air is poorer and the summer radiation of heat from buildings and pavements far greater than in the more open outer districts. Infant mortality increases as you approach the center of any city.
In the more central localities, which are the chief rental areas, the conditions are all against the safety of life and limb. The traffic dangers from playing in the streets, and in going to and from school, are constant. Each day takes its toll.
Every child has the RIGHT to a home of its own.
The child raised in a rented house or apartment is CHEATED.

19.1 According to the National Association of Real Estate Boards (NAREB), "the child raised in a rented house or apartment is CHEATED."

Many others regarded government promotion of public housing as disturbingly anti-American, and various outraged groups representing the building industries lobbied Congress incessantly. G. M. Stout, president of the Atlanta Real Estate Board, cast the public housing question in familiar ideological terms of individualism, self-reliance, and frontier manhood: "The working classes of this country will rue the day when they are housed in Government-owned, Government built, and Government-regulated houses. Masters house their slaves, but free men house themselves. Those who are descendants of pioneer American stock will not regard as 'Home' a unit in a fine building, built at taxpayers' expense, in a slum clearance project" (Stout 1935 in Schnapper 1939:343). Other special interest groups accepted public housing but urged greater local control of the program or promoted the use of particular building materials. In response, supporters of public housing struggled to deliver a symbolically acceptable product.

Yeomanry in an Apartment Complex

Public housing promoters faced a double challenge: they wished to appear unthreatening to private real estate interests, but they also wished to create desirable housing environments. They needed to link the attempts of others to enshrine the single-family home to their own efforts to propose a form and rationale for large-scale housing projects comprised of apartments. Although the form of the American public housing project is usually seen as derivative of workers' housing experience in Europe, distinctively American cultural factors also played significant roles. In the United States, the public housers sought to design projects to maximize their aesthetic distance from the existing urban fabric of lightless and airless tenements, yet also to maximize the cultural continuity with older notions of village greens and individual homes.

The rather unexpected link of housing project to home and village comes across clearly in the language employed by many housing pioneers. Clarence Perry, whose influential Neighborhood Unit plans addressed everything from districts of single-family homes to slum-clearance sites intended for apartments, believed that good settlement structure entailed both shared public space and carefully delineated boundaries. He justified the size of his model slum clearance proposal by observing that "it is large enough to permit the replanning of blocks so as to enable the maximum exposure of apartments to light and open spaces" (Perry 1933:51). Like those who subsequently planned public housing, Perry intended the slum-clearance neighborhood unit to demarcate territory that had been safely purged of the dependent poor. Perry (1929) called this type of neighborhood unit "a village engulfed by an expanding city" (53), a healthy enclave protected from the incursions of human and automotive threats. In this way, armed with the superblock, many of the same neighborhood attributes that the National Association of Real Estate Board saw linked exclusively to districts of single-family homes could be extended. Public housing projects, too, could be a protected and privileged enclave.

Noted housing reformer Edith Elmer Wood argued that "if urban life is to endure, it must find a way to recapture some of the nerve-relaxing security of the countryside" (Wood 1939:34), a goal seemingly shared by most public housing advocates in the 1930s. Jane Jacobs dubbed them "decentrists" in recognition of their retrograde pursuit of a past American rural ideal, their presumptions of self-sufficiency, and their love for self-contained communities. In the tradition of American exclusionary zoning, such projects rejected any inclusion of commercial facilities. Moreover, by consciously abandoning streets in favor of superblocks, these settlement designs also turned housing units inward to promote the illusion of isolation and rural privacy. In reality, designers achieved self-containment without recreating privacy; they mimicked the village green at the same time as they rejected the village.

Public Housing as Neighborhood Design

Decentrist or not, neighborhood unit ideals and village metaphors deeply affected the design ethos of subsequent public housing projects. As a 1941 report by the Boston Housing Authority put it, "the building of a housing project should not only clear away the greatest number of sub-standard dwellings possible, but it should help to rehabilitate the neighborhood by virtue of its plan, by virtue of its open spaces, landscaping, play areas and juxtaposition of its modern buildings. In size, a project should be sufficient in itself to withstand encroaching blight from all sides" (Boston Housing Authority 1941). Like Riis and Veiller, public housing designers regarded openness itself as a moral virtue. At the same time, they wished to build self-sufficient island settlements capable of defending themselves. Such settlements served as the spatial corollary to the underlying economic imperative of early public housing, which required that tenants be "independent and self-supporting." Yet, because large public housing projects were large multi-family complexes and not little houses on the prairie, public housing's most ardent backers struggled to find ways to make the settlement form of public housing consistent with established American domestic traditions and values.

Nathan Straus, administrator of the United States Housing Authority beginning in the late 1930s, valiantly tried to reconcile public housing with mainstream American ideals and preferences for single-family homes and yards. He wanted each family in public housing to cultivate a garden plot, and he preferred dwellings with private entrances that would foster a sense of "turf" and belonging (Straus 1944:154). In a related manner, Straus fought to keep USHA projects at low densities, preferring "individual houses at the rate of twelve families to the acre" (a figure drawn from English Garden City practice). "It has been amply proved," he noted, that this threshold of density "is most conducive to well-being and happiness," since it permitted each family "breathing space, play space, room for a small garden." As a concession to land costs, however, he was willing to settle for "row houses or two- or three-story apartments at a density of twenty-five to sixty families to the acre" (53, 56), and most housing authorities built their projects according to these compromised ideals.

Even at higher densities, Straus believed that sound community design for public housing entailed self-contained communities that could mimic small-town social interactions. In the USHA booklet *Housing and Recreation* (1939), Straus extolled the ideal of the New England village, arguing that "these early American communities, with daily life centering about the village green, can teach us much in the design and planning of public housing projects" (3). Five years later, in *The Seven Myths of Housing* (1944), Straus asserted that many public housing projects had successfully mimicked this culturally resonant town common: "Old and young alike find that the center of life is the open play area of the housing project as it once was the village green. There, children play in safety, mothers sew and gossip as neighborliness is awakened and civic pride grows apace" (163).

19.3 In 1945 the Boston Housing Authority's photographer depicted the Charlestown public housing development to resemble the central green of a patriotic town.

Whatever the power of vestigial collective memories of the colonial town common, asserting the metaphor did little to reproduce the social relations that once gave rise to such settlement design. As built, housing projects deliberately eschewed the spatial and institutional qualities of either a traditional New England town center or a contemporary urban neighborhood. Clarence Perry's mixed-use neighborhood unit gave way to a single-use residential environment lacking either commercial or civic facilities, just as the initial ideals of low-density developments with private entrances and private yards gave way to apartment blocks surrounded by ill-defined "open space." Public housing designers retained some vestige of the town common, but dispensed with the town.

Despite such shortcomings, early project designers persistently attempted to plan, photograph, and promote project open space as a programmed vestige of the lost New England town common. The elaborate annual reports of the Boston Housing Authority from the early 1940s, for example, depicted the Charlestown project to emphasize its courtyard flagpole, while neatly framing the distant view of the Bunker Hill Monument. The caption emphasized that the project was "New Spacious and Open" but older indicators of patriotism also remained prominent. Boston Housing Authority designers outfitted other housing developments with reassuring reminders of gardens and white picket fences and gates, even though the buildings themselves were multi-family brick structures. The BHA repeatedly and pointedly juxtaposed these sorts of images against others showcasing the discredited past of filthy alleyways and deteriorating tenements. Taken together, the imagery did more than promote modernity and progress; it did so in ways that simultaneously supported nostalgia for the settlement forms of a small-town past. Public housing attempted to do more than destroy the slums; it also aimed to rebuild the village. Such housing projects may now be regarded as the epitome of modernist site planning, but their designers—and their tenants—consistently refused to abandon their last links to the pastoral ideals of house and garden.

Public Housing as a Moral Imperative

Well into the mid-20th century, promoters of public housing relied on the melodramatic metaphors of 19th century tenement reform. To build public housing was to embark on a spiritual transformation, delivering huddled masses "out of the shadows" and "into the sun." The spirit of Jacob Riis remained alive and well. In Boston, official assessments of conditions continued to invoke polar opposites of darkness and light, filth and cleanliness, despair and hope. The Authority publicly phrased its mission in religious terms: public housing was a "crusade to rid the city of substandard areas" and a "mandate from destiny" to prove that Boston was not "past redemption." In this pursuit, the Authority believed itself to be a bastion of both "good morality" and "good business" (1945).

During the early 1950s, as the Authority completed construction on its last 17 large family public housing developments, it gradually turned away from its metaphors of redemption. It sited most of its postwar projects on vacant land rather than on cleared slums, so it was easier to resist retrofitted rhetoric. As before, however, housing officials struggled over ways to reconcile the form of public housing with the ideals of single-family homes. In its *Primer for Use of Local Housing Authorities* (1948), the Massachusetts State Housing Board extolled the "advantages of

GROUP HOUSING GIVES LOWEST RENT

19.5 This prototypical design for "Group Housing" is rendered to resemble a rambling colonial house, but is really multi-family housing located on a superblock.

the row house" over apartment buildings, since "row houses give the privacy and livability of a single-family home" and would "provide the tenants front and back yards" (13–15). Similarly, its 1948 booklet, *Massachusetts Housing for Veterans*, featured a model of "Group Housing" rendered to mimic a large, shuttered, and clapboarded neocolonial single-family home. By this point—more than a decade after project building had commenced across the country—such retrograde images surely strained credulity. These designs may have reflected wishful thinking or ideological preferences, but they bore little relation to the actual practice under way in large American cities. In Boston, as elsewhere, most postwar housing projects consisted of walk-up apartment buildings with shared entryways and stairhalls, or elevator highrises—not rowhouses or single-family homes.

The Stigmatization of the Projects

Meanwhile, a settlement structure based on open space and premised on its contrast to surrounding slums meant one thing when the residents within were regarded as the deserving working class and quite another thing once the projects became viewed as a domicile of last resort.

Public housing design during the 1950s and 1960s lost any vestigial connection and orientation to traditional forms of American urbanism, and the metaphors of village and enlightenment disappeared from public discourse. The heyday of the large project superblocks came just as their chosen clientele ceased to be the favored upwardly mobile working poor who initially populated the projects and had inspired their creation. In the late 1940s, a study by the National Association of Housing Officials found up to 90 percent of those who had been forced to vacate public housing because of excess income had moved on to homeownership (163). By the mid-1950s, however, fewer and fewer families could act on such an aspiration. Whether or not they were sent to public housing as desperate refugees from urban renewal initiatives, entry into public housing ceased to connote a positive gain in status. Once intended as a reward mechanism for carefully vetted nuclear families with stable records of employment, public housing projects became transmuted into coping mechanisms (or even containment vehicles) for the very poor, usually segregated by race. Correspondingly, as forms of settlement, housing projects lost all remaining vestiges of links to earlier forms of high-status space. What was once touted as the urban heir to the village green became little more than ill-maintained treeless expanses of asphalt-covered "open space."

Back to the Village? Public Housing in the New Millennium

For more than 30 years, public housing projects in most large American cities have been allowed to decline, victimized by inadequate financing, incompetent management, widespread vandalism, and sustained public apathy. Once sought as sources of uplift and enlightenment, the metaphors for public housing instead emphasized wastelands, war zones, or imprisonment. Housing authorities accepted responsibility for helping many households that the private sector simply would not, or could not, house. With little new public housing being built, especially

19.7 At the West Broadway development in Boston, project management and maintenance collapsed during the 1970s.

19.8 At the "Vaughn Residences at Murphy Park" in St. Louis, developers seek to attract the middle class back to a site that once served as public housing (see buildings at rear).

after 1980, federal preferences for admission to the limited resource of public housing went to those whose need was most desperate, including the homeless. These changes exacerbated the long-term decline in incomes that had been under way since the 1950s and left housing projects with the highest rates of unemployment-per-acre in the country. According to Flynn McRoberts and T. Wilson, as of 1990, nine of the nation's ten poorest neighborhoods were in public housing projects (*Chicago Tribune*, January 24, 1995:1, 6).

Despite the concentrated poverty and the frequency of dire accounts in the media, this is not the end of the story. Instead, the rather improbable coda to this symphony of woe is the ongoing attempt by housing officials and designers to reverse the decline of public housing and to restore—neighborhood by neighborhood—some of its initial cachet.

Beginning in the mid-1990s, the HOPE VI program in the U.S. Department of Housing and Urban Development provided an unprecedented source of funds for overhauling dozens of the nation's most "severely distressed" projects. Meanwhile, and completely consistent with this first impulse, Congress passed a landmark public housing reform bill. Known formally as the Quality Housing and Work Responsibility Act of 1998, the legislation gave much greater leeway to housing authorities to give housing preference to those earning up to 80 percent of area median income, clearly implying that public housing ought to be forcibly returned to its initial incarnation as a haven for working families.

These new policy directions have already had important implications for the structure and meaning of housing projects as forms of settlement. Just as early public housing promoters during the 1930s and 1940s had emphasized the continuity between project design and dominant cultural ideals of home and village—at a time when admission to public housing was meant to be seen as a reward for good citizenship—so too today's HOPE VI proponents

stress the need to reintroduce the dominant ideology of the single-family home and traditional streetscape back into public housing. These redevelopment efforts are deliberately intended to transform the most notorious examples of failed urban public housing into mixed-income communities that can attract and hold the sorts of upwardly mobile working families that once dominated the earliest projects. It is not enough to renovate or modernize; the intent is wholesale transformation at the level of symbol and metaphor.

Housing authorities (and their architects) clearly see housing and settlement design as encoding a system of values. They are all too aware that in order to be successful in attracting back a more middle-class population, any redesign must succeed by ridding the project of all its old meanings and connotations. It is not enough to remove the literal meanings through name changes, new signage, and mobilization against graffiti, although these matters are crucial. Nor is it enough to transform the buildings in ways that merely obliterate any recall of the rhythms, repetitions, and roofscapes of the original project. Increasingly—prodded by an aesthetic partnership between HUD and the Congress for the New Urbanism, a network of designers and others advocating for a return to pre-modernist design principles—designers are going even further in their efforts to restructure public housing in ways that can shift its meaning. Ultimately, in many HOPE VI projects, housing authorities, and their designers seek a level of reimaging that permits a shift in architectural type and invites entirely new metaphorical associations. In an extreme case, such as Boston's Orchard Park, the transformation of the original 1942 project into its salsa-suburbia incarnation as Orchard Gardens Estates is startling enough to be unrecognizable. Old projects, once designed in distinctive ways (ostensibly to demonstrate their distinct superiority over the cold-water flats of surrounding slums), are now being transformed into reassuringly familiar landscapes, even if those landscapes bear no particular relationship to surrounding areas.

19.20 By 2000, Boston's Orchard Park project had been largely demolished and reborn as Orchard Gardens Estates, replete with a traditional streetscape and pre-modernist images of house and garden.

Now, instead of a contrast with the slum, the key symbolic shift entails the maximum possible repudiation of the evolved form of public housing itself. This re-imaging of public housing, achieved through a manipulation of symbols, is intended to foster and permit a corresponding socioeconomic transformation of occupancy. As public housing is reconceptualized to approach the norms of private homes, the tensions between the two settlement forms stand revealed but not resolved.

References

Boston Housing Authority. *Rehousing the Low Income Families of Boston: Review of the Activities of the Boston Housing Authority, 1936–1940.* Boston, MA: Boston Housing Authority, 1941.

———. *Annual Report, 1944–1945.* Boston, MA: Boston Housing Authority, 1945.

Bruner, Jerome. *Acts of Meaning.* Cambridge, MA: Harvard University Press, 1990.

Folsom, M. W. *A Home of Your Own.* Chicago, IL: National Association of Real Estate Boards, 1922.

Franck, Karen A. "Changing Values in U.S. Public Housing Policy and Design." In *New Directions in Urban Public Housing*, eds. David P. Varady, Wolfgang F. E. Preiser, and Francis P. Russell. New Brunswick, NJ: Center for Urban Policy Research Press, 1998.

Franck, Karen A., and Michael Mostoller. "From Courts to Open Space to Streets: Changes in the Site Design of U.S. Public Housing." *Journal of Architectural and Planning Research* 12,3(Autumn 1995):186–220.

Goodman, Nelson. "How Buildings Mean." In *Reconceptions in Philosophy*, eds. Nelson Goodman and Catherine Elgin. Indianapolis, IN: Hackett, 1988.

Handlin, David. *The American Home*. Boston, MA: Little, Brown, 1979.

McRoberts, Flynn, and T. Wilson. "CHA has 9 of 10 Poorest Areas in U.S., Study Says." *Chicago Tribune*, January 24, 1995:1, 6.

Perry, Clarence Arthur. *The Neighborhood Unit: A Scheme of Arrangement for the Family-Life Community*. In *Neighborhood and Community Planning*. Regional Survey of New York and Its Environs 7, monograph 1. New York: Committee on Regional Plan of New York and Its Environs, 1929.

———. *The Rebuilding of Blighted Areas: A Study of the Neighborhood Unit in Replanning and Plot Assemblage*. New York: Regional Plan Association, 1933.

Riis, Jacob. *How the Other Half Lives*. New York: Dover, 1971 [1890 original].

———. *A Ten Years' War*. Cambridge, MA: Riverside, 1900

———. *The Peril and Preservation of the Home*. Philadelphia, PA: George W. Jacobs, 1903.

State Housing Board. *Primer for Use of Local Housing Authorities*. Boston, MA: State Housing Board, 1948.

———. *Massachusetts Housing for Veterans*. Boston, MA: State Housing Board, 1948.

Stout, G. M. "What Price Low-Cost Housing?" *National Apartment Journal* (May 1935):10. Quoted in M. B. Schnapper, ed., *Public Housing in America*. New York: H. W. Wilson, 1939.

Straus, Nathan. *The Seven Myths of Housing*. New York: Alfred A. Knopf, 1944.

———. *Housing and Recreation*. Washington, DC: United States Housing Authority, 1939.

Vale, Lawrence J. *From the Puritans to the Projects: Public Housing and Public Neighbors*. Cambridge, MA: Harvard University Press, 2000.

Veiller, Lawrence. *A Model Tenement House Law*. New York: Russell Sage Foundation, 1910.

———. *A Model Housing Law*. New York: Russell Sage Foundation, 1920.

Weiss, Marc A. "Own Your Own Home: Housing Policy and the Real Estate Industry." Paper presented at Conference on Robert Moses and the Planned Environment, Hofstra University, June 11, 1988.

Wood, Edith Elmer. *Introduction to Housing: Facts and Principles*. Washington, DC: United States Housing Authority, 1939.

Transplanting the New Jersey Turnpike to China

Thomas J. Campanella

20

Iconic American built environments have taken root far from Yankee soil, as have other examples of popular culture. China has been particularly fertile ground for the reproduction of American spatial and architectural prototypes, in spite of the enormous cultural and political differences between the People's Republic and the United States. The skyscraper, born in 19th century Chicago, has flourished in Shanghai and Shenzhen. Exclusive gated communities have been built on the outskirts of nearly every major Chinese city, featuring plush villas with maids' rooms and two-car garages. American-style theme parks have opened around the country, some of which celebrate the American landscape itself, with scale replicas of the White House, the United States Capitol, Mount Rushmore, even the World Trade Center. And Mickey Mouse is waiting in the wings; it is only a matter of time before Disney establishes a beachhead on the Chinese mainland (there is already a Disneyland under construction in Hong Kong, and a Shanghai park has been rumored for several years).

20.1 Model of United States Capitol at Beijing World Park.

The transfusion of material culture back and forth between societies, the channels by which exchanges occur, are complex and often obscure, particularly in the present age of light-speed communication and globe-spanning media. This is especially the case when an intermediary is involved, as is the case with Hong Kong and the Chinese mainland. Since the early 1980s, the Hong Kong property development community has functioned as a broker and conduit channeling Western ideas about architecture and urbanism into China. Hong Kong investors, many of whom were educated in the United States and Canada or have extensive family ties there, have been major players in the mainland building and property markets and are often the principal backers of major skyscraper and shopping center projects there. Beijing's immense Oriental Plaza, the largest shopping center in China, is perhaps the most infamous— built amidst a storm of controversy by Hong Kong development tycoon Li Ka-shing. Equally significant is Hong Kong's lead role in residential property development on the mainland, where investors have built hundreds of luxury housing estates and suburban gated "villa" communities since 1985.

Suburban villa developments, aimed at China's rapidly rising professional and entrepreneurial elite, draw from a particularly eclectic array of antecedents. There have been some extraordinary hybrids over the years. Initial plans for Beijing's Rose Garden Villa, for example, featured a medley of architectural neighborhoods such as "European," "American," and "Japanese." There was even a "Space" district, with vaguely deconstructivist folly-houses meant for homebuyers with a "space-age kind of outlook." More typical—and most popular with the new elites—is a style that may be described as wedding-cake Baroque, with florid plaster details and an abundance of statuary. In such developments even patrolled entry gates (all of these projects are gated in some way) become architectural confections intended to convey—however clumsily—status, arrival, and prestige.

20.2 New gated community in Zhongshan, a booming city in the Pearl River Delta.

20.3 Sales brochure for
Country Garden Villas, a
Hong Kong development in
suburban Guangzhou.

But behind the sugary Continental façade lies a substrate of American bedrock. As patterns of settlement on the land—as cultural landscapes—China's gated villa subdivisions borrow chiefly from American precedent. Exposing this lineage sometimes requires peeling back several layers; other times it is explicit, and even a selling point. Of course, there is a good amount of metamorphosis and adaptation that occurs as these cultural prototypes are imported. The changes are often subtle, but more frequently the model undergoes a clear transformation or translation prior to being absorbed into the Chinese mainstream. The best example of the latter is a recently completed gated community in Beijing that is actually named "Orange County," modeled on the suburban California community. "Orange County" is an exception to the general rule; most villa projects are similar to American prototypes only in the larger sense. Up close they commonly present a variety of eclectic details of local, national, and even international origin. As a U.S.-based agent of the Chinese developer put it to Mike Anton and Henry Chu of the *Los Angeles Times*, March 9, 2002, "We wanted to create a whole environment that was in the American style." The success of "Orange County" and similar projects has helped seed interest among American developers in tapping the vast Chinese market for residential housing—a move that could well precipitate the wholesale export of American suburbia to the People's Republic. The U.S. National Association of Home Builders has already held a major conference in China; as an executive director of the Association succinctly put it, "There are 200 million potential customers for single-family housing."

20.4 Entry gate and security guards,
Country Garden Villas.

China's burgeoning upscale suburban communities are an example of what Robert Fishman has termed "global suburbs," exclusive enclaves where "the relations of economic and cultural domination that characterize the global economy" are cultivated and reproduced. Residents of such places were at first indeed the advance guard of globalization—foreign expatriate professionals working in China. But increasingly in the last decade most buyers have been young Chinese professionals increasingly fluent in the emerging vocabulary of global capitalism and "eager to imitate," writes Fishman, "the spatial patterns of privilege in the dominant global society, the United States" (2002:7). Few mechanisms have been as effective in popularizing American privilege than the United States media and entertainment industries. Blockbuster Hollywood films and syndicated television programs such as "Baywatch," "Hunter," and "Growing Pains" have disseminated images of an idealized American world—youthful, affluent, modern—that stokes a craving in China for certain architectural and spatial settings associated with that lifestyle, from the shopping mall to the suburban home.

A key element in this transfusion is the private automobile—arguably the single most cherished status symbol in the New China. Although its vehicle fleet is small compared to the United States, China's rapid motorization has been a prime factor in urban decentralization and sprawl. The number of motor vehicles in China (including taxis, trucks, and other commercial vehicles) rose from a mere 1.7 million in 1980 to 18 million in 2001 (National Research Council 2003). In that same period, the number of private passenger vehicles grew at an average annual rate of almost 20 percent, and more than 28 percent during the boom years of 1991–96 (Riley 2002). It is estimated today that there are as many as 8 million private automobiles in China, and some forecasts see as many as 50 million Chinese motorists by 2020 (Wiseman 2001). This surge has already overwhelmed transportation infrastructure in most cities—especially Guangzhou, Shanghai, and Beijing. Auto ownership in the Chinese capital is escalating by as many as 100,000 vehicles a year, despite astronomical operating costs and a chronic shortage of parking in the city center. The number of privately owned automobiles in Beijing passed the 1 million mark in the spring of 2002. Between January and April that year some 90,000 people sat for their driver's exams, raising the total number of licensed drivers in Beijing to nearly 3 million, according to the Xinhua News Agency, May 22, 2002.

China's motoring revolution has already had a tremendous impact on the landscape. The nation's highway system is nearly ten times the size it was in 1990, and the *Washington Post Foreign Service* reported on June 6, 2002, that transportation planners are working to connect every major city to a 54,700 km highway grid similar in extent to the American interstate highway system. Guangzhou's urban road network has been extended at a rate of 9 percent annually, and Beijing is quickly becoming a concentric version of Los Angeles. A succession of massive ring roads have been looped around the capital, leapfrogging a running tide of development (Hook 2003). Each new road is, of course, meant to accommodate more vehicles and ease congestion. But as often happens, the new infrastructure only encourages more people to take up driving, and is quickly overwhelmed itself. Beijing's expressways are already packed, and at present only a mere 12 percent of the city's population drives (Dorgan 2003). It is very likely that thousands more will purchase automobiles as the fifth and sixth ring roads—both already under construction—are completed in time for the 2008 Olympics. It is impossible to tell whether it is the surging number of motor vehicles or the extensive road building that is driving China's motoring revolution; as these examples suggest, it is likely some combination of both chicken and egg.

The automobile is largely an American artifact, and so too the emerging spatial order of automobility in China. There are strip malls and towering billboards, big-box retail outlets and gas stations that seem to have been lifted straight out of suburban Dallas or Atlanta. The highways themselves bear more than a passing resemblance to American interstates—even the road signs are rendered in familiar green and white. The reason for this is clear. Unlike the more convoluted processes of transference that imported American residential prototypes, China's new era of highway building can be largely traced to a single individual—an extraordinary Hong Kong engineer-cum-developer named Gordon Y. S. Wu. Wu helped put China on the high road by building a highway—the Guangzhou-Shenzhen Expressway—that was inspired by, of all things, the New Jersey Turnpike. One of the first and most influential modern roads in the People's Republic, the Expressway has had a dramatic impact on the physical landscape of the Pearl River Delta, China's fastest-growing and most economically powerful region. The road continues to serve as a touchstone for a nation as smitten with the automobile as Americans were in the 1950s—the very decade in which Gordon Wu studied in the United States and toured its embryonic highway system.

Gordon Wu was born into a family of cars. His father owned the largest taxi fleet in Hong Kong, and was affluent enough to give his son a first-rate education. Gordon was shipped off to Princeton in 1953. The teenager boarded a ship bound for California and, several days later, passed beneath San Francisco's Golden Gate Bridge. It was a transformative moment for the boy. Marveling at the soaring span above, he knew then and there that engineering would be his future. Gordon was an average student at Princeton. Nothing in the curriculum fired his interest as much as a new road that roared across the meadowlands a few miles from campus. The New Jersey Turnpike, completed only two years before, stretched 118 miles from the Delaware River north to the George Washington Bridge. In the 1950s the road was considered a landmark of the motor age and an engineering masterpiece. Even its steel overpasses—all 400 of them—used state-of-the-art structural techniques. New Jersey's governor, Alfred E. Driscoll, called the Turnpike "the finest highway in the world" (Anderson 1996–2004). It set standards that would be applied to interstate highways for decades—from carriageway width and curve radii to the ubiquitous green-and-white highway signs. Moreover, the road stimulated residential development all along its route, transforming a landscape of woodlands and dairy farms into an embryonic suburban kingdom. To a young boy from dense and teeming Hong Kong, this was a sleek vision of future things.

As Gordon Wu related in an interview April 16, 1999, in the summer of 1955, he and three of his classmates drove a brand-new Buick to California, following U.S. Route 30 through the Midwest and over the Rockies. The journey carried them across a national landscape on the threshold of the motor age. America glowed with the heady optimism of an unprecedented economic boom, its young veterans basking in the glory of a good war fought well. They bought suburban homes in places like Long Island's Levittown, and acquired brand-new cars to get them there. In Congress a bill was making the rounds that would eventually emerge as the Federal-Aid Highway Act of 1956, authorizing $25 billion to build a "National System of Interstate and Defense Highways." The frayed tapestry of New York City was being stitched anew by Robert Moses, the city's inimitable master builder. In 1955 Moses was at the apogee of his career. He had already built a dozen bridges and tunnels and more than 600 miles of highway across the metropolitan region, and just won a battle over the Cross Bronx Expressway.

In the spring of 1955 Gordon Wu had a chance to meet this American Haussmann. It was no small event for a young man filled with an aspiration to build. Gordon was part of a group of civil engineering students invited by a construction industry professional society—The Moles—to a dinner and lecture by Moses. Afterward the guest of honor met with the student engineers and talked about roads, and about getting things done.

Gordon Wu graduated from Princeton in 1958. He made his way back home to Hong Kong with an Ivy League diploma in hand and a head full of ideas. In his studies of history he learned how the Erie Canal changed the course of American empire during the 19th century, tapping a vast and bountiful hinterland into the port of New York. Canals, railroads, roads—these meant access, and access lubricated the wheels of commerce. Gordon had toured the greatest highways of the age—engineering marvels of their time. He saw firsthand the extraordinary "seeding" effect these roads had on regional development. He watched as the most ambitious road-building campaign in human history geared up. He had driven across America and met the greatest builder America had ever known. Now Gordon returned home to help his father launch a real estate venture known as Central Enterprises Company, Ltd. Not long after, he founded his own engineering office—Gordon Wu and Associates—and then started a construction company to build what he designed. He founded the company in 1963 and called it Hopewell Construction, Ltd., after a suburban New Jersey town near Princeton.

Gordon Wu soon distinguished himself in one of the headiest periods of urban development in Hong Kong's history. By the late 1970s he was among the most accomplished builders in the British colony. Gordon and his engineers developed a technique of high-rise building construction—the concrete slip-form method—that made it possible to erect a floor every three days. He attained a summit of sorts in 1980, when he crowned the Hong Kong skyline with the 66-story Hopewell Centre—the tallest building in the territory at the time. The soaring white cylinder, topped with a rotating restaurant, was the opening act in what would eventually become the most spectacular skyline in the world, exceeding even New York's for sheer thrust and exuberance. After Hopewell Centre, Gordon began casting about for opportunities across the border, in the long-closed People's Republic of China.

The mainland had only recently begun to open its doors, even to neighboring Hong Kong. After Mao Zedong's death in 1976, Deng Xiaoping became paramount leader of the People's Republic. He began a bold effort to restructure the Chinese economy, shunting aside Maoism and its centrally planned economy for a hybrid of socialism and capitalism. Termed "socialism with Chinese characteristics," the new economic order encouraged free enterprise and entrepreneurialism. To create Petri dishes for foreign investment, several special economic zones were established in the vicinity of Hong Kong. It was thought that by building an experimental city in close proximity to the British colony, China could learn capitalism from a master. Hong Kong became broker and agent to a world yearning to trade with mainland China, and by the mid-1980s cross-border trade and commerce was booming. The first and largest of the special economic zones, Shenzhen, grew from what had been a sleepy fishing village to a busy metropolis in less than a decade.

The Shenzhen growth machine sent shockwaves throughout the Pearl River Delta. Zhuhai and Guangzhou—the old city of Canton—were soon themselves designated special development zones. A tide of foreign investment flooded in from Japan and the West, and even more from Hong Kong businessmen with family connections to delta towns and villages. The region was on the verge of becoming China's golden triangle. But there were obstacles. For one, the Delta lacked even a single modern highway, though it was laced with an extraordinary network of rivers and canals, a natural infrastructure that had enabled the Cantonese to trade with the West for hundreds of years. Even through the Republican and Communist eras, these water routes and a handful of rural roads met the region's transportation needs. But as the economy roared to life in the 1980s, people and goods began moving about like agitated molecules. Every year between 1978 and 1986 the number of bus passenger trips in the region nearly tripled, with many towns and villages being served for the first time ever (Vogel 1989:221–22). Factories and industrial plants were being built farther away from the historic water routes, increasing traffic on an already severely overloaded road network—little more than a maze of county roads and obsolete bridges, many of which were unpaved and nearly all were crowded with pedestrians, oxcarts, and farm equipment.

Worse, the economic engine of the Pearl River Delta—the corridor between Hong Kong and Shenzhen in the south and Guangzhou to the north—lacked a mainline arterial, a "main street," so to speak. It took container trucks seven hours to get from one city to the other—a distance no more than that between New York and Trenton, New Jersey. It was clear that sustaining the economic viability of the Pearl River Delta would depend in large part on building an efficient transportation network. To Gordon Wu, that meant one thing: big roads. He had a delta solution all worked out in his head even before the opening of the Chinese economy. It was one that would have put a smile on the face of Robert Moses. If Deng Xiaoping opened China's door to the world, Gordon Wu would roll an asphalt carpet to its front door—a multi-lane expressway that would track the low-slung east flank of the delta all the way from Shenzhen to Guangzhou. He had in mind a prototype: the New Jersey Turnpike. He would build its Chinese sibling, right down to details like guardrails and green-and-white signs.

Wu rolled up his blueprints and took them to Beijing. To his dismay, few were impressed. The railroad ministry opposed the plans categorically, pointing out that China had few trucks and fewer cars; trains would do well enough to carry China into the future. But Wu was tenacious. He argued that while rail was perfectly suited to a centrally planned economy, the emerging entrepreneurial scene—fluid and dynamic—demanded a much finer "grain" of regional penetration. With good roads, container trucks could take goods straight from factory to buyer. Villages and *dan wei* (cooperatives) far from a rail line could tap into the economy and contribute to regional—and national—growth. He explained to senior ministers how the American interstate highway system worked, how it was built, and how roads like the New Jersey Turnpike had reconfigured the economic geography of North America. He even led a delegation of officials—including China's deputy minister of highways—on a road trip across the United States. Finally, after months of negotiating, Gordon gained the endorsement of both the central government and Guangdong's provincial authorities. Then, in June 1981 he signed a Letter of Intent with the Guangdong Provincial Bureau of Communications and the Provincial Highway Construction Company. Gordon had a green light.

He knew it would not be easy. The Pearl River Delta contains some of the most densely settled places in China. It is also very wet, with a tropical monsoon climate drawing some 80 in of rainfall annually. Throw a stone in any direction, anywhere in the delta, and it is likely to land in water. More than 1,000 miles of rivers, creeks, and canals drain a hydrologic system that extends across an area of 425,700 square km—roughly the size of California (Neller and Lam

1994:438). The geographer George D. Hubbard (1929) called the Pearl River Delta "drowned topography"—a vast coastal plain submerged over the course of millennia and tilting toward the South China Sea. By his estimation the extent of this submerged plain was second only to that of the mighty Yangtze River. It would be a challenge to build a wooden footbridge across land like this, let alone a six-lane expressway. The roadbed would have to be taken over everything from duck ponds and rice paddies to busy shipping channels. There was also the matter of getting around or through densely populated villages and townships. In the path of Gordon's road lay factories, housing developments, orchards and farmsteads, and ancient villages. A right-of-way would have to be painstakingly assembled, piece by piece.

As Gordon's hand-picked team of engineers in Hong Kong worked out the details of the road itself, negotiators hammered out a right-of-way with local officials and landholders along the route. In many ways this was the most difficult and exhausting part of the highway project, and it dragged on for a solid decade. The deal-making required a lot of *guanxi* (personal connections), and it often took place over banquets lubricated with copious amounts of *mao tai*—a potent Chinese liquor. But when the banquets were over came the bill. Yes, the gracious officials would indeed allow Gordon to build his road through their jurisdictions, but not before they received a hefty sum for all their trouble. Where the road was forced to cross land leased to private companies or individual farmers, Wu was told that he had to negotiate with the users on an individual basis; the officials would do nothing to help, though they could easily have done so by condemnation.

The reason was simple: affected landholders (who ranged from owners of orchards and duck farms to appliance factories) would soon themselves receive a visit from local officials, who urged them to bargain hard with the "rich foreigners." In fact, most of the compensation eventually paid each landholder by Gordon's company lined the pockets of corrupt bureaucrats. It was highway robbery, literally. At one point Gordon and his builders were even pressured to alter the route of the road—not away from a densely settled area, but straight toward one! Again, corrupt local municipal leaders had figured that doing this would force the highway builders to acquire and demolish scores of buildings, paying out immense sums in compensation, which was then skimmed. In an even more extreme case, developers gained wind of the coming highway—or were tipped off—and proceeded to erect lavish villas smack in the path of the road. Doing so multiplied the value of the land, enabling the leaseholders to then extract a bloated payout in compensation for their "losses."

In spite of these roadblocks, Gordon was able to patch together a workable if costly corridor for his highway. Now came the actual construction. Some two dozen rivers and canals intersected the route, and all along was boggy land upon which nothing could be built without extensive drainage and filling. As a result, much of the road had to be raised above grade. For this reason, more than a third of the superhighway's total mileage was placed on pylons. The bridges and raised sections were constructed mainly of pre-cast concrete, requiring an astonishing 1.5 million cu m of mix. A total of 43,341 beams were used, some individual members weighing as much as 90 tons. A beam launching gantry was designed in-house by Wu's engineers to facilitate assembly. The gantry lumbered along the construction route like a giant mechanical spider. Even with so much of the road elevated, an immense amount of earth had to be shifted about to produce a smooth path for the roadbed—something like 30 million cu m of earth was cut and filled, a quantity sufficient to bury 3,000 football fields 6 ft under.

Despite these and other challenges, the road was completed in only 22 months. At the peak of operations, more than 30,000 men and women labored on the project—often around the clock. The Guangzhou-Shenzhen Superhighway was finally opened in July 1994; its visionary builder was hailed a hero. Just like its New Jersey inspirant, the superhighway began stimulating development all along its route. Gordon had meant the road to do just that, only he hoped to harvest a good bit of the new energy along its flanks. He did so by retaining options for each of the superhighway's interchanges, where he planned to build an ingenious multilevel flyover-cum-shopping mall. Together, these would make available some 10 million sq ft of retail space. The malls were meant to be revenue producers on their own, but were also intended to spur suburban development in the vicinity, serving as the nuclei of several new townships. It was a vision of utopian sprawl straight from New Jersey and one that has indeed helped hasten the physical transformation of the delta from a largely pastoral landscape of farms and villages into a scene of unmitigated sprawl—something that Rem Koolhaas has called a "bastard metropolis." The footprint of the road and the development it has stimulated is stunningly revealed in aerial and satellite photographs, in which Gordon Wu's superhighway appears like a mighty dragon sprawling across the landscape.

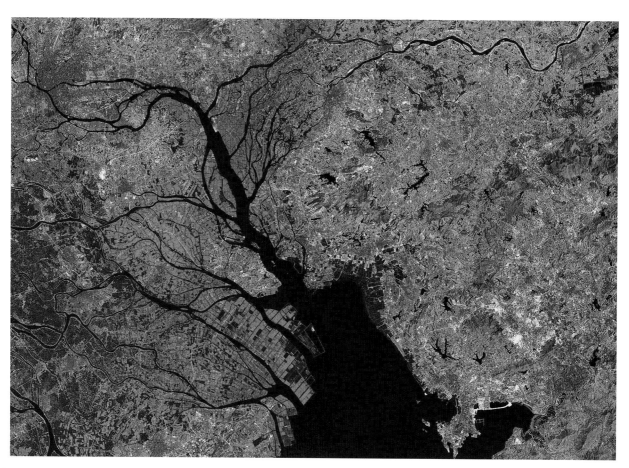

20.6 Landsat image of the Pearl River Delta. The curving band of urbanization on the right side of the Delta reveals both the route and immense impact of the Guangzhou-Shenzhen Superhighway.

Gordon Wu had much more in mind than this single stretch of road, however important. The superhighway was only part of a great highway system he envisioned for the Pearl River Delta and beyond, one that would create a single, finely tuned economic engine out of this vast region. His plan was to build a great circumferential highway around the delta—the economic core of southern China—by pairing the Guangzhou-Shenzhen Superhighway with a second road that would run from Guangzhou south along the west side of the Delta to the Zhuhai Special Economic Zone and former Portuguese colony of Macau. In the north, the two routes would be joined by a 38-km ring-road orbiting Guangzhou (completed in 2002), while in the south (at the bottom of the letter "A" formed by the east and west roads), a causeway would be constructed to bridge the gaping mouth of the Pearl River itself. This "road across the ocean" would run from Zhuhai and Macao across the water to Lantau Island in Hong Kong, site of Chek Lap Kok airport and its extensive highway and rail links. The Chinese penchant for numerology quickly suggested a name—"one bridge, three connections" (Hong Kong, Zhuhai, and Macao). As with the Guangzhou-Shenzhen Superhighway, Gordon was inspired here too by a landmark of American engineering—the Chesapeake Bay Bridge and Tunnel. In fact, he pointed out in an interview, if the Bridge-Tunnel were pulled taut and shipped to China, it would fit almost perfectly between Zhuhai and Hong Kong.

Much of Gordon's trans-delta system has already come into being, and the regional highway network he first envisioned in the 1980s is swiftly taking form. Because of financial problems related to the Asian economic meltdown in the late 1990s, Hopewell Holdings was only able to build the Guangzhou-Shenzhen Superhighway and a beltway around Guangzhou, but it retains a limited interest in the other roads, and provincial authorities have picked up construction where Gordon left off. The Shende Highway on the delta's west flank, for example, has largely been built, although as a "Class I highway" rather than the limited-access expressway Gordon intended. The highway will eventually be plugged into the Guangzhou Ring Road and extended south beyond Zhongshan to connect with China's National Road 105 from Zhuhai.

Here lies the jewel of the system—the cross-Delta causeway that would be the crowning achievement of Gordon Wu's life of building. By 1997 Gordon had already succeeded in building a reduced-scale prototype of the great crossing—a road-bridge linking Nansha, a small city south of Guangzhou to the Humen district of the booming industrial city of Dongguan, one of the largest producers of computer hardware in the world. Built almost entirely of steel, the road-bridge is 16 km (9.9 mi) long with a main span of 888 m (triple 8 is an auspicious number in Chinese culture, as "eight"—*ba*—sounds like *fa*, a character signifying wealth or fortune). It remains the largest cross-Delta structure on the Pearl River, though it would be dwarfed by the proposed crossing to Hong Kong.

Gordon had to wait two decades for his big Delta bridge idea to reach a point where historical forces were aligned to push it toward reality. In 2000 he was appointed chairman of Hong Kong's powerful Port and Maritime Board, giving him a bully pulpit from which to promote the bridge. A study by a pair of researchers at the Chinese University of Hong Kong published in the spring of 2002 estimated that the bridge would boost the entire Delta economy by some U.S.$14 billion, stoke Hong Kong's economic growth by as much as 1.7 percentage points, and add 25,000 jobs for Hong Kong residents on the west side of the Delta (Cheung 2002). Then, in March 2003, Beijing sent a delegation from the State Development and Reform Commission to investigate the proposed bridge and study its effect on economic flows. Not long after the group submitted its final report to the State Council, it was announced in the *People's Daily* online, August 12, 2003, that a coordinating group would be established to study economic, hydrological, and environmental factors related to the Delta crossing. A completion date of 2007—in time for the 10th anniversary of Hong Kong's return to China—has been laid out.

Significantly, there is already precedent in China for just such a project, serving Hong Kong's chief competitor, Shanghai. The Hangzhou Bay Bridge across the Yangtze River Delta, which broke ground in June 2003, will trim some 120 km off travel between Shanghai and Ningbo. Making the $2 billion project a reality was itself a gargantuan undertaking, and preparatory work was begun more than a decade ago (Hoon 2003). Yet Gordon's causeway is still years away from being built.

While a broad coalition of developers and other private-sector groups have lined up behind the project, and it has received the full endorsement of China's central government, it remains unclear where the financing for construction would come from. Also uncertain is whether the future revenues from bridge tolls would be adequate to pay off the debt incurred in construction. The layout itself has been controversial. Four different alignments have been tested over the last decade, and the Y-shaped scheme favored by the Hong Kong government inadvertently cuts nearby Shenzhen out of the loop. There is also a panoply of environmental issues stacked against the road-bridge. For one, the west side of Lantau Island—where the causeway would make landfall—is home to the 800-year-old fishing village of Tai O and breeding grounds for an endangered species of white dolphin. Moreover, the simple administration of such a link would require a degree of transparency and cooperation between Hong Kong and Guangdong Province that may still be years away. There is also the specter of terrorism, a universal concern since the September 11, 2001, attacks on the United States. However massive the causeway may appear to be, to a suicide bomber in a boat it is little more than a filament across the water; even a small explosive device could do enough damage to close the entire span.

And what of China beyond the Pearl River Delta? Gordon Wu had plans for that, too. Though the Pearl River Delta is blessed with fertile land and easy access from the sea, it is separated from the rest of China by a belt of mountains to the north. If, reasoned Gordon, a highway could be hacked through this barrier, the delta could gain access to a much larger hinterland. The highway would be like an asphalt river draining a vast economic watershed. In fact, Gordon had just this in mind. The Chinese land mass is drained by three great river systems: the Huang or Yellow River runs through the north China plains; the mighty Yangtze cuts through the heart of the nation; while the south is served by the Xi or West River—of which the Pearl River is a part. But not all of China has been equally blessed by such life-giving waters. The vast country south of the Yangtze, north of Guangdong, and east of the Yunnan Plateau, for example, is unserved by any major, sea-bound rivers.

This shortcoming of geography was nothing Gordon Wu could not fix with his calculators and earthmovers. His plan was to drive a superhighway from Guangzhou north to Hengyang, the southernmost navigable point on the Xiang River and the major transportation hub of Hunan Province (the Xiang flows into Dongting Lake, which is in turn connected to the Yangtze River by canal). From there the highway would beat a path due north, terminating at the city of Yueyang on the eastern shore of Dongting Lake and a stone's throw from the Yangtze itself. The road, to be called the Guangzhou-Yueyang Expressway, would be China's missing "fourth river"—a 6-lane, 600-mile-long asphalt passageway hacked through a mountain range and spanning the administrative boundaries of hundreds of townships and municipalities. The plan was as outrageous as it was brilliant. The road would not only provide Guangdong access to resource-rich lands all along its route, but by driving all the way to the Yangtze River it would allow the southern province in on a share of the riches flowing toward Shanghai.

The Shanghainese are very covetous of the Yangtze, which is commonly described as their very own "dragon" (Shanghai itself being the dragon's head, not surprisingly). What Gordon had proposed was a regional economic coup as dazzling as Hannibal's elephant ride to Carthage. Shanghai could only watch as a steady flow of container trucks diverted all manner of goods and products south rather than east. In fact, Gordon Wu had another well-engineered coup from the pages of history in mind—New York's Erie Canal. The canal changed forever the economic geography of the United States. Before its completion in 1825, New York was a prosperous port city but one whose national and global significance paled in comparison to Boston and Philadelphia. The building of the Erie Canal was an epic gamble meant to change this by connecting the Hudson River to the Great Lakes. It would be a water-road stretching 363 miles across the entire width of New York. It succeeded beyond anyone's expectation. The canal not only opened up the western part of the state, but put the Midwest and all its agricultural riches within a week's canal ride of the port of New York. With an almost unlimited hinterland at its back door and the sea out front, New York quickly outstripped Boston and Philadelphia and emerged as America's empire state.

Wu was convinced the Guangzhou-Yueyang Expressway would do for the Pearl River region what the Erie Canal did for New York. The road would extend the Hong Kong–Guangdong hinterland far into China's interior, bringing large areas of Jiangxi, Hunan, Guangxi, and even Sichuan Province into its economic orbit. It would bring access to one of the country's most populous regions, home to some 300 million people. When Gordon Wu first proposed this road in 1982, many dismissed it as a fantasy that would require a mandate from heaven to build. But today, like the delta loop he envisioned, it is rapidly becoming reality. Guangdong authorities have adopted Wu's route and are currently constructing an expressway to the northern boundary of their province. About 60 miles of the highway will pass through steep terrain, and at least one major tunnel is scheduled for completion this year. Hunan Province has picked up the baton and is building its section of the highway to Hengyang, funded in part by the World Bank. Completion of the route from the Guangzhou ring road to the Xiang River at Hengyang will likely be completed by 2005. Hong Kong will then have tapped China's greatest river, thanks to a man whose passion for building highways was nurtured 50 years ago and half a world away.

*Portions of the second half of this chapter appeared, in earlier form, as an essay in *Harvard Asia Pacific Review* (Summer 2003).

References

"Beijing's Private Autos Top One Million." Xinhua News Agency, May 22, 2002.

"Bridge Spanning Hong Kong, Zhuhai, and Macao To Be Set Off." *People's Daily* online, August 12, 2003.

"In China, a Rush to Get Behind the Wheel." *Washington Post Foreign Service*, June 6, 2002.

Anderson, Steve. "The Roads of Metro New York: New Jersey Turnpike, 1996–2004." *http://www.nycroads.com/roads/nj-turnpike/*.

Anton, Mike, and Henry Chu. "Welcome to Orange County, China." *Los Angeles Times*, March 9, 2002.

Cheung, Gary. "Bridge to Lift Delta Economy by HK$110 Billion." *South China Morning Post*, April 23, 2002.

Dorgan, Michael. "Chinese Racing to Buy Lower-Priced Cars." *Detroit Free Press*, March 3, 2003.

Fishman, Robert. "Global Suburbs." Paper presented at the First Biennial Conference of the Urban History Association, Pittsburgh, PA, 2002.

Hook, Walter. "Should China Motorize?" Electric Vehicle World (*www.evworld.com*), open letter from the executive director of the Institute for Transportation and Development Policy, January 18, 2003.

Hoon, Lim Siong. "Bridge Building Faces a Cash Crunch." *South China Morning Post*, July 19, 2003.

Hubbard, George D. "The Pearl River Delta." *Lingnan Science Journal* 7(1929):24.

National Research Council. *Personal Cars and China*. Washington, DC: National Academy Press, 2003.

Neller, R. J., and K. C. Lam. "The Environment." In *Guangdong: Survey of a Province Undergoing Rapid Change*, eds. Y. M. Yeung and David K. Y. Chu. Hong Kong: Chinese University Press, 1994.

Riley, Kevin. "Motor Vehicles in China: The Impact of Demographic and Economic Changes." *Population and Environment* 23,5(2002):480–88.

Vogel, Ezra. *One Step Ahead in China: Guangdong Under Reform*. Cambridge, MA: Harvard University Press, 1989.

Wiseman, Paul. "China's Roads are a Crash Course." *USA Today*, September 3, 2001.

Wu, Sir Gordon Y. S. Interview with author, April 16, 1999. Hong Kong.

Landscape Ecology and Cities

Laurie Olin

21

How we conceptualize aspects of the world is a significant issue in the design and planning of human settlements. While this may seem obvious, I do not think it is to many practitioners of architecture, landscape architecture, and planning today. The first step in any analytical process, especially if it is intended to lead to prescription, is that of description. We must be able to see and describe the subject under consideration sufficiently so that we can work with it effectively. Only with an adequate grasp of particular details and events can one generalize and make inferences, leaping intuitively to test hypotheses.

As part of this process designers and planners often use analogies and metaphors as devices to help develop concepts or to explain and discuss the structure and form of cities. Different ages have been partial to particular, popular metaphors drawn from religion, art, and science. Despite the merits or differences of each, one common characteristic has been an emphasis upon an implicit assumption of "wholeness," of complete and contained forms. There has been a recurring use of particular formal patterns and analogies in the discussion, criticism, history, and theory of urban form. Whether one considers artistic notions of composition employed in the Renaissance, mechanical models in the Enlightenment, or organic metaphors of the 19th and 20th centuries, there has been an implicit assumption that a city can be conceived as a "thing," a single organism or composition, a whole interconnected coherent structure that suffuses, supports, or gives shape and form to its overall urban situation (Lynch 1981:73 ff). While this may be true of paintings, sculptures, buildings, and landscapes at the scale of gardens or a farm, it is not necessarily so for a city.

One person or a small group of individuals *can* conceive, design and construct all of these products except for the latter, a city. So too, one purpose can give shape and form, one set of principles can dictate the arrangement of complex organs and features of an animal or plant. These social and natural products are bounded, self-contained, working entities, separate from others, yet whole. Larger settlements, especially the major cities of the world, however, do not behave like individual organisms, nor can their structure be described or planned sufficiently by these earlier methods or analogies. Cities are too extensive, too polyvalent, too multilayered, and too multi-centered. They are driven by numerous (oftenconflicting) decisions, authors, and systems. Most settlements are not really coherent single structures (by almost any measure). The lack of a single author, plan, design, or purpose produces patterns, structures, and physical/formal solutions that are more analogous to the activity and results that can be observed and described in the ecology of a forest or region of mixed and diverse habitats, or even more particularly in a cultural landscape—one with a mixture of natural and human structures and activities.

21.1 An urban landscape: San Francisco, California, seen from Diamond Heights.

A useful way, therefore, to perceive of large and especially modern settlements or cities that is in itself an evolution or development from earlier scientific and organic analogies is to consider them in terms of Landscape and the emerging study of Landscape Ecology. While such an approach may have its limits and drawbacks, it will ultimately prove more helpful both in our ability to describe certain aspects of our cities and to intervene as planners and designers.

Several fundamental concepts of Landscape Ecology can be seen in the situation of cities. These pertain to notions regarding patches, corridors, and matrixes, dynamism and instability, energy flow and interaction between populations, the effects of complexity versus simplicity in the face of crisis, and non–scale-dependent events. Non–scale-dependent events in nature are those whose mathematics and structure are similar to each other regardless of size. Originally developed as part of chaos theory, fractal-based geometries of self-replication can be seen in phenomena as different as the dynamics of cigarette smoke at one scale and the air currents and patterns of weather systems and hurricanes. Other structures such as animal bones, blood circulation systems, and buildings have limits to their effective size that are dependent upon the mathematics underlying the structures of their physical materials, crystals, or molecules.

Urban examples of size-dependent structures, i.e., where the mathematics and geometry determine limits to function or effectiveness, would be the capacity, volume, and effectiveness of the flow in circulation systems such as roads, bridges, walkways, sewers, or aqueducts. A non-size-dependent phenomenon, or one that could operate similarly at various scales, would be those events dependent upon the laws of thermodynamics, say wind and heat. A size-dependent phenomenon would be the possibility of the presence of a certain animal or bird species which requires a territory of a minimum acreage of old-stand forest for its diet, home, and behavioral traits. A non-size-dependent event would be the in-migration of a particular group of foreign nationals to a region or city.

Reflecting on urban projects upon which I have worked at various scales over a 40-year period, I conclude that no matter what the project, whether large or small, public or private, there was always another scale above and below that upon which my colleagues and I were working. In fact, every plan and project was always only a patch or a scrap, an incomplete fragment of some larger whole, and this larger urban situation was both a collage and a palimpsest of such partial structures interacting in space and time in much the same manner as natural communities and systems in a landscape. While it is obvious that a city is not a forest or a coral reef, I have come to see settlements and especially major cities as landscapes, albeit of an urban form.

I have not always seen things thus. Entering architectural practice at the beginning of the 1960s it was clear that a lot was wrong with the models of Ed Logue, Ed Bacon, and Victor Gruen then in use. The massive urban renewal projects and destructive Eisenhower-era interstate highway system savaged one city after another and sent many people off in search of alternatives. Pre-industrial, indigenous, and vernacular architecture, as well as primitive and prehistoric communities were studied avidly by my generation. Aldo Van Eyck's fascination with Dogon settlements in Africa, Bernard Rudofsky and Sybil Moholy-Nagy's presentation of buildings created without architects, Thomas Sharpe, Ian Nairn, and Gordon Cullen's presentation of villages in England and Western Europe as models of community and civitas, were like catnip to designers at the time. Mayan ruins and Japanese farms (as presented by Norman Carver) and all manner of development and settlement patterns were studied by my colleagues who had become disenchanted with contemporary developments in the American— and to some degree Western European—urban condition. Even architectural historians such as Vincent Scully and Christian Norberg-Schultz and critics such as Rayner Banham and Kenneth Frampton shifted their interests from single buildings and individual architectural personalities to larger ensembles, communities, and cities with more than passing references to landscape and ecology. This atavistic study of ancient sites and primitive societies was an attempt to make a break from the perceived formal traditions and habits of the moment. While it was educational, this activity rarely produced models that helped in coming to grips with the situations facing professionals in highly evolved and large 20th century cities.

One perceptive theorist swimming against this tide was Christopher Alexander who, before he moved to California in 1965, wrote a remarkable two-part essay, "A City is Not a Tree." In it Alexander argues that the analogy of a tree used by some of his contemporaries to describe the structure of cities was "comparable to the compulsive desire to neatness and order that insists the candlesticks on the mantelpiece be perfectly straight and perfectly symmetrical about the center." Instead he proposes "the semilattice, by comparison is the structure of a complex fabric; it is the structure of living things; of great paintings and symphonies." While he had difficulty fully articulating just what his alternative structure would be like, he was onto something in his antagonism toward categorical zoning and the separation of uses practiced then and still much in vogue. In the face of a predilection for single unified compositions he advocated instead schemes that exhibited overlapping, simultaneity, and multiple connectivity.

Other personalities as diverse as J. B. Jackson, Ian McHarg, William H. Whyte, Kevin Lynch, Theo Cosby, and Spiro Kostoff spent decades of their mature careers seeking to analyze and explain and in some cases even codify principles that took into account the immediate

world around them and situations far more complex and advanced than those of primitive societies. Some offered keen insight into human behavior, others broad resource management tools, or strategies for the arrangement or determination of the desirable scale of particular ensembles of activities. Each has contributed to our understanding of the nature and structures of cities. Despite offering help for one particular sort of situation or another, none, with the possible exception of Lynch, has offered adequate help to those of us in practice faced with the design and planning of significant chunks of urbanity.

My own speculation upon the structure of settlements and cities beyond a consideration for buildings, their situation and obligations, came after I left New York and returned to Seattle in 1969. For two years I lived and worked part time along with a group of artists and designers in the Skid Road community, eventually publishing in 1974 a small study that was largely a tract opposing the City Planning Agency and government who were intent upon leveling much of parts of that city known as Pioneer Square and the Pike Place Market. The major insight I gained was that the residents of Skid Road formed a society distinct from that of the larger, parent society in the city around them. Furthermore, rather like one population of plants or animals living in close proximity with another in a natural setting, there were various interactions and conflicts between these two communities. While sharing some resources, the spatial organization as it related to these impoverished and in many cases, homeless individuals—

where they slept, ate, socialized, acquired goods or income, their daily routine—was developed in a very coherent way within, beside, and on top of the structure that was being used by the rest of the community. When I mapped it I realized that the world of a Skid Road bum was remarkably analogous to that of the territory of many of the wildlife species I was familiar with from my experience in the wilderness of Alaska and readings in field ecology. In my essay in human ecology, *Breath on the Mirror* (1972), I was reluctant, unlike some popular journalists and behavioral scientists of the time, to push the analogy too far. I still am. For me it's merely a useful and revealing way to see or describe things.

A few years later I had the privilege to live, work, and study in both England and Italy. Some of my conclusions are presented in *Across the Open Field* (2000). I found much to learn from their cities, villages, countryside, parks, and gardens, not the least of which was that an ecological perspective seemed inevitable in attempting to relate the multiple phenomena that comprise each of these environments. Nevertheless, ecological literature available in the 1970s was heavily oriented to wilderness populations and remote, largely undisturbed natural settings and was difficult to press into service regarding cities.

Today I realize that the lens through which I have consistently examined architecture, villages, towns, and cities is that of *the relationship of any particular thing or event to its setting*, whether urban or not. By this I mean something other than contextualism or landscape as they are generally construed. The theoretical model I was circling around had yet to emerge in the literature available to professionals like myself who were not in the social or life sciences. Today, it exists. It is known as "Landscape Ecology," and there are numerous proponents in Europe and America. Three of its most accessible texts are *Landscape Ecology* (1986), by Richard T. T. Forman and Michel Godron; *Land Mosaics: the Ecology of Landscapes and Regions* (1997), by Richard T. T. Forman; and *Landscape Ecology Principles in Landscape Architecture and Land-use Planning* (1996), by Wenche E. Dramstad, James D. Olson, and Richard T. T. Forman. What separates these works from much of what went before is that they are devoted to the study, description, and the development of theory regarding the nature of inhabited, developed, disturbed, and settled lands. Much of this study is concerned with what takes place in so-called natural areas adjacent to or within settled lands of agricultural, forestry, suburban, and urban development, not some remote archipelago or wilderness. In so doing, a vocabulary and methods have been developed to describe and study the life within ordinary settled landscapes and to recognize the constituent parts, interactions, problems, and issues posed by different arrangements, shapes, and sizes of those elements.

From these and other writings one may consider some principles of Landscape Ecology:

- A landscape is a living system.
- Living systems exhibit three broad characteristics: structure, functioning, and change.
- Landscape structure is the spatial pattern or arrangement of landscape elements.
- Functioning is the flow or movement of animals, plants, water, wind, materials, and energy (in cities add people, money, goods, ideas) through the structure.
- Change is the dynamics or alteration in spatial pattern and functioning over time.
- The structural pattern of a landscape is composed entirely of three types of universal elements: patches, corridors, and matrices. These each have variability in size, character, texture, etc., but form all landscapes, no matter how diverse.
- Patches can be big or small, varying in shape, and number.
- Corridors can be straight or curvy, narrow or broad.
- A matrix is an extensive interconnected similar association, fabric, community, or material.
- These are all scaleless concepts and are not size dependent.

Why or how can such seemingly simple premises be of use in urban design? Or even first, how do such notions come into play in the planning and design for landscapes in general; what are the issues and goals; and then what are the supposed results? How could such notions translate through analogy into practice in urban situations?

The elements or building blocks of a landscape—patches, corridors, and matrices—together form mosaic patterns of great variety and at all scales. In recent studies it has been determined that context often has a greater effect upon patch functioning and change than the internal characteristics within a patch (Forman 1997:285). Context includes adjacency, neighborhood, and location, all of which establish spatial structure and the potential for interaction between units. If one of the most fundamental laws of geography is that all things are related but near things are more related than distant ones, then the spatial arrangement of elements will affect the interchange and flow of energy, nutrients, wind, air, gasses, water, animals, vehicles, and people. Because particular species and individuals "find some habitats more suitable, many locomotion-driven movements are directional, toward patches of the same type" (Forman 1997:287).

People, of course, do not behave as mechanically as soils. Animals and winds also move all over the place, up and down slope, as well as back and forth, leading to flow-webs or multiple movements between ecosystems. While an infinite number of ecosystem arrangements and patterns may be theoretically possible and a bewildering number of apparently different looking or unique neighborhoods, landscapes, or sets of individual features seem to occur, in fact a limited number of common general configurations exist.

An extraordinary body of field research in recent decades has developed data about the effects of spatial arrangement and scale upon ecosystems, as well as a typology of fundamental spatial patterns. These patterns may be considered under the following terms: regular, aggregated, linear, parallel, and associated. While it is obvious that these patterns will be limited by the simple mathematics of three-dimensional geometry and the fundamental law of physics that only one object may occupy a given space at a time, the resulting physical combinations—linear chains of patches, spider-like star clusters of patches around a matrix, or corridors linking patches between matrices (of one or different types)—the results in terms of effects, benefits, or problems has not been clear or obvious. As one study pointed out, while only seven common elements (fields, clearings, woods, hedgerows, rivers, roads, and house clearings) were common in 25 different landscapes considered, the differences in their arrangement, extent, and configuration produced markedly different results in the biological and aesthetic as well as social and economic character (Dramstad, Olson, and Forman 1996).

Although it is not possible in the context of this chapter to fully develop the supporting data, it is arguable that pursuing this point of view and the methodology of landscape ecology would be of great use in urban and suburban design. In some ways both traditional town planners and so-called New Urbanists have intuitively utilized some of these principles. One example is the concept of buffers, which can be found in ecosystems possessing more than two associations, such as when the plants and animals of two biophysical, ecological communities, such as a prairie or meadow and a forest, are separated by a transition "buffer" zone, or community of plants and animals, which is neither. A seashore would be such a zone, with its own particular characteristics and inhabitants existing between the incompatible worlds of ocean and dune or upland, which have their own plants and animals, which cannot thrive in either of the other zones. Such areas are seen as both separating areas of difference and as joining them, while maintaining their own character. An interesting example of this as a cultural product in the rural world is the "hedgerow," which is a barrier or fence between adjoining agricultural fields. It has the biophysical characteristics of a forest edge or transition zone, being neither a woods nor a field, and as such has contributed a remarkable ecological diversity and richness to agricultural landscapes wherever it has been employed. What, one might ask, could be an urban equivalent? Commercial strips along arterials and boulevards or parkways come to mind as possible answers. By analogy these have often been introduced between different and seemingly incompatible land uses because of their potential ability to reduce some sort of negative reaction or to absorb or prevent the flow of something—a predator, seeds, flooding, or some social nuisance such as pollution, noise, or an unpleasant sight—from one sector or place to another.

It is the eschewing of single systems and the embrace of multiplicity and layered interactions and the limited spatial vocabulary and arrangement possibilities that provide useful models and analogues. There are many examples of the correlation between this body of theory and that of our contemporary understanding of urban situations.

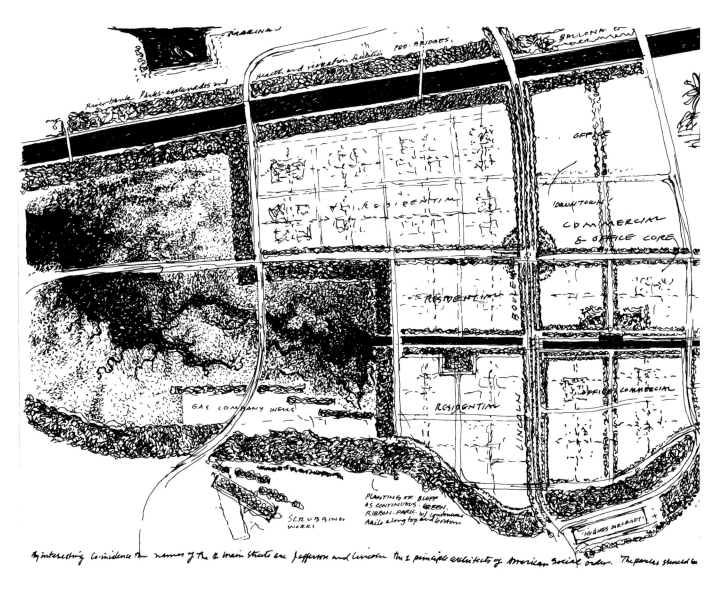

21.4 Ink drawing of early concept for Playa Vista development, Los Angeles, California.

Several urban projects that I have worked on with my office and others can be seen to embody analogies to some of the most fundamental spatial and structural properties considered in landscape ecology. It should go without saying that many other issues were involved, and that these proposals can be seen and described in other ways. My point, however, is that fundamental notions derived from Landscape Ecology were useful to me in the early stages of conceptualizing these plans.

PLAYA VISTA, LOS ANGELES, CALIFORNIA

This 1,000-acre site is now under development with significant portions in construction. It has been presented in other contexts, even (whether appropriately or not) by others as an example of "New Urbanism," a premise I do not particularly share. I prefer instead what might well be termed "Old Urbanism." Located on a former industrial site near the Pacific Ocean

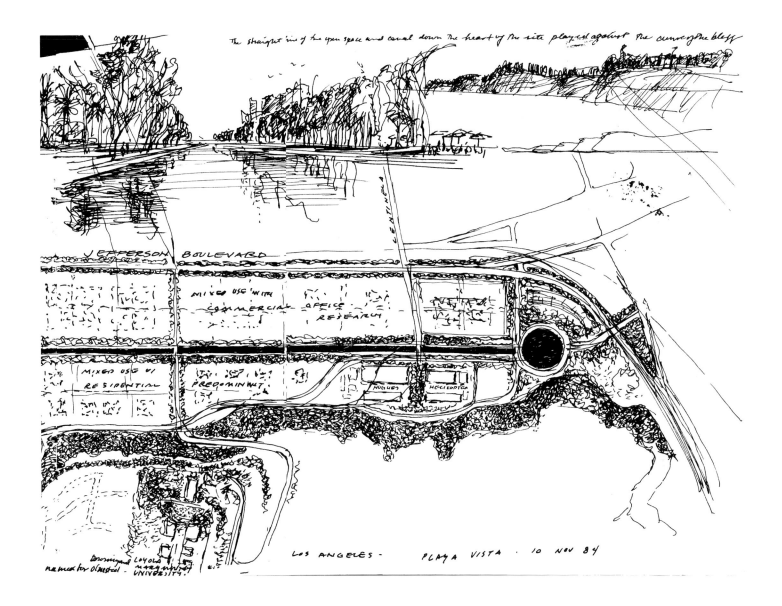

The straight line of the open space and canal down the heart of the site played against the curve of the bluff

JEFFERSON BOULEVARD

CENTINELA

MIXED USE WITH
COMMERCIAL OFFICE
RESEARCH

MIXED USE W/
RESIDENTIAL

PREDOMINANT

HUGHES

HELICOPTER

named for Olmsted —
University.

LOS ANGELES ·   PLAYA VISTA ·   10 NOV 84

at Marina Del Rey, most of this site lies within the city of Los Angeles near the international airport, LAX. Although I worked on this project off and on for about twelve years with a large number of talented architects, planners, engineers, attorneys, ecologists, economists, developers, and politicians, it is safe to say that the first of several evolving plans we produced grew out of this first plan sketch made during my initial site visit.

In the first plan one can see the concepts of matrix, corridors, and patches applied to the tract overall, and an understanding that the tract was to constitute a new large precinct grafted into the patchwork of the adjacent surrounding city. There is a substantial amount of generalized texture indicated, a matrix of sorts of urban fabric. This represented normal streets, buildings, yards, and sidewalks—the blocks and houses, apartments and condos, shops and businesses—which were to fill out the bulk of the development. This was to be more of a normative extension of what the rest of Los Angeles was made of, but we hoped with an increase in density and quality, sort of a better version of numerous urban fragments which had

been produced there between World War I and World War II. Although I did have particular models of architecture and street trees in mind—a sense of local character within this matrix—they were not germane to this level of diagram.

The western portion of the site consists of a large patch. This was to be a reconstructed wetland adjacent to Ballona Creek and the ocean. With the exception of a road traversing it on a causeway, it was to be a pure setting for natural processes and wildlife habitat with no human intrusion. Since wetlands are biologically among the most important and fecund of all physiographic situations this was a particularly strong and unconventional proposal in Los Angeles in 1986.

Also in this scheme was a mile-long corridor connecting the eastern end of the development with that of the west, providing a situation for people, vegetation, and by implication animals (mostly birds).

A mixed-use plan was developed, with housing and commercial interests. The latter included the retention of Howard Hughes's historic aircraft factory buildings, which were pressed into a new use as sound stages for such films as "Labor Day"and "Titanic" a few years later as the plan progressed.

This first plan, however, met with political opposition, and the ownership of the project changed. Working with the next owner and a different design group I managed to increase the size of the wetlands from 45 acres to 90, and to shift the long corridor south to be adjacent to the Westchester bluffs which we had preserved from development in the initial plan. This increased its ecological utility by allowing wildlife to move back and forth from the hillside to a stream I now proposed to create as well. An amenity to the community, it was an ecological improvement as well. To make up for this shift a series of new small neighborhood parks and squares were introduced into the residential matrix on a fairly regular basis. This peppering of small parks also helps to take pressure off the stream corridor for active human recreation and play space, thereby helping to improve its biological utility. A rich street plan formed an integral and intertwined aspect of this matrix.

This plan is now under construction, and I am happy to say at the time of writing the wetland is partially built and has won an award from the EPA. The first phase of the western housing and its parks are under construction, and the commercial properties at the East End are in design with construction expected to commence within in 2004.

Rebstock Park, Competition and Bebaungsplan, Frankfurt, Germany

This proposal forcefully developed a scheme that can be analyzed in terms such as those of patches, matrix, and connectivity. As at Playa Vista this project was also located on a former airfield and industrial site, in this case just west of the historic center of the city. The initial pattern of buildings in our scheme conceptually grew out of, extended, and transformed those we found in Ernst May's well-known Siedlung plan of the 1930s immediately adjacent to the east of our site. In an experiment to create a structure for this large urban development that was not based upon current or traditional geometries and urban design habits, the New York-based architect Peter Eisenman and I looked for other sources of form. We came upon intriguing recent developments in the descriptive language and diagrams of the science of sudden events such as avalanches and catastrophes. This led us to speculate upon the nature of transformative events as expressed physically, which in turn led to concepts and aspects of folding. We were attracted to analogues regarding the possibilities "both-and" or inclusiveness rather than those expressing old familiar pairs of opposed qualities, such overworked dualities and polarities as hard/soft, open/closed, formal /informal, natural/cultural. This was also a conscious experiment to see if we could conceive of the project in a way other than that of a normal figure/ground relationship, which has had such a determinist effect upon much of urban design in recent decades. While helping to depict issues of scale and texture, and especially the nature of urban open space, in our view this supposedly "contextual" device (figure/ground) popularized by Colin Rowe, Fred Koetter, the Krier brothers, and others has too often limited designers' considerations to volumetric matters and building arrangement as derived from the work of Camillo Sitte and Otto Wagner at the beginning of the last century.

At the time we were speculating upon such issues of arrangement and form and other topics such as storm water management, aquifer recharge, cold (fresh) air drainage from a greenbelt (recently developed for Frankfurt by Bernard Lassus and others), urban agriculture, wildlife habitat, traffic, housing, schools, recreation, and jobs, and daily use patterns for different age groups were also addressed. Seasonal parking for the nearby Messe (Frankfurt Book Fair and Exposition), major regional public recreation facilities and community gardens were also added to the mix. It seemed to us that conventional notions of urban form and geometry were inadequate to accommodate such multiple interactions. Ecological analogues, however, seemed very suited to our needs.

21.7 Ink drawing of parking fields, recharge canals, habitat hedgerows of Rebstock Park development.

After winning an invited competition and developing a master plan for the site, a set of regulatory planning documents, or Bebaungsplans, have been developed and approved for this site by the City of Frankfurt. Construction thus far has been stalled, largely as a result of changes in national and municipal finances and government leadership resulting from German reunification, as well as recent financial woes of the principal developer.

Nördlisches Derendorf Competition, Dusseldorf, Germany

In this subsequent project Eisenman and I worked from a different but related departure point. For a quantity of new social housing and an exhibition/trade center to the north of the altstadt and its historic streets of tall, thin, row houses we conceived of the project and the buildings as analogous to a landscape of mountains and valleys. The streets were seen as canyons and cliffs, and in fact were rather normal looking. The buildings were hills, sloping

21.8 Model of Dusseldorf mixed-use development proposal.

away from the streets and forming green valleys, which served as private and semiprivate open space in a traditional manner, in essence as back yard park corridors. The whole was a matrix, not that dissimilar from the earlier conventional urban fabric to the south. This project can be seen as being composed of nearly all one matrix, albeit one of parallel corridors: a ridge and valley landscape, with good solar orientation and air movement.

Not only did we not win the competition, but also it seems that the city fathers, or at least the architectural jury, hated our scheme and expressed the view that it was grotesque. I am convinced it was much more "normal" than they understood.

Mission Bay, San Francisco, California

By the end of the 20th century the United States had become an extremely conservative and contentious (at times seemingly retarded) scene for urban design, planning, landscape architecture, and architecture. For reasons of scale, finance, entitlement, and politics the owners

21.9 Mission Bay development plan, San Francisco, California.

and design team with whom I have been working were not able to achieve large patches of open space within this 200-acre urban development, but with San Francisco Bay immediately to the east this seemed acceptable.

Earlier plans emphasized single qualities—creating a patch by opening up China Basin in a quasi-Venetian manner, or creating a matrix with the maximum density and a hierarchy of streets and small squares. My colleagues and I, instead, have resorted to the production of a maximum amount of interactive edge conditions and to an emphasis upon connective corridors. We have also attempted to develop a vibrant matrix of mixed-use development that includes a considerable amount of pedestrian and private garden resources. A key element or event in landscape ecology is something known as an "ecotone," which is the edge of boundary between two different ecological communities. Kevin Lynch would have called this a "seam." In natural settings such edges are the most active in terms of all manner of transactions between species and communities of plants and animals. Several key decisions were made regarding context. In addition to adjusting this new urban fabric to address the Bay, our planning team has utilized the humanist-derived block dimensions used by Vara, who established the layout of the original mission and Pueblo nearby, rather than the extraordinarily long blocks and orientation of the 19th century industrial area.

CONCLUSION

When engaged in urban design, designers and planners make fragments and episodes at various scales. These parts may or may not be physically or conceptually complete formal structures, but inevitably at another scale of consideration they will always be seen as fragments of a larger mosaic. Knowing how a collection of such fragments can complement and support each other to produce a larger environment that supports many diverse lives and purposes is highly desirable. This is especially true if one accepts the notion that the language, metaphors, analysis, and conceptual models we use affect the structures and communities that we build.

REFERENCES

Alexander, Christopher. "A City Is Not A Tree (Part II)." *Architectural Forum* (May 1965):58–61.

Dramstad, Wenche E., James D. Olson, and Richard T. T. Forman. *Landscape Ecology Principles in Landscape Architecture and Land Use Planning*. Washington, DC: Island Press, 1996.

Forman, Richard T. T. *Land Mosaics: The Ecology of Landscapes and Regions*. Cambridge: Cambridge University Press, 1997.

Forman, Richard T. T., and M. Godron. *Landscape Ecology*. New York: Wiley, 1986.

Lynch, Kevin. *Good City Form*. Cambridge, MA: MIT Press, 1981.

Olin, Laurie. *Breath on the Mirror, Seattle's Skid Road Community*. Seattle, WA: By the Author, 1972.

———. *Across the Open Field, Essays Drawn From the English Landscape*. Philadelphia, PA: University of Pennsylvania Press, 2000.

Scully, Vincent. *American Architecture and Urbanism*. New York: Praeger, 1969.

Settlements After Now

Michael Sorkin

22

The urban population of the world is currently growing at the rate of 150,000 a day. This means that we are adding the equivalent of 50 cities of one million—50 Dallases, Detroits, Jiddahs, or Guatemalas—or five megacities—five Cairos or Tokyos—a year. I mention these dire statistics simply to assert that any discussion of contemporary shelter and settlements descends—in the first instance—from necessity. Although our cities and our dwellings embody our cultures and their histories succinctly and intrinsically, the press today is above all quantitative.

We have the intellectual and economic resources to solve this crisis and, for the most part, there are no technical problems to impede us. The real problem is distributive, an issue of justice and will. This observation is scarcely fresh—Friedrich Engels, for one, made it more than 150 years ago—but it remains in the background of these discussions. Just as the history of shelter writes the history of our mores and social structures, so it records the history of our politics, our greed, and our efforts to be fair.

Modernity has, nonetheless, changed these equations. Those black garbed anti-IMF demonstrators in Seattle, Washington, or Prague, hurling bricks through the windows of McDonald's and Starbucks, have surely located the appropriate symbols of a system at once narrow, homogenizing, and concentrating, yet global. The context of settlement today can no longer be located in isolation from the space of these worldwide flows of capital and ideology that shape our cities more profoundly than any other influence.

However we resolve issues of equity, there is no way to solve the shortfall of shelter other than via the construction of new cities. Hundreds of these will be needed to house the world's burgeoning population. Hundreds more will be needed to rehouse the immiserated masses stuck in the hypertrophied, apraxic megacities that we've produced. Without exception, these new cities will be global, linked by physical and virtual skeins of commerce, communication, and movement, to the rest of the world. But, they will be obliged to solve many more problems locally both to survive and to flourish.

In the globalizing environment, the pressures—at both high and low ends of the development scale—increasingly make no difference. Sprawl, the near universal urban development default, spreads in both underdeveloped and developed versions—the Mexico City or the Silicon Valley models—and national and municipal authorities, almost without exception, seem powerless or unwilling to stop it.

Part of the issue is a lack of clear-cut alternatives: we suffer from a shortage of suitable paradigms for settlement. The current repertoire includes modernist mass housing models, suburban strategies, devolutions of the garden city (including so-called new urbanist models), corporatist mega-models á la Pudong or Canary Wharf, and a limited number of *ex-nihilo* new town strategies—as practiced, for example, with mixed success around Cairo. Finally, and most prominently, the indigenous functionalist minimalism of the *favelas* and squatter communities that ring the cities of the developing world—the real terrain of this explosive growth—must be cited. While arguments can be made for the efficacy and logic of each of these types, all are fundamentally lacking in key qualities, ranging from sustainability to physical character to social dynamism and equity.

One of the difficulties engendered by the neo-liberal economic regime those protesters in Seattle were out to trash is its faith in the invisible hand. This laissez-faire economic compact translates—in the urban and architectural realm—into a suspicion of planning, framed in any way other than as the physical means of accommodating market forces. The flexibility and continuous relocations and shifts demanded by the global market distrust permanence in general and slowly accumulated urban organization in particular. Such short-range focus is no friend of great cities.

Ironically, this impetus to impermanence and the reduction of planning to a set of marketing protocols is abetted by the contemporary, postmodern, academic, and theoretical mood. To begin, the failures of modernist urbanism (and of the modern fantasy of a universal subject meant to inhabit it) have left us not simply shy of the solution but of any solution that aspires to the comprehensive. Of course, the radiant city model got no less than it deserved, but we are left to confront the same problem it sought to solve with one fewer means at out disposal.

This generalized suspicion of planning conceived as a top-down, command practice is not simply the outgrowth of a single ill-conceived model but of an array of local and community struggles against its imposition. Today, the hegemonic apparatus is not less one-dimensional or authoritarian, it has simply gone underground, been virtualized, codified outside the visual field. Part of the task of the recovery of the planning process will be to revisualize it, to make its effects legible. This will involve—as in Seattle—a vigorous critique of the mystified meanings of choice in an environment of so-called free trade, of remorseless commercial propaganda, or of lax "as-of-right" planning strategies.

Here in the academy, we have surely abetted this reticence to confront the problem of new settlement directly. For close to 50 years, our most prominent discourses have undercut the relevance first of intentionality and later—a logical development—of authority. This cutting loose of the fixity of intentions and texts, while obviously thrilling as an analytical site, has only reinforced our suspicion of master narratives, received ideas, and the ethical stability of places and situations. However, if narrative can be embodied in the stones, stucco, and spaces of the city, there is no more complicit and masterly narrative in culture. Cities depend on their accumulations of singularities and on the legibility of historic masses of compacts to function and to thrill.

Four imaginary projects from my studio attempt to revisit the idea of settlement and shelter from several fresh perspectives. They assume a number of cultural and environmental defaults and constitute both practical proposals and polemical interventions into the questions we are discussing today and tomorrow. All of them address issues raised by globalization but view it as an inevitability that harbors both threatening and promising components. None of them, however, attempts to pose as a universal solution, however concretely they recognize the universality of the problems they confront.

The planning of settlements in the new millennium confronts two great threats. The first of these is environmental, the breakneck degradation of the environment and the mismanagement, squandering, and maldistribution of global resources. Whether one supports the view that cities are the product of agriculture or vice versa, history is clear on the intimacy of the initiating relationship between the local supply of resources and the growth of fixed settlements.

This economic idea of locality is worth revisiting. We have been working on the idea of self-sufficiency in cities and looking again at the import replacement model, so beloved of command planners and Jane Jacobs. Although I do not harbor any fantasy of complete urban self-sufficiency, the calculation is an excellent way to begin to inventory the environmental weight of a town or city. In thinking about this, I draw on the notion of the ecological footprint, pioneered by William Rees in Vancouver. If we are to move towards a globally sustainable environment and towards increased local autonomy simultaneously, calculating the requirements for self-sufficiency in food supply, water, energy, oxygen, culture, etc. will be crucial.

Such a calculation will also open the door to fresh considerations of physical differences in cities. If globalization has a deleterious effect on the character of cities, it is in the risk of homogenization, the effacement of the *genius loci*. I do not believe that the solution to this problem—especially in the context of new cities built from scratch—is to attempt to resuscitate historic forms totally wrested from their originating contexts of meaning. This risks the devolution of urbanism into a species of symbolic decoration and the willful ignorance of more resonant and sustainable approaches.

However, if the history of settlements does have anything to teach us, it is that a process-based view of the interaction of culture and environment is the royal road to urban invention. Bio-regional character and necessity inflected by the daily habits of citizens has always lain at the heart of settlement form. Here we really can learn from the millenia. Not necessarily directly but from their strategies and practices of compaction, of climate modulation, of neighborhood formation, of local interdependency, of movement, of scale, and of expression. Often these solutions can be far more radical than current thinking. Looking back to Çatal Höyük or the Chaco Pueblo, for example, we find complex settlements that solve the problems of circulation and distribution without either corridors or streets, an amazing configuration.

The creation of meaningful difference in the hundreds of cities that the global economy will produce entails not simply a reliance on the "natural" processes of response to climate, topography, local materials, or cultures. Indeed, adequate difference cannot be assured by the fictions of autonomy however useful they are environmentally, politically, economically, or culturally. All cities will have to confront the forceful particulars: global capital, environmental quality, shifts in production, and reconfigurations of the family into other forms of affinity.

But this still leaves us short of the means of producing the kinds of differences that distinguish Fez, from New York, from Prague. New cities will not simply require similar differences of degree, they will be obliged to acquire them swiftly and "artificially." To me this means that the production of new settlements will rely—more intrinsically than ever—on frankly artistic strategies for the production of meaning. This is a study we have neglected almost completely. Yielding either to arguments of tradition or necessity, the visionary discourse is almost completely marginalized. But, if our cities are to exhibit the exemplary differences so manifest in the historic settlements we are seeing at this conference, they will require vision more than ever.

I do not advance the view that visionary urbanism must or can proceed from the pure realms of invention. Indeed, I am not certain of the existence of such a realm. I am, however, interested in two particular sites of potential for such renewal. The first is historic. As I have suggested, good cities represent accumulations of compacts, which—like the growth of a forest—take on successive series of forms and ecologies. Although much current architectural ideology is prejudiced towards dynamism and the irrationalities of untrammeled growth, so many of our greatest cities—including those mentioned above—have achieved a form of completion, a climax as the foresters would say.

Conceptually speaking, this homeostatic situation has tremendous relevance for the creation of self-sustaining new cities. Such cities will necessarily be limited in their growth and will always be subject to an on-going inventory of their sufficiency and their environmental efficiency. The problem with engaging the precedent of climax is in defining the creative utility of the observation. We remain too much in thrall of the formal specifics of satisfying historic environments and miss both the possibilities to inflect them as sources rather than principles or patterns for copy *and* the possibility that their meanings have simply shed too much depth to retain relevance.

How can we then loosen the grip of historicism and its translation into the preservationist regulatory environment that—paired with its evil twin, laissez-faire edge-city suburbanism—so stifles invention. Certainly, the dramatic infusion of an environmentally based set of ambitions will help tremendously as will the inculcation of the fantasy of self-sufficiency. Parenthetically, I believe that this latter insistence on a constant inventory of a city's capacities will abet—both via its scales of participation and the substance of its continuous decision-making—the progress of democratic governance. As many have observed, the urban is the logical register of enfranchisement, independence, and resistance for citizens of the global system.

The second great sphere of invention is the accidental. As social entities, cities are great accident-producing machines, propinquity engines that advance both freedom and sociability by engendering encounter. This same prospect of invention through juxtaposition characterizes the physical city. Ecologists call a region of overlap between separate ecologies an ecotone. Cities have equivalent territories—urbitones—in which scales, populations, and formal typologies abut and mix. These are sites of potentially tremendous inventive possibilities—zones of genetic fluidity—and our new cities must proceed with the logic of and preference for such places of experiment. While the stabilities of urban form are a critical counterweight to the profligate shifts in our cultures of life-style and inhabitation, the city cannot remain static any more than it can acquiesce to its dissolution.

Weed, Arizona (1994)

Weed, Arizona, is a proposal for a small new city that grew from an investigation of possibilities for the conversion of the American military economy by reusing existing bases as sites for new cities, in this case a small piece of the Yuma Proving Ground. The idea is to transform one great national enterprise, militarism, to another—urbanism.

Located on an existing artificial lake created by a dam on the Colorado River, the site adjoins a large, irrigated, agricultural area. The town is dimensioned by the bearing capacity and character of the land, by proximity to water, and by a neighborhood structure loosely configured

to a ten-minute walking radius. A series of intersecting, branching spines provides pedestrian streets, and an element of order, and surfaces for different styles of movement, including a slow-motion transit system. Automobiles are relegated to the periphery of the city.

This urban morphology is meant to be responsive to the fresh possibilities raised by environmental best-practices, by new modes of knowledge-based, small-scale, flexible, craft-intensive manufacturing, by specialized agricultural production, and by the radical reordering of relations of proximity brought on by electronic space. The city is predicated on a fantasy of compatibility, on the waning of zoning by use or by class. Both the city and its architecture are structured as "lofts," a condition at once flexible and resistant. Weed's architecture investigates the integration of a "generic" day-lit, walk-up, cross-ventilated condition with buildings of larger scale and special use.

22.2 Weed, Arizona project. Site plan showing neighborhood structure.

22.3 Weed, Arizona project.
Detail of circulation channel
and spines, tennis courts, and
water's edge.

Weed investigates new ratios between built, blue, and green space. While the availability of water makes possible extensive greening of the territory within the city, the absolute density of the town means that the total area of green space is small. Intended to be as sustainable as possible, Weed seeks self-sufficiency in agriculture, water, energy, oxygen, waste treatment, jobs, and education. Located at a very particular convergence of landscape, culture, technology, and architecture, dense and pedestrian, laced with water and greenery, Weed seeks to offer non-coercive variety within a very specific formal context, spaces to support activities both predictable and un-envisioned.

NEURASIA (1996)

Neurasia is a project for an imaginary city built along a line somewhere between Hong Kong and Hanoi. The idea is an old one: a linear city. In this version, the connective tissue is a transportation and technological armature that organizes transfer between modes of movement and isolates disruptive uses. Cities are to spring up along this armature according to local bearing capacity and need. Distance between towns is to be calculated to enhance local self-sufficiency, maximize unbuilt space, and to respect the character of the place.

Each town along the line is organized in a series of village-scale neighborhoods, each distinct. A priority to pedestrians is achieved with an intense layering of means of motion. Within the city, there is an abundance of small-scale agriculture, sufficient to support the local population. Complex networks of green and blue space serve farming, recreation, oxygen production, environmental cleansing, and thermal regulation. At the center of the city—per Asian tradition—lies a void. The drawings here represent a portion of one of the cities that has sprung up along the line.

22.4 Neurasia project. The system of cities showing the formation of two new towns along the linear spine.

22.5 Neurasia project. Detail of village structure with circulation network and a portion of a commercial and civic center.

22.6 Neurasia project. Detail with a mall village/neighborhood.

22.7 Aerial view, House of
the Future.

House and Retirement Communities of the Future (1999)

As generals are said to always prepare to fight the last war, so architects too often design for a previous social paradigm. The nuclear family—still the organizing type for most of our housing—now comprises less than half of the households in the United States. The House of the Future (in this rural incarnation) is therefore a co-housing scheme, meant to accommodate between a dozen and twenty people, living in a variety of chosen arrangements. The "house" is organized into a group of double units that share a "living machine," a bio-remediation device for the treatment of wastes. Shared space is dedicated to kids, to communal activities, and to workspace for those inclined to a more social environment during the day.

22.8 Plan of double unit,
House of the Future.

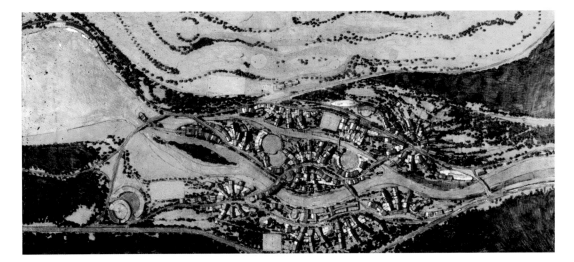

22.9 View, House of the Future.

The retirement community continues the rural idyll but has the scale of a small village. Cars are left at the periphery of the community and internal transport is by foot, bike, or electric bubble car (a robotic version is seen making an automated delivery). The village is clustered around several centers that provide services and community facilities and is surrounded by recreational areas, including (of course) a golf course for those who actually have retirement time on their hands.

Dwellings are of a row house type. Each unit has a green house for gardening and thermal control, and each row shares a living machine for the treatment of its wastes. The buildings are constructed of highly insulated, soybean-derived plastic panels. This material is not simply fully renewable, it can—should the social security check fail to arrive on time—also be eaten.

22.10 Site plan, Retirement Community of the Future.

22.11 Row house plans
with greenhouses and living
machines, Retirement
Community of the Future.

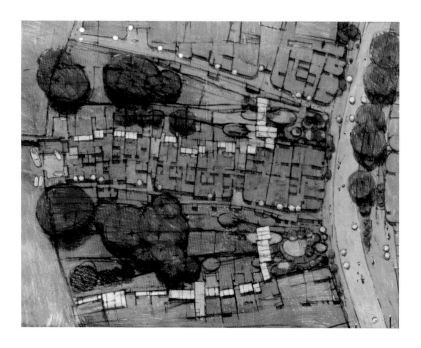

22.12 Row houses with
living machine, bubble cars,
and aerogel windows,
Retirement Community
of the Future.

21st Century Nomadism and Settlement

Denis Cosgrove

23

Human settlement, like most apparently simple concepts, eludes unambiguous or universal definition. Knowledge of the archaeological, historical, and geographical variety in the structures and forms of actual human settlements should generate caution against such attempts. Nevertheless, and perhaps inescapably, there is a tendency to assume an often unexamined hierarchy of settlement types. Greater significance and currency tend to be given to permanent settlements over transient sites, while larger and more complex structures are privileged over smaller, simpler ones. Solid and enduring constructional materials (which until the advent of entirely synthetic materials have had their own declension, from stone through metals, bricks, and wood, to more flimsy materials) are more highly valued than those involving minimal or impermanent structural intervention in the natural environment. The scale, complexity, and monumentality of cities give them prominence over towns, villages, hamlets, and encampments. The choice of study objects in this volume reflects these principles of selection. To some extent, they are an inevitable outcome of a literate community's intimacy with written culture and urban life. More generally, they may be a function of meanings implicit in the concept of "settlement" itself.

In their material expressions, urban societies are indeed more complex than societies dependent upon direct and unmediated use of natural resources for food and shelter. But we are informed enough today of the lived complexity of aboriginal worlds to be wary of attributing any absolute superiority in cultural sophistication of the former over the latter. More significantly for this discussion, nomadism, until recently taken as the very mark of primitivism in many non-urban societies, is today the condition of increasing numbers of people in the most highly urbanized, modern societies. As such, it calls into question some assumptions we continue to hold about the nature and meanings of human settlement. This condition calls for a more detailed reflection on those assumptions and on contemporary relations with the un-settlement of mobility and nomadism. Some of the consequences of conventional hierarchies in human landscapes may act to restrict our embrace and understanding of conditions of settlement that have been developing throughout modernity, that characterize much of our daily experience, and that will continue to intensify in the future.

Settlement and Mobility: "Othering" the Nomad

The process of settling implies an antecedent state of movement. Settlement is dialectically related to mobility. Philosophically, the West is heir to two divergent views on movement and rest. The dominant Aristotelian view was of perpetual but ordered motion in the celestial world and of the urge toward stability in the elemental, produced by the fixedness of the earth, at rest as

333

the settled center of the cosmos. A subordinate but ultimately more accurate perspective from the point of view of modern physics was that of Epicurus, best expressed by the poet Lucretius in *De Rerum Naturae*. This posited a cosmos composed of indestructible atoms, in constant motion, only transiently coming together to produce fixed material forms. Here motion is the more fundamental state and settlement is always transient and provisional (Wright 1995). In social thought, it seems, the West has remained more wedded to the Aristotelian than the Lucretian view of what is the natural state of things. One expression is the long-standing cultural rejection of those whose lives are characterized by mobility and who fail to subscribe to a recognized mode of settled occupance, thus defined in some respect as nomads (Irons and Dyer-Hudson 1972). Such groups have been consistently "othered" by settled communities: their difference—in this case in the way they occupy space and connect home and territory—used to define and delimit the identities of both parties. Othering generally involves a negative regard, as has typically been directed toward nomadic lives (Cresswell 1996). Settlement is connected socially with permanence, rootedness, stability, and depth, and these things tend to be privileged over transience, instability, and surface (Relph 1976). This is true in Western social thought, whose evolution was among peoples largely devoted to permanent agriculture with subsidiary pastoralism and to urban government. Home and community are deeply felt and strongly valued, and they are closely associated with both permanent settlement structures—house, village, neighborhood—and with circumscribed or formally bounded territories—personal property, parish, township, city, nation. To those holding to such values, others, whose lives do not conform to this mode, are at once unsettled and un-settling.

In the imagined geography of the Classical *polis*, such others lay beyond the boundaries of the city and its cultivated fields—restless and dangerous barbarians who occupied "primitive" structures such as caves, tents, or huts. In the Renaissance reworking of Classical texts or in the complex stadial theories of the European Enlightenment, the most "primitive" of peoples, on the lowest rungs of an assumed human evolutionary ladder, were regularly pictured as nomadic wanderers, lacking collective purpose, pulled hither and thither by the exigencies of the natural environment upon which a hunter-gatherer life depended. Rykwert (1981) discusses the myth of architecture's origins among the earliest "settled" people. Even in the late 19th century, the European cultural memory of Rome's decline and destruction at the hands of mobile and migrant peoples remained strong. Thus the Russian writer Grigoriev, in an 1875 work entitled *Nomads as Neighbors and Conquerors of Civilized States*, claimed that nomads "are warlike and disposed to raiding, which makes them dangerous neighbors for sedentary nations" (Noyes 2000:48), while the British geographer and strategist Sir Halford Mackinder in his influential 1904 essay, "The Geographical Pivot of History," framed global history as a struggle between nomadic peoples of the Eurasian interior and the settled nations of its periphery who are constantly threatened by the "Asiatic hammer striking out of vacant space" (Mackinder 1904:426). The nomad's significance within Western consciousness was further intensified with European overseas colonization. These assumptions and experiences entail contradictions for thinking about settlement today.

Before examining these, we should recognize that as threatening as unsettled, mobile peoples beyond the boundaries of settled territory might be, the nomad's or vagrant's presence within the boundaries of fixed settlement has always been regarded as equally subversive to the connection of settlement and social order. The peasant or slave moving outside the circumscribed bounds of her owner's estate, the merchant or mariner in a foreign port, the gypsy at the cottage door, the tramp in the suburb or the hobo panhandling on the city street, the court defendant "of no fixed abode," the welfare claimant or economic migrant in temporary accommodation—all are conventionally unsettling figures in the landscape. Each has commonly been the subject of negative stereotyping within the simplified dialectic of settlement equals permanence, rootedness and inside-ness; mobility equals transience, superficial attachment and outside-ness. The fates of generations of Jews, gypsies, and other travelers testify to the tragic consequences of an overly narrow privileging of "settlement."

Modernity and Mobility

Over the past half-millennium, the processes of modernization, powered by the restless energy and ever-increasing mobility of capital, first in the hands of merchants, later of industrialists and financiers, and by the demands of consumption cultures, have intensified and transformed the dialectic of settlement and mobility. It is a complex story, from which I note but one or two salient moments. From the earliest days, capital investment's capacity to uproot and displace settled peoples, rendering them mobile and migratory, has been recorded and regretted by both authorities and social commentators. Thus, in Elizabethan London, the increased number of vagrants was a matter of public comment and state concern. The homeless and the mobile seemed to grow in numbers as the city prospered; most were former rural dwellers, displaced by the intensification of farming and the wool trade's conversion of fields to pasture. They also included veteran soldiers and sailors, always an unsettling group whose mobility resulted from fighting on behalf of the settled, and who thus lay a disturbing moral claim on the attention of the latter. Uprooting, displacement, and consequent vagrancy, even if impermanent, increased steadily across Europe as agricultural modernization was followed or accompanied by industrialization and as cities struggled to accommodate the mobile in new settlement forms: suburbs, planned towns, workhouses. Nineteenth century social welfare debates were dominated by questions of settlement, largely because of the sheer numbers displaced from their former occupations and the dynamic nature of the new urban forms to which their movements gave rise (Polanyi 1957). The most dramatic global consequence of this un-settlement was the transoceanic migration of millions of Europeans, accompanied in the century's closing years by Japanese, Chinese, and Indians, to settle in the Americas, Australia, and Africa. Human migration caused by economic disruption continues to intensify into the new millennium and shows no sign of abating.

Such movement is not merely the temporary uprooting of the poor and the dispossessed, although that has always been a significant part of the story. Restlessness, impermanence, and mobility are characteristic features of modern life for large numbers of prosperous people—the average American household moves its home more than once each decade and Europeans are catching up. Even when a locational move is not involved, the internal and external spaces of the home are regularly transformed to meet the needs of a more transient lifestyle. Permanence of human settlement may no longer be a normal condition, if ever it was. It is this that forces us to consider the meaning and values we attribute to settlement. We can do so best by understanding the complex cultural connections of settlement and mobility within modernity. These emerged most starkly in the context of overseas colonization at the turn of the 20th century when new settlements were carved out of lands declared available to Westerners precisely by virtue of the supposed vagrancy of their indigenous populations, as a solution to the unsettlement caused by modernization in Europe.

Europe's 19th century unsettling played a major role in the functioning of those European empires that reach into the memory of many still alive today. These were colonial as much as commercial enterprises, providing locations for resettling people from the metropole into overseas "colonies," modern continuations of the classical Roman *colonia* or estate where land was settled, tilled, planted, and farmed by citizens—often former soldiers—who would make the stoutest defenders of the motherland. Such settlement of course entailed expropriation. Direct removal of previously settled agricultural peoples was rare (but not unknown); more commonly the lands thus settled were constituted as wild, uncultivated or improperly cultivated, or they were *terra nullius*; in sum, they were un-settled. In point of fact, they were almost always used productively, but in ways that Europeans simply did not recognize as constituting a form of settlement, ways that frequently involved patterns of movement on the part of the users that left no trace in the form of permanent settlement structures. Such non-European, non-modern, societies were negatively defined as "nomadic."

Nineteenth century colonists and commentators were at once repelled and fascinated by the idea of the nomad. From stadial theories of civilization, enunciated by writers such as Turgot and Taylor, there was wide acceptance that nomadic peoples represented a "lower" stage of human evolution, and as such they were to be found in marginal environments, at the furthest reaches of the earth. Such theories, popular from the mid-17th to the mid-20th centuries (and by no means fully extinguished even today) ranked human societies according to an evolutionary hierarchy from the most primitive to the most advanced, using such measures as literacy, monotheism, settled agriculture, money, trade, and urbanism (Huntington 1959). Hunting and gathering were supposedly followed by pastoralism, settled agriculture, urbanization, and civilization. For many, these "stages" could be mapped circumferentially away from Europe, regarded as having reached the culminating stage of human progress (see Heffernan 1994:328–43). Geographical location alone was sufficient cause to render such peoples exotic—at once dangerous and exciting (Driver and Martins 2005). Nomadic peoples were easily "orientalized," with all the complexities of cultural identity, gender and sexuality attribution, and power relations that the term implies (Said 1978). Orientalism, as a "colonialist" discourse, attributed nomadism as a generalized classification to such diverse groups as the Tuareg, Bedouin, Kalahari Bushmen, or Plains Indians, paying little attention to the specificities of their livelihood or to the complex and highly regulated patterns of movement and rest that their modes of occupancy involved. By the early 20th century, to be sure, anthropologists had begun to reveal something of the spatial and environmental logic of such livelihoods, but the dominant cultural response in the West remained negative. The nomad was simultaneously seen as a threat to social and spatial order and therefore to be "settled" as part of the complex process of colonial expropriation, yet celebrated as an iconic figure of freedom from the constraints of settled, bourgeois Western life. The nomad became an ambiguous and liminal figure—socially, spatially, sexually—readily romanticized in T. E. Lawrence's *Seven Pillars of Wisdom* or Rudolph Valentino's *Sheik of Araby*. The equivalent figure within the metropole was perhaps the dandy or urban *flâneur* who wandered apparently aimlessly in the city's streets and squares, associating with others of dubious moral and sexual status, and equally disconnected from settled existence.

Such romantic fantasies were not reflected in the harsh colonial response to nomadism, which consistently involved enforced settlement of nomadic societies in permanent camps and villages and inducements to practice permanent cultivation (that is, when individuals were not corralled as labor on plantations or farms or in mines). Thus both French and Italian colonial governments sought to control the movements and ultimately to settle the peoples of their North African colonies, the latter in literal concentration camps in 1920s Cyrenaica (Atkinson 1994:328–43). The positive consequence of this, from the point of view of the colonialist, was that the lands over which these peoples had formerly traveled and had held and regulated in usufruct could now be declared open and uncultivated, turned into state lands and sold off to European colonists. The processes of expropriation on the American Plains in the 1890s or in Australia well into the 20th century was little different: the enclosure and forced settlement of the indigenous population on "reserved" lands with the declared intention of "civilizing" them through the experience of settled agriculture and the offices of Christian missionaries. This was accompanied by the simultaneous release of their former territories for settlement by people of European origin, themselves having commonly been uprooted by the processes of modernization in the metropoles.

The ironies of settlement values entailed by this process are clearly apparent in the case of German colonization in South West Africa. John Noyes (2000) has recently reminded us of the conventional conflation within "nomadism" of two sets of phenomena: livestock rearing and spatial mobility. This both reflected European theories of social evolution that privileged "settled agriculture," and reduced the agency of societies so defined by attributing to them high levels of dependence upon the natural landscape. Colonists in German South West Africa (Namibia) interpreted the practices of indigenous pastoralists such as the Herero, closely geared to the seasonal availability of forage for their herds, as nomadic, and viewed them through lenses crafted by Herder's description of "half-wild hunters and nomads" or Schiller's "nomad hordes of the Tartar steppe" (Noyes 2000:49). The Herero were figured as subject to their cattle, passively submissive to the needs and desires of beasts and wholly dependent upon their natural environment. The German imperial government adopted the standard colonial practice of forced sedentarization which, it argued, would remove the beast from the Herero by removing the Herero from the beast: converting them to Christianity, locating them in stone built houses and introducing them to cultivation. In the rhetoric of the day, this would "instill in them a sense of permanence . . . *Heimatsgefühl*, the feeling for home" (Noyes 2000:56). The grazing lands thus vacated could be available for German settlers.

The small farmers who represented the first wave of German settlement faced the contradiction that they themselves were migrants, unsettled and mobile. However, they claimed a cultural superiority from their own *Heimatsgefühl*, which they carried with them as Germans extending the territorial scope of the fatherland. They adopted a romantic view of German rural culture that emphasized settled and continuous connection with the land through inheritance of family property as the moral foundations of civil life. A further contradiction emerged however with the relatively rapid realization that the fullest commercial value of the territory obtained from the Herero actually did lie in large-scale cattle rearing rather than small family farming, and this the modernizing colonial authorities began to promote. The replacement of African modes of cattle rearing by European pastoralists was justified on the modernist grounds that the latter would be more "rational," tied into global trading circuits rather than the simple amassing of cattle for local social status. But European pastoral methods actually reduced productivity, while they entailed the supplanting of small European farming settlements by large-scale ranches, introducing conflict into the heart of the settlement process itself. As Noyes points out, "modernization alone was not enough to mobilize mass sentiment for the colonial project . . . a landscape was needed that could be superimposed on the German landscape, promising new freedoms, the expectation of profit and, above all this, the retention of an integral national identity in a new territory" (2000:62).

21ST CENTURY NOMADISM AND SETTLEMENT LANDSCAPE

The imaginative, even ideological, power that Noyes's conclusion attributes to the European image of a settled agrarian landscape within Western evaluations of social space has certainly diminished over the past half-century. The numbers involved in agriculture, nearly half the population even in industrialized countries at the turn of the 20th century, are today diminutive in every part of the West. But the settled rural landscape retains a residual power to evoke sentiments of attachment and belonging and to act as an image of familial and social order. "Settling down" on a self-sufficient family farm, harmonizing human construction with nature visually or functionally, and preserving the forms of past settlement as heritage, all serve as redemptive, if romantic, responses to the distopic aspects of modern, especially urban, life. The most immediate expression of this cultural attachment in today's settlement landscape is the occupation of former agricultural structures by residents with no functional connection whatsoever with the land. A defining feature of the "post-modern" landscape of every developed country, and increasingly elsewhere, is massive growth in the equity value of traditional rural homes and related settlement structures such as barns, mills, and animal houses. The flow of new investment into rural structures is impressive, converting them to new uses as family homes, offices, and workplaces, connected locally by means of improved rural roads and freeways to urban centers and suburban malls, and globally through the use of modern telecommunications. Much of the contemporary rural settlement landscape of every Western country is a façade, offering the appearance of an unchanging assemblage of vernacular structures behind which function has been utterly transformed. Their architectural form and decoration are determined more by contemporary aesthetic and functional considerations rather than by historical integrity. They mask a social life of very high mobility lived in contradiction with the appearance of rooted permanence. Tight zoning regulations frequently bind whole regions as areas of high landscape value and heritage significance, distinguishing them from more active parts of the rural landscape where modern, commercial agriculture is practiced and where the creative destruction of landscape structures is allowed to operate more freely. Creative destruction has been regarded by some theorists as capital's solution to the "spatial fix" that emerges from the contradictions between "settled" structures and increased velocities of capital circulation needed to realize surplus value (Harvey 1985; Smith 1990). In this respect that distinction between countryside and city, which has structured so much of western social, political, and architectural discourse since the time of the Greek *polis* is no longer meaningful in any of its traditional senses. All settlement is today effectively urban: the rural village or hamlet is little more than a spatially separated and architecturally distinct suburb.

In some regions this is dramatically obvious. The Italians refer to the northeast region inland from Venice as *la città diffusa*, a single urban settlement zone (Ludoviana 1990). It is structured around a scattering of ancient cities—Padua, Treviso, Vicenza, Pordenone—set within a long settled agrarian space (Detragiache 2003). Their historic centers are today highly conserved gems of pre-modern urban settlement form. They are surrounded by suburban apartment zones largely dating from the mid-20th century and are connected by a network of railways and roads of radically varying capacity. These roads are lined with a dense mesh of modern factories, workshops, storage units, office blocks, and retail sites, whose architectural forms are individual expressions of a dominantly functionalist style (Dal Pozzo 2002). Many are built on family-owned properties of a few hectares whose owners still cultivate fields up to their parking lots. The rural landscape, fragmented but still structured in large measure by the patterns of Roman colonization, is scattered with hamlets, churches and their *campanili*, villas, farmhouses, and barns, dating from every one of the past seven centuries, most no longer used for traditional purposes but housing high-tech design studios, company headquarters, and similar "postmodern" functions. New houses, indistinguishable in many respects from those being constructed in the Loire valley, the German Palatinate, Worcestershire, England, or New Jersey, stand in fields of vines and corn surrounded by a shelter belt of fast growing exotics such as the *Leylandiae* or ancient olives uprooted from Puglia and replanted as decorative elements. Like citizens across the West and much of Asia, their proprietors watch television from Atlanta or London, eat delicacies from Kenya and California, dress in fashions determined in Paris and New York as well as Milan, and take holidays in New Zealand and Peru. Actually and virtually, they are radically mobile, their physical settlements only tenuously connected to those historic processes which initially structured the landscape and which have long underpinned the concept of colonization and settlement.

The disjuncture between the meanings, forms, and experiences of settlement apparent in such regions of the contemporary world is profound. But it simply reflects a much more generalized modern condition: modern nomadism. I am not suggesting that every person today is continuously nomadic, and certainly not in Noyes's sense that conflates nomadism with pastoralism. But we need a term that captures the significance of personal mobility and actual movement as dominating features of modern social life and their connections with settlement. Neither *vagrancy* nor *migration* fulfils this need. The former implies a lack of either purpose or employment, the latter a form of movement that remains subordinate to fixed points of origin and destination. At a banal level, some movement is a necessary condition of all human life. But today human movement has virtually lost its qualities of void or gap between the fullness of the places that it connects, i.e. of being the vacancy between settlement events. Movement is increasingly a primary condition of existence, and movement is filled with activities that were formerly tied to a settled place.

Consider, for example, the way that the various functions of the traditional American family home of the 1940s were "settled" in specialized spaces: reception hall, family room, dining room, den or office (with the household telephone), kitchen, bedrooms, and bathroom. Not only have the boundaries between these functions tended to blur within domestic space, as kitchen and dining room conflate, as children's rooms become living rather than merely sleeping spaces, as the family room disappears, but increasingly the functions formerly settled within the home have spilled out of it and dispersed onto the road. The most obvious of these are eating and speaking on the phone. It is not uncommon for the average American household to eat out three times in a week, and most meals at home are taken casually and often individually. Eating for many modern people is more akin to grazing than to formal dining (perhaps the conflation of humans, pastoralism, and nomadism is not entirely exhausted). Less remarked upon are

23.3 The postwar suburban tract house already presented itself in a "ruralized" setting and initiated the process of allocating significant space to the automobile and allowing internal space use to become nomadic.

other migrations. For example, the use of motels, whose location and design precisely articulate a conception of settlement as subordinate to mobility, increases annually as the average annual number of nights slept in one's own bedroom declines.

This is not to suggest that the home has lost its significance; indeed, some activities such as office work have increasing presence there. It is rather that activities once settled in specific places are now footloose. Above all, they take place "on the move." Cordless phones in every room of the house and cell phones beyond make communication entirely mobile. New technologies extend this mobility to Internet access and entertainment media. In the design and selling of automobiles ever greater attention is paid to their multiple uses in motion: ease of drinking and eating, entertainment and communication systems, even their flexibility and comfort for sleeping. The popularity of the SUV, whose size and flexibility reflect the multiple demands of families in motion during significant periods of their lives, is a clear reflection of this process—it is at once the camel and tent of the 21st century.

Mobility is not confined to any one class, although as with all innovations it tends to be more immediately and widely apparent among the wealthy. There has always been a small part of society that is nomadic in the sense that I am using the term: merchants, scholars, diplomats, mariners, and soldiers who I mentioned above. And some among the very wealthy have long occupied a number of houses or migrated between residential hotels. But the numbers now moving regularly over long distances and for sustained periods are now enormous. The scale and continued growth of global tourism are familiar, but we rarely consider in finer detail the varied guises that the tourist now adopts. Among Europeans, North Americans, East Asians, Australians, and New Zealanders it is widely accepted today that young people between the ages of 18 and 25 will spend a year or more travelling globally before or after their college years. Increased flexibility of lifetime career patterns and delay in the age of parenting allow such

23.4 The Sports Utility Vehicle (SUV) is designed to accommodate an increasing number of formerly "settled" life functions.

adventure to be repeated at intervals into the fourth decade of life. As parents, many of these people will spend regular periods in one or more "second" homes, owned, rented, or timeshared. There will also be regular business conferences and conventions, together with social gatherings and reunions, all of which require travel and accommodation in order to bring together people widely scattered by their life choices. The houses they buy and sell will be regarded as much as financial investments as settled "homes." And in their retirement years many will use the equity generated in the housing market to buy a "recreational vehicle," spending months, if not their entire lives, migrating between different RV resorts and extended family visits. Families are increasingly dispersed nationally and internationally, a phenomenon by no means confined to the wealthy. Long distance movements of whole clans between Britain or the Gulf and the Indian subcontinent or Caribbean, between the U.S. Midwest, Mexico and Central America, between Germany and Turkey or Holland and Indonesia are regular and constant.

THE POVERTY OF SETTLEMENT

So pervasive are these phenomena of scatter and mobility, both short and long haul, that the locations of greatest social deprivation today are those of least mobility and most fixed settlement. It is in farming, fishing, mining, and manufacturing regions whose environmental or spatial marginality denies them capital investment, that the traditional architectural and social forms of settlement and settled life survive. Hill farms in northern Europe or Appalachia, fishing towns on the Oregon or Scottish coasts, former coal mining villages in southern Belgium, or "rust-belt" manufacturing cities in Ohio all exemplify these aspects of conventional settlement. The city of Buffalo, NY, for example, has lost some 40 percent of its mid 20th-century population but frequently figures high among American cities on such measures of settled community as attachment to place and neighborhood or closeness of family and friends. Nevertheless, the loss of the young, the educated, the skilled, and the entrepreneurial from these places produces a cycle of impoverishment familiar from earlier stages of modernist un-settlement and dispersal, for example, in southern Italy, the islands of the Aegean or Atlantic Britain. The paradox of

23.5 The contemporary urban landscape reflects settlement as a pause within a continuously mobile life: downtown Beverly Hills, California. Ca. 1960.

modernity, apparent in landscape since its first naming in the 18th century as *picturesque*, that the most visually appealing settlements, those which appear most rooted and stable—in a word, settled—are also the poorest and least developed, remains clear in both the landscapes of today and in our response to them.

Modern nomadism dominates the material as much as the social landscape of contemporary settlement. The most noted and criticized geographical feature of the contemporary city is its spatial extensiveness, and within its vast horizontality, the proportion of space devoted to movement. The continuously urbanized area of Los Angeles is similar to that of Italy's *città diffusa*: over 5,000 square miles. These cities are no longer exceptional; the effective area of settlement of every major city is now many times larger than its continuously built-up surface. The explosion of the city into highly fragmented and separated functional zones, connected principally by road vehicles, and the movement and parking surfaces devoted to them, has been a principal subject of urban architectural, environmental, and social criticism for the past half century (Auge 1995; Davis 1992). There is little new to be said about a phenomenon that has generated some of the most compelling geographical metaphors of our time: urban sprawl, conurbation, megalopolis, edge city, "thirdspace" (Dematteis 1984; Soja 1996). Therefore, rather than bewail once more the baleful impacts of the car and its ancillary infrastructure on an ideal of settlement, we might consider what the modern city's complex of parking lots, freeways, malls, airports, convention centers, motels, and recreational spaces is telling us of ourselves and our continued embrace of nomadism as a mode of existence.

In Praise of Nomadism

In discussions of settlement we seem largely to ignore the evidence that nomadism is a widely preferred form of human existence. The ecological image of the deeply rooted,

23.6 The "new urbanism" deploys the architectural rhetoric of "settlement": Main Street, pedestrian spaces, and homely façades to mask the "nomadism" of capital, goods, and people that have brought it into being and sustain it. The Grove retail mall, Los Angeles, California.

permanent settlement, whose close social, economic, political, and environmental integration finds expression in an architectural harmony of built form and the presumed social harmonies of community continues to inform popular urban ideals. The New Urbanism has capitalized on this sensibility, offering the illusion of settlement by excluding as far as possible the physical evidence of hypermobility (Katz 1994). But it is a sham; the residents of such places accept the social regulations that sustain the illusion of settlement, but once beyond the spatial boundaries of what is effectively one more functional zone within the dispersed city, they participate as fully in contemporary nomadism as everyone else. Such settlements recall the picturesque villages constructed by 18th century landlords in the Europe of agricultural revolution, housing the farmworkers on newly capitalized estates in model settlements designed to appear as timeless expressions of traditional rural order (Cosgrove 1996). Like New Urbanism's settlements needing access to the freeway, these were commonly built on or near new toll roads, evidence of the mobility their form sought to obscure.

Nomadism is always a method of connecting and regulating access to spatially scattered material and social resources through patterns of human movement. Contemporary nomadism is no different. Its means of transport are more sophisticated and faster, the patterns of human migration today more complex and often more individually chosen. But perhaps we need to acknowledge that, despite conventional usage, nomadism is not the opposite of settlement, it is merely a specific form of settlement necessitated by the spatial distribution of the resources required for a chosen form of existence. As we choose to mobilize an ever greater array of resources within the course of a human life, and those material and social resources are scattered over a wider area, settlement elements also scatter and greater investments of time are made in accessing them. Inevitably, nomadic lifestyles replace settled ones for ever greater numbers of people. The real distinction between 21st century nomadism and that of former times lies in our ability to enrich and elaborate the times and spaces of movement themselves. Thus, increased numbers of activities whose performance formerly required settled location (eating, listening to music, searching for information, holding a conference) can now be undertaken in motion. Twenty-first century nomads occupy moving settlements. Perhaps the SUV is the true settlement space of the new millennium.

References

Atkinson, D. "Nomadic Strategies and Colonial Governance: Domination and Resistance in Cyrenaica, 1923–1932." In *Entanglements of Power: Geographies of Domination /Resistance*, eds. Joanne P. Sharp, Paul Routledge, Chris Philo, and Ronan Paddison. London: Routledge, 1999.

Auge, Marc. *Non-places: Introduction to an Anthropology of Supermodernity*, translated by John Howe. London: Verso, 1995.

Cosgrove, Denis. *Social Formation and Symbolic Landscape*. Madison, WI: University of Wisconsin Press, 1996.

Cresswell, Tim. *In Place/Out of Place: Geography, Ideology and Transgression*. Minneapolis, MN: University of Minnesota Press, 1996.

Dal Pozzo, Luca, ed. *Fuori Città, Senza Campagna: Paesaggio e Progetto nella Città Diffusa*. Milan: FrancoAngelli, 2002.

Davis, Mike. *City of Quartz: Excavating the Future from Los Angeles*. London: Verso, 1992.

Dematteis, G. *Le Metafore della Terra*. Milan: Feltrinelli, 1984.

Detragiache, Angelo, ed. *Dalla Città Diffusa alla Città Diramata*. Milan: Franco Angeli, 2003.

Driver, F., and L. de Lima Martins, eds. *Tropical Visions in an Age of Empire*. Chicago, IL: University of Chicago Press, 2005.

Harvey, David. *The Urbanization of Capital: Studies in the History and Theory of Capitalist Urbanization*. Baltimore, MD: Johns Hopkins University Press, 1985.

Heffernan, Michael J. "On Geography and Progress: Turgot's *Plan d'un Ouvrage sur la Géographie Politique* (1751) and the Origins of Modern Progressive Thought." *Political Geography* 13(1994):328–43.

Huntingdon, E. *Mainsprings of Civilization*. New York: New American Library of World Literature, 1959.

Irons, William, and Neville Dyson-Hudson, eds. *Perspectives on Nomadism*. Leiden: Brill, 1972.

Katz, Peter, ed. *The New Urbanism: Toward an Architecture of Community*. New York: McGraw-Hill, 1994.

Ludoviana, Francesco, ed. *La Città Diffusa*. Venice: Daest, 1990.

Mackinder, Sir Halford. "The Geographical Pivot of History." *Geographical Journal* 23(1904):421–44.

Noyes, John K. "Nomadic Fantasies: Producing Landscapes of Mobility in German Southwest Africa." *Ecumene* 7(2000):46–68.

Polanyi, Karl. *The Great Transformation: The Political and Economic Origins of Our Time.* Boston, MA: Beacon Press, 1957.

Relph, Edward. *Place and Placelessness.* London: Pion, 1976.

Rykwert, Joseph. *On Adam's House in Paradise: The Idea of the Primitive Hut in Architectural History*, 2nd ed. Cambridge, MA: MIT Press, 1981.

Said, Edward. *Orientalism.* London: Penguin, 1978.

Smith, Neil. *Uneven Development: Nature, Capital and the Production of Space.* Oxford: Blackwell, 1990.

Soja, Edward. *Thirdspace: Journeys to Los Angeles and Other Real-and-Imagined Places.* Cambridge, MA: Blackwell, 1996.

Wright, M. R. *Cosmology in Antiquity.* London: Routledge, 1995.

Materials Matter
in Urban Architecture

David Leatherbarrow

24

"I think that in every building, every street, there is something that creates an event, and whatever creates an event is unintelligible."—*Jean Baudrillard*

Few would deny that the building is one of the definitions of human settlement. Together with law, language, and customs, architecture contributes both to the formation of towns and cities and to their capacity for expression. Some architects, however, see the building as more than this. Some have convinced themselves that the built work and its designer have a more determining role, that their task is to provide settlements with their basic order. The individual and social patterns they accommodate and represent follow from this—no small claim. This ambition can be seen in the work of designers who blur the distinction between urban and architectural design in order to see the city or its parts as susceptible to substitution by "big architecture." Rem Koolhaas (1995), to name only the most famous of this group, has asserted that the building's "bigness" alone can constitute the urbanity of our time: "bigness no longer needs the city: it competes with the city; it represents the city; it preempts the city; or better still, it *is* the city" (515).

24.1 L'Institut du Monde Arabe, Paris, France, Ateliers Jean Nouvel, 1981–87.

There are two obvious ways of reading this statement. One is that Koolhaas intended it to be less prescriptive than polemical, that his aim was to challenge basic assumptions, to disabuse us of our presumed certainties so that new possibilities of urban order could come into view. Another way to read the text is to view its hyperbole as a way of diverting attention from the somewhat discouraging fact that many of the cities and urban areas that have yielded to over-sized insertions in the recent past are far from satisfactory. In many cases they are plainly miserable. In the last couple of decades nearly every major city in the USA has demolished one or another of the "big" projects of the postwar years. When not demolished, these projects have been retrofitted with imagery of earlier architectures. Past failures do not exactly inspire confidence in renewed claims for *architecture as the city*.

Faced with this realization, it might seem wise for architects to retreat from the city and concern themselves with the individual building only: its interiors, external appearance and immediate vicinity—extending their interest no farther than the adjacent sidewalk, forecourt, yard, or garden. Retrenchment of this sort has the double appeal of limited exposure and greater control. It signals a retreat nonetheless. A better alternative involves differentiating types of concern an architect can have for the city: that one accept a distinction between awareness and responsibility, the first of the city, the second for the building (Leatherbarrow 2000:170 ff). Neither hesitancy nor conservatism would be required for the adoption of this two-part premise, for understanding could certainly include criticism. Indeed, it should. Quite possibly, it must. It is hard to imagine how a design could be developed in the absence of judgments that are critical of existing conditions; that is, if the project's aspirations are restricted to accepting and affirming what predates it. Moreover, once it is granted that no city or city district is lacking problems, it becomes clear that all sites can be imagined otherwise. This means recognition of the need for change does not devolve from an architect's unbounded ambition but from awareness of the inadequacy of existing conditions when contemporary interests are taken into account.

Seen in this light, project making could be defined as a limited means of approximating a condition that ought to be. Approximation is implicit in understanding, for every description, interpretation, and evaluation invokes a particular point of view that not only orients but prompts project proposals, each moving toward (approximating) a desired condition. Yet, while both survey work and design testify to local and contemporary interests, they can be separated along the lines I suggested; the attentiveness of the first results in descriptions that can be verified, while the productivity of the second results in proposals that are more or less persuasive.

In the past few decades arguments for the importance of urban understanding in architecture were often developed out of criticism of the modern movement, especially the so-called international style architecture of the middle decades of the 20th century, frequently described as anti-urban because its prejudice in favor of free-standing objects led to the disruption of existing patterns. Many buildings from this period give vivid evidence of this sentiment.

Even more forceful are the polemical writings of figures such as Le Corbusier and Wright, whose comments on the traditional city never involved ringing endorsement. But their writings should not be taken at face value. Like Koolhaas (and providing him with a rhetorical model) they overstated the problems they faced and the originality (epochal significance) of their solutions. Moreover, their dismissive statements conceal levels of understanding and engagement that are remarkably discerning—much more so than recent attempts to "recover," "restore," or "renew" the traditional town through appropriation and imitation of its familiar patterns and motifs (as in post-modern projects). Urban understanding is apparent in the built work of not only such first-generation modernists as Le Corbusier, Frank Lloyd Wright, Mies van der Rohe, and Richard Neutra, for example, but also in that of a number of those to follow: Eero Saarinen, José Luis Sert, and the Smithsons come immediately to mind. Forgetting for a minute what these architects wrote, looking carefully at their ways of working with the city, one can discover their projects accepted a double constraint, that of acknowledging what remained relevant from the past and imagining what would be required for the future because circumstances had changed. This approach parallels the awareness-responsibility division introduced above, suggesting that the urban understanding many seek in current practice has antecedents in the modern tradition.

Must architects who endeavor to see and use the city as the framework for their projects choose either an apocalyptic or a nostalgic vision, between the final substitution of the city by "big architecture" and the restitution of its familiar forms through the strategies of "new [old] urbanism"? If we refuse the choice between a city that is unlike any that has ever been and one that reminds us of what we've always known, we will need to find another horizon of reference for contemporary architecture. My suggestion rests upon a simple observation: cities and buildings are not only spatial, geometric, and dimensional (patterns), but also *material*. Might the material aspect of cities and architecture clarify their relationships to one another? What is the relationship between city form and architectural construction?

Glass and Clay

"Then along came those nasty English and spoiled the game for our knights of the drawing board. They said, 'Don't design, make. Go out into the world and see what is wanted. And when you have fully grasped that, go and work at the forge or the potter's wheel.'"
—Adolf Loos, *Glass and Clay*

In 1998, during his presentation at the Jerusalem Seminar, Jean Nouvel argued for architecture's "non-image," proposing that our "extreme aspiration is that of [the] human as conjurer, who can make anything appear or disappear at will according to need or desire; who can travel instantly to any location by lighting up windows on the world, or by even-faster self-propulsion" (83). To substantiate, or at least buttress, his claim Nouvel repeated Paul Virilio's observations on contemporary technology: "Speed and technology eliminate barriers between people and nature, between the world and the universe." Prompting these comments on technology and place were references to both the diaphanous works of James Turell and Nouvel's own recent projects in Paris: the Fondation Cartier (1991–94) and Institut du Monde Arabe (1981–87). In all three there was a severe reduction—near elimination—of the separation between people (the "world") and nature that architecture had traditionally instituted. This was because "people want there to be nothing—nothing at all—between the heavens and us . . . we want an absence of materiality to put us in touch again with the non-synthetic world," by which, I gather, he meant nature. Nouvel did not assume that this new connection or newly

24.2 Fondation Cartier,
Paris, Ateliers Jean Nouvel,
1991–94.

close connection would require retreat from the city, for not only was a new contract with nature to result from the elimination of matter, but also a new form of engagement with the city, one of connectivity, flow, and immediacy. Glass, the most immaterial of materials, would be the key to restoring the linkage between architecture and both natural and urban life, as if the world-nature linkage were to occur within the world of the city.

The same year Nouvel offered these comments about architecture in direct connection with nature and the city, Peter Zumthor proposed an interpretation of the relationship between the building and its milieu that seems radically opposed to Nouvel's. Writing about his Thermal Bath at Vals, he explained that: "the building takes the form of a large grass-covered stone object set deep into the mountain and dovetailed into its flank. . . . Mountain, stone, water . . . building in stone, building with stone, building into the mountain, building out of the mountain, being inside the mountain—our attempts to give this chain of words an architectural interpretation . . . guided our design for the building and step by step gave it form" (1996:9–10). Instead of the absence of materiality proposed by Nouvel, here we have palpability in abundance, materials in their full concreteness—mountain, stone, water—as if architectural space resulted from the hollowing out of preexisting substances. Zumthor offers not a light, but a solid, weighty, thick, and heavy architecture. If the first, Nouvel's, proposes pure passage from the building's interiors to its environment because virtually nothing divides them, the second approximates pure connectivity by virtue of the absence of any gap between them—not trajective but substantive spaces and situations.

While this pairing would seem to present us with yet another opposition and choice, the fact that both Nouvel and Zumthor argued for continuity—through transparency in the first case and materiality in the second—suggests that when the two are seen as similarly dedicated to interconnectivity they offer a more subtle understanding of the relationship between the building and its environment. I shall introduce three terms to elaborate what is common in their understanding of the city-architecture relationship: sedimentation, saturation, and surplus. The first two differently contribute to the constitution of the third, which measures the cultural content the city has to offer. My working premise is that materials matter no less in cities than in buildings. The key difference is that they are often *shown* in building and only *given* in cities.

TRACES OF LIFE

"I am convinced," Zumthor wrote, "that a good building must be capable of absorbing the traces of human life and thus of taking on a specific richness" (1998:24). This passage implies, although it does not state, that the building's materials (more than its dimensions and geometries) allow this absorption. Architectural richness results from stone, steel, timber, and glass "taking on traces of human life." The passage also suggests that the building, or its materials, would not possess this richness were this deposit not to occur. That is a sobering thought for architects, for the basic ambition of design is to arrange and schedule all the techniques that will give the building its meaning, quality, and substance. Zumthor's statement makes room for the contribution of other, non-technical or non-professional agencies of enrichment and articulation. One way to form a fuller understanding of what he suggests is to ask what might resist the accumulation that defines a good building. What kind of architecture prevents absorption or resists sedimentation? What inhibits construction materials from escaping their pre-occupancy poverty?

The opposite of receptivity is expressivity. Against an architecture that tolerates additions to its finished surfaces one could pose buildings that insist on the adequacy and fullness of their *own* expression. Zumthor is sharply critical of talkative architecture. "I frequently come across buildings that have been designed with a good deal of effort and a will to find a special form, and I am put off by them. The architect responsible for the building is not present, but he talks to me unceasingly from every detail, he keeps on saying the same thing, and I quickly lose interest." Good architecture should not constantly talk, it should keep itself silent, for only then will it "receive the human visitor" (1998:32).

Zumthor was not the first architect to argue for semantic restraint in design, nor was he the only one to fault chatty designs. In 1924 Le Corbusier famously criticized the excesses of French decorative art, rejecting "chairs that are charming [and] intelligent, but too talkative . . . If chairs and armchairs extinguish Picasso, Legér, Utrillo, Lipchitz, then chairs and armchairs

24.4 Caplutta Sogn Benedetg, Sumvitg, Graubünden, Peter Zumthor, 1985–88.

24.5   Kunsthaus Bregenz, Bregenz, Austria, Peter Zumthor, 1990–97.

are insolent . . . are extremely loud" (2001:63). In these same years Adolf Loos argued for the reticence (*Verschwiegenheit*) of urban images: "the house should be reticent on the outside and unveil its entire richness on the inside" (1982:129). More recently, Tadao Ando echoed these arguments in advocating for a taciturn architecture: "my aim is to limit materials, simplify expression to the maximum, eliminate all non-essentials, and in the process interweave in my spaces the totality of the human being" (1996:458). In different ways, and in consideration of furniture, façades, and other architectural forms, Le Corbusier, Loos, and Ando recommended an architecture that silences itself in deference to the sorts of articulation that result from the impress of practical affairs. Settings that are talkative, chatty, noisy are the ones that are incapable of absorbing the specific richness Zumthor sees in good buildings because they are so fully dedicated to declaring their designer's message and meanings.

Zumthor's desire for semantic restraint would seem to recommend an architecture of expressive materiality. Were this the case, he would appear to be adopting a familiar position once again. As long ago as the 17th century architects argued that the beauty of the building could be positively determined by the "richness" of its materials, as in Claude Perrault's celebrated distinction between positive and arbitrary beauties, his demotion of proportions to the latter category and advancement of *la richesse de la matiere* to the former. Since that time many other architects have sought to derive significance and beauty for their buildings through the selection and refined treatment of materials, especially those that are rare, vividly qualitative, or unusual. In this tradition Loos represents something of an exceptional figure, for while his buildings are clad in strikingly beautiful materials (mainly on the inside), he asserted with great insistence that "all materials are equally valuable." On his account, only the merchant, not the architect, sees a kilogram of gold as worth more than a kilogram of stone (Loos 1982:63). If we feel awe before a granite wall, the sentiment that overwhelms us arises from our estimation of the labor required for the wall's construction and finishing, not from valuation of the material itself. Value or significance arises not from things, but the ways they are handled, worked, or treated. Loos, like Ruskin, saw in the architectural surface the marks of human hands. Works that were judged beautiful were those that revealed evidences of uncoerced craft in their production. Architecture can be eloquent if the designer first recognizes the preliminary poverty (also the potentials) of unfinished materials—not their (natural) richness. If a preconception of quality prevents the free exercise of finishing, the result will lack the specific richness that makes a work wonderful. Here, by an indirect route, we return to Zumthor's argument for "traces." Zumthor once asked if the effort and skill put into the construction of a building were not inherent parts of the thing itself. His answer was yes, or in reverse, that in the world of artifacts there is really no "thing in itself." In a work of architecture nothing exists apart from the efforts and intentions that brought it into being and visibility. "The notion that our work is an integral part of what we accomplish takes us to the very limits of our musings about the value of a work of art, a work of architecture" (1988:12).

But traces of labor are not all that the materials of the building were meant and seen to absorb. When he imagined "architecture exposed to life" Zumthor also envisaged prosaic and pedestrian affairs as the subject matter inscribed onto the pages and chapters of the building's history. Patina is a narrative composed through the use and misuse of settings: "the innumerable small scratches on surfaces, of varnish that has grown dull and brittle, the edges polished by use" bear witness to the lives lived within specific settings (1988:24). Here, too, Zumthor repeats Loos: "I did not grow up, thank God, in a stylish home . . . there was the writing table! There was an ink stain on it; my sister Hermine had knocked over the inkwell when she was a little baby . . . every piece of furniture, every thing, every object had a story to tell, a family history. The house was never finished; it grew along with us and we grew within it" (Loos 1982b:23–24).

The finishes and forms specified in design and construction are undone in life, but the result is not only deformation, not only negative. Although wear and tear result in subtraction, they also allow for a significant sort of addition. Over time and through use architectural settings accrue legibility as they chronicle the patterns of life they accommodate. Time does not pass in architecture, it accumulates. If it passed it would leave no trace. But the reverse is true. Every thing around us exhibits signs of its history, its development or deterioration. All physical things, especially bodies and buildings, offer themselves to visual experience as a sedimentation of signs of actions and behaviors. If a face is recognizable it is because time has written onto its skin or surface signs of the ways it has conducted itself in the world. In a famous passage from *The Notebooks of Malte Laurids Brigge* (1949) Rainer Maria Rilke observed this kind of record on the inner wall of a Parisian building that had been brought to light by the collapse of the other sides of the structure. Between the supporting timbers that had been "rammed slantwise" against the bared wall he could see vivid, if torn and fragmented, traces of the lives that had been lived within:

> the stubborn life of these rooms had not let itself be trampled out. It was still there, it clung to the nails that had been left, it stood on the remaining handsbreadth of flooring, it crouched under the corner joints where there was still a little bit of interior. One could see that it was in the paint, which, year by year, it had slowly altered. . . . But it was also in the spots that had kept fresher, behind mirrors, picture, and wardrobes; for it had drawn and

redrawn their contours. . . . It was in every flayed strip, it was in the damp blisters at the lower edges of the wallpapers. . . . And from these walls . . . the breath of these lives stood out. . . . There stood the middays and the sicknesses and the exhaled breath and the smoke of years. . . . The sweet and lingering smell of neglected infants was there, and the fearsmell of children who go to school, and the sultriness out of the beds of nubile youths. To these was added much that had come from below, from the abyss of the street. . . . And much the feeble, tamed domestic winds, that always stay in the same street, brought along; and much more was there, the source of which one did not know. (46 ff)

The "it" to which Rilke refers in this passage is the life that was lived in these apartments. *It* was generally apparent in the materials but made particular in their specific qualities, their dulled, frayed, and blistered qualities, "drawn and redrawn" by the behavior of those who tenanted the rooms, and by the influences from the street below, and more besides. It—life— was inseparable from the things against which its movements were played out.

As Zumthor suggested, events and settings are not two aspects of a place, the first performed and the second planned, the one resulting from practical, the other from professional decision making. Instead they are bound together in reciprocal dependence, for without the resistance offered by things, life would have no way of making itself apparent, of making itself present, of occurring. Zumthor used the word *resistance* in two senses. The first indicated the critical posture taken by architects and architecture. It indicates the building's standing against the corrosive tendencies of contemporary culture, the "waste of forms and meanings." Zumthor's second sense of the term is more difficult to grasp because it is paradoxical. Resistance indicates the ways that buildings, or their materials, make life visible (even possible) by offering obstacles

24.6 Thermal Bath Vals, Vals, Graubünden, Peter Zumthor, 1990–96.

to unbounded and unstructured movements or flows. Architecture reveals life to itself by giving it limits and resisting its forces. Absorption or sedimentation is the process whereby the movements and energy of practical life encounter and come to rest in the spaces and surfaces of a setting. Perfectly ambient movements are never apparent. Thanks to the building and its capacity for resistance, however, the patterns of life obtain both definition and legibility. The wall's capacity for resistance, its readiness to serve as a counterforce to all kinds of movement in the environment, is also its potential for articulation and expression.

EVENTS AND THEIR EFFECTS

Jean Nouvel, unlike Peter Zumthor, proposed an architecture for our time that was light, not heavy, changeable, not permanent, dematerialized, not materialized. The proposal was not offered ideologically but in recognition of cultural and professional history. "Today," Nouvel observed, "we can produce a single sheet of glass which is ten meters long and three meters wide. We enter into a kind of architectural Darwinism in which our knowledge is used to eliminate useless matter and to increase performance in the areas of loading, lightness, and insulation" (1998:76). To ignore this fact and the possibilities it suggests is to retreat from the reality of the current condition. But an ethics of contemporaneity was not all that prompted Nouvel's turn toward a dematerialized architecture, toward ephemeral effects. Technical progress leads toward a non-technical goal: renewed contact with nature. This progressive reductionism is supposed to bring us into closer contact with the natural world, for the absence of "things" means the unobstructed presence of the environment.

No truism of architectural history is more commonplace than the notion that the use of glass in modern architecture established a new connection between the architectural interior

24.7 Fondation Cartier, Paris, Ateliers Jean Nouvel, 1991–94.

and the exterior world. The window wall is the most conspicuous and frequently discussed evidence of this achievement (see Leatherbarrow and Mostafavi 2002:39–78). When José Luis Sert addressed the problem in a short text called "On Windows and Walls" (1967), he saw the development of new modes of construction as an opportunity to rethink the ancient tradition of joining exterior to interior through openings in the wall: "For thousands of years, from the doors of caves until recently, all windows . . . served the triple function of providing light, ventilation, and view. It was only with the lightening of structures . . . that the window could be radically transformed and its triple function re-examined. . . . Large sheets of glass gave birth to the 'picture window.' This established a partial separation of the functions of view and light from that of ventilation" (192).

What might have been seen as an achievement—"the all glass front"—was for Sert the beginning of a serious problem. As curtain walls for office buildings gained wide acceptance "façades of anonymity" started appearing throughout the world. No city these days is without an entire crowd of them. But Sert never advocated abandoning curtain wall construction. The task was to use the new materials and methods but also recognize the long-standing desire for identity through difference. "We still need walls and windows of some kind," he observed, but "can we not find an architectural vocabulary that will permit greater variety?" His solution was to reintroduce the differentiations that existed before the window-wall, distinguishing elements that accommodated views from those that modulated the intensity of light (or created shadow), and from those that regulated the flow of air into the interior. This meant treating the glass wall as if it were not all of a piece, as if it were aggregate or composite, as if—ironically—it were like masonry construction.

But there are other ways of achieving variety. Nouvel, for example, has sought to assimilate the window wall into the natural world so the (environmental) changes of the second would give animation to the first. He calls this "putting nature to work."

Nature, for Nouvel, is not an object to be viewed, but an element that can "structure" the building. He wants the pane of glass to be more than a picture of the landscape. The metaphorical "interpenetration" inside and outside is also inadequate to his sense of contact with nature. His aim is to have the building and the environment work together, operate as one, and perform their task jointly. That task is to bring architecture to life. His strategy is to let the qualities of the ambient landscape saturate his surfaces so completely that they become the qualities of the building itself. For this to happen two types of change must occur: first, the building must be dematerialized; and second, light must be seen and treated as if it were matter.

In an interview with Jean Baudrillard, Nouvel outlined a new sense of transparency. He said he is less interested in spatial continuities and unimpeded views than the play of ephemeral effects (Baudrillard and Nouvel 2002:61–62). Traditional architecture always played with permanent effects. Now impermanent effects are possible: "working with transparency involves nothing more than working with matter to give a building different appearances." It is not clear in this passage if the matter to which Nouvel refers is light or glass. His aim, I take it, is to see the two as one. Transparency is a kind of evaporation, it is the means by which the building allows itself to be absorbed into the atmosphere or, in reverse, the means by which the atmosphere completely saturates the building's surfaces, making them co-extensive with its unbounded expanse.

24.8 Fondation Cartier,
Paris, France, Ateliers Jean
Nouvel, 1991–94.

With reference to the same effect on the canvases of Georges Seurat and Paul Signac, Nouvel described this architecture as a kind of "cosmic pointillism." From the earliest years of the movement, neo-Impressionist painters demonstrated a strong interest in industrial imagery, particularly their surfaces of steel and glass near bodies of water. Signac asserted that the urban world was his central preoccupation. An example of his interest might be *Gas Tanks at Clichy* (1886). He was not alone; in fact, a number of painters focused on the industrial zones at the city's periphery. Bleakness characterizes these scenes, for they are often empty landscapes, without focus or hierarchy. Typically the terrain is rendered in blue, gray, and white. Regardless of the colors used, however, light suffuses everything seen.

Describing Seurat's conté crayon drawing *Scaffolding* (1887), Robert Herbert (1991) observed that light mediated between the construction's geometry and the space's "mysterious layers of depth." Patches and patterns of shadow and light fluctuate from foreground to background in the compressed depth of the image, such that "the play of light and dark threatens to push us . . . into a realm of enigma" (262).

24.9   L'Institut du Monde Arabe, Paris, Ateliers Jean Nouvel, 1981–87.

It was precisely this unstable or enigmatic quality of surfaces saturated with light that Nouvel has sought to achieve in architecture. The capacity of glass to mirror its surroundings was just as important as its transparency. Speaking of his Arab Institute in Paris he stressed the ephemerality of its appearance; its image, he said, changes under different conditions, rain, fog, cloud cover. Architects of our time are trying to capture "variations in time, the seasons, the movements of visitors, etc." This effort is not for the sake of novelty but of relevance. Once the building and its materials transcend themselves into the atmosphere the old deadening permanence of architecture is abandoned and the building joins step with the pace of contemporary life.

ARCHITECTURE EXCEEDING ITSELF

While the areas of difference between Zumthor and Nouvel's conceptions of architectural materiality are obvious and undeniable, points of convergence also exist.

The first point of convergence concerns architecture's relationship to its ambient surroundings. The necessity of interconnection between the building and its milieu is not immediately apparent for either of these architects. Zumthor's desire for the "completeness" of the architectural object, for example, would seem to mitigate against engagement and for independence. When defined as whole and entire unto itself, the building is free from entanglements with its location. In many places he seems to be arguing for the autonomy of the architectural object. Likewise, Nouvel's emphasis on the contemporaneity of the building might suggest an essential separation from contexts that date from earlier times. He has frequently claimed that the traditional city has been "blown apart" in the modern world. Demographic shifts, technological change, and globalization have contributed to the disintegration of traditional patterns. A radical break with past forms would therefore seem to be inevitable. Further, Nouvel sees himself as heir to the tradition Le Corbusier inaugurated: the traditional city represents the "pack donkey's way." Yet, both architects envisage the constitution of the part (the building) as a condensation or crystallization of salient aspects of the whole (the environment). Where they differ is only in the aspects of the environment they choose to stress.

24.10 L'Institut du Monde Arabe, Paris, Ateliers Jean Nouvel, 1981–87.

Zumthor views the surrounding milieu as a pattern or framework of practical affairs. The city is an ensemble of life's typical situations. His short text "The Body of Architecture" narrates his participation in a number of these: observing others in a hotel lobby, feeling isolated on the streets of a 19th century suburb, wandering through a museum, and so on. His fragments allude to the different ways these situations are structured: socially, linguistically, topographically, and architecturally. Although architecture is one of the most permanent of these structures, all of them have the same subject matter, which Zumthor calls "life." His argument about "traces" takes this "context" as the building's primary horizon of reference. It is also the source of the building's more legible articulation, its richness.

Nouvel, by contrast, views the surrounding milieu as the natural world, as a play and variation of environmental phenomena: wind, rain, and, most importantly, light. His use of glass and his treatment of other materials are always in the service of reducing the separation between what has been built and what precedes and follows all constructive acts—nature. The capacity of materials to receive, reflect, and modulate light is so significant that it determines the building's dimensions and geometries. A theater built out of metal, plastic, and glass, he said, cannot be the same as one built out of stone. The ways in which these new materials catch light and orchestrate its effects redefines our conception of theatricality. Were the landscape not "put to work" in the project, these changes would not be so dramatic; but once the building is co-determined by forces outside itself, its essential character results from something other than just design intentionality.

Zumthor's horizon of reference is social, and Nouvel's is physical. The first finds richness in the sedimentation of practical affairs; the second looks for qualities that result from the saturation of surfaces by natural light. Zumthor's frequent use of stone and Nouvel's of glass would seem to reinforce this opposition.

24.11 Kunsthaus Bregenz, Bregenz, Austria, Peter Zumthor, 1990–97.

That the matter is not so simple becomes clear when one realizes that neither architect really narrowed his choices in this way, nor did either dogmatically abbreviate the full spectrum of materials. Zumthor's Kunsthaus in Bregenz, Austria, for example, has all the materials and many of the qualities one might find in a building by Nouvel. Likewise, Nouvel's use of timber in the Genoscope de Lanaud building or the Les Thermes project in Dax, France, develops the very same qualities Zumthor achieved in his timber-clad buildings (in the Archaeological Museum in Chur, Switzerland, for example, or his own studio). Materials matter to these architects because of the ways they can be treated. Neither stone nor glass possess any particular "truth," nor is one or another singularly apposite to our time. The whole matter rests on the ways they are shaped and transformed, the ways they become what they had not been before, the ways they exceed themselves.

Both architects argue for materials becoming more than they were and for an architecture that offers to experience much more than the architects themselves could have designed, more perhaps than they could have foreseen. Baudrillard's epigraph alludes to the "unintelligible" foundation for events and effects. Nouvel, along the same lines, recognized the significance of aspects of the project that were never rationalized: "when you talk to a developer . . . there are a ton of questions . . . and then there are those things that remain unsaid. . . . What remains unsaid . . . signifies something vital" (Baudrillard and Nouvel 2002:8). Zumthor, for his part, observed that "the most important things are often those one doesn't see." "When we look at buildings which seem to be at peace within themselves," he said, "they seem empty. . . . It is as if we could see something on which we cannot focus our consciousness" (Zumthor 2001:25, 1998:17).

Perhaps something of this understanding of architecture exceeding itself was implied in Koolhaas's statements about oversize architecture: "Bigness transforms the city from a summation of certainties into an accumulation of mysteries" (Koolhaas 1995:501). Such

24.12 Caplutta Sogn
Benedetg, Sumvitg,
Graubünden,
Peter Zumthor,
1985–88.

mystery has potential that is analogous to the capacity of materials: "If urbanism generates potential and architecture exploits it, Bigness enlists the generosity of urbanism against the meanness of architecture" (515). Both the generosity of the town and the yielding readiness of materials give architecture opportunities to surpass its own intentions.

Both Zumthor and Nouvel also subject architectural space to the order of historical time. This has already been implied in the observation about the limits of design's foresight: if the building is enriched by agencies outside the specifications of the project, this occurs after the completion of the construction. Put differently, as agencies of articulation outside the compass of professional instrumentality, both sedimentation and saturation accomplish their results in the building's open and extended history. Construction does not end, it begins the process of articulation. Rilke's phrase is apposite here: surfaces that we find legible are "drawn and redrawn" over time. Once taken up in the adventure of construction and use the materials of a building invite, register, and finally recall kinds of conduct that increasingly saturate their surfaces with traces of recurring modes of behavior and environmental influence. This makes each surface something of a clock, calendar, and chronicle. Space in architecture is not measured by inches, feet, and yards alone, but also by minutes, days, months, and years. The (temporal) processes of sedimentation and saturation bring its surfaces into visibility. But the vectors of architectural time do not only point toward the past; each trace also prompts or invites subsequent events. The chronology that is particular to urban architecture allows its heritage to be renewed through acts of appropriation that obey no obligation to the past other than its use for purposes of redefinition. In the built world past, present, and future do not line up one after the other like soldiers in formation, but bend that line back onto and out from itself such that both directions overlap *in the present*. While it may seem sensible to distinguish two agencies at work in the process of sedimentation whereby architecture accrues and extends history—human and environmental forces—only their compounded effects give it its proper voice.

Architecture's Debt to the City

The difference between figure and ground, or outlay and supply, is not absolute. Not only are they convertible, but they coexist. In many paintings traces of background color can be seen *through* the foreground figures. The sedimentation to which Zumthor referred and the saturation sought by Nouvel never completely conceal the materials of the building, their assimilation into the life of the milieu is always incomplete. As long as it stands, the building resists the environment. In urban architecture materials that are alternately seen and un-seen interpenetrate one another, but the latter also escape the limits of the former; otherwise they could not continually serve as their supply. Viewing the city as a big building, or as the outcome of design work is like seeing the background as if *it* were the figure. From this angle, its withdrawing character is ignored and its capacity to fund the project's visible richness is wasted. The city and environment surpass design intention and produce effects that cannot be foreseen. Although they exceed intention, they enrich intuition.

Urban and natural phenomena act in ways that run counter to received wisdom and expectations, but at the same time they grant to both expectation and understanding their greatest reward. Finally, while the city gives itself to architecture and experience as something that contravenes what might be reasonably expected, it also endows experience with richness of content. Despite their differences, the materials that make up the buildings of both Zumthor and Nouvel come to life by drawing from a territorial source that is as abundant as it is non-architectural.

References

Ando, Tadao. "Light, Shadow, and Form." In *Tadao Ando Complete Works*, ed. Francesco Dal Co. New York: Phaidon, 1996.

Baudrillard, Jean, and Jean Nouvel. *The Singular Object of Architecture*. Minneapolis, MN: University of Minnesota Press, 2002.

Herbert, Robert. *Georges Seurat 1859–1891*. New York: Harry N. Abrams, 1991.

Koolhaas, Rem. "Bigness or the Problem of Large." In *S,M,L,XL*. New York: Monacelli, 1995.

Leatherbarrow, David. *Uncommon Ground*. Cambridge, MA: MIT Press, 2000.

Leatherbarrow, David, and Mohsen Mostafavi. "Window/Wall." In *Surface Architecture*. Cambridge, MA: MIT Press, 2002.

Le Corbusier [Paul Boulard, pseud.]. "Le Salon de l'Art Décoratif au Grand Palais." *L'Esprit Nouveau* 24(June 1924). Cited and translated in Caroline Constant, *Eileen Gray*. New York: Phaidon, 2001, 63.

Loos, Adolf. "Building Materials." In *Spoken into the Void*. Cambridge, MA: MIT Press, 1982a.

———. "Interiors in the Rotunda." In *Spoken into the Void*. Cambridge, MA: MIT Press, 1982b.

———. "Heimatkunst." In *Trozdem*. Vienna: Prachner, 1982c.

Marion, Jean-Luc. *The Crossing of the Visible*. Palo Alto, CA: Stanford University Press, 2004.

Nouvel, Jean. "Presentation." In *The Jerusalem Seminar in Architecture*, ed. Kenneth Frampton. New York: Rizzoli, 1998.

Rilke, Rainer Maria. *The Notebooks of Malte Laurids Brigge*. New York: Norton, 1949.

Sert, José Luis. "On Windows and Walls." In *José Luis Sert*, Knud Bastlund. New York: Praeger, 1967, 192.

Zumthor, Peter. "The Hard Core of Beauty." In *Thinking Architecture*, trans. Maureen Oberli-Turner. Baden, Switzerland: Lars Müller, 1998.

———. "A Way of Looking at Things." In *Thinking Architecture*. Baden, Switzerland: Lars Müller, 1998.

———. "Stone and Water." In *Thermal Bath at Vals*. London: The Architectural Association, 1996.

———. "I Build on My Experience of the World." *Detail* 1(2001):25.

Contributors

Wendy Ashmore is Professor of Anthropology, University of California at Riverside, Riverside, CA.

Tony Atkin is Principal, Atkin Olshin Lawson-Bell Architects, and Adjunct Associate Professor of Architecture, University of Pennsylvania, Philadelphia, PA.

Augustin Berque is Professor of Geography, École des Hautes Études en Sciences Sociales, Paris.

Suzanne P. Blier is Professor of History of Art and Architecture, Harvard University, Cambridge, MA.

Larissa Bonfante is Professor of Classics, New York University, New York.

M. Christine Boyer is Professor of Architecture, Princeton University, Princeton, NJ.

Edmund Carpenter is an author and anthropologist, New York.

Thomas J. Campanella is Professor of City and Regional Planning, University of North Carolina at Chapel Hill, Chapel Hill, NC.

Denis Cosgrove is Alexander von Humboldt Professor of Geography, University of California Los Angeles, Los Angeles, CA.

T. J. Ferguson is Partner in Heritage Resources Management Consultants, and Adjunct Professor of Anthropology, University of Arizona, Tucson, AZ.

Stephan Feuchtwang is Professor of Anthropology, London School of Economics & Political Science, London.

Stanislaus Fung is Senior Lecturer in Architecture, Faculty of the Built Environment, University of New South Wales, Sydney.

Tsutomu Iyori is Professor, Graduate School of Human and Environmental Studies, Kyoto University, Kyoto.

PIETRO LAUREANO is consultant to UNESCO, founder of IPOGEA, an architect, and Professor at the University of Basilicata and Bologna.

DAVID LEATHERBARROW is Professor of Architecture, School of Design, University of Pennsylvania, Philadelphia, PA.

DAVID O'CONNOR is Lila Acheson Wallace Professor of Egyptology, New York University, New York.

LAURIE OLIN is Principal, Olin Partnership, and Practice Professor of Landscape Architecture, School of Design, University of Pennsylvania, Philadelphia, PA.

JUHANI PALLASMAA is Principal, Juhani Pallasmaa Architects, Helsinki.

GREGORY POSSEHL is Professor of Anthropology, University of Pennsylvania, and Curator of the Asian Section, University of Pennsylvania Museum of Archaeology and Anthropology, Philadelphia, PA.

ROBERT W. PREUCEL is Associate Professor of Anthropology, University of Pennsylvania, and the Gregory Annenberg Weingarten Associate Curator of the American Section, University of Pennsylvania Museum of Archaeology and Anthropology, Philadelphia, PA.

JOSEPH RYKWERT is Paul Philippe Cret Professor of Architecture Emeritus, School of Design, and Professor of Art History, Emeritus, University of Pennsylvania, Philadelphia, PA.

MICHAEL SORKIN is Principal, Michael Sorkin Studio, and Director of the Graduate Program in Urban Design, City College of New York, NY.

LAWRENCE VALE is Professor and Head of the Department of Urban Studies and Planning, Massachusetts Institute of Technology, Cambridge, MA.

GORDON R. WILLEY was the first Charles P. Bowditch Professor of Central American and Mexican Archaeology and Ethnology, Harvard University, Cambridge, MA. He died in 2002.

Index

193, 206, 246–48

Ming Dynasty, 107, 124, 132, 136

Mingming, Wang, 113, 116, 118

Mission Bay, San Francisco, *320–21*

Mission Hill (public housing project, Boston), 276

Miyakawa, Eiji, 100

Moche Valley, Peru, 29

Mohenjo-Daro, 69–83; Great Bath, *69*, 70, *72*, 73–74, 77–81

moieties, 215; Bororo, 5; Plains Indians, 10; Kotyiti, 203

Moses, Robert, 291, 297–99

Mount Athos, 260, 262, 267; Athos, 267, *268*, 271

Murgia Timone, 236

Mycerunus, 91

Nabatean, 238

Naram-Sin, 92

Naranjo, 48–49

National Association of Real Estate Boards (NAREB), 279, *280–81*

Neanderthals, 2, 4–5

Nebuchadnezzar, 94

Negev Desert, 238

Neimeyer, Oscar, *101*, 102

Neolithic, 235-37

Neurasia, 328, *329*

New Jersey Turnpike, 295, 297, 299

New Kingdom, 56, *59*, 65

New Mexico, 7–9, 185–90, 241–42, 246

New Urbanists, 313

New York City, 11, 182, 277–78, 297–99, 304–305, 310, 317, 325, 339

1914 Model Housing Law, 278

nomadism, 333, 336–37, 340, 343–44

Nördlisches Derendorf Competition, Dusseldorf, *319*

north-south axis, 42, 44, 48

Nouvel, Jean, 102, *247*, 349, *350*, 351–52, 356–63; and *transparency*, 357, 359

Noyes, John, 334, 337–38, 340, 345

NWT hieroglyph, 7

oasis, 227–32, 235, 239; model, *229*; societies, 219

Okinawa Island, 135–36, 140–41, 146–47, 149

"Orange County," China, 295

Orchard Park, Boston, 289, 290

orient, 260, 262, 265–67

Oriental Plaza, 294

orientation, building and settlement, 7–9, 43, 46, 50, 107, 116, 194, 198–99, 277, 321; landscape, 9; solar, 320; historical, 107, 132, 286

Ortiz, Alfonso, 242

Palenque, 44, 50

Paleolithic, 4, 213–16

Parmentier, Richard, 200

Parthenon, 260, 267–68, *270*, 271

Pearl River Delta, *294*, 297–300, *302*, 304

Perry, Clarence, 282

Petra, Jordan, 236, 238–39

Pharaoh Uadji (Djet), 90

phenotype, extended, 13, 17, 20, 104

Piacenza (bronze model of a sheep's liver) 155

Picuris, 187, 191

Peirce, Charles Sanders, 200

Pike Place Market, 310

Pitjantjatara, 4–5

Playa Vista, Los Angeles, 314–16, *314*, *316*, 317

plaza, Maya, 44; Pueblo, 187, 194, *197*, 198–201, *202*, 203, 205; Zuni, 248–49, *251*, 252–53, *254–55*; Oriental Plaza shopping center, Beijing, China, 254

postmodern landscape, 338

Pueblo Revolt mesa villages, 185, *186*, 187–89, 192–96, *197*, meaning of 199–201, 205

privies, 77

Pudong, China, 323

Pueblo Indians, 185, 188

Pushkari, Ukraine, 4

pyramids, Virú, 29; Maya, 30–31, *36*, 40, 42, 47; Cahokia, 32; Egypt, 62, 65, *85–87*, 88, *90–91*, 94

Quiriguá, 44, 46–50

rancheria settlement, 195

Rebstock Park, Frankfurt Competition and Bebaungsplan, *317–18*

Rees, William, 325

Rénan, Ernest, 259, 267

Riis, Jacob, 277–78, 282, 285

Rilke, Rainer Maria, 354–55, 362

Ritter, William, 259, 261, 263, 268, 270–72

Rome, 10, *24*, 35, 38–40, 91, 154, 157–58, 161, 171, 259–62, 334

RV resorts, 342

Ryukyu Kingdom, 135–36, 146

Sabloff, Jeremy A., 32, 34, 44

sacred landscapes, Chinese, 107; Okinawan, 136, 144–45, 147–49; Pueblo, 202

Salimobiya (warriors), 249

Sanders, William T., 29, 37

Saqqara, 88, 90–91

Sargon of Akkad, 94

Satsuma Daimiate, 136, 139–40, 145

Sayil, 44

Scorpion King, 90

sebkha (oases), 220, *224–25*, 227–28

Seefa forest, 139, 141, *142*, *145*, 146–48

Seibal, 44, 46

Sert, Jose Luis, 349, 357

settlement archaeology, 7, 24, 41

settlement form, 8–9, 12, 283, 285, 290, 325, 335, 339

settlement patterns, 29, 32; Mayan, 37; Mesa Villages, 190; landscapes, 309

Shalako, 9, 249

Shanghai, China, 293, 296, 303–304

Shenzhen, China, 293, 298–99, 303; *see also* Guangzhou-Shenzhen Superhighway

Shibam, Yemen, 232, *233–34*, 235, 239

Shuri Castle, *136*, 143

Siberia, 215–16

"signs in history," 200–201

Sitte, Camillo, 263, 318

Skertchly, J.A., 175, 177–78, 184

Smithson, Alison, and Peter Smithson (of Team 10 Architects), 349

spiral, Chaco Canyon, *8*, Danhomè, pattern of urban renewal, *173–74*, 183

solar, Pueblo, 7–8; Maya, 42–43; Egypt, 58–59, 61, 65; tomb, 227, orientation, 320

Song Dynasty Encyclopedia (Lie shu), 124

space syntax, 195, *196*, 199, 205

stela (stele, stelae), Xunatunich, 31; Tikal, 42, 44; Amenhotep III, 58; Ur-Nammu, 86, *88*

Straus, Nathan, 283

Sumerians, 85–87, 92–95; language of, 91

SUV, 341–42, 345